T0202259

The Game Designer's Playbook

The Game Designer's Playbook

An Introduction to Game Interaction Design

Samantha Stahlke
Pejman Mirza-Babaei

OXFORD
UNIVERSITY PRESS

Great Clarendon Street, Oxford, OX2 6DP,
United Kingdom

Oxford University Press is a department of the University of Oxford.
It furthers the University's objective of excellence in research, scholarship,
and education by publishing worldwide. Oxford is a registered trade mark of
Oxford University Press in the UK and in certain other countries

© Samantha Stahlke and Pejman Mirza-Babaei 2022

The moral rights of the authors have been asserted

All rights reserved. No part of this publication may be reproduced, stored in
a retrieval system, or transmitted, in any form or by any means, without the
prior permission in writing of Oxford University Press, or as expressly permitted
by law, by licence or under terms agreed with the appropriate reprographics
rights organization. Enquiries concerning reproduction outside the scope of the
above should be sent to the Rights Department, Oxford University Press, at the
address above

You must not circulate this work in any other form
and you must impose this same condition on any acquirer

Published in the United States of America by Oxford University Press
198 Madison Avenue, New York, NY 10016, United States of America

British Library Cataloguing in Publication Data
Data available

Library of Congress Control Number: 2022937904

ISBN 978–0–19–884591–1

DOI: 10.1093/oso/9780198845911.001.0001

Printed and bound by
CPI Group (UK) Ltd, Croydon, CR0 4YY

Cover image: Samantha Stahlke

Links to third party websites are provided by Oxford in good faith and
for information only. Oxford disclaims any responsibility for the materials
contained in any third party website referenced in this work.

For our families
(Yes, that means you too, Svetlana)

Foreword

When someone first explained to me that "UX" design in game development was shorthand for "User eXperience" design, my instinctive reply was, "So, you mean game design?"

I don't remember clearly how the exchange went after that. Probably they shook their head, cleared their throat, and fidgeted, politely working around my awkward naivete to explain the subtle distinctions we normally point to in methodology and purpose. Upon reflection, I believe what they should have said was, "Yes, in the same way that when I say biology, I also am talking about science."

I am a game designer, but in a smaller team, that often means I also contribute to the game and studio in many other ways. Writer, business developer, product manager, level designer, system designer, producer, quality assurance, localization coordinator, casting director, and of course UX designer. I write "of course" because there are very few methods of achieving good game design without (consciously or unconsciously) executing good UX and interaction design.

Understanding the user experience is the fundamental requirement for understanding how and why a game *works*—mechanically, aesthetically, emotionally, artistically. Some designers shuffle towards creating their desired experience more instinctively, with pure trial and error, embracing 'iteration' without considering how analysis might save them time and effort. But the best designers I know employ a vast vocabulary with a wide array of tools, all striving to somehow peer through the plastics and metals of the physical artifacts, strip away the clouding of vaguely-worded feedback, and clearly perceive the player's true experience. They see not only the player's mental state, but the dynamic shifts it undergoes while playing, and all the many intricate variables that contribute to those transformations.

In the early days of Kitfox, while we were still part of Execution Labs, I was introduced to Pejman, as the UX Research Director who offered insights and support to all of the teams there. More recently, Samantha and Pejman were able to provide research resources to analyze how players responded to *Boyfriend Dungeon*'s characters, increasing our confidence in writing and character design. The game undoubtedly owes some portion of its success to their team.

When I heard they were writing this book, I knew I'd want to read it as soon as possible. I wish I had been able to take advantage of the lessons and best practices described in this book for my entire career, but I'm glad I can start now! I'm envious of all the young designers who can tuck this into their toolbox immediately and have that much more to work with as they begin their craft.

To the designer holding this book in your hand right now, I wish that it brings you courage and good fortune. The user experience is often a hydra of a problem, with every curiosity replaced by two more in its exploration. I believe this book can help all of us game designers decide which questions are worth asking, and benefit more from the knowledge they expose. They say there is no such thing as a finished piece of art, only that which has been abandoned. . . but equally, perhaps there is no such thing as a complete understanding of user experience, only those questions we are brave enough to ask.

Be brave.

Good luck.

Tanya X. Short

Preface and Acknowledgments

We decided to write this book for many different reasons. A desire to share what we've learned about game interaction design with aspiring designers around the world. Wanting to create an educational resource that could reach beyond our own students. A frustration with the dearth of textbooks containing puns and edgy takes on the gaming industry that no one asked for. Most importantly, we decided to write this book to share our passion for games and what makes them tick with a diverse audience. No matter whether you're a student of design, a curious gamer, or a professional on the hunt for puns and edgy takes, we hope this book can provide you with some useful knowledge, helpful examples, and inspiration for your own work.

If you're wondering why *we* decided to write this book, the long version of that story includes an ill-fated midterm exam, a few oddball research projects, and several bowls of ramen. The short version of that story is that the "we" in question, Samantha and Pejman, have been working together since 2015 in both academic and commercial work. After co-authoring several articles together and collaborating in a few teaching endeavours, Pejman suggested that they write a book about game interaction design. Samantha agreed with this idea, because she has poor impulse control. And, after a few years of writing, interviews, writing, editing, writing, compositing, and writing, you're about to (hopefully) delight in the result of that collaboration.

Creating this book has been both a challenging and rewarding journey. When we set out to write it, we knew that it would be difficult to pull together a volume that managed to capture our combined advice on game interaction design while also teaching and working on our research. What we didn't anticipate was that most of our writing would end up taking place during the pandemic lockdowns, which made the effort overwhelming at times. Luckily, we are fortunate to have the most wonderful, understanding friends and family that anyone could hope to imagine. There are many people who have supported us through this journey, and this book would not have happened without their support.

We would like to thank Dan Taber, our Commissioning Editor at Oxford University Press, and his team, particularly John Smallman, Katherine Ward and Charles Bath, for guiding and encouraging us from the initial discussion we had about this book all the way to final release.

Throughout the book we highlight design examples and screenshots from various commercial games. We would like to thank the many developers and publishers who responded to our inquiries about including material from their games—as well as in some cases providing confirmation on features or design decisions mentioned in our writing.

The book also features interviews with experts from the game industry and academia; some of them are mentors, advisors, and friends of the authors. We would like to thank them for their support and contributions to this work: Jason Avent, Kris Alexander, Osama Dorias, Jason Della Rocca, David Galindo, Ario Jafarzadeh, Mark Laframboise, Regan Mandryk, Graham McAllister, Romana Ramzan, Steven Smith, and Cherry Thompson. We would like to especially thank Tanya X. Short for writing the foreword of the book.

We would also like to thank our colleagues at Ontario Tech University for their support. We especially want to thank our students in the game development and interactive media program and our amazing team at UXR Lab for inspiring us every day. Special thanks also go to Ame Gilham for helping us with the indexing. And in a rare moment of practicality, we should mention that everything discussed in this book represents our own views and opinions, and not necessarily those of our current or past affiliated organizations.

We both wish to thank our family and friends for their love, care, and encouragement. Samantha thanks Svetlana for constantly putting up with her antics and not telling anyone where they hid the jewels back in '69, and Emilian for teaching her a level of friendship expressible only in mixtapes and comics about Russian spiders. She also thanks Helen (and Mu & Ivy), Atiya (no u), Josh, and Owen for being amazing friends and excellent members of the travelling percussion band she has yet to tell them about. Pejman thanks his family, particularly his parents, Edina, and Rùm for their constant support, love, and shared fondness for Victoria sponge.

Lastly, we thank you, the reader, for picking this up to read—we hope you enjoy it!
- Samantha & Pejman
gamedesignplaybook.com

Contents

Contents

1

Caveman Arcade

Leave any group of humans unattended for any significant amount of time, and you will return to find that they have done something. If for a few minutes, perhaps you return to a number of smaller groups exchanging pleasantries amongst themselves. If for a few hours, perhaps you return to a group of newfound friends tossing around a ball of some sort, wondering why you've left them there with seemingly no instruction. If for a few thousand years, perhaps you will return to find that they have invented the internet.

That's the peculiar thing about humans—even when our basic needs are met, or rather especially when our basic needs are met—we opt to do *something* instead of nothing. Both individually and collectively, our curiosity and desire for stimulation constantly nag at us to *do something*. Idle hands rarely stay that way for long. Fingers drum subconsciously in anticipation of our next action. Then, they reach for something, maybe a pen, a musical instrument, a paintbrush, or a computer. Even trying to do absolutely nothing is an act in itself, a meditation that allows us to reflect on ourselves or seek some form of spiritual fulfillment.

Maybe it is this constant desire for *something* that has resulted in the rich library of recreational activities humans have come to enjoy. When we are safe, rested, and well-fed, we watch movies, listen to music, travel, read, write, draw, exercise, and talk with friends. And, of course, we play games. Naturally, our work here explores video games in particular, though the act of play is far from exclusive to digital games. Someone who has never picked up a controller in their life will almost certainly have played a board game, engaged in sport, or pretended to go on an adventure as a child.

Even the act of tossing crumpled paper into a wastebasket can be transformed into a friendly competition, as boredom and imagination unite to transform an office into a basketball court. Probing the underlying reasons

The Game Designer's Playbook. Samantha Stahlke and Pejman Mirza-Babaei, Oxford University Press.
© Samantha Stahlke and Pejman Mirza-Babaei (2022). DOI: 10.1093/oso/9780198845911.003.0001

for what makes the act of play specifically so compelling, and what benefit games might have to human development, is an interesting challenge.

One theory could be that games allow us to practice vital skills in a safe environment. Perhaps tossing the paper into the wastebasket evokes some primal state where the accuracy of a projectile could be the difference between having food for the night or starving. However, this is not a book about evolutionary biology, anthropology, or ballistics. The question of why humans invented games, or first came to enjoy them, is a fascinating one to be sure, but it is not our primary focus. Instead, here we examine the question of what makes games fun today, and how different design choices can make a game more or less enjoyable. As a matter of course, we hope to create more fun and engaging experiences; in essence, we strive to build a better wastebasket.

1.1 What's in a game?

So ingrained in our culture is the notion of games and play that most people have an intuitive sense of what makes up a game. Formally speaking, games are often defined as a structured form of play comprising rules, which dictate the actions available to players and how they are performed; boundaries, which delineate the "game space" from the real world; and outcomes, which result from playing the game. Consider table tennis: as an oversimplification, the rules of the game specify that players can hit the ball with their paddles, and a player scores if their opponent fails to return a volley before the ball hits the ground. Spatial boundaries define the game as occurring within the vicinity of the table. The outcome of a match is such that the player with the most points is declared the victor.

Attempting to define games with this level of rigor leads to some matter of debate in terms of what should be labelled as a game, as opposed to a "toy," or simply "play." Does a lack of definite rules mean that children playing a "game" of pretend aren't really playing a game at all? Is a game like *The Sims* no longer considered a game per se, since no final outcome or objective is prescribed to players?

While there is certainly a place for this sort of debate, here we assume a more colloquial definition of the term. Indeed, the principles described in this book can be applied in the design of anything that might be called a game, whether digital or otherwise. For our purposes, we can loosely define a game as any interactive experience where participation is a goal in itself.

There are two key points in this understanding of what defines a game. The first is interactivity, which distinguishes games from other non-interactive

Figure 1.1 Many digital games blur the line between "game-like" and "toy-like" play. Left: in *The Sims* games, players have full customization over their Sims' virtual lives. Where one player might create a living room, another might opt for the objectively superior bear shrine. Right: a perfectly normal day in *Garry's Mod*.

Credit: *The Sims 3* was developed by Maxis and published by Electronic Arts. *Garry's Mod* was developed by Facepunch Studios and published by Valve.

entertainment media, such as books, movies, or television. Games are inherently participatory experiences; during play, players' actions affect the course of a game in some way. In turn, the resulting changes affect which actions are available to players, and their strategy in performing those actions.

The second defining quality of games is the notion of the experience itself motivating engagement. Though the completion of a game often promises some reward in the form of a satisfying conclusion to a story, a feeling of mastery, or plain old bragging rights, players do not play solely for the privilege of viewing an ending screen. Instead, the goal of engaging with a game is experiencing all it has to offer. This creates a particular delineation between games and productivity software; replaying a favourite game is hardly unusual, but rewriting the same paper in a word processor is a special kind of torture reserved only for the most extreme of masochists.

Obviously, this understanding of games is quite broad, easily encompassing examples like *The Sims* or imaginary "games" that might otherwise be subject to lexical controversy. Moving forward, this understanding is sufficient for comprehending and applying the design principles discussed. For those less familiar with the subject material who wish to learn more about the formal study of games as systems, you may refer to the readings suggested at the end of this chapter.

Regardless of structural specifics, interaction lies at the core of every game. Games provide players with opportunities for interaction; they give players something to *do*. Likewise, interaction shapes the course of a game. Such changes might be as straightforward as incrementing a player's score, or as complex as requiring characters to adapt to the death of a simulated companion. Interaction can take many forms, have any number of consequences, involve multiple players at a time, and evoke a potent cocktail of delight, surprise, and frustration.

The nature of player interaction can vary wildly depending on the game in question. In sport, interaction is literal, physical, and immediate. A soccer player, for instance, has the objective of guiding the ball across the field to score. To achieve this goal, they kick the ball toward the opposing team's net. Interactions in sports are "designed" to the extent that they are restricted by the rules of a given game, but are most influenced by the characteristics of human motion and the physical objects with which they are played.

In board games, player interaction retains a physical component, but is in many cases symbolic of some imagined scenario. In *Monopoly*, players exchange play money symbolizing multi-million-dollar real estate deals, moving tokens on a two-dimensional board representing New York City. Here, there is more room for "designing" what player actions mean in the context of the game state. Since interaction is metaphorical to a degree, an arguably greater deal of creative freedom exists. Physical interactions can be used to represent imaginary or impossible scenarios.

Digital games offer an even greater level of abstraction between the physical actions taken by players and their meaning in the context of a game. With a game's world having few or no tethers to the physical reality of the player, the possibility space of interaction design for digital games is enormous. When controlling a virtual character, a single button press can be used to trigger an acrobatic motion, a response in conversation, or the firing of a weapon.

Naturally, this spectrum of interactions from the literal to the abstract is far from absolute. Games played in the physical world often have in-game consequences divorced from reality: despite the imagined stakes, real-life dismemberment is thankfully not required to enjoy a round of laser tag. Likewise, some digital games design their interactions to have varying degrees of analogy between players' physical movements and in-game actions.

A purely abstracted model of interaction may reduce every possible action to a button press on a keyboard or game controller. By contrast, games played using a peripheral such as the Microsoft Kinect (may it rest in peace) can map the motions of a player onto their character exactly. Still others adopt a hybrid approach, for instance, requiring players to physically swing a controller as a proxy for their character's sword while mapping locomotion to a series of button presses.

The importance of good design in these interactions is practically self-evident; over the course of a session, players may execute hundreds or thousands of individual actions shaping their experience. Common actions, such as moving a character, might be repeated hundreds of times on their

PLAN NO. 211212

Figure 1.2 Games are often described as occurring within the "Magic Circle," a concept delineating the game space from reality. Thus, the very same action occurring inside the magic circle has a very different meaning when performed outside the magic circle. Inside the magic circle of bowling, throwing a bowling ball at things to knock them over is how you score points. Outside the magic circle, the very same action just means you're a "bad houseguest" and "should have returned the key when we kicked you out last October, Jerry."

own. It is thus vital that these actions are satisfying and enjoyable to sustain player engagement.

Within the first few minutes of a game, players will often perform many key interactions for the first time, solidifying their initial impressions of the experience. The first time a player fires their weapon in a shooter, for instance, they can immediately gain a feel for the game's physics, aiming difficulty, and realism in gunplay. A sufficiently well-designed interaction can keep players coming back to pull the trigger again and again, even after hundreds of hours of play. Conversely, a slight imperfection in the look or feel of this action might make players grow disenchanted or outright frustrated with a game's combat after a few hours.

The sheer variation possible in crafting a library of player actions conveys the complexity and nuance of game interaction design. The task of creating and refining these actions poses a number of challenging questions. How can we design interactions which contribute to player satisfaction and enjoyment while simultaneously blending with the greater game experience, so as not to be intrusive? To what degree should each action have a noticeable impact on the game's world, and what degree of permanence should these impacts have? How can we effectively communicate the consequences of players' actions without overwhelming them, or giving an impression of condescension? How can we isolate what makes a given interaction "fun," when the definition of "fun" in itself is so nebulous and elusive?

It is the job of an interaction designer to answer these questions, along with the dozens more that arise with any design task, and deliver a satisfying experience. This requires an intimate understanding of player needs, preferences, and motivations, as well as foundational knowledge built from existing designs. A good starting point, therefore, is to assess how games, and the way we play them, has evolved throughout the course of history.

1.2 A (relatively) brief history of game interaction

Five thousand years ago, as ancient civilizations blossomed in northern Africa and the Middle East, people invented and played games. In our first few millennia as a society, early humans began practicing agriculture, economics, and law, while simultaneously exploring the arts and creating the first known games. These games ranged in strategic complexity, and varied in their cultural or religious significance. For many of these games, only fragmented artifacts survive; the exact rules long since faded or changed throughout the generations to become a distant cousin of their past selves. Nonetheless, from what does remain, we can glimpse at the origins of what would eventually become the rich landscape of games we know today.

Some of the earliest artifacts related to games are small tokens unearthed at burial sites in southern Turkey dating back to the third millennium BCE. Carved from stone to resemble creatures, projectiles, and pyramids, the tokens are thought to have functioned as game pieces, similar to other objects found throughout Mesopotamia from the same period. However, little is known about their exact meaning, with no records existing to describe the games that might have been played with these pieces.

More substantial remnants exist for games played in Sumeria and Egypt around the same time. Arguably the most notable of these creations is the *Royal Game of Ur*. Also known as the *Game of Twenty Squares*, the *Royal Game* featured race-to-the-end gameplay, with boards dating back to the twentieth century BCE found throughout the Middle East and the Mediterranean. Another game originating in this era is *Senet*, an Egyptian creation thought to have been symbolically tied to the afterlife.

Figure 1.3 Board games invented in antiquity, clockwise from top left: *Senet*, an Egyptian game thought to represent a journey through the afterlife; The *Royal Game Of Ur*, rumoured to have been connected to personal fortune-telling; *Pachisi*, ancestor to *Sorry!* and more blatantly *Parcheesi*; *Go*, perhaps the game with the longest-standing ruleset.

Credit: Image of Senet by the Metropolitan Museum of Art (CC0). Image of *The Royal Game of UR* by BabelStone at the British Museum (CC0). Image of *Go* cropped from a photo by Goban1 (public domain). Image of Pachisi by Daniel Schwen at the Children's Museum of Indianapolis (CC BY-SA 4.0). All original images obtained via Wikimedia Commons.

Despite the fact that many ancient rulesets are assumed to be lost forever, we can already see commonalities in design between these games and their modern counterparts. Carved tokens marched along boards crafted from wood and stone. Marked tetrahedra or sticks were tossed to determine players' allocated movements across a game board, injecting chance and serving as a primitive form of dice.

Though separated by thousands of years, the *Game of Twenty Squares* is not so different from a contemporary race-to-the-end game like *Sorry!*. Stripped to their most essential description, both involve rolling dice to move tokens across a game board. Of course, it should be noted that *Sorry!* is more or less identical to the game *Pachisi*, played in India for centuries before its re-imagining and popularization in the West. Regardless, it is telling that the basic components and interactions associated with board games thousands of years ago still exist in successful games today.

These commonalities are not to suggest that there exists some magical set of interactions, outside of which there is no room for innovation. Hundreds of new board games are released each year which push the boundaries of tabletop design, promote social play, and rethink classic interaction paradigms. Take the idea of a game board, for example. In its most basic form, a game board is a static surface used to track the location of tokens. But why should a board limit itself to a fixed configuration? Why should it serve as a backdrop, rather than an active part of play?

Modern game design explores the answers to such questions, often subverting convention by putting a twist on classic mechanics and modes of play. The static game board is rethought in titles like *Terraforming Mars*, which allows players to change the board's contents during play to simulate shifting the geography of an alien world. In *Carcassonne*, players build the board from individual tiles as the game progresses, creating different layouts with each playthrough. Both of these games, along with dozens of others, present refreshing iterations on the notion of board-based designs. It is a fascinating lesson in the nature of human creativity that the precursors of such ideas can be traced back to antiquity with relative ease.

In addition to board games, sport also played a role in the recreation and tradition of ancient cultures. Perhaps the most famous example is the ancient Olympic Games, which began in Greece around the eighth century BCE as part of a religious festival. Athletes competed in several events which remain popular in some form to this day, including footraces, boxing, javelin, and an early version of mixed martial arts known as *pankration.*

Many team sports are also older than one might think, with roots leading back centuries. Consider football (soccer), for instance, whose earliest recorded ancestor is a game played in China over two thousand years ago. Similar games were played in Japan, Greece, and Rome, all before a standard ruleset was codified in England in the mid-nineteenth century. Safe for modernization of the equipment used and formalization of rules, there is surprisingly little which separates the ancient Chinese game of *tsu-shu* from the football we know today.

Likewise, many of the board and card games invented hundreds of years ago are strikingly similar to their contemporary iterations. *Go*, frequently cited as the oldest game played according to its original rules, is thought to have first appeared as early as four thousand years ago. Chess was invented around the seventh century CE, spreading from India and Persia throughout

Asia and Europe. The first playing cards, printed around the 1300s, mirrored the earlier invention of playing tiles or dominoes in China before the turn of the first millennium. In the centuries that followed, cards would be used to create hundreds of games, many of which are still played today, such as Patience (or Solitaire) in the late 1700s, Poker in the 1830s, and Rummy in the 1890s.

Before the invention of computers, all game interaction was necessarily physical and mostly literal in nature. Though creators and players alike were always free to experiment with fanciful themes, games were still limited by the physical objects they were played with, and the capability of their human operators. Rule complexity was restricted by what human players could be expected to memorize or reference while maintaining reasonable gameplay pace.

Within these confines, a great deal of variety still exists. Simplicity can certainly prove itself a virtue in terms of widespread appeal and longevity. *Snakes and Ladders* can hardly be said to have much depth, and yet it is a veritable mainstay of family board game collections, particularly due to its easy learnability for young children. At the other end of the spectrum, *Dungeons and Dragons* has spawned entire volumes dedicated to explaining lore and the rules of play, with individual game campaigns lasting hours or days.

The realm of game design was always a diverse one, long before the digital age. Human imagination is, for all intents and purposes, practically unbounded, and games have always been free to take advantage of this fact. That said, certain experiences that we now take for granted as a part of digital games are impractical or impossible to achieve otherwise. A physics-based puzzle would require the fabrication and assembly of all required components. Large-scale first-person combat would necessitate hiring a troupe of trained actors, or else coordinating a group of colleagues for a friendly neighbourhood siege—hardly fodder suitable for a Wednesday night on the couch after a long day at work. No matter the level of creativity, confining ourselves entirely to real-world interactions imposes inherent limitations on what can be achieved in authoring a particular experience.

These limitations were shattered remarkably quickly as humans began using computers to make games in the mid-twentieth century. The first patent for an electronic game of sorts, called the *Cathode-Ray Tube Amusement Device*, was issued in 1948, and described a system where players would adjust the path of an electrode beam to hit manually placed targets. Little is known about how functional the initial prototype or prototypes were, as the device never reached the market. It is debatable whether the invention even qualifies as a video game by modern standards, since it involved no real computation, rather serving as a user-controlled display of sorts.

Computer games more or less as we know them today date back to the 1950s, created largely as academic curiosities. The first is often credited as *Noughts and Crosses* (OXO), a version of *tic-tac-toe* created by then-PhD student Alexander Douglas at Cambridge University in 1952. A more well-known example is William Higinbotham's 1958 game *Tennis for Two*. Played on an oscilloscope, *Tennis for Two* was a one-of-a-kind attraction for visitors to New York's Brookhaven National Laboratory; this was long before video games entered the realm of mass production. Four years later, in 1962, a group of programmers at MIT developed *Spacewar!*, a two-player dogfight set in outer space.

Figure 1.4 Early digital games, from left: *Spacewar!* on a PDP-1 computer at the Computer History Museum in California; An arcade cabinet running *Pac-Man*; Legendary *Donkey Kong* player Steve Wiebe participating in the *Kong Off 3* tournament in 2013.

Credit: Image of *Spacewar* cropped from a photo by Joi Ito (CC BY 2.0). Image of *Pac-Man* by Peter Handke (CC0). Image of Steve Wiebe by Datagod (CC BY-SA 4.0). All original images obtained via Wikimedia Commons.

It would take another decade after *Spacewar*'s creation before video games hit the mainstream in the early seventies. From this point onward, the story becomes far more intriguing for game aficionados, replete with all manner of exotic hardware, interpersonal drama, and economic crisis. Here, we will focus on how the evolution of interaction modes and user experience (UX) design brought us to the present day. For those eager to learn more of the vaudeville aspects of game history, some additional readings exploring the subject are provided at the end of this chapter.

No discussion on the history of games would be complete without mention of *Pong*, Atari's 1973 creation that kickstarted the arcade age, eventually bringing about classics like *Pac-Man, Galaga, Space Invaders, Donkey Kong, Dig Dug, Frogger*, and hundreds of others. Arcade cabinets would serve as an introduction to digital games for countless thousands throughout the seventies and eighties. At the time, this marked a massive leap in design and player understanding; games no longer had to physically play out on tabletops, fields, or rinks. Instead, they could live in virtual space, creating a system comprising user, game, and machine.

This new mode of gameplay necessarily introduced a layer of abstraction, requiring an input device of some sort for players to communicate their intended action. Interaction was now metaphorical in some way; rather than physically moving tokens around, a button press would serve as a proxy for firing the weapon on a spaceship. These early devices needed to be simple and easy to learn above all else; with the popularization of home PCs still a decade away, most people had little or no prior experience operating a computer. Early arcade cabinets used dials, switches, and buttons to facilitate user input—interaction paradigms which were already established thanks to devices such as radios and television remotes.

Obviously, such designs were due at least in part due to the novelty of video games and computers in general; the notion of a gamepad was completely alien at the time. Most importantly, though, designers needed to take advantage of what people already knew. The first *Pong* cabinets didn't feature two analog sticks, as a modern audience might expect, but rather a pair of dials. It would be a long journey from these early controls to the sophisticated gaming-specific peripherals that would emerge decades later.

Both technological limitations and economic motivations shaped the experience design of arcade games. The limited computing power available imposed constraints on the complexity of game mechanics and graphics, and the scope of game content. Commercially, turnover needed to be incentivized; one player snagging a few hours of game time on a single quarter was hardly profitable. Both of these pressures favoured shorter play sessions, where a relatively small amount of content could be packed in to boost excitement, and revenue could be maximized.

Consequently, arcade titles could give explicit time limits, or more commonly, dole out a fixed number of lives and let difficulty curves naturally kick players out of the game as their skills faltered. There was a finality associated with the game over screen, at least, until another coin was offered up, with save states out of the question on public machines. And yet, the bragging rights that came with high scores, and the tantalizing possibility of making it just a bit further next time, kept players coming back again and again. Echoes of this thinking still live on in the "one more try" microtransactions found in modern free-to-play puzzle games.

Game experience design would evolve substantially over the next several years, as the advent of home consoles and computers changed how video games were consumed. Instead of making small purchases to spend a short amount of time playing, game copies could be purchased outright. This notion, coupled with the larger scope made possible by increased computing power, led to longer experiences that could be enjoyed over hours, days, or weeks. Home computers also made the craft of game development more accessible, leading to a flood of new industry talent and a veritable explosion in design creativity.

Looking back, many of these early efforts would have been criticized extensively by contemporary standards, technological limitations aside. The transition from coin-operated games to home titles marked a substantial shift in design thinking. Some aspects of the arcade mentality didn't translate well to at-home games, and some of the experiences created for home consoles were unlike anything attempted before. People craved more depth and diversity than mere high scores could provide; they wanted games to build fantastical worlds, tell stories, and let them play with friends.

Hardware design also had its ups and downs throughout this period; imagine holding a Nintendo 64 controller and thinking it to be the state of the art, with its three grips and clunky alternate holding positions. Following the turn of the millennium, rapidly increasing computing power allowed games to become increasingly complex and realistic, allowing game interactions to become more sophisticated in kind.

Forty years ago, watching a few enormous pixels teleport across the screen at the nudge of a clunky joystick was a marvellous delight. Today, we demand immediate responsiveness and fluid motion, often accompanied by lavish animation and rendering that approaches photorealism. With so many computational shackles removed, designers can tweak the timing of every footfall, injecting feedback and personality into every interaction. This freedom has allowed games to become the polished, thoughtful, and satisfying experiences beloved by players everywhere.

Twenty-first-century computing didn't just change the way games looked and felt, but redefined the role games play in our everyday lives. Smartphones and other mobile devices have rendered games ubiquitous, playable anywhere and anytime. Streaming has brought video games on par with traditional sports in terms of viewership. Virtual reality, after years of speculation and sci-fi fodder, has finally established a footing as a platform in its own right. Each of these avenues provides us with more ways to play games, and more opportunities for designers to create innovative and engaging experiences.

The meteoric rise of video games to become arguably the most pervasive form of entertainment prompts a rather obvious question—why? What makes games so very contagious?

Entire volumes could be written (and in fact have been) on player motivation and the psychology of games alone. Throughout this book, we will explore how individual design choices can contribute to a game's appeal, but for a start, consider the many mental, physical, emotional, and social opportunities that a game experience has to offer. Games can move us to laughter, tears, joy, and frustration. They challenge us, in tests of both wit and reflexes, and drive us to reach mastery. Games carry the promise of escapism, telling stories that lift us from the humdrums of reality into a world of our own making. We can use games as tools to tell stories, spread awareness, or share ideas. They allow us to connect with the people we love, and make new friends along the way. Perhaps it is a combination of all these factors that makes games so compelling.

Perhaps our infatuation with games is simply a product of that interminable human appetite for purpose, the desire to *do something*.

1.3 How to use this book

If you've read the whole chapter up to this point, you already have an idea of what we'll be discussing in the rest of the book. For those of you joining us from the cover, or finding this volume open and abandoned in a coffee shop, this is a book about interaction design for video games. More precisely, it is a book about learning to think like an interaction designer, following a user-centric ethos. You will learn how to critically analyze your own designs and those of others, and how to view those designs from the player's perspective. This book will also provide a brief introduction to the study of human-computer interaction, and how to apply general design standards to the task of crafting game interactions.

If you are already a practicing game designer, this volume will help refine your knowledge of interaction design, as well as providing practical examples and designer perspectives for your reference. If you work in another area of game development, the knowledge presented here will help you to communicate more effectively with your design team. If you're a student, this book will provide you with a comprehensive overview of game interaction design and give you an early start in applying a user-centred approach. Lastly, if you're reading this out of pure interest, or a passion for gaming in general, hopefully this book will help you better understand the inner workings of game design, and perhaps inspire you to create something of your own.

This work focuses heavily on the practical application of interaction design. Each chapter will focus on dissecting the design of commercial games, practical exercises, and interviews with experts working in the games industry and games research. Every topic will explore both positive and negative examples taken from existing games, noting what can be learned from successful designs, and how those less successful could be improved to better serve players' needs. Additional materials are suggested at the end of each chapter to further develop your knowledge. You will also find exercises throughout which allow you to practise the concepts introduced, and serve as a starting point for your own work.

Each chapter is written to function on its own, with no particular background from prior chapters necessary for understanding. However, if you are relatively new to game design, we suggest beginning with Chapter 2 to establish some of the terms and ideas used throughout the rest of the book. Chapter 2 will also provide a detailed look at what sort of content you can expect from the sections that follow.

Regardless of where you begin your journey with the remainder of this book, remember that our goal is the same throughout; to create something memorable and magical for our players.

Good luck, and have fun!

Further reading

Game Design Workshop by Tracy Fullerton (4th ed., CRC Press). ISBN: 978-1138098770.
A systems-oriented overview of game design with lots of useful exercises.

Game Development Essentials: An Introduction by Jeannie Novak (3rd ed., Nelson Education). ISBN: 978-1133708797.
A general volume on game development with a focus on industry examples and profiles.

Blood, Sweat, and Pixels by Jason Schreier (Harper). ISBN: 978-0062651235.
Behind-the-scenes drama, agony, and inspiration from the game development industry.

The Ultimate History of Video Games by Steven Kent (Three Rivers Press). ISBN:978-0761536437.
An older, but comprehensive overview of how we got here.

Sources on the history of games

Brown, W. Norman (1964) The Indian Games of Pachisi, Chaupar, and Chausar. In Penn Museum's *Expedition Magazine* (Spring 1964), pp. 32–35.

Computer History Museum (n.d.) Timeline of Computer History: Graphics & Games. Accessed online at www.computerhistory.org/timeline/graphics-games/.

Finkel, Irving L. (2007) On the Rules for the Royal Game of Ur. In *Ancient Board Games in Perspective*. British Museum Press. ISBN: 9780714111537.

Goldsmith, T.T., et al. (1948) Patent for *Cathode-Ray Tube Amusement Device*. US Patent No. 2455992.

International Olympic Committee (n.d.) Welcome to the Ancient Olympic Games. Accessed online at www.olympic.org/ancient-olympic-games.

Murray, H.J.R. (1913) *A History of Chess*. Oxford University Press. 2015 reprint ISBN: 9781632202932.

Parlett, David Sidney. (1990) *The Oxford Guide to Card Games*. Oxford University Press. ISBN: 9780192141651.

Piccione, Peter A. (1980) In Search of the Meaning of Senet. In *Archaeology* (33), pp. 55–58.

Sağlamtimur, Haluk and Massimino, Martina G.M. Wealth Sacrifice and Legitimacy: The Case of the Early Bronze Age Başur Höyük Cemetery. In *Proceedings of the 10th International Congress on the Archaeology of the Ancient Near East*, pp. 329–342.

Stewart, Mark. (1998) *Soccer: A History of the World's Most Popular Game*. F. Watts. ISBN: 9780531114568.

Exercises

Digital devolution

Take a digital game of your choosing and re-imagine it as a board game. You can use any game you like, but as a starting point we advise choosing something simple, such as a classic arcade game like *Asteroids* or *Pac-Man*. Try to answer the following questions at minimum:

- How many players is the game designed for?
- What is the objective of the game?
- How does one turn play out?
- Can you describe a full ruleset?
- What do the board and any pieces/cards/and so on look like?

To express your design, use writing, sketches, and some simple physical pieces if you have supplies handy.

Fusion cuisine

Take two games, either board or digital, that you're very familiar with (e.g., have played for several hours), and envision what they'd look like if combined into a single game. Create a one-page mockup illustrating the spirit of the final game in writing, sketches, edited screenshots, and so on. Here are some questions to get you started:

- What is the name of your abominable hybrid?
- What mechanics does it borrow from each game?
- What is the overall storyline?
- How will the game look?

(Continued)

15

(Continued)

- What does a "slice" of gameplay look like in a couple of sentences?
- How does the game set itself apart from each of its inspirations?
- What are some new ideas that emerge in bringing the two games together (e.g., mechanics, characters, and so on)?

If you're feeling incredibly ambitious, you can try your hand at prototyping a rough version of your game physically (if your fusion is a board game) or prototyping a couple of key interactions in a free game engine like Unity (if your fusion is a digital game).

2

The Parlance of Play

If you were awake at any point between 1995 and 2005, you probably heard the word *interactive* tossed around left and right as one of the era's most pervasive buzzwords. Much like the phrases *big data, machine learning,* and *pumpkin spice* defined the 2010s as a technocratic vision of AI-powered autumn-scented everything, the word *interactive* conjures up an image of digital acceleration in the late 90s, when computers landed in every middle-class home and the nascent internet was busy rediscovering music piracy.

Pristine rows of jewel CD cases lined the shelves of every electronics department as the direct-to-consumer software business took off, promising the latest *interactive experience* that could help you write a book, edit photos, teach your child math, do your taxes, or simply have a terrifying cartoon dog tell you how to use your computer.[1] The word *interactive* is not limited to computers lexicographically, but if I asked you to think of something *interactive*, you'd probably imagine an app or a computing device. But why is that?

At an incredibly basic level, computers are tools. Our experience with tools is defined by how we use them, and computers are somewhat unique in this regard because they are capable of using us back. They can communicate with us, and dynamically respond to our actions. You can use pen and paper to write, or you can use a computer. If you use a computer, you can take advantage of things like spelling and grammar suggestions, word prediction, and so on: it reacts to what you have done. This is not possible with passive tools like pen and paper, at least, not without the assistance of potent psychedelics.

We can define this distinguishing characteristic more formally by specifying that there is two-way communication between humans and computers. We communicate with computers by using input devices, such as typing

---

[1] Some may prefer us to forget about Microsoft Bob entirely, but that will never happen.

The Game Designer's Playbook. Samantha Stahlke and Pejman Mirza-Babaei, Oxford University Press.
© Samantha Stahlke and Pejman Mirza-Babaei (2022). DOI: 10.1093/oso/9780198845911.003.0002

on a keyboard. They communicate with us via output devices, such as displaying words on a screen. This two-way communication does not occur with something like pen and paper. This is where we return to our beloved action-oriented terminology; we *act* on passive tools, whereas we *interact* with computers.

2.1 Making humans and computers play nicely

Different sources from different fields have a colourful spectrum of definitions for the words *interaction*, *interactive*, and *interactivity*. Debating these definitions here would be a remarkable waste of time, and so we will establish our own quick addition to this rainbow before moving on. An *interaction* is a reciprocal exchange of information between entities. Typing on a keyboard and seeing letters appear on screen is an interaction. Talking to someone is an interaction. Poking a rock with a stick is not an interaction, unless the rock has something to say in response. Something is *interactive* if it can be interacted with. A smartphone is interactive. A person is also interactive. A rock is not. *Interactivity* refers to interaction between things. We can speak of interactivity among people, interactivity between people and computers, or interactivity among computers. Sadly, we cannot speak of interactivity between rocks and sticks, which may explain their poor attitudes toward the study of human-computer interaction.

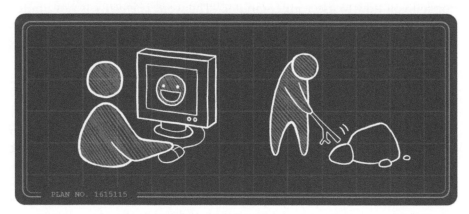

Figure 2.1 On the left, an interaction between a human and a computer. On the right, a sad and lonely human looking for a friend. Little do they realize that the real friendship was the stick they found along the way.

If you're reading this book, it's almost certain that you've already had several dozen interactions with technology today. In fact, feel free to take a quick glance at your phone and check Twitter, Instagram, Tik Tok, or whatever other social media phenomenon is currently at the forefront of your personal zeitgeist. We'll still be here when you get back. After all, since this book is not interactive in itself, it lacks the means to lose its patience with you.

The interactions we have with computers are rich and diverse—even those we have come to take for granted. Through mice, keyboards, and touch-screens, you can beckon forth any tidbit of information you desire from the entire body of human knowledge. You can receive messages from friends, dismiss messages from colleagues, check the weather, shop for umbrellas, learn how to make lasagne, read a novel, write a novel, order takeout, ogle the missteps of a public figure, admire the world's largest cat, play games, design games, and be reminded to call your mother (it's really the least you can do). The possibilities that such interactions afford us are objectively ridiculous in scope; it's no surprise that these devices have become indispensable on such a short timescale.

Even discounting our use of smartphones and personal computers, we still have countless interactions with digital products in our daily lives. We browse for movies on our televisions, set timers on our ovens, let our thermostats decide when they can save power, tell the lights to turn on when we get home, and pop little pods into our coffeemakers, relying on them to know the rest.

Our experience with different interactions can be as wildly different as the interactions themselves. We might have a pleasant time using our phone to play a casual game, or a miserable time trying to figure out the secret sequence of buttons that puts a universal remote in pairing mode. An individual's perception of the quality of an interaction will vary depending on their needs, preferences, and prior experience. What may be a minor inconvenience to one person may be immensely frustrating for another. What might be obvious to an experienced user may be inscrutably confusing to a novice. Different people experience the same interaction differently.

Interactions do not simply spring out of nowhere for us to criticize. They are designed, with varying amounts of thoughtfulness and success, to help us accomplish tasks, entertain us, and delight us. Interaction design encompasses everything from outlining an app's user workflow to laying out the buttons on a coffeemaker. Interaction design is in software, and in hardware. It's choosing fonts and colours, creating icons, and making widgets. It's research, prototyping, implementation, and testing. Interaction design is about understanding users' needs, identifying what they need or want to do, and creating the best possible experience for them to do so.

We must also recognize that the immediate effect of an interaction is merely one aspect of its significance. Multiple interactions can support a larger goal for the end user. Further, the design of these interactions can have an impact beyond individual users, serving a broader purpose.

Let's examine how the impact of an interaction can extend beyond its short-term consequences with a quick example. Imagine a navigation app that uses data about traffic flows and local construction to minimize driving time as opposed to route length. One interaction you have in using the app might be searching for your workplace on the map. This might immediately provide you with an estimation of travel time, and the option to plan a route. In conjunction with other interactions, this can support the larger goal of saving time on your morning commute. At a macro scale, the app might aim to help reduce emissions by shrinking the amount of time vehicles spend on the road.

Interaction designers need to consider each level of impact in their work. Good interaction design follows a *multilayered* approach: it considers how an interaction can immediately satisfy a user, how that interaction supports the user's overall goal, and how it can help fulfill the broader purpose of the experience they are creating.

We're not here to talk about navigation apps or coffeemakers, though—we're here to talk about games. Everything we've just discussed applies just as much to games as it does to smart appliances, word processors, social media sites, or any other interactive product.

This may not be obvious at first. Games and productivity applications, after all, offer vastly different experiences. Though the interactions contained therein will vary accordingly, the core philosophy of interaction design in games is still the same. Just as in other applications, interaction design in games is about creating a satisfying user experience. The multilayered approach discussed previously also applies to games, and can be employed to help create a more cohesive experience.

At first glance, it may be difficult to see how a single game interaction has any long-term impact. The act of play is having fun in the moment, fleeting, and can be aimless. Some games do not even provide players with any explicit direction or goals, having no win condition. How can we view the impact of interactions in such games as multilayered?

Consider the sandbox game *Minecraft*. Though *Minecraft* does have an ending of a sort, it never pushes players toward any specific goal. Aside from basic survival mechanics, players need not accomplish anything in particular to play, as is standard in the sandbox genre. And yet, we can still view the interactions in *Minecraft* through the lens of multilayered design.

Take a single interaction from the game's core gathering and crafting mechanics, mining diamonds. This provides multiple immediate delights for the player—the excitement of seeing a rare resource, the satisfaction as the block is slowly chipped away, the plucky sound effects that play as it is mined successfully. However, the consequences of this interaction also support players' larger goals. Though no explicit goals are given to the player,

Minecraft creates an environment where players define their own goals, such as building a mansion or having a full suit of expensive armour. Interactions to acquire resources support these goals by giving the player more materials to build and craft with. Taken together, this interactive loop of resource acquisition, crafting, and consumption supports the game's larger purpose: immersing players in a world that serves both as an escapist fantasy and a creative outlet.

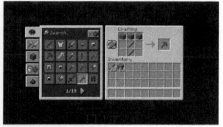

Figure 2.2 "Layers" of interaction in *Minecraft*: resource collection (top left), crafting basic tools (top right), and building a base (bottom). In this case, the base is a jungle hideaway used by one of the authors when she's not busy griefing her friends in the server.

Credit: Minecraft was developed and published by Mojang Studios.

It is important to note that many games have purposes beyond entertainment. Researchers and creators alike have explored the use of specially designed games for education, therapeutic purposes, physical rehabilitation, and professional training, among other applications. Such endeavours are commonly referred to as "serious games."

Having broader goals beyond creating a fun experience is far from unique to serious games, however. Many commercial games explore serious subjects, aim to educate players in some way, or seek to have some form of social benefit. This is especially true in recent years, as designers have sought to tackle issues like war, mental wellness, and grief in nuanced ways. Mental health in particular has been explored by a number of games that help to destigmatize individuals' struggles and provide an empathetic experience for players. *Celeste, Night in the Woods*, and *Hellblade: Senua's Sacrifice*, for instance, all feature main characters dealing with mental wellness issues, providing sensitive, informed representation. Designing games that aim to provide something more than entertainment gives interaction designers the additional challenge of figuring out how to support these broader impacts even in moment-to-moment gameplay.

Understanding how better interaction design can help enhance both immediate player enjoyment and a game's intended overall impact is the focus of this book. Together, we will examine how a game's individual interactions come together to create a fulfilling user experience. Our discourse will involve examples primarily drawn from commercial games in the consumer entertainment space. However, the design principles discussed apply not only to commercial entertainment games, but serious games, gamified applications, and games for social change. Each chapter explores a different area of applied interaction design in games, aiming to provide a complete overview of how thoughtful interaction design can be employed to create better game experiences. If you'd like an overview of what is explored in each chapter, you can find a brief outline in Section 2.5.

Before we dive into the specifics of game interaction terminology and how interaction design is practiced in the industry, let's look at how successful interaction design manifests in popular games.

2.2 What successful game interaction design looks like

You're clung to the side of a cliff, squinting through the downpour of a tropical storm. The weather had changed in an instant, and what you thought would be a routine expedition has quickly become a perilous journey into the unknown. As lightning crashes behind you, you take one final desperate leap, grabbing onto the top ledge and hauling yourself to safety. You look around, awestruck by the beauty of the jungle sprawling out around you. Without glancing at your map, you have no idea where you are, but you do know that you'll remember this feeling of discovery for a long time.

Gameplay in *The Legend of Zelda: Breath of the Wild* is packed with moments like this. Though prior games in the series had typically given players carte blanche to roam most of their landscapes freely, *BotW* was the first Zelda game to feature a sprawling world that was open by design. Boss fights can be completed in any order, and artificial boundaries are never thrown at the player to say: "We're not ready for you to come here yet." Nintendo aimed to create an experience for players to feel immersed in a fantasy world where they have absolute freedom.

This is achieved brilliantly through the game's world design, but that feeling of freedom also owes a great deal of its success to how its core navigation mechanics are implemented. Navigating in *BotW* isn't just about holding forward to run; in going from one place to another, players have a litany of tools at their disposal and actually interact with the environment during travel. Players can run, climb, glide from high ground, surf downhill atop a shield they're carrying, ride a horse, or conjure pillars of ice to cross dangerous waters. Climbing especially proves itself an indispensable part of the game's discovery-driven feel. With rare exception, players can climb any vertical surface. Cliffs, trees, buildings—where a sheer ten-metre vertical wall would say "this is the level boundary" in most any other title, in *BotW* it beckons "if you can make it up here, you're bound to find something amazing." With each leap up a cliffside, players reinforce their agency and anticipate the sight of some new landscape, delivering on the absolute freedom that *Breath of the Wild* seeks to achieve.

Figure 2.3 A diverse set of landscapes in *Breath of the Wild* supported by an equally diverse navigation toolkit. Besides running around, the player can use a paraglider to fly (left images) or climb to reach a vista atop a tower (top right) or cliff (bottom right).

Credit: The Legend of Zelda: Breath of the Wild was developed and published by Nintendo.

Plenty of games don't aspire to grant players total freedom; sometimes, they aim to emulate a carefully crafted film where the player is cast in the lead role. The *Uncharted* series is famous for creating such experiences, where players are taken on a veritable thrill ride as action hero Nathan Drake. Designing the flow of interactions to fit a tightly linear, scripted path is critical;

players must be guided to take the same basic path with the correct timing, but still feel a sense of control over what happens. Naughty Dog achieves this in the *Uncharted* games by pushing the player in the right direction without relying on the invisible walls, obnoxious quest prompts, and "follow this path exactly" UI (user interface) that have become frustratingly ubiquitous in modern action-adventure titles. Players are guided by topography, the placement of objects in individual areas, colour cues in the environment, dialogue from characters, and dynamic obstacles thrown at them in a believably coincidental but entirely deliberate manner. Even though players know they are being led from setpiece to setpiece, the organic feeling of each decision they make to run, shoot, climb, and drive their way forward preserves the magic of the experience.

Both the *Uncharted* and *Legend of Zelda* games are what you might refer to as "traditional" in terms of their form factor and expected player habits. Both are usually played on relatively roomy screens, and players have access to peripherals like headsets and gamepads. Players generally play for an hour or more at a stretch, and may return to the game once or twice a day at most.

The same cannot be said of mobile games, at least, not typically. Most users will be playing on a small screen, without audio, for a few minutes at a time. Without access to more complex input methods, mobile games need to rely on touch input, necessitating simple controls. In a saturated market with so much competing for our limited attention during short periods, games try to keep the player coming back over and over, creating a routine. Successful games in this space reflect these considerations in their interaction design. *Angry Birds*, one of the first breakthrough hits in the mobile marketplace, gave players a series of short, snappy levels where everything they needed to know was visible at once. Controls were as simple as they could get, with players swiping across the screen to slingshot their avian ammunition into action. Though such an interaction may have been a lacklustre click-and-drag for a PC game, as a gestural control, it is incredibly satisfying to execute. Action is immediate and provides a torrent of enjoyable feedback to players through visual and sound effects, score pop-ups, and character animations.

Many games in the mobile space use an onslaught of feedback for every interaction to give players an accelerated sense of reward. *Candy Crush*, the first massive hit in a long string of *Bejeweled* clones (naturally, *Bejeweled* itself was a clone of *Shariki*), uses this strategy to the extreme. Every move, every use of a power-up, and every completed level is met with a saccharine combination of joyous sound effects, harp riffs, animated text, bursting particle effects, flashing lights, and congratulations. Of course, *Candy Crush* employs this sort of spectacle alongside prompts to spend real money in-game that are hardly subtle, and a tightly controlled reward schedule for repeated play.

This creates an experience which is objectively shallow and manipulative more than anything else, and yet players keep returning. Here, we will treat games like *Candy Crush* with care, as examples to be learned from, but not emulated. Quality interaction design isn't just about ensuring success, it's about respecting the needs and boundaries of our players.

Figure 2.4 In *Candy Crush*, players are bombarded with constant affirmations that their every swipe is a gift from the heavens. It's an undeniably engaging feast for the eyes (and ears), but ignoring all that hindbrain stimulation, it's also a ploy to keep players coming back and eventually shelling out some cash. Getting confetti for completing the guided tutorial on your first try feels a bit like winning the Nobel for changing a lightbulb without getting mustard on your shirt.

Credit: Candy Crush was developed and published by King.

Ethical commentary aside, recent design trends and shifts in the marketplace have also created opportunities for innovation. Twenty years ago, touchscreens were mostly a promising oddity. Today, most people cart one around in their pocket, and the clunky stylus-driven games of old have been replaced with slick, fluid experiences. But mobile gaming is just one avenue that's helped to diversify the nature of game interaction; other advances, such as the still-emerging space of virtual reality and the rapidly growing world of esports, are also changing the ways we play.

Many innovative games have been released for VR in the past few years, though none have quite matched the fanfare of Valve's latest entry in the *Half-Life* franchise. *Half-Life: Alyx* earns well-deserved praise from fans and critics alike for its atmospheric level design, combat, story, and soundtrack.

Perhaps the most important reason *Alyx* shines as a VR title, however, is the sheer attention to detail in making each interaction feel as natural and satisfying as possible. Playing *Alyx* doesn't feel like playing a first-person shooter that's been ported to VR. Interactions that are impossible to execute in high fidelity with a gamepad are fully realized with gestural controls.

The act of looting, typically relegated to button presses out of necessity, is replaced with physically rifling through desk drawers and plucking grenades off the toolbelts of dead foes. Players are given the sensation of having telekinetic powers with the gravity gloves, a piece of in-game tech that allows objects to be hooked in and grabbed from afar. Gunplay is most often up-close and personal, having players scramble to grab a new magazine and reload their weapon manually without relying on a character's animation to do it for them. The game switches flawlessly from adventure, to first-person shooter, to survival horror and back again. It manages to do this without skipping a beat or feeling disjointed because its experience minimizes the barrier between real-life action and in-game interaction so effectively.

Games like *Alyx* show us that good interaction design doesn't just mean incrementally improving on convention to deliver solid experiences. Good interaction design can mean respecting players' expectations while simultaneously surprising them with innovations that expand our understanding of what games can accomplish.

2.3 The field of game interaction design

Many areas of game development are tricky to describe academically. They are multidisciplinary, needing to reconcile subtle differences in terms and methods from the domains that inform them. Like the game industry itself, they are constantly changing. Pieces of knowledge can rapidly evolve significantly or become completely obsolete. Interaction design may be one of the most fickle of them all, with trends flaring up and dying out in what seems like an instant.

Irrespective of its mercurial nature, however, a broad discussion of the field is still helpful. Reflecting on the research domains that have contributed to interaction design helps to explain the reasoning behind generally accepted ideas. Keeping an eye on progress in these domains can also help to identify developments that will eventually gain traction in game interaction design.

Naturally, as a child born of many different fields, game interaction design has inherited a great deal of terminology, alongside inventing some of its own. Understanding this language establishes common ground for communication between professionals, and breaking down examples to analyze them in an abstract way. So, how do we speak (formally) about game interaction?

2.3.1 *The language of game interaction design*

We have already established the abstract definition of *interaction* as a reciprocal exchange of information between entities. In other words, one entity communicates with another, and the other communicates back based on the information received. In games, one entity is the player, and the other is the game. The idea of mutual information exchange applies to two or more entities, rather than two alone; in a multiplayer game, many players and the game itself will all participate in the communication of information.

Everything we *do* in games is an interaction. We communicate with a game by using some input device like a controller or mouse and keyboard, and the game communicates the result through some output device, like a screen or speaker. We issue the command of "run" by pushing forward on the left analog stick, and the game shows us our character running forward. We issue the command of "eat" by clicking on food in our inventory, and the game plays a crunching sound effect. Sometimes, these interactions bleed into the real world. If we issue the command of "invite player," we're reaching out to another human. If we issue the command of "buy premium currency," we're making a huge mistake and should probably require a password to prevent late-night impulse purchases.

By abstracting the concepts of "action" and "effect," we can create a common model for all game interactions. Since we are ultimately creating an experience for players, we will centre our viewpoint around the player's perspective. We will call this breakdown the *player interaction model*. The player interaction model describes the steps involved in an interaction from beginning to end:

1. **Game communicates information about state to player.** Before deciding what to do, players need to know what is going on in a game. This means the game must communicate about things like the surrounding environment, available resources, and so on.

   Example: Displaying the player's current health on-screen using heart icons.

2. **Player decides what to do.** Based on the information available, the player decides what they want to do. Depending on the game, this might mean running, jumping, swimming, flying, shooting, crafting, building, talking, cooking, or vandalizing another player's territory.

   Example: Noticing you are low on health and deciding to drink a potion.

27

3. **Player communicates desired action to game.** The player communicates their intent to the game via the input device used (e.g., mouse and keyboard).

   Example: Clicking a health potion in your inventory.

4. **Game reacts to action.** Based on the player's input, the game updates internally to reflect changes in its state as a result. This might mean things like changing the position of objects in the world or updating resource values.

   Example: Increasing the player's health.

5. **Game communicates result of action to player.** Feedback needs to be provided on the effects of their actions for players to know how the game's state has changed as a result. This might include sound effects, animations, particle effects, controller vibration, voice clips, or simply updating the heads-up display (HUD), among any other forms of feedback the game can provide.

   Example: Playing a sound effect and updating the display of the player's current health.

You will notice from this breakdown that it forms a cycle quite neatly. The consequences of one interaction change the game's state, the communication of which to the player is updated accordingly. Based on this new information, players decide what to do next, creating a cycle of communication between player and game as the player takes one action after another.

You may also notice that steps 2 and 4 do not involve direct communication. These steps are where the player decides what to do (reacts to information from the game) and the game updates itself (reacts to information from the player). Interaction design focuses on refining the communication that happens in steps 1, 3, and 5 to provide a better experience for players. Each of these steps relies on reaching across the boundary between player and game. Bridging the gap between a player's brain and a game application is accomplished through the devices we have mentioned, like controllers and screens, and often supported by virtual elements, like menus and HUDs. We can refer to these points of contact as *interfaces*: things that facilitate the interaction between player and game.

Formally speaking, you may hear of four basic types of interaction. These four categories are not mutually exclusive, rather being used to help describe the combination of qualities that define different interactions. We will not use these terms extensively in this book, but it is helpful to understand them, and they can be useful in helping to identify the types of actions that players need to take in games at a high level.

PLAN NO. 12151516

Figure 2.5 The cycle of game interaction. The game communicates with players through visuals, sound and other forms of output. Players communicate with the game by providing input through peripherals, gestures, or some other means of control. This back-and-forth surrounds every interaction players have with a game. In the previous case, the player notices they're low on health and decide to heal—and if they arrive at a point where they're low on health again, the cycle repeats itself.

Instructing is the act of giving a command to a system. In a game, this might be something like hitting the reload button, selecting a weapon from a menu, or typing an action in a text adventure.

Conversing is engaging in a dialogue. In games, this might mean talking to other players over voice chat, or asking a non-player character (NPC) about the local area.

Manipulating is interacting with virtual objects. This type of interaction has always existed in games (e.g., opening doors, pushing crates). Input methods like touchscreens and VR controllers have helped to create more high-fidelity representations of these interactions in games (e.g., by allowing you to reach out and grab a door handle instead of pressing a button to open it).

Exploring is movement through a virtual environment. Many games, particularly shooters, action-adventure games, role-playing games (RPGs), platformers, and other games with a first- or third-person perspective, are heavily reliant on this type of interaction for the player to move through a game's world.

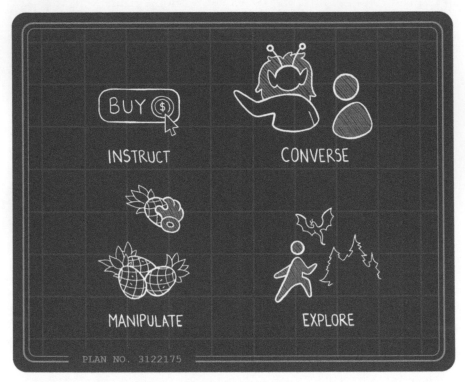

Figure 2.6 Four types of interaction. Instruction is giving an explicit command, such as hitting a button to purchase something from an in-game merchant. Conversing is engaging in dialogue, such as receiving a tip on the local goblin invasion from your friendly neighbourhood butterfly lion elf. Manipulation is interaction with virtual objects, such as laboriously creating a stack of tropical fruits. Exploration is moving through a virtual environment, whether the depths of the ocean, the outer reaches of space, or a forest filled with dragons.

Like many concepts in game interaction design, this terminology is borrowed from the broader domain of interaction design, itself a descendant of sorts to human-computer interaction. In fact, game interaction design borrows a great deal more from other domains than you might first imagine.

2.3.2   *Fields related to game interaction design*

As a hugely multi-disciplinary industry, game development has stolen the lunch money of many different fields during its rapid growth. Game interaction design is no exception, existing at the intersection of software engineering, understanding human behaviour, and the study of game systems. Here you will find a brief description of some of the fields that have contributed heavily to the space of game interaction design. If you're curious to know more about any of these areas, you might want to browse some recent research, or leaf through an introductory textbook, to get an even better footing with the groundwork for interaction design. If you're feeling particularly thorough, go ahead and obtain a doctorate in one or more of the following subjects before continuing this book.

> **Game design** in general describes the design of all manner of game systems, from core mechanics, to story and mission structures, to AI behaviours, to cinematics, and everything in between. Level design is often included under the terminological umbrella of game design as well, though "game designer" and "level designer" are typically separate jobs at all but the smallest of studios. If you like, you can think of game interaction design as a subset of game design. We're not so picky about definitions in this book, and we promise not to tell.

> **Human-computer interaction (HCI)** is a field that aims to understand our relationship with computers. HCI is a broad domain that encompasses everything from evolving new design methods, to developing new hardware, to observing how people use technology in their everyday lives. The body of knowledge that has emerged from the study of HCI has a substantial influence on game interaction design. The concept of user-centred design (UCD), for instance, which demands a focus on user needs and attitudes throughout the design process, is essentially a prerequisite for good game interaction design. More information about UCD is provided in Chapter 10.

> **User experience research** centres on evaluating the effectiveness of interactive systems. Of particular interest is games user research (GUR), which focuses on understanding user experience (UX) in games. As with any design discipline, evaluation is an essential part of game interaction design. Interaction designers should have at least a basic understanding of GUR methods as a result. The overview of evaluation methods given in Chapter 11 can serve as a starting point for those unfamiliar with the field.

Ludology is an overly fancy Latin-inspired portmanteau referring to the study of games, particularly viewing games as formal systems. Ultimately, every interaction we design is a pathway for players to alter the state of a game system. As an interaction designer, you will need to have a solid understanding of how a game's subsystems relate to one another to create meaningful context for presenting interactions to the player and providing feedback.

Cognition, psychology, and social science help us understand how people think, behave, and interact with one another. Communication is an essential part of any interaction, whether between two players or players and the game itself. Research in human cognition and psychology can help us to design interactions that will elicit the perceptual and emotional responses we want our players to experience. Understanding social interactions and cultural norms also help us in knowing what players expect from successful communication.

Like every other part of game development, game interaction design also shares a relationship by association with computer science. Typically, interaction design specialists will be fairly removed from the technical programming aspects of a development pipeline. The exact skillset you need to practice interaction design in the industry may vary depending on the needs of your studio and the role you are asked to assume, bringing us to the next topic at hand.

2.3.3 *Who does this sort of thing in game development?*

While the title of "Game Interaction Designer" does exist in the industry, you will rarely find such specialized titles outside of very large studios with several hundred employees. The more common specialist role associated with interaction design is that of the UX designer, a job that overlaps heavily with interaction design while having a focus more on the gestalt of the game experience. UX designers are commonly found at medium-to-large development studios, especially those with a player-centric design ethos. Plenty of UX professionals would argue that a dedicated UX designer is necessary on any team with half a dozen people or more. With the tight budgets and timelines of game development, this is often not the case in reality.

For smaller studios and independent developers without UX designers, interaction design is usually rolled into the responsibilities of game designers. This can be a natural fit for smaller projects, as a designer can sketch out plans for how players will interact with a game's systems during the conceptualization and refinement of those systems.

Even if interaction design is not an explicit component of your role at a studio, it may still relate heavily to the work that you do. If UI programming is part of your job, you will probably work closely with interaction designers, or be asked to take on some design responsibility yourself at a smaller studio. 2D artists and graphic designers will often be tasked with creating elements of a game's graphical user interface, and may be granted significant influence over a game's interface design. Animators and sound designers play a substantial role in shaping the feedback that game interactions provide. A solid understanding of how this feedback will affect player decision-making and convey the correct tone is essential in such work. Lastly, programmers responsible for implementation need to understand exactly how the interactions they create should proceed and why, helping to prevent small technical changes from unintentionally muddying design intent.

In a perfect world, anyone who works in game development should have a solid understanding of game interaction design, seeing as how it permeates most every aspect of a player's experience. Of course, this statement smacks of a self-centred specialist fanaticism in much the same fashion as "everyone is a UX designer" or "management needs to know engine programming." And yet, such dogmas are more idealist than self-centred; everyone on a development team really does contribute in some way to UX, and management really should understand the technical details of development to some degree. The point here is that, though dedicated interaction design is certainly a specialist role, the field of interaction design is useful to understand regardless of your job title.

2.4 How can we define successful game interaction design?

Good interaction design begets a good game experience, as we have already explored at a high level. But beyond appreciating specific instances of well-crafted interactions, how can we create a universal assessment of game interaction quality?

Quality, like fun, can be a frustratingly nebulous concept in game development. Some comparisons have obvious conclusions; players will prefer a game with responsive controls over one with input lag, and view the former as being of higher quality. More subjective questions lead to more divided responses, though. Some players will enjoy visual novels with heavy narrative content and cutscenes interwoven through exploration, while others will lean on the skip button and resent the lack of "real gameplay." Some players will love the flurry of a fast-paced online shooter, while others will stay away to play something they find less stressful.

A skilled designer will keep the characteristics and preferences of their target audience in mind throughout the development process—an ethos aptly referred to as *user-centred design*. We can apply this user-centric approach to give a much clearer definition of "success" with respect to game interaction design. Given that we know who our target players are, we can consider five questions about any given interaction from the player's perspective:

1. **"Would I want to do this?"** The initial appeal of an interaction determines whether players will be inclined to try a new experience in the first place. Here, it is essential that the designer knows the preferences of their target player, and appeals to past positive experiences where possible. A sequel in a franchise, for instance, should use familiar elements to bring back returning players, while incorporating some changes or additions to keep things exciting and create new fans.

2. **"Do I know how to do this?"** Players need to understand the steps taken to complete a specific in-game action, whether intuitively or through explicit instruction. If they cannot understand what needs to be done, they will frustratedly search for the information elsewhere, or quite possibly give up entirely. Consider an enemy vulnerable only to fire; cues in its design (e.g., resembling wood or ice) or in-game hints can help players understand what to do. Without such information available, relying on the player to "just know" may result in frustration as they swing a sword repeatedly to no avail and eventually give up.

3. **"Can I do this?"** This question asks about an interaction's usability. Burying a needed command in six layers of menus, having unjustifiably complex control mappings, and failing to provide any feedback on whether an action was successful are all excellent ways to ensure that nobody will ever be able to enjoy your game. Understandable interfaces, thoroughly tested control schemes, and abundant feedback will all improve the usability of the interactions they support.

4. **"Is it fun to do this?"** Fun is that other nebulous concept we mentioned earlier. Like the initial appeal of an interaction, whether something is perceived as fun depends a great deal on user preference. It is generally impossible, or at least wildly unreliable, to attempt evaluating this question as a self-proclaimed design expert. More so than any other characteristic, fun requires real players to validate.

5. **"Would I want to do this again?"** Even if the answer to each prior question is resoundingly positive, this last point can prove the swift death of any interactive experience. What might be fun at first can wear out its welcome, a party game played once and left to collect virtual dust on its digital shelf. Retention and replay value are both dependent on creating interactions that not only hook players in, but create long-term appeal.

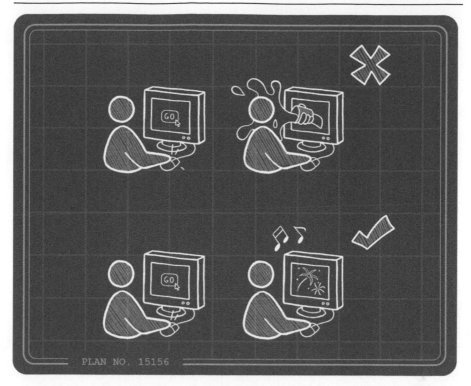

PLAN NO. 15156

Figure 2.7 Top: you generally want to avoid giving users a negative experience on purpose, unless of course you're employing a bit of tactful punishment to make something like a boss fight more rewarding in the end. Bottom: using pleasant feedback can help to make an interaction more satisfying.

If players can say yes to each of these questions, then our design is successful. This concept bears resemblance to many such models in HCI and game design, often referred to as layers or levels of experience design.

For readers familiar with HCI, this discourse has no doubt brought upon flashbacks of diagrams featuring pyramids, nested circles, or a gaggle of arrows, and no apology on our part can fix the cacophony of geometry rattling around inside your head. But whether this is the first time you've seen a breakdown of user experience, or you've already seen a dozen different ones this week, the takeaway is the same. The number of layers, the terminology, and the nightmarish shapes used to contain them are irrelevant. What matters is that successful interaction design means fulfilling the needs of your players from the moment they see your game to the end of their first playthrough and beyond.

2.5 What to expect from the rest of this book

Becoming a game designer is like becoming a surgeon, albeit with significantly fewer lives and significantly more unnecessary meetings hanging in the balance. Learning the theory is all well and good, but if you ever want to get anything done, eventually you have to start cutting things open. This is a book about dissecting games to see how they work, and how we might mess about with the bits inside to improve them.

Each chapter is loosely centred on one of these bits, like narrative or feedback. We'll examine how different games tackle the aspects at hand, and derive general advice based on how existing titles succeed, fail, or fall somewhere in between. If you're looking for a leisurely read, then feel free to move through the chapters in order, or pick whichever strikes your fancy and go for it first. If you're currently six hours from release and desperately trying to fix your UI before your Steam listing goes live, fear not—each chapter functions as a standalone read (and you, hypothetical developer, are probably looking for Chapter 4).

If you're not sure where you'd like to start, here's a few vignettes to give you a feel for what each chapter is all about.

At the insistence of that one friend you have, you finally break out your gamepad to try your hand at *Dark Souls 3*. The game sticks a sword in your hand, slaps some instructions down on the ground in front of your character, and pushes you in front of a giant knight-turned-demon-turned-dragon. After being obliterated continuously for the better part of an hour, you question your sanity, your will to live, and your friendship. Aren't tutorials supposed to be easy?

Our first experiences with games, particularly in learning how to play and overcome the challenges thrown at us, are explored in Chapter 3.

Sometimes, the way a game looks and feels can draw us in before we've even scratched the surface of what it has to offer. One of the best examples of this phenomenon is playing *Ori and the Blind Forest* for the first time. The visual design and soundtrack of the game are both stunning, but what really makes the experience so satisfying is its feedback. With every step, leap, and glide, your character Ori is a spectacle of fluid animation and cheerful foley. Even when you've failed a challenging gauntlet of platforms are watching Ori wink out of existence, you can't help but admire the resultant explosion of light, sparks, and sound. Chapter 4 is all about designing satisfying and informative feedback that keeps players coming back for more.

Back in the early 2000s, schoolchildren everywhere became briefly obsessed with *QWOP*, a browser game that had you frantically bashing your keyboard in a fruitless attempt to make your character run by controlling, of all things, the muscle groups in their legs. The developer of *QWOP* moved on to create *Getting Over It With Bennett Foddy*, an equally sadistic game where players control a character stuck in a cauldron whose only means of locomotion relies on swinging a sledgehammer. Both games are frustrating, neither obeys any established convention, and yet they're nonetheless incredibly compelling. How a game's controls can be designed to meet, or pleasantly subvert, our expectations, is the focus of Chapter 5.

Even if we discount challenge, or the usual definition of "fun," games still have a wealth of experience to offer. Like literature and film, gaming is a medium for storytelling, rife with opportunities to make us laugh, cry, and reflect on our own lives. *The Last of Us* is a game about the apocalypse, and the rise of the undead. But at its core, it is a story of grief, acceptance, love, and an exploration of what it means to be a parent. In the first few minutes of the game, the protagonist, Joel, holds his daughter as she dies. Eventually, circumstance brings him together with Ellie, a young orphan whom he grows to love. As you watch Joel and Ellie effectively become father and daughter, it can be difficult to understand how such powerful emotional moments spring from a game that could have just been about shooting zombies. Chapter 6 looks at how games can design impactful narratives that leave a lasting impression on players.

The remaining chapters that form the middle part of this book focus on relatively recent developments in game design. The promise of virtual reality, glimmering in system-selling, innovative titles like *Beat Saber*, is the focus of Chapter 7. If you remember the spectacle that was several thousand people trying to control a Pokémon game on Twitch via text chat, you'll enjoy examining the interactive potential of livestreaming with us in Chapter 8. Lastly, Chapter 9 looks at how artificial intelligence is shaping our experiences by giving us more thoughtful in-game companions, manipulating us to spend our money, and even doing some of the creative work for us (remember *No Man's Sky*?).

If all this talk of the games that are already out there is making you yearn to create something yourself, then you may want to start with Chapters 10 and 11, which discuss prototyping and evaluation respectively. Finally, Chapter 12 speculates about the future of game interaction design. If you are curious to see our design guidelines for developing games for the Smell-O-Vision (yes, it's finally coming), you may find this chapter especially interesting. Alternatively, for our mid-twenty-first century readers, you might want to pause and laugh at our vision of the future before burning this book for warmth.

As you embark on your journey to probe the depths of interaction design, and perhaps one day create a game yourself, always keep the player's perspective in mind. Game interaction design is both science and art; it is about respecting the laws that govern our perception and behaviour, while creating something that surprises and delights us.

Expert Profile: David Galindo—Food for thought

Founder, game designer, and lead programmer at Vertigo Gaming Inc.

Many of us spend our lives chasing a dream, whether it's something we've always known, or something we've just discovered. For David Galindo, that dream has always been making games. He started out working on hobby projects in junior high, hoping to eventually turn his passion into a career. If games didn't work out, he liked the idea of becoming a journalist, leading to an undergraduate degree in communications and a gig as a movie reviewer for IGN.

Before making the leap to work on games full-time, one of David's other jobs was serving as the lone barista at a bustling hospital coffee shop. "Customer service changes you," he says with a chuckle, "because you have to deal with *people*." In dealing with all sorts of people in all sorts of moods, he says ideas for gameplay dynamics began to emerge—dynamics he brought to life in the game that proved to be his breakout hit.

Cook, Serve, Delicious! is a restaurant sim, catered to challenge-hungry players looking for an occasionally punishing test of their reflexes. It was David's biggest game to date, but with a budget just shy of $10k, he describes development as "scrappy," pulling together what he could to fund the game's art and music. He programmed the game himself, despite having no formal training: "I'm a very rudimentary coder, but I can code enough to get my ideas going [...] If it works, it works." And *CSD* worked more than well enough; after a late 2012 release bolstered by some signal boosts from Giant Bomb and Steam Greenlight, it sold tens of thousands of copies.

David hoped to break even, but the game's performance had returned his original budget a few dozen times over, leaving him with a windfall to fund future projects. One was a city-builder, ultimately shelved when David realized that he'd need to act fast if he wanted to make a sequel to *CSD* while the original game was still popular. He'd go on to create two such sequels, the first of which came out in 2017. Working on *CSD 2*, David says that all that cash helped immensely in terms of things like art, but as an independent designer, "having a big budget doesn't really do a lot for me gameplaywise." In finding a way to move the series forward, he figured the second game might make the first one obsolete. But with a more arcade-style arc, *CSD 2* stood alone as its own experience. Unfortunately, not all fans of the first game liked this change, and David had to deal with a small but vicious crowd of review-bombers amidst mostly glowing praise.

Eventually the reception of *CSD 2* evened out to near-universal positivity, particularly after continued efforts to update the game. But the experience of dealing with hate had stung, and David describes work on the third game as "coming from a place of anger" at first. That anger quickly turned into a much more productive drive to simply focus on what he wanted, something he says made development a lot more fun. While David is cautious about the applicability of such free-spirited design in general, it certainly worked for *CSD 3*, which became a wildly hectic and widely loved game featuring food trucks run amok in a futuristic apocalypse.

Having capped off the trilogy, David says one of the most surprising things in retrospect is the diversity of players he managed to attract, ultimately helping *CSD* to become more inclusive. Despite initially targeting hardcore players, he received interest from casual players hoping for a more toned-down experience, leading to "chill" modes. He also fielded requests for accessibility features, such as adding toggles for screen-shake, and siren sound effects, which caused anxiety in some players. In terms of accessibility and challenge, David thinks that *CSD 3* is "pretty close to achieving that ideal balance," a goal which has helped to inform his design philosophy: "It's planning for the power user, and also the user that just wants to chill and have fun."

After the runaway success of the *CSD* games, David says he's ready to move forward and experiment with new ideas. Having made it as an indie, he describes success as "both exciting and scary at the same time." Getting attention means making money, but bigger budgets mean bigger risks, and more players means more people to please.

When we sat down with David—and his adorable cat, Pretzel—he was working on two new projects, one of which is top secret as of this writing. The other is *ChefSquad*, a new twist on the restaurant genre designed for streamers to play with their viewers. He's releasing *ChefSquad* for free, as less of a business move and more an exploration of livestreaming's interactive potential: "We're just doing it because we're having fun." The game itself is a large-scale co-op experience, where a host streamer "hires" a group of viewers as helping hands in a virtual kitchen. While he originally envisioned *ChefSquad* as a Gordon Ramsay-esque barrage of barking orders, David's since shifted gears to make the game feel like more of a team effort, promoting a sense of community between the host and their viewers. He describes the game as experimental: "It's not set up to be 'fun' [...] This game is so dependent on the streamer's personality and their engagement with the audience."

David's propensity to experiment with new gameplay dynamics reflects on his approach to design, which is best described as playful. He loves to surprise people, whether working in little half-jokes that leave the punchlines up to the player, or setting a match to conventional expectations like he did with *CSD 3*. Grinning, he mimics an unsuspecting player—"I thought I was playing a cooking game, not a robot apocalypse game!"—and his joyful response, "Ha, gotcha!!"

When thinking about the phrase *interaction design* specifically, David has a fresh interpretation focused on interactions not only between game and player, but between the people *surrounding* a game. This doesn't just include players, but also content creators like streamers, and the entire online audience consuming content related to that game. Successful game design, he says, is about capturing the interest of all those people: "You want to engage the audience. And you're always asking yourself how to do that. That's what game design is all about. How to keep the audience engaged for as long as possible. And keep them entertained, and having fun, and doing something that they've never quite seen before." Today, David says achieving that goal is more difficult than ever, thanks to rising standards of quality and an increasingly packed marketplace. "It's the easiest it's ever been to make a game," he says, "but it's the hardest to succeed at it."

Given his status as the celebrity chef of gaming, we simply had to discuss food with David as well, both in games and in general. When we asked him about his favourite food, he struggled to settle on one dish, having had many memorable experiences trying new foods for the first time with friends. After meeting up with the Zach behind Zachtronics—developer of games like *SpaceChem* and *Opus Magnum*—at PAX, Zach insisted he try a popular Japanese street food. Failing to find a restaurant in town that served it, Zach invited David over to his house for a home-cooked version

(Continued)

(Continued)

of okonomiyaki, a dish that eventually worked its way into the *CSD* games. David has similar stories of meeting up with other familiar names, like streamers Northernlion and Kate LovelyMomo, who introduced him to many of the Korean foods that made it into the series.

David says he's learned a lot about the foods we eat in his experience, carefully working to respect the history and cultural meaning of the dishes represented in his games. As you can imagine, this effort involves a lot of background research and community outreach, in the interest of accuracy and avoiding offensive content. David recalls a few instances of his discoveries, from renaming ingredients to omit historical slurs, to carefully checking for any religious significance that might affect how a dish should be represented. With food playing such a central role in the human experience, crafting games centred around the subject is a great deal more nuanced and complex than one might think at first. David feels that the space of cooking in games is still very much unexplored, and although he's done with *CSD*, he assures us that his next project will still involve cooking in some way.

"But to answer your question," he says, returning to the point that sparked our chat, "Pizza!"

Further reading

Interaction Design: Beyond Human-Computer Interaction by Jennifer Preece, Helen Sharp, and Yvonne Rogers (4th ed., Wiley). ISBN: 978-1119020752.
A thorough introduction to the field of interaction design in general, and a great resource for design methods and exercises.

The Human-Computer Interaction Handbook edited by Andrew Sears and Julie A. Jacko (3rd ed., CRC Press). ISBN: 978-0429103971.
A book featuring many diverse applications of HCI. Of particular interest are Chapters 31 *Why We Play* and *User-Centred Design in Games*.

Exercises

Decomposing interaction

Take two games you have played in the same genre (e.g., RPG) and pick an interaction common to both games (e.g., casting a spell). For each game, break down that interaction based on the model discussed in Section 2.3 (game state communication, decision, input, reaction, feedback). Write a couple of sentences and/or draw sketches for each step.

After breaking down each interaction, write out a point-form list explaining differences between how each game implements the interaction. Reflect on what works (or what doesn't) for each game, and be sure to identify any areas where one game's implementation improves on a similar design element from the other.

Everyone's a critic

Take a game you adore, and pick out one of your favourite singular interactions. Can't get enough of hand-clicked cookies in *Cookie Clicker?* Now's your chance to express your love.

Answer each of the questions posed in Section 2.4, trying to highlight what makes that interaction really shine. Now, do the same thing for an interaction you can't stand in a game you absolutely hate. Compare your answers for both interactions. What makes your opinion of them so different? How could the negative interaction be improved to become more engaging?

Marvelous mundanity

Pick an action from the real world—preferably a fairly routine one—and think about how you would transform it into a game interaction that is fun and engaging. What would the context for this interaction be? What mechanics would it support? Write some notes and sketches to illustrate how the interaction would play out over the five stages of the model discussed in Section 2.3.

3

The Long Con

As designers, we want our games to be successful. You'll hear many different definitions of success in the games industry, depending on whom you ask. As a first impulse, you might assume revenue to be the most reliable metric. Indeed, the livelihood of a professional game designer is dependent on sales. The purchase decision marks a turning point where *potential players* become *players*, making the leap from being interested in a game to financially invested in one. In a market where players cannot possibly be expected to open their wallets for each of the thousands of games on offer, we fixate on convincing players that our games are worth their money.

And yet, money is far from the only way to measure a game's success. Two games with equal revenues are not necessarily equally beloved. A player might drop an expensive game from their repertoire after just a few hours, but spend the equivalent of days on end with a cheaper title if it offers a more compelling experience. Ultimately, players are often more judicious with their time rather than their money; time, after all, is almost uncontestably the more valuable resource. The decision to buy is merely the first step in a player's journey with a game; high sales do not guarantee critical success, user satisfaction, or a secure future for the studio responsible.

In the long run, sustained success is far more desirable than achieving a single flash-in-the-pan hit. To ensure longevity, a developer needs to produce a series of games that have a lasting impact on players, or else a single title capable of holding onto players long after its release—look no further than *Minecraft* for an example taken to the extreme. Maybe, then, our efforts should not be focused solely on convincing players that our games are worthy of their hard-earned cash. Instead, we should ask how the experiences we create can convince players that our games are worthy of their time. But how can we keep players invested from beginning to end, and perhaps beyond even that?

The Game Designer's Playbook. Samantha Stahlke and Pejman Mirza-Babaei, Oxford University Press.
© Samantha Stahlke and Pejman Mirza-Babaei (2022). DOI: 10.1093/oso/9780198845911.003.0003

A critical realization is that players' needs can shift drastically as they progress through a game. Over time, players evolve from requiring instruction and assistance, to freedom, challenge, and sufficient engagement for long-term replayability. If we can understand and account for these changing needs accordingly, then we can provide experiences capable of calling players back time and time again.

3.1 Baby steps

Upon first taking the plunge with a new title, players have very little knowledge, if any, of how it works. A game's introductory phase is thus responsible for teaching players the basics and providing a hook to sustain continued interest, a combined effort often referred to as *onboarding*. Early on, novelty can serve as a key factor in capturing player attention, as new mechanics and content are continuously introduced. With these additions comes the necessary process of player learning, and the potential pitfall of a game becoming overwhelming if it introduces new demands too quickly or with too little instruction. Conversely, a "hand-holding" approach may seem condescending, or bore players whose skill quickly exceeds the challenge offered by a game.

During the first phases of a game, the novelty of seeing a game's mechanics, world, and characters for the first time can help keep players engaged. After they come to grasp the basics, a game can no longer depend on this initial novelty to preserve engagement. From this point forward, new content can be introduced sparingly to ensure players will still have something to discover. However, without a limitless budget, it is impossible to continuously surprise players to keep their attention. Ultimately, the pattern of basic interactions players will repeat over and over—the core game loop—must be compelling enough to sustain player interest. Setting players up to understand and enjoy this core loop is something that needs to happen during onboarding.

The act of shepherding players on their journey to learn a game's mechanics poses several challenges. What do players need to learn, and when? How much instruction is too much? How can we convey information to the player? How do we keep things interesting while preventing confusion or frustration? And most importantly, how do we make sure that we leave a great first impression in the first place?

This is an intimidating gauntlet of challenges to be sure, and yet all can be addressed by accounting for characteristics of a game's target audience and basic interaction design principles. With these factors in mind, let's use this chapter to discuss our first task in designing a complete experience—helping players learn what to do.

3.1.1 *What do players need to learn, and when?*

The idea of a tutorial is simple; it is the part of a game intended to teach you how to play. As a designer, you might view your goal here as making players aware of what they can do, and telling them how to do it.

The most obvious way to accomplish this is to create an "information dump": list out instructions for everything players can do before the game starts. Such an approach is reminiscent of reading the rulebook before setting up a new board game. You are told what actions are available and how to perform them, and then proceed to start playing. If you have ever played a platformer where every one of the controls was written out for you at the start with no context, then you've seen this approach in action.

There are several problems with this method. Let's list off just a few:

- Reading a list of actions is neither interactive nor particularly engaging.
- Presenting everything at once can and will overwhelm players with information, and they will likely forget some instructions.
- Some information may be irrelevant until much later in the game, leading to confused and potentially impatient players.
- Players are robbed of the chance to discover things for themselves.

Thankfully, this type of instruction is not exceptionally common in modern commercial titles, though it can still prove a tempting pitfall for novice designers. After all, why not just get the tutorial over with so players can get to the "real" game, with its carefully crafted challenges dependent on a pre-existing knowledge of the mechanics?

The problem with this mentality is that it fails to acknowledge the learning process as a fundamental part of the player experience. Our initial assessment of our goals is incomplete. We still need to make players aware of what they can do, and how they can do it. But we need to convey information effectively, so that players aren't overwhelmed or confused. Arguably more importantly, we need to make learning engaging and rewarding. This will make information stick by keeping players interested and reinforcing what they've learned. It will also ensure that a player's first impressions of our game will be something other than flashbacks to the monotony of an ill-delivered high school arithmetic class.

Sadly, the concept of an information dump isn't the only pitfall we will encounter on our search for a satisfying learning experience. Taking a "finished" game and tacking on half an hour of unskippable tutorial prompts is not good design. Forcing players to read a manual and then throwing them into the fire is not good design. There is an unmistakable pattern in poor tutorial design, and that is the disconnect between tutorial and game. To make learning a rewarding journey for players, our first step is to stop thinking of "the tutorial" as some separate entity. Instead, we should view player learning as a continuous process, and focus on making sure that each lesson we teach is engaging and fits within the broader context of the game.

There is no blueprint for accomplishing this flawlessly—creating the "perfect tutorial," if you like—but there are a few critical pieces of advice which will take us from a poorly crafted learning experience to an effective and engaging one.

1. Make learning part of the game.

Humans, by and large, love to learn new things. Presentation makes all the difference, though, which is why you'll find plenty of people enthusiastic to watch *Planet Earth* and equally unenthusiastic to relive particularly drab memories of their schooling. This effect doesn't just apply to content which is overtly educational; it applies to any situation where one must absorb new information. An epic fantasy novel is much more engaging to read when it pursues worldbuilding through action, as opposed to 40 pages of expository dialogue and an extensive glossary. A science fiction movie is more entertaining to watch when we learn about its technology by watching characters interact with it, rather than spending 10 minutes listening to an academic explanation. Learning is made more enjoyable by being skillfully blended within the context of the complete experience which it supports.

This axiom is true of games, as well. Players pick up a game to play it, and if the initial learning curve doesn't feel like part of the experience they were hoping to get, you risk losing them—even if the rest of the game delivers that experience perfectly. Packing a boring tutorial onto an otherwise fantastic game is like welding a rusty tricycle to a Maserati; it detracts from the entire package. Ideally, learning should be integrated into players' experience to the extent that this disconnect disappears entirely. Finessing this integration has been, for the most part, an area of continuous improvement in game design over the past several years.

In the first *Assassin's Creed*, players are given a tutorial sequence after an introductory cutscene. During the cutscene, the characters use the word "tutorial" liberally, making it rather obvious that the next few minutes of gameplay will focus on memorizing keybinds before users move on. The tutorial sequence itself takes place in a foggy void, as opposed to the richly detailed environments of the main game. Characters contained therein are faceless, while a disembodied voice instructs players on how to move around, fight, and use their special abilities.

This tutorial isn't terrible; it's paced relatively well, gives players a chance to try things out as they are introduced, and equips players with the knowledge they need to get started in the rest of the game. However, it does feel quite disconnected from the rest of the experience, and not just in terms of environment. Players have little freedom during this sequence, especially in comparison with the rest of the game. The game's narrative is temporarily on hold, save for a small amount of exposition about its technology. These disconnects cause somewhat of a delay in the ability of new players to fully immerse themselves, and on a second full playthrough, make the sequence feel unnecessary in the greater context of the game.

Assassin's Creed II, on the other hand, integrates its tutorial into the game much more smoothly. Basic interactions are taught during a scripted sequence that kicks off the game's narrative. Players are told to watch as another character handles a few enemies, but are free to jump into the fight themselves. A few control bindings are taught inventively, and somewhat humorously, by having the player temporarily take control of their ancestor as an infant. Once the player gains control of their ancestor as an adult, signifying the beginning of the game's main arc, they learn how to combine moves in combat, loot enemies, and interact with friendly characters. These interactions don't occur in a foggy void, either. Instead, the player's character gets into a fight with some rich kids, as a friendly character shouts encouragement. The player learns looting to grab some coin off their unconscious rivals and pay a doctor for medical services.

Figure 3.1 In the original *Assassin's Creed*, players learn controls in a void while other characters explicitly refer to the sequence as a "tutorial program" (left). In *Assassin's Creed II*, learning is more grounded in the game's world, as players are instructed on fight combos whilst wailing on a group of rich kids (right).

Credit: *Assassin's Creed I* and *II* were developed and published by Ubisoft Entertainment.

While it's still relatively obvious to the player that they're learning something, that learning occurs much more organically. Learning happens in the game's world, with character and story development unfurling alongside. And as a boon to new and returning players alike, there's a decent amount of freedom in this initial sequence, or at least a great deal more than its equivalent in the first instalment. This makes the learning process feel less contrived, more enjoyable, and more engaging in the greater context of the game.

In general, we can do a few things to make learning feel like a more cohesive part of the game experience. Learning should occur in the game's world, not outside of it. In games with a significant story component, players should learn about aspects of that story, such as characters, plot, and worldbuilding, as they learn to play. Give players some freedom, and never arbitrarily restrict actions that haven't been taught; limitations should have an in-game reason, such as lack of equipment. Remember that a player's attention can be mercilessly fickle. Your game needs to be a cohesive, engaging experience from beginning to end.

2. Do, show, tell.

Just as there are different ways to teach in a classroom, there are different ways to teach in a game. In school, you were probably given information in lots of different ways: reading, listening, looking at diagrams, and interactive exercises. In games, we can identify three main ways of teaching players. Each of these methods can be used regardless of the information we're trying to convey, whether it's a control binding, a character's personality, information about enemy behaviourbehavior, or something else entirely.

First, we can *tell* players that information in writing or through a voice clip. This is a very straightforward method of instruction which leaves little ambiguity, though it can feel a bit heavy-handed if relied on as the sole channel for everything the player is expected to learn. This method is often useful as a backup reference for the player, or a source of additional non-vital information, such as an in-game encyclopedia. An example is *Subnautica*'s PDA, which provides the player with written and voice entries detailing the game's lore and the behaviour of its denizens.

We also *show* players information by guiding them to witness an event in the game's world. This is an excellent way to give players knowledge of enemy behaviour, environmental hazards, and so on, while still feeling natural. Watching something transpire in the game's world and learning from it creates a moment of discovery. Even for communicating a very basic piece of information, this method can be very effective. Consider the opening sequence of *BioShock*, when players first enter the underwater city of Rapture. As part of the introduction, players watch from the (relative) safety of the bathysphere as a Splicer enemy first calls out to and then kills a man stranded in the area. From this experience, players learn to view cries for help as potentially suspicious, and gain knowledge of the behaviour and movement patterns of this enemy type. Viewing this atmospheric vignette is far more engaging than if the player had simply received a radio transmission telling them to watch out for humanoid silhouettes shuffling around.

Figure 3.2 In *BioShock*, players often learn something about enemies by witnessing their behaviour from a safe place before being thrust into their presence.

Credit: *BioShock* was developed by Irrational Games/Ghost Story Games and published by 2K Games.

Our last option is to create an opportunity where players need to *do* something that they will learn from as a result. This is the approach which is most directly engaging for players. If we can minimize the degree to which we explicitly prompt players to take the desired action, we can create the impression that the player has discovered something completely on their own. However, we also run the risk of players getting stuck, depending on what we expect them to do, and the cues provided to guide them in the right direction. Sandbox games and games with survival elements commonly give players to discover many interactions on their own. In *Don't Starve*, for example, little explicit information is provided as to what players need to do to survive. Players discover things such as the impacts of climate and the effects of different in-game foods for themselves.

Strictly speaking, it may be better to think of the three categories as inactive (tell), active (show), and interactive (do), though these terms are far more easily confused. It is also important to note that different methods can and should be used in combination. A good rule of thumb is that, for anything you *tell* or *show* players, you should also have them *do* something which reinforces their knowledge immediately or soon after. Many games blend the *tell* and *do* approaches in the initial learning phase to follow up a clearly written or spoken instruction with an interactive demonstration that the player has learned the required skill. From the cantankerous drill sergeant in

Figure 3.3 In *Don't Starve*, players are put into a trial by fire, learning the consequences of their actions through experimentation. Left: if the player's sanity falls low enough, shadowy apparitions appear and hint at their threatening nature, later revealed as they gain physical form and attack the player. Right: if left unchecked, several different factors can lead to an untimely demise.

Credit: *Don't Starve* was developed and published by Klei Entertainment.

Call of Duty: *Warzone* to the titular character in *Cooking Mama*, this "do as I say" method of instruction is effective and quick, if often a little inelegant.

3. Get the pacing right.

There are few games that draw as many comparisons as the *Souls* (or "Soulsborne") franchise, yielding an obnoxious number of claims that some game or other is "the *Dark Souls*" of its genre. The temptation is typically triggered by difficulty; the *Souls* games have gained well-deserved notoriety as some of the most punishingly hard titles in the mainstream. However, *Dark Souls* isn't just a difficult game to play; it's also a difficult game to learn.

In *Dark Souls 3*, the first thing you do is create a character. There's a lot of complexity here for new players to take in at once, with little in-game advice or hints. But let's set this aside and chalk it up to something players can research on their own. The game's first area, the Cemetery of Ash, serves as a tutorial for the basic actions players have available, primarily relating to combat. There are 16 prompts before the game's first boss fight, informing the player of 20 different actions, the vast majority of which correspond to unique control combinations. Most of these prompts come a few metres apart on the ground, and so players will read most of them in just a few minutes.

Apart from practicing these moves of their own accord, the game throws twenty or so grunt-type enemies at the player before they arrive at the first boss arena. It should be noted that none of these enemies require the player to successfully execute most of the actions taught, other than the basic attack (with blocking and dodging *almost* necessary). It should also be noted that only about a dozen of these encounters occur along the main path most

Figure 3.4 In *Dark Souls 3*, players are faced with dozens of control prompts in quick succession (top) before being quickly confronted with a boss (bottom), with scant opportunities for practice that don't involve meeting the business end of a massive spear.

Credit: *Dark Souls 3* was developed by FromSoftware and published by Bandai Namco.

players will take. And then there's a boss fight. The challenge of this fight doesn't just come from its difficulty. It comes from the fact that new players are trying to remember the fifteen or so different combat control bindings that they had to read during the ten minutes prior. The first major fight in *Dark Souls* isn't just a challenge of dexterity and timing. It's practically a vocabulary quiz of control combinations.

For a contrasting approach, let's turn to a game which is objectively the *Dark Souls* of platformers and has gained a reputation for challenge in its own rite: *Hollow Knight*. Though the former is a 3D action RPG and the latter a 2D metroidvania[1] platformer, both feature boss fights as a core part of their

---

[1] A metroidvania, so named after the *Metroid* and *Castlevania* series, is a subgenre of action-adventure, typically featuring a large open world which is initially heavily restricted in terms of player access. Different parts of the world "open up" as players gain new abilities that allow them to explore or overcome obstacles in new ways.

experience and both have a reputation for being difficult. Unlike its more notorious companion, however, *Hollow Knight* is far less difficult to learn.

The player is dropped into Hallownest, the game's world, with relatively little fanfare. While controls can be read from the pause menu, the game assumes that players will discover the basic actions available for themselves. With only three meaningful actions at the start (run, jump, attack), all bound to single inputs, this isn't much of a stretch. The player is given a few environmental obstacles, a few enemies, and then reads about how to heal. For the next several minutes of gameplay, these are the only actions available, apart from talking to NPCs. Most new players will have defeated several dozen small enemies before arriving at the first boss.

By this point, the game has given ample opportunities to practice movement and combat along the initial area's critical path. The result is that the first major fight is a challenge of execution rather than memory. During *Dark Souls'* first boss fight, you might find yourself asking, "How do I execute a special two-handed attack again?" *Hollow Knight*, on the other hand, doesn't leave the player wondering which single button corresponds to the single attack available for the first boss. The informational complexity of *Hollow Knight* ramps up much more gradually, despite still creating a significant challenge for players.

Figure 3.5 *Hollow Knight* offers an introduction with a relatively gentle pace for new players, while giving players who know what they're doing an opportunity to jump ahead with relative ease. Early areas give plenty of low-risk opportunities to get used to its platforming controls (left) and introduce comparatively docile enemies (right).

Credit: *Hollow Knight* was developed and published by Team Cherry.

In speaking of challenge, you'll often hear the term "difficulty curve": a description of how challenge grows and changes during a game. A smooth difficulty curve is one that gradually becomes harder over time, increasing challenge to match player skill. A steep difficulty curve accelerates quickly, requiring players to practice before moving on or else fail repeatedly on their road to mastery. Drawing out such a curve is an excellent exercise to understand how challenge evolves over time in different titles.

We can use this same tool to understand the pace of instruction in a game. Put another way, we can visualize a "complexity curve" tracking how much new information is delivered to players over a given section of gameplay. This helps us to understand how much we are asking players to take in, process, and remember over time, watching out for any spikes that might cause an undesirable hiccup in understanding or memory.

In these terms, *Hollow Knight* has a very gradual complexity curve leading up to the first boss fight, whereas the same curve in *Dark Souls 3* is nearly vertical. *Dark Souls 3* hits the player with significantly more information in a significantly shorter amount of time, creating a much higher cognitive load for the first boss fight.

This isn't to say that the tutorial in *Dark Souls 3* is terrible—though it certainly is less accessible to unfamiliar players than that in *Hollow Knight*. That first boss in *Dark Souls* does force the player to learn, albeit in a far from forgiving way. The point here is that the flow of information *can* be smoothed out without sacrificing difficulty. And for returning players, despite its more gradual complexity ramp, the opening of *Hollow Knight* is far from sluggish. While it's not as quick to reach the first boss as *Dark Souls*, players familiar with the game can still arrive at the fight quickly and progress at their own pace. In this way, *Hollow Knight* affords players a bit more freedom as well.

But what can we take away here as general advice for pacing our delivery of information to the player?

First, mechanics should be introduced as they are needed, rather than all at once. The benefit of such an approach is twofold; firstly, it prevents players from forgetting knowledge introduced far in advance of its application. Second, it allows for new content to be introduced throughout the game, helping to extend a game's novelty factor and facilitate moments of additional player discovery.

Nintendo mastered this style of delivery long ago with the *Mario* games, famously introducing a new idea such as a power-up or environmental gimmick at the beginning of an area and continuously building on its use. The indie darling *Celeste* demonstrates this pattern near flawlessly, introducing one or two new environmental gimmicks in each main chapter and recombining them to create successively more difficult challenges without overwhelming the player with new things to remember. By the end of the game, players need to know how to interact with and take advantage of a myriad of different obstacles, but the pace of their introduction makes players' learning of those obstacles a much less frustrating journey.

Another important thing to note is that pacing should consider the prior experience of your target audience. If you can correctly assume that your

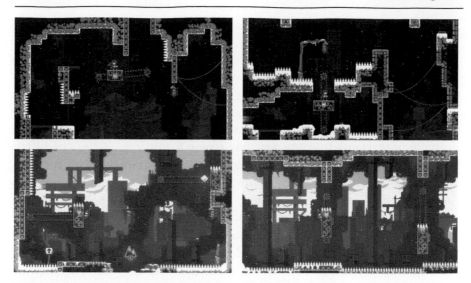

Figure 3.6 In *Celeste's* first chapter, a moving platform mechanic is introduced (top left). Toward the end of the chapter, that mechanic is used in increasingly complex ways, such as requiring the player to time jumps off the platform to gain a boost in momentum (top right). Later in the game, this mechanic is reintroduced and combined with other elements to create an even greater challenge as the player navigates vast gaps with hazards awaiting at any false move (bottom).

Credit: Celeste was developed and published by Extremely OK Games.

players have extensive experience in the genre, or with previous titles in a series, pacing can be increased. If you are targeting novice players or young children, pacing should be slowed. Matching pacing to your target audience is always a good decision. An even better one, however, is to give players some flexibility in how they will experience this initial learning phase. Provide a chance for less familiar players to move forward at their own pace, while letting stronger players surge ahead.

4. Give players enough instruction (but not too much).

A concept strongly tied to the pacing of learning is the level of instruction given. Just as pacing can vary between inaccessibly fast and painfully slow, level of instruction can vary between confusingly absent and mind-bendingly excessive. Suppose that we want to teach the player how to jump, by pressing the A button on their gamepad. We might provide no explicit instruction, and assume that the player will figure this out for themselves based on experience, or some clue in the environment. We might provide a low level of instruction, with an on-screen icon of the A button accompanied by the text "jump." We might provide a high level of instruction, having a character read out dialogue about the importance of jumping and working in half a dozen phrases akin to "Remember, if you're ever *feeling low*, you can *press A* to *reach new heights!"*

The risk associated with providing a greater level of explicit instruction is the perception of unnecessary hand-holding, a particular risk for players with a degree of prior skill. In some games, a high level of instruction, at least initially, is warranted. In the first few research missions of the chemistry-themed puzzler *SpaceChem*, the player is given written instructions for every action they should take. This includes things like placing nodes on an on-screen contraption, and controlling the speed of the game's simulation. Given that the mechanics and terminology used in *SpaceChem* are quite niche, this walkthrough is appropriate for new players. Flexible pacing and the freedom for experimentation helps to prevent this level of instruction from feeling restrictive.

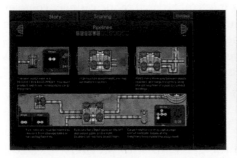 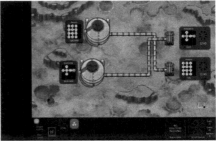

Figure 3.7 In *SpaceChem*, players are given manual-style instructions before a new mechanic is introduced, and then given an in-game assignment which requires them to demonstrate a basic understanding of that mechanic.

Credit: *SpaceChem* was developed and published by Zachtronics.

A high level of instruction is not always as justified, or welcome by players, however. Critics and players alike voiced complaints that the tutorial in *The Legend of Zelda: Skyward Sword* suffered from excessive instruction. The game's introductory section has a habit of explaining even the simplest mechanics over an agonizing series of dialogue boxes. One sequence has an NPC lamenting their lack of skill in picking up barrels, prompting the player to pick up a nearby barrel themselves. This triggers another dialogue sequence filled to the brim with control prompts. The act of carrying a barrel is turned into a miniature mission where the player is made to slowly amble into the next room before sitting through more dialogue praising their immense skill at having pressed two buttons over the past three minutes.

You might call this "death by instruction," where instructions are stretched out and repeated for even simple actions. Simple lessons don't demand that players are repeatedly hit over the head with instruction before being allowed to proceed. Unfortunately, this misstep is often accompanied by sluggish pacing, and the resulting combination of slowness and verbosity is a union most unholy.

Simply toning down the level of instruction can be an appropriate remedy for this issue. This is often a question of stepping back and asking what instructions are strictly necessary for players to learn the intended information.

For some games, the answer may be none at all. Sandbox titles like *Minecraft* and *Terraria* often have little in the way of explicit instruction, leaving players to discover many things about the world and what they can do on their own. As discussed previously, relying on players to "do" things themselves creates brilliant moments of discovery, at the risk of unintentionally creating gaps in player knowledge. Just as too much instruction can cause frustration, too little can cause confusion.

As a general takeaway, there are a couple of rules we can use to determine what level of instruction is appropriate. Very young players might struggle with complex instructions, and require a more gradual introduction of content. Inexperienced players will generally need more instruction, while more experienced players may find that too many instructions make a game slow and uninteresting. Casual players with only a few moments to devote at a time might be prone to forgetting what they've learned between sessions, whereas more serious players can consume and reinforce more knowledge in a single sitting.

For interactions which are common in similar games and display sufficient external consistency, the overall need for instruction is lowered. For interactions introduced later in a game, assuming a fair degree of internal consistency, then the level of instruction required for "new" additions can be reduced as a game progresses. Such advice might seem rather obvious, and yet, when a game's level of instruction fails to meet the needs of a given player, disaster can ensue.

There's an infamous anecdote from the annual trade fair Gamescom of a journalist struggling to play the first few minutes of *Cuphead*, an arcade-style action platformer. Our journalist gets stuck at the point where the game expects him to perform a mid-air dash after jumping to reach a high platform. There are two prompts on screen at once explaining how to jump, and how to dash. After a few failed attempts to reach the higher platform it becomes clear that he doesn't understand that the moves are to be used in combination, attempting to reach the platform by jumping alone. Finally, after nearly two full, painful minutes, and well over a dozen attempts, he finally performs the moves successfully in combination.

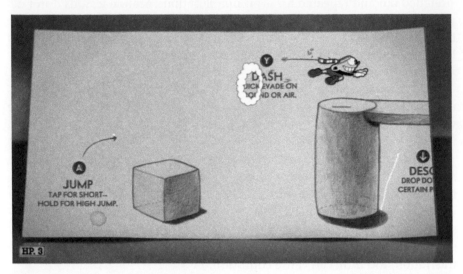

Figure 3.8 The tutorial that launched a thousand angry commenters. The trick, though it's not so tricky, is to execute a dash around the apex of the player's jump. Unfortunately, if you're not very experienced with platformers, this might take a few tries. Or, if you're an unlucky games journalist, the most painful few minutes of your professional career.

Credit: *Cuphead* was developed and published by Studio MDHR.

Many things have been said about this incident, many of them unforgivably cruel to the journalist in question. Of the actual discussion, some claim that the game's instructions are more than adequate, and that additional prompts would be excessive and annoying. Others claim that the design of the tutorial was lacking (and indeed, *Cuphead*'s developer did make some slight adjustments to the section in question before its eventual release). Some responses also noted that *Cuphead*'s tutorial needs to be taken in the context of its target audience: veterans of the genre with the necessary knowledge to overcome any ambiguities. Each of these points is justified to a degree, particularly the point about the experience of the target audience.

Regardless of where you stand on *Cupheadgate*, though, finessing level of instruction isn't always a black-and-white question of removing or adding instructions. Contextual instructions can be used to prevent a tutorial from feeling condescending to skilled players, while lending a helping hand to players if they are struggling. These additional instructions, layered on top of what a game will offer no matter what, may be triggered by different conditions, such as players taking a certain amount of time to complete an expected action, or failing repeatedly at a particular task.

Many games provide this sort of help, delivered through prompts that appear after a certain time or an AI companion that waits until a player seems "stuck" before giving some piece of advice. In the action-adventure game *Undertale*, some boss fights introduce new combat mechanics following a brief initial description. If players repeatedly take damage, failing to use the new mechanic properly, the boss character will give them additional hints. Players that catch on quickly won't need to sit through unnecessary instruction, and players that would otherwise become frustrated have access to additional information.

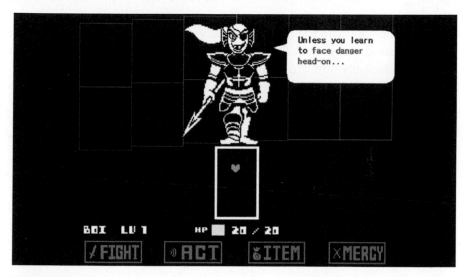

Figure 3.9 In *Undertale*, fearsome knight and renowned fish lady Undyne gives the player some not-so-subtle hints about how her battle will work: use directional inputs to face her attacks with your shield.

Credit: *Undertale* was developed and published by Toby Fox.

Contextual hints are also used in *Civilization V*, to give players, particularly those who may not have completed the game's optional tutorial, prompts for the actions available. On starting a new game, if players fail to "found a city" on their first turn for more than 20 seconds or so, a hint pops up informing players how to start their first city and where in the user interface this action is located. Along with this hint, the player is given options to learn more, or ask not to be given this reminder again. Experienced players will likely never see this hint in the first place, and novice players are given the freedom to learn additional related information if they choose. Just as with pacing, adding flexibility to the level of instruction players receive where possible is an excellent strategy to keep a game's introduction accessible without alienating skilled players as a consequence.

5. Minimize punishment during learning.

Picture this: you're learning to play a new action game. You're familiar enough with the genre, but still getting used to the controls, and you're learning more with every fight. The game throws a few waves of enemies at you, some aerial combat, and even a boss fight. You're about 30 minutes in when an enemy finally gets the better of you, and your character dies. And then the game takes you back to the very beginning, for another half hour of learning those same ropes again before you're granted the privilege of saving your progress.

This could sound all too familiar if you've played *Nier: Automata*. Even in the famously difficult *Dark Souls 3*, that first tutorial boss we talked about earlier is mercifully quick to return to when players inevitably succumb on their first few (dozen) tries. Fortunately, *Nier* does have difficulty settings, so it's not impossible for players to reduce their chances of repeatedly losing 30 minutes of their time, at least temporarily. Unfortunately, players' objections to this type of design in general are often met with a resounding chorus of something along the likes of "this isn't a game for babies" by more skilled players.

Apart from its obvious toxicity, this kind of gatekeeping often shouts over a less-than-ideal design choice. Regardless of how difficult a game is intended to be, there should be some semblance of a safe environment present for learning to take place. This doesn't necessarily mean that players shouldn't be allowed to fail—but they should be able to quickly return to whatever bested them, at least at first.

Undertale cheekily riffs on the idea of a safe learning environment, while still successfully providing one. Players' first experience takes place in the Ruins area, where they speak "to Toriel" for help, Toriel being an NPC guiding the player through their first steps. She quite literally holds the player's hand for the first stretch of the game, with sarcastically tense music playing the moment she steps off-screen for the player to navigate for themselves.

It is possible for the player's character to die in combat during their initial journey, but location-based save points are placed to prevent losing too much time in the process. Toriel's almost comically motherlike demeanour sets up the game's first boss—herself—brilliantly. As the player takes damage, Toriel worsens her aim on purpose to avoid hurting them. While it is technically possible for the player's character to die during this fight, this change makes the first boss fight a safe environment for learning in itself, while also developing Toriel's character and helping to establish some of the

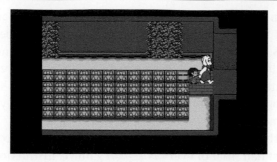

Figure 3.10 Handholding in tutorials is usually undesirable, unless it's literal and adorable.

Credit: Undertale was developed and published by Toby Fox.

game's quirky charm. This doesn't come at the expense of eventual difficulty, either; some of the later boss fights carry all the punch one would hope for from *Undertale's* bullet hell inspirations.

Just as with instructional pacing, punishment during learning is often conflated with a game's challenge in general. Calling a game intentionally difficult and imploring players to "get good," however, is no excuse for failing to provide players with a reasonable opportunity to learn the ropes and get good in the first place.

6. Don't force players through anything repetitive or unnecessary.

There is little more vexatious than being forced through unnecessary instruction while playing a game. The longer the period of instruction, the more frustrating it becomes, and this frustration is only magnified on replay. In other words, nobody wants to sit through a boring, unskippable tutorial, especially if the information is something players already know.

A classic unfortunate example in this regard is the *Pokémon* series, nearly every mainline entry of which bears a lengthy tutorial section at the start. The player's experience is effectively on rails for the duration, while taking in heavily instructional dialogue and scripted battle sequences interrupted by heavily instructional dialogue. The game also limits access to many abilities that returning players are already familiar with, slowly making them available after players have read through (you guessed it) heavily instructional dialogue.

For first-time players and especially children—who form a substantial part of the series' target audience—there is nothing wrong with this format. Although it leans extensively on the "tell" method of instruction, it is integrated with the story and flows naturally into the main arc of gameplay. The tutorial is slow by design, to avoid overwhelming and eventually alienating new players, who are often young children.

59

The problem here is that in this crusade for simplicity, Game Freak have created one of the most notoriously tedious gameplay experiences for returning players. For anyone replaying a Pokémon game, or moving on from another game in the series, the game's tutorial is agonizingly slow. After an extended montage of sighing and button mashing to shave seconds off the display of dialogue, players breathe a sigh of relief upon finally being allowed to play the game "for real."

Despite all the charm of its world and the appeal of its core mechanics, close to the first half hour of every *Pokémon* game is instruction unnecessary for a substantial portion of its players. Luckily, the latest entry in the series to date, *Pokémon Sword and Shield*, has taken steps in the right direction, automatically skipping the tutorial for catching Pokémon if the player takes the initiative to catch one for themselves sufficiently early on.

Simply giving players the option to skip through instructional content or access it as a separate experience can be an acceptable, even favourable, solution. This is certainly not a new idea; the original *Half-Life* offers players the option to select the training room when starting a fresh game, skipping explicit instruction for controls and the like otherwise.

The "optional, but separate" teaching approach is often suitable for games that have a great deal of interplay between resources and gameplay systems. Certainly, this optional but separate content should be something substantially more interactive than reading through a manual. For new players, a guided experience to learn these interactions while introducing content gradually is great. However, it's not something that should be repeated ad nauseum with every playthrough or scenario. It is relatively common to see this approach taken successfully in games that have significant strategic or management elements. For instance, the strategic roguelike *FTL: Faster than Light* and management simulation *Planet Zoo* both have dedicated tutorial missions intended for single-use play, or to refresh player memory.

Figure 3.11 The opening missions of *Planet Zoo* provide an introduction to map navigation, taking care of animals, and building exhibits.

Credit: *Planet Zoo* was developed and published by Frontier.

Only playing through a game's introduction once, or being able to bypass it altogether, however, is not the only way to prevent boring players with repetitive content. Furthermore, in many cases, such a design may be undesirable for exacerbating that gap between "tutorial" and "game." In a heavily story-based game or RPG, for instance, you may want to create a parallel between the player's learning and the learning or growth of their character in-universe. By necessity, then, this initial phase becomes an "unskippable" part of any future playthroughs.

Pacing and enjoyment of such a sequence then becomes critical, especially for games where replayability is especially important. Consider the *Elder Scrolls* series, open-world action RPGs where restarting with a new character to explore different playstyles is commonplace. The fifth entry in the series, *Skyrim*, packs about half an hour of heavily scripted introductory content, featuring a lengthy unskippable cutscene followed up by a laundry list of instructions delivered during a forced linear journey through the game's first area.

Figure 3.12 You might finally be awake, but the nightmare has only just begun.

Credit: The Elder Scrolls V: Skyrim was developed by Bethesda Game Studios and published by Bethesda Softworks.

Much like the case of *Pokémon*, though paced quite slowly, there is nothing overly frustrating about this introduction as a first exposure to the game. However, in an open-world game that emphasizes freedom, and one that practically begs for multiple playthroughs at that, it is nothing short of a slog for returning players, and does a poor job of conveying the freedom it promises to new players. It is hardly surprising that one of the most popular community-made modifications (mods) for *Skyrim*, called *Life Another Life*,[2] is designed to replace Bethesda's lengthy intro with a shorter one more akin to previous games in the series, such as *Morrowind*.

That is not to say that pulling off a lengthy, but still rewarding, introduction is impossible. Another modern open-world adventure with RPG elements does just that—Nintendo's *The Legend of Zelda: Breath of the Wild*. *BotW* starts players off in the Great Plateau, a tutorial area within the larger kingdom of Hyrule, after a brief introduction to its controls. Players are gently guided to a character that will inform them of their early objectives, and upon completion, the main story begins and the rest of Hyrule is opened to them.

The crucial difference here is that *Breath of the Wild*'s introductory experience is far from linear. The Great Plateau is a microcosm of the entirety of Hyrule, mirroring its open-world gameplay on a smaller scale. New players will find themselves subtly guided through geography and carefully placed resources to complete tasks and learn about the world in a relatively gentle way at their own pace. Returning players can complete the requisite tasks in any way and any order they wish, with the ability to explore freely as opposed to being forced onto the same linear path they've already experienced. With a more relaxed design that promotes player freedom without creating a dangerous or confusing environment for new players, *Breath of the Wild* accomplishes a broadly appealing and effective in-game introduction.

3.2 A masterclass in learning

The very best games are those which excel in all aspects of their design. A game may be lauded for its art direction, but fall flat on account of lacklustre gameplay. Engaging gameplay may be tainted by a clumsily written story, or ruined by an inscrutable user interface. Few titles can fully deliver on every dimension of the game experience. When a game does manage to accomplish this, it becomes not only beloved by its players, but rightfully revered by designers.

Portal 2 is just that: a game that does everything well, flawless to many and respected by all. But its success isn't just down to innovative gameplay, clever writing, and stunning creative direction. It's also because *Portal 2* teaches players to become masters of its mechanics without even realizing it. The opening sequence of the game is brilliant, giving an introduction gentle enough for complete newbies and engaging enough to appease series veterans on their fourth playthrough.

---

[2] According to the community site Nexus Mods, *Live Another Life* has over 5.7 million total downloads as of May 2022.

The game starts with little fanfare, as you awaken from stasis in the Aperture Science facility. A wry robotic narrator quickly instructs you in basic movement before putting you back to sleep. When you open your eyes again, uncountable years have passed, and a friendly robotic companion breaks you out of stasis with the intention of helping you escape. To do this, you'll need to explore the facility and work your way through its "test chambers," a series of physics-based puzzles. Thus begins our main story and our main gameplay loop of solving puzzles to move through Aperture's labs.

The first test chambers are heavily geared towards learning basic puzzle mechanics, such as moving objects and interacting with the environment. Most importantly, they teach you how to understand, operate, and manipulate portals, the central element of the game's puzzles. At any one time, two portals can exist in a level: one orange, and one blue. Anything that enters one portal exits through another. First, you're introduced to this with two portals that are fixed in place, walking through one and exiting through the other. Then, you can press buttons that change the position of one of the portals, leaving the other fixed in place. You then find a portal gun capable of freely placing blue portals, while orange portals remain fixed in predetermined positions. Finally, you find the dual-portal gun, allowing you to freely place portals of both colours for the remainder of the game. All of this is packaged into half a dozen puzzles, or around the first 30 minutes of gameplay.

Let's examine how this opening sequence, and subsequent learning throughout *Portal 2*, fits within the guidelines for player learning we've established.

> **Make learning part of the game**. *Portal 2* teaches its mechanics inside its test chambers, making learning part of the core puzzle-solving experience. Chambers that introduce new material aren't disconnected from those that serve as regular challenges, nor are they presented any differently. Players learn during what feels like regular gameplay. Any explicit instructions are delivered to you by characters in the game, not disembodied prompts on the screen. This is true not just of the opening sequence, but whenever a new puzzle mechanic is introduced. These qualities make it difficult to draw a line between "tutorial" and "gameplay." You could say that the entire game is a tutorial of sorts. You could also say that *Portal 2* has no tutorial at all.

> **Do, show, tell**. Players learn the very basics of movement and early exploration with the "tell/do" combination. Characters give instructions, and players immediately follow them. However, this method is quickly eschewed in favour of a heavily interactive approach which pushes players to discover things for themselves. Clever environmental design is

Figure 3.13 The opening sequence in *Portal 2*, as well as its initial puzzles, serve as a seamless in-world tutorial. Players awaken in a serene chamber for instruction on basic controls (top left) before quite literally dropping into the ruined laboratory (top right). The very first puzzles have players control the opening of portals in fixed positions (bottom left) before finding a gun that they can use to place a blue portal (bottom right). (After a short spell longer, players find a gun that can place both portals at will.)

Credit: *Portal 2* was developed and published by Valve.

used to show you something that practically begs for experimentation, and you learn something new as a result. When you pick up the single-portal gun for instance, you are in an alcove surrounded by "portal-able" white walls. Even firing the gun randomly, you will quickly learn that you can open portals on these surfaces, while being unable to do so on others. Successfully opening and stepping through a portal will allow you to progress further. You're given an obvious opportunity to experiment, and a simple task to move forward, all without being told what to do. Most all new mechanics are introduced in this manner.

Get the pacing right. New information during the opening sequence is delivered without any sort of time pressure, giving new players time to absorb it. Depending on their skill level, though, more experienced players can run through more quickly, preventing it from becoming tedious. The game's pacing truly shines as it progresses, however. Complexity increases in tandem with the difficulty of its puzzles: new mechanics are introduced only after players have demonstrated some mastery of those they already know, right as they are needed to progress further through the game. These new mechanics are peppered continuously throughout the game, making sure you always have some new mechanic to play with. Over the course of a dozen or so hours total after seeing their first portal, you'll be introduced to turrets, laser redirection cubes, bridges made of light, trampoline-like platforms, paint you can use to alter the environment, and more.

Give players enough instruction (but not too much). Players learn most mechanics through experimentation, guided by careful environment design. When they do receive instruction, it's interwoven with dialogue which is otherwise amusing or relevant to the story. At certain points, characters will offer additional or more explicit instructions after some time has passed. This gives new players a bit of extra help without making more skilled players feel as if the game is drowning them in instruction.

Minimize punishment during learning. It is impossible for the player's character to die in *Portal 2* until about halfway through the first chapter, after they have already picked up the single-portal gun. The first hazard introduced is a pool of acid, a static part of the environment that is easily avoided. If players do succumb, they'll reload to lose less than 30 seconds of progress, as the game autosaves at the beginning of each new test chamber. Players can also freely save the game at any point, a choice that works well in a puzzler that encourages players to experiment.

Don't force players through anything repetitive or unnecessary. This is where the game's charm helps to make it an instant and easily replayable classic. Even if you know exactly what's coming, if you like *Portal 2*, you'll like replaying its opening sequence. The writing, story progression, and environmental design throughout are top-notch, and frankly worth experiencing for the dialogue alone. What's more, after the first time it is completed, players can skip to any chapter in the game, providing additional flexibility should they wish to return to the experience.

Perhaps the greatest thing about *Portal 2*'s "tutorials" is that they don't compromise on anything the game has to offer. Its immersive world, engaging gameplay, snappy dialogue, and rich artistic direction are all on full display during even the most basic of lessons. Learning in *Portal 2* isn't really a tutorial at all. It's a collection of immaculately timed opportunities for player discovery that form an indispensable part of the game's experience. *Portal* should serve to remind us that there is no trade-off between fun and efficacy when it comes to learning: as designers, we can have our cake, and eat it, too.

3.2.1 *Final thoughts*

First impressions are powerful, in life and in games. A player's first 20 minutes with your game will likely decide whether they return for several hours more, leave it to be forgotten in their catalogue, or uninstalled entirely. Stripping away the flash and spectacle of visual effects and catchy intro music, this first 20 minutes is focused on one thing: teaching players what your game is all about. Players need to learn how to play, but also how a game's world works, how its characters interact, and so on. Critically, they also learn what to expect from the rest of their time with the game. This is why slipshod tutorials are so damaging; players will assume that the remainder of their experience will reflect their first few minutes whether you intend them to or not.

Recognizing the importance of the onboarding phase and player learning is an important first step in designing a successful initial experience. Keeping in mind the key factors that will shape this experience—integration, communication method, pacing, instruction level, error forgiveness, repetition—is the next. In sculpting the initial experience of your own game, you should revisit games that left a particularly notable (or notably bland) first impression on you personally, and consider studying some of the titles referenced in this chapter.

The big-picture takeaway is this: a player's first interactions with your game need to reflect the highest quality on offer throughout the entire game experience. The vital learning that occurs during this stage needs to be not only effective, but engaging. After all, players are there to play—you need to let them.

Expert Profile: Romana Ramzan—Player champion

Producer at No Code Studio

Romana Ramzan has always loved games. But she didn't see a path for herself in the subject until her fourth year of university, when she found out that games research was an option for her undergraduate thesis. A year of game research and Romana was hooked, proceeding to earn a PhD in games for health a few years later.

During her PhD, she taught at her university and worked as a freelance UX researcher with a consulting firm. After graduation, she entered the industry as a "Player Champion"—a title she fondly describes in connection with her focus on understanding user behaviour—at Scottish developer Denki. A little over a year later, with the 2-hour commute from her native Glasgow conflicting with her desire to start a family, Romana left Denki to settle down as a university lecturer. Eventually, the industry would call her back, and today she works as a producer at No Code, the studio behind the BAFTA-winning sci-fi thriller game *Observation*.

The thing that brought Romana back to the industry is what excites her most about her work: its fast-paced, iterative nature. "I was bored with stability," she says of her decision to return to the industry, describing it as offering more opportunities to keep up with the day-to-day reality of game development. One of her favourite things about her role is solving problems: "It's those unexpected challenges that pop up. And you need to do some investigation, and find a solution, and learn something that makes other people's jobs easier." Those other people are a big part of what she does, especially as a producer, and Romana says that for her, picking a job is just as much about the people as it is about the work.

This people-centric attitude extends to her view of interaction design, which she describes as a recipe that's "65% UI design and 35% user research." That user research element is key, she argues, to the vital task of understanding your players: "If you don't have that understanding of who you're making [your game] for, then how do you come up with the design itself?"

Having worked on UX both in and out of games in her time as a freelancer, Romana says that many challenges are common to the design of games, productivity apps, and websites. The foremost such challenge is a tendency for developers to assume that users will behave in the same way as them, or exhibit the same preferences. She mentions an example of a kids' nutrition website she'd been involved with evaluating, which ran into a number of usability issues as a result of failing to include younger potential users early in the design process. Romana mentions that historically, one of the biggest problems related to understanding users in games is designing an effective "onboarding" experience that introduces players to the experience they can expect from a game. This obstacle, and others like it, is compounded by a lack of firm, standardized game design approaches; of course, true standardization in this respect is both impossible and undesirable given the subjectivity and creative freedom of designing games.

In the face of all this subjectivity, Romana says that the best designers are those who are eager to learn, driven to constantly improve, and can stay open to feedback. A good designer needs to "adapt, to be able to take things on board and learn. But also have a broad understanding of the bigger picture, and not just making the assumption that 'Because it's something I like, everyone else is going to like it as well.'" Occasionally, though, she says designers need to know when to go with their instincts and push forward on something important to them. This is where the qualities of leadership and communication enter the equation. Romana talks about the importance of making sure that the entire team feels heard and involved in the design process, emphasizing that design decisions need to be given as explanations instead of commands: "If you can explain why you're doing it, it means that the team as a whole buys in to what's being done." For her, becoming a successful designer is about having people skills on both sides of the screen: understanding and respecting your players as well as your team.

Outside her main career, Romana is heavily invested in bringing promising new developers into the fold, reflecting on her days as an educator and her involvement in organizing game jams. For many people, though, seeing a path into games can be difficult. One obstacle is the perception of games as childish or a waste of time,

(Continued)

(Continued)

incentivizing parents to discourage their kids from pursuing a job in the industry. Romana says this perception can be exacerbated by longstanding family attitudes or cultural factors, noting that growing up as a girl in Pakistan, she observed a social favouring of two "stereotypical career paths," doctor and engineer. She chuckles in recounting how she described her university studies to her grandmother, joking that she felt "redeemed" after earning a PhD, even if some family members didn't really understand the subject of her work.

Another barrier for aspiring designers is a lack of representation. Romana has always loved playing games, but growing up, games didn't offer relatable role models for her. She describes an inability to find "a character who embodies my experiences." While this dearth of representation didn't deter Romana from studying games, she points out that it's a gross oversight on the part of the industry. Speaking about underrepresentation, particularly of women and Muslims, she asks, "Why are we neglecting such a large group of people?" She notes that addressing this neglect presents creative opportunity, asking what a game might look like if it starred the "opposite" of Lara Croft, the beloved upper-class, pistol-wielding girl next door. Romana says that shifting our thinking in this respect is essential to foster a more inclusive climate: "If we're going to encourage change in the industry, we need to show it with the kind of products we're putting out as well."

Between social attitudes about gaming and a lack of representation, Romana fears that passionate, talented individuals might get left behind: "There must be so many people out there who don't realize that this is something you can do." She's optimistic about this changing for the better, though, noting that diverse voices are becoming more prominent in games and the stories that they tell. Romana says this is especially true for indie developers, while the slower machine of AAA development is still largely focused on turning out instalments of established franchises. Simultaneously, increased efforts toward accessibility and internationalization are helping to lower barriers to entry for players of all backgrounds. Romana hopes that in her work, she can help to "make the industry a better and welcoming place for others," for instance, by encouraging people from underrepresented groups to participate in the game jams she helps to organize. "If you have a voice," she says, "then you have to use it."

During her second stint in the industry, Romana says that one of the most educational experiences she's had is parenthood. She rhymes off a striking list of similarities between being a developer and being a parent: impostor syndrome, the need to "wear many hats," managing different personalities, being organized, and of course, "mitigating risks where possible." She's currently entertaining the notion of giving a GDC talk about her experience, noting that "moving forward from tantrums" is a key skill for both parents and developers to learn. In the meantime, she sees every new project as an opportunity: "Every time you make a game, the next time you make one, you think surely it's going to be easier [. . .] And lo and behold, it's not, because the landscape is continually shifting, and progressing, and changing." For Romana, that change is a central part of the fast-paced industry she's grown to love, and she's eager to embrace whatever challenges come next, and the people that come with them.

Further reading

Design and Development of Training Games, edited by Talib S. Hussain and Susan L. Coleman (Cambridge University Press). ISBN: 978-1107280137.
While this book is oriented specifically towards games *for* learning, it communicates a great deal about learning *in* games.

Flow: The Psychology of Optimal Experience by Mihaly Csikszentmihalyi (Harper). ISBN: 978-0061339202.
The seminal volume on the *flow state*, often precipitated in games as an ideal balance between game challenge and player skill. More of a general psychology interest volume, but an important concept in game design, especially for keeping players enchanted with their experience. Of particular interest is Chapter 4 (The Conditions of Flow).

Exercises

Returning student

Pick a game with a tutorial you think could be improved; if you're at a loss for examples, feel free to dig into some of the flawed tutorials we've explored so far. For each of the six rules outlined in this chapter, jot down a couple of notes on whether the tutorial follows or deviates from that rule. Use this as a starting point to reimagine an improved version of the tutorial, writing down notes and sketches on how you would change it.

Reflect on your improved version of the tutorial and revisit each of the six rules. Are there any that your new design still deviates from? Can you justify this, or further improve your design?

Super Mario school

If you've never played a *Mario* game, now is the time to borrow a copy from a friend to get the gist of it, lest you be out of the loop in approximately 20% of all theoretical game design examples.

Assuming you have some familiarity, come up with an idea for a new powerup for a 2D *Super Mario* game that alters Mario's movement in some way (it's okay if your idea turns out similar to one of the very many powerups that already exist). The powerup doesn't have to directly change the way that Mario runs around; it could also be some kind of environmental puzzle-solving tool.

Come up with a short tutorial level aimed at teaching players how to use your new powerup. Try to minimize any explicit instructions given and teach the player through scenarios that hint at what they could try to do. Sketch out your level on graph paper, and try to include at least 2 - 3 small challenges that will help players learn and test their knowledge of your power-up. You can also sketch your level digitally, or mock it up in *Super Mario Maker*.

After you're done designing your level, try to walk through it, noting down what players would be thinking/learning along the way. Try to look at the bigger picture and see if your tutorial level teaches players everything you want them to know. Should you add anything? Condense anything? How could your tutorial be even more engaging?

4

Say What you Mean

At its core, interaction *is* communication. Interaction is fueled by the exchange of information. When this exchange succeeds, it blends into the background of the larger experience it supports. When it breaks down, it becomes the subject of intense frustration. Failures in communication are universally recognized as a common curse, birthing the likes of schoolyard rounds of broken telephone and the phrase "lost in translation". Panaceas for our communication woes form some of the more optimistic threads of science fiction, from Douglas Adams' Babel fish to the TARDIS translation matrix in *Doctor Who*. The communication of information is a subject inextricable from every interaction we experience. Game interaction is no exception, and as we have already discussed, two-way communication between game and player is what drives the cycle of player action and game reaction.

There are many ways to categorize the ways that games communicate with us. One is by placement; that is to say, whether a piece of information is given to us inside the game's world (e.g., a character shouting) or outside it (e.g., an icon on the HUD). Another is by type, such as whether the information in question is a number or a description. We might even categorize by importance, depending on how essential different pieces of information are for players to know. No matter which delineation we choose, it's important to note that such attempts at categorization are rarely mutually exclusive. For instance, if we separate communication based on placement, how do we categorize a very much player-controlled menu that's visible on a TV very much *in* a game's world?

For the purposes of organizing this chapter, we'll be loosely separating communication based on when and how it occurs. First, there is information about a game's state that is conveyed continuously (typically outside a game's world). An example is an always-visible UI element showing players how much health they have left. We refer to this type of communication as *continuous communication*. Second, there is communication that occurs in direct

The Game Designer's Playbook. Samantha Stahlke and Pejman Mirza-Babaei, Oxford University Press.
© Samantha Stahlke and Pejman Mirza-Babaei (2022). DOI: 10.1093/oso/9780198845911.003.0004

response to player action or significant in-game events (often inside a game's world). An example is a red flash on-screen triggered the moment a player takes damage. We refer to this as *responsive communication*. It is important to note that the same element can serve up both continuous and responsive communication—when that always-on health bar updates in response to damage, it's communicating responsively.

If you recall the core model of game interaction discussed in Chapter 2, we can think of continuous and responsive communication as the first and last steps of that model. First, players obtain information about a game's state via continuous communication. Then, they decide what to do and act on that decision by providing input. The game processes this input, and finally, provides responsive communication that helps players to inform their next decision. Each and every transfer of information from game to player can influence a player's actions, and the experience they have.

In designing our means of communicating information to players, several questions must be answered. What do we need to tell players? How will we represent information? What do we need to do to grab players' attention? How can we make communication accessible? How can we preserve utility while making things beautiful? This chapter will explore these questions, examining how we can design both continuous and responsive communication effectively.

Our first order of business is understanding the tools we have at our disposal for communicating with players; in other words, how people process information.

4.1 Communication and the senses

Sometime around your first year of primary school, about the time you were learning to share your safety scissors and avoid eating crayons more than once or twice a week, you were probably taught that humans have five senses. Like so many other lessons from our early years, this is a lie told to make things a bit simpler, and ostensibly give teachers more time to confiscate art supplies before they could be consumed.

The truth is that, depending on your definition of "sense," the list of human senses is somewhere between seven and well over a dozen entries long. On top of the standard quintet of sight, hearing, touch, taste, and smell, we might list balance, temperature, pain, and awareness of needs like hunger and thirst, to name a few. These channels all serve the same core purpose—transmitting information.

In theory, any of the senses could be co-opted to communicate information during gameplay. And as tempting as it may be to have players lick an electrode and taste their current stamina percentage, some channels are best left untouched, at least for now. Here we'll be sticking to how we can represent information within the reasonable and ethical bounds of modern technology.

4.1.1 *Keeping an eye on things*

Humans are often described as visual creatures. When we record information, we usually do it visually. We write things down, type them up, and draw sketches. Sight is just *easy*. Typical human vision has a ridiculously high bandwidth for transmitting information. It allows us to jump between concepts quickly, and rapidly identify sudden changes. Vision is, for better or worse, the king of representing information.

In games and elsewhere, there are several visual cues and channels that can be used to communicate information to the player.

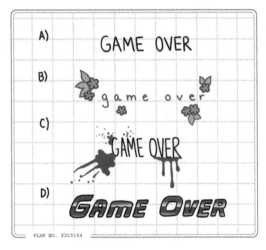

Figure 4.1 Something as simple as stylizing text for a "game over" can say a lot about your game, such as A) "We're very boring people," B) "Dying is just a part of living, man," C) "Written and directed by Quentin Tarantino," or D) "It's 1986."

Text. Text isn't just for labels and subtitles; if used well, it can provide snappy feedback that players understand at-a-glance. Obviously, reading paragraphs in such situations is untenable, so you'll have to be prudent with your choice of words. Think of the stylish *K.O.* at the end of a *Street Fighter* match, or the flashy, colour-coded words of praise (or insult) that pop up after each note in the *Dance Dance Revolution* games.

Shape and iconography. Shape creates meaning in a game from a combination of existing game conventions, real-life parallels, and its own

PLAN NO. 931514

Figure 4.2 Icons play off our cultural and real-world associations to convey or imply meaning at a glance without relying on language, such as "health" (left column), "stamina" (middle column), or "magic" (right column).

in-universe elements. The shape of characters and objects can provide simple, quick indicators of intent; usually, round is friendly (think Mario) and pointy is mean (think Bowser). Probably the most recognizable and ubiquitous use of shape in games is to encode information using icons in a game's HUD. Icons might function as labels (like a bullet next to an ammo counter), creating less clutter and taking up less space than text while also eliminating the need for a translator. Icons can also serve double duty, simultaneously telling you what they represent and its current state, like the heart icons forming the health bar in the *Legend of Zelda* games. Furthermore, repeating a symbol can help to build associations in a player's mind—such as emblazoning health pickups with the same icon used to represent health in the HUD.

Size. Just as in the real world, size implies power in a game's world. The giant tower in the distance is probably significant, and the boss you're fighting right now is probably on the order of a dozen or more times the size of your character. Something about the stone creatures in *Shadow of the Colossus*

Figure 4.3 The three size-based gut reactions encoded into the instincts of every living thing.

just wouldn't feel right if their sizes were on par with frogs instead of buildings. Like shape, size is also used to encode information in a game's UI, often by masking away an element to represent a proportional amount (such as a refilling health bar or a pie-wheel timer showing an ability cooldown).

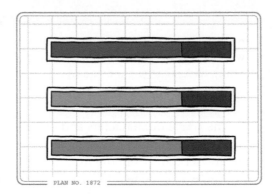

Figure 4.4 Assuming you have unimpaired colour vision, can you guess what each of these status bars would probably represent? Which is stamina? Which is mana? Which is health? While not a bulletproof assumption, given these three colours, the mapping that first comes to mind is probably red for health, green for stamina, and blue for mana.

Colour. Many of our existing associations with colour can quickly convey information; for instance, red might mean warning, heat, or something related to health depending on the context. As we'll see shortly, using colour on its own is a generally terrible idea for accessibility reasons, but is helpful as a supplementary cue. Another way that colour can be used effectively is within a game's world, used to create contrast that doesn't rely on players' ability to identify a particular hue. For example, the *Portal* series uses white walls to help guide players through exploratory sections of the game. White walls contrast otherwise dark environments, while letting players know that the portal gun may be used to reach them.

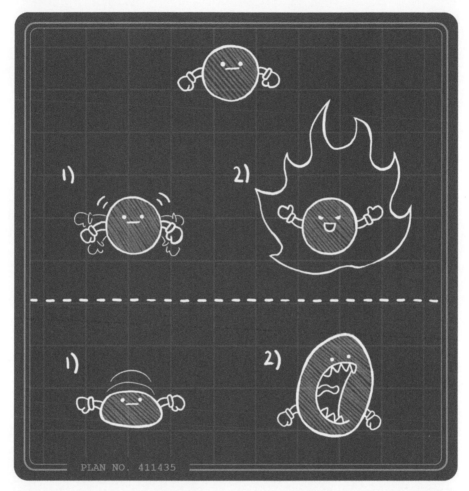

Figure 4.5 Motion can convey information, particularly intent. An enemy might vibrate in anticipation of bursting into flames, or squish down before springing back up to take a mighty bite out of you.

Motion. Quick motion can quickly grab players' attention, alerting them to sudden changes. Screen-shaking and particle effects can be used to create spectacle for a calamitous event or supernatural ability. Intense motion should generally be used sparingly to avoid overwhelming players or creating a false sense of importance, but motion doesn't always have to be extreme to be effective. Relatively subtle animations can be used to telegraph enemy attacks, and slight motion in a game's UI can be used to tell players how quickly something like an energy meter is depleting or refilling.

4.1.2 *In one ear and also the other*

Hearing is quite distinct from vision in the fact that we are incapable of easily turning it off. You can close your eyes, but it's far more difficult to close your ears, as anyone with young children can attest. Perhaps this is why hearing can feel so primal. Noticing a flicker of motion in your peripheral vision may well be unsettling, but it doesn't compare to a sudden and unexplained bump in the night. This isn't a book about evolutionary biology, so we'll disregard the obvious survival reasons behind this. Suffice it to say, though humans may be visual creatures, we are also creatures profoundly impacted by sound.

Just as there are different ways to communicate information visually, there are also different ways to communicate information with sound in games.

Speech. As the audio analog of text, speech can be used not only for conversation and voiceover, but also for feedback. A pat on the back from Wheatley in *Portal 2*, or a slap in the face from GLaDOS, can provide an immersive, amusing, and rewarding bit of feedback for players. An important thing to remember here is that voice lines can quickly feel repetitive if overused. The voice of the exosuit in *No Man's Sky*, for instance, feels repetitive when it triggers an identical voice line multiple times per minute in harsh environments. In general, you should exercise caution if using a limited collection of voice lines to provide frequent feedback, and give players the option to adjust or disable vocal feedback while providing alternate means of conveying the same information.

Sound effects. A sound effect occurs in response to some event or change, whether in a game's world or its internal state. The bell of a town crier can lend a game's world a greater sense of life. A delightful riff can reward you for picking up that latest breadcrumb on your collectibles list. Spatial audio, which uses stereo sound to tell players *where* a sound is coming from, can provide important guidance or warnings in-game. So varied are the applications of sound effects that their design is an entire volume on its own. Many game sound effects become iconic, as blips or jingles that instantly communicate the intended message while being pleasant or amusing. The alert sound from *Metal Gear Solid*, jump tone from the original *Super Mario Bros.*, health station foley from *Half-Life*, and treasure jingle from *The Legend of Zelda*; if you've heard them once, you'll never forget them, and each conveys its intent with style.

Music. Sound effects are typically concrete in their source and timing; the effect is prompted by some event in the game or its world, and is (usually)

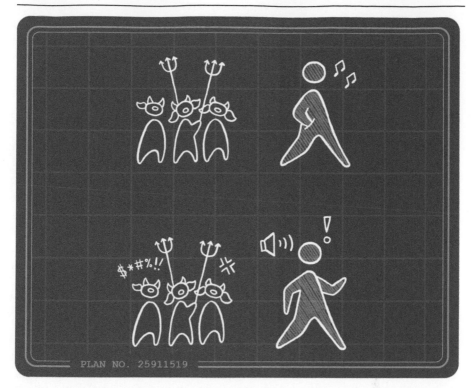

PLAN NO. 25911519

Figure 4.6 Audio is an important cue for anything that happens outside a player's field of view. Unless the local goblin invasion has invested in some serious stealth training and pricey slippers, you probably want to give the nearby mobs a bit of auditory flair.

easy to trace and interpret if designed well. Music is far more abstract: outside of rhythm games, there is rarely a simple 1:1 relationship between the features of a game's music and its events. Instead, the character created by melody, instrumentation, tempo, and key communicate the *feeling* of the current situation. Frantic, pounding music implies dire combat. A somber, minimal melody in a minor key communicates a character's loss, or a feeling of desolation. Changes in music communicate changes in state, quickly putting the player on alert or at ease and helping to shape their mindset. The *Pokémon* games, for instance, shift to a more desperate track during battle if the player Pokémon's hit points are critically low. Another example is the use of unique tracks during boss battles in games like *Undertale*, which can put players in a focused state while creating a memorable tone for each fight.

Ambience. You might think of ambience as a subcategory of sound effects, not necessarily traceable to any given event or change, but nonetheless adding character to a game's world. Chirping birds can create the feeling of a serene meadow without having to animate all manner of sparrows and jays. Whistling wind and faraway creaking can help to fill in the atmosphere of a dark environment. Though you generally won't be using ambient sounds to convey strategic information to players, they can still be extremely effective in communicating the nature of an environment and, like music, help to build the right mindset for players as a result.

4.1.3 *The other, spookier senses*

Although sight and hearing are certainly the easiest senses to appeal to in terms of available hardware and information bandwidth, we are not limited to these channels alone to convey information in games. While taste and smell are sadly (or perhaps fortunately) out of reach for the time being, it is possible to tap into a couple of our other senses to accentuate existing audiovisual feedback.

Haptics. Communicating information through touch in games is referred to as haptic feedback. This is commonly implemented via the rumble motors present in most gamepads, and used as a secondary cue to cue excitement or danger. A massive gateway shaking open during a cutscene, a character taking sustained damage, or a natural disaster are all common triggers to feel such feedback in action. While some more exotic peripherals for touch feedback do exist, such as bulky haptic vests or fancy VR gloves with little force-feedback triggers in the fingers, controller vibration comprises a majority of the haptic feedback that most players will experience.

Your typical gamepad rumble doesn't communicate much beyond "something's happening right now!" With specific hardware devices, the communication can be much more nuanced, and help to make interactions feel more grounded in reality. The Nintendo Wii's controller, for instance, can use force feedback to make something like swinging a tennis racket in *Wii Sports* feel much weightier. Though they have since shifted somewhat from the focus on motion control, Nintendo's Switch console experiments with richer haptic feedback with HD Rumble. A criminally underused feature, HD Rumble relies on actuators that can move weights inside a controller on a precise linear path, as opposed to the rough cyclical motion of standard controller vibration. The effect of this feature in games like *1-2-Switch* is the ability to roughly approximate things like resistance and weight through the feel of the controller in the player's hand.

VR development is another area where haptic feedback has become increasingly relevant. Since many games in VR rely on mapping their controls to realistic motion—reloading a gun in *Pavlov VR*, swinging a crowbar in *Boneworks*—haptic feedback can help lend in-game objects a sense of weight and force. Subtle controller vibration in *Beat Saber* helps the imaginary swords you're holding feel powerful, giving a sense of resistance as your blade bites into each virtual block.

Balance and motion. We are fortunate to possess a rather sophisticated ability referred to as the *vestibular sense*, granting awareness of the body's balance, orientation, and movement. To the delight of young children everywhere, this ability is easily fooled with the likes of a blindfold, swivel chair, or cruel friend who reneges on their promise not to spin the playground carousel too fast. This ability is also easily fooled by holding a screen in front of someone's face and displaying a moving first-person camera while they remain stationary. If we see motion, we expect to feel motion, and vice versa.

Seeing immersive motion without the appropriate physical sensation often leads to nausea and headaches, especially in VR. Assuming you don't enjoy seeing your name printed above the word *defendant* in block letters, deliberately throwing off players' sense of balance as a proxy for some sort of extreme controller rumble is a horrific idea. Nonetheless, it *is* possible to actively communicate character movement to players through the vestibular system without risking motion sickness from a general audience. Doing so requires special hardware; arcade racing games, very expensive flight simulators, and gimmicky seated virtual rollercoasters all accomplish this with seats that can shift or tilt on demand.

Proprioception. Proprioception is from the Latin meaning "to grasp oneself," and refers to our awareness of position, and the position of our limbs relative to our body. Unless you intend to visit your players individually and move their hands and feet for them during play, this is not a sense that can be directly used for communication. In conjunction with other senses, however, it can help to convey spatial information in-game. Imagine, for instance, a pitch-black environment in VR. Players feel for walls with handheld controllers, receiving haptic feedback if they hit something. In combination with awareness of the position of their own hands, players can quite literally feel out their surroundings.

4.1.4 *Putting it all together*

It should be clear by this point that we are spoiled for choice in terms of our communication options. The channels we choose to convey information will be heavily dependent on what that information is and its importance. Usually, there are multiple viable solutions to communicate any given piece of information, with creative freedom playing a significant role and no singular ideal solution existing. Nonetheless, we can apply some general rules of thumb based on what we are trying to communicate.

Data science prescribes standard categories for classifying information based on its type: qualitative, or descriptive, and quantitative, or numerical, with further specifiers for different sorts of numeric data. We don't require this level of rigour for our purposes, so we'll stick with simpler terminology in the interest of being a bit more specific to games. At a very high level, we can identify three basic types of information you might convey to players: *quantities* (e.g., remaining hit points or ammunition), *descriptions* (e.g., what an item does, whether a character is hostile), and *locations* (e.g., where your next objective is). For each data type, we can establish some general guidelines in how it may be represented to players. Here, we'll be focusing primarily on audiovisual cues; without highly specialized hardware, other sensory channels should be viewed as secondary supports in representing information.

Quantities: "you have this much left." Communicating a player's remaining mana in Morse code via controller rumble is generally a recipe for frustration. If you want players to have a relatively accurate idea of any number, it must include some sort of visual representation. If an estimation of the value is sufficient during gameplay, then you can opt to use a proportional display, like a meter that fills or depletes as the value changes. Many games use these types of displays to represent character health; everything from the *Elder Scrolls* games to *Street Fighter*. It is important to note that the size of such a display will affect the granularity of a player's estimate; a very large meter will allow for more precise estimates than a very small one.[1]

If you want players to know the exact value you wish to communicate, then you should usually provide actual numbers on-screen. The role-playing subgenre of Japanese role-playing game (JRPG)s, which can demand players have a precise understanding of their damage output, often uses such displays in combat. *Xenoblade Chronicles*, for instance, displays a floating number on-screen corresponding to the damage of each attack as it is executed. If the value you want players to know exactly has a relatively small range or possible number of values, you can avoid an explicit numeric display by using a clearly divided visual display. An example is icon-based health bars, such as that used in *Hollow Knight*, which can tell players exactly how much health they have left without needing to show players an actual number.

Descriptions: "this thing is evil." Depending on what you are trying to describe, any of the channels described throughout this section might be appropriate. For descriptions that require substantial detail, such as the

---

[1] This is for two reasons. First, there is something called the "just noticeable difference," a quirk of human perception defining the smallest possible change that we will notice and something data visualization designers always need to consider. Between two displays of different sizes used to represent the same value, the same change in value will appear larger on the larger display, and is thus more likely to exceed the visual "just noticeable difference." Second, a smaller display will have lower resolution and thus less ability to even display small changes in the first place due to necessary rounding in its pixel size.

PLAN NO. 315211420

Figure 4.7 Four different ways to represent a player's health total. Quantities might be represented using written numerals, discrete gauges (like filled or unfilled icons), or a continuous gauge (such as a health bar).

function of an item, some form of text should usually be included. Simpler descriptions, such as the type of an item in the player's inventory, might be easily conveyed through iconography. In general, icons are preferable to text if their designs are easily interpretable (and additional information can always be given in a separate, more detailed view).

This label-maker approach, while certainly functional, is not always the most engaging way to communicate information. Simple descriptions like "this character is hostile" or "this area is safe" are often best communicated in subtler ways, such as changes in music or cues in environmental and character design. Sometimes, the more direct approach of explicitly tagging things is necessary to avoid confusion—imagine if enemy characters in *Overwatch* looked identical to teammates except for facial expressions. However, if a more creative approach is feasible, it can create memorable moments. Suddenly hearing combat music in *Skyrim* and seeing an angry mob of vampires turning the corner ahead is far more engaging than noticing red icons on a minimap.

Locations: "it's over there." As you might expect, the answer to this question is usually "just show them." Icons on a compass or minimap are certainly the most straightforward way to communicate the location of something in any game where players navigate a virtual space. Spatial audio, however, can also be incredibly effective, and can be used when giving players an explicit map location would be inappropriate (e.g., the location of a nearby enemy revealed by the sound of their footsteps). Audio can also

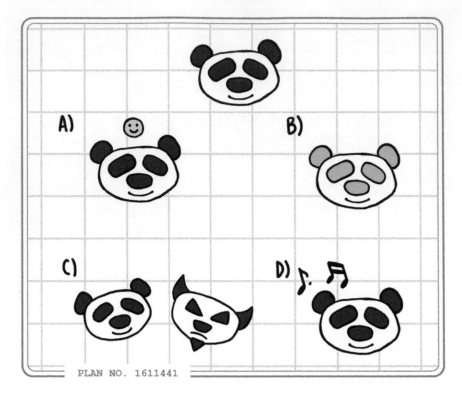

PLAN NO. 1611441

Figure 4.8 If you wanted to communicate the quality of "friendly" in association with a character, you might A) use iconography, B) use colour, C) contrast that character with a less friendly-looking fellow through shape, or D) play happy music in their presence.

be used in situations where players are meant to discover a location with the assistance of something like in-game radar.

Another distinction we can make is that each of these data types can be involved in either continuous or responsive communication. For instance, a player's remaining health might constantly be displayed on screen, but sudden changes in that value (taking damage or healing) will carry additional responsive feedback, such as animations and sound effects.

A key distinction between continuous and responsive communication is that continuous communication serves as a reference for players, while responsive communication serves as an alert. This means that, in general, continuous communication should be unobtrusive, avoiding things like excessive visual motion or loud audio effects. Responsive communication, on the other hand, should grab players' attention, using things like motion, sudden visual change, sound effects, and haptic feedback.

Returning to our previous example, the health bar in a game's HUD is a form of continuous communication. It should be easily visible for reference, but shouldn't distract players by flashing or animating when nothing of interest is happening. If health is critically low, an additional unobtrusive effect could be used, such as a dimming effect at the edges of their character's vision.

If players suddenly take a large amount of damage, that change should be communicated responsively to alert players to the change. This might mean showing an animation of their character staggering accompanied by a bloody particle effect, a flash on their health bar, a sound clip of the character shouting, or a short burst of controller rumble.

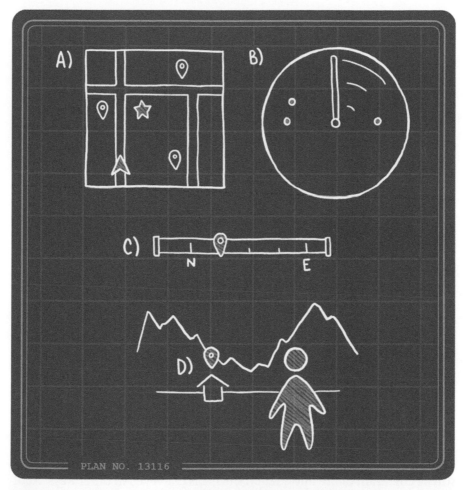

Figure 4.9 Locations might be represented or highlighted via A) minimap, B) faux radar, C) a HUD compass, or D) UI elements overdrawn in a game's world.

Another thing that affects how much attention we should try to grab with our communication is the importance of the information in question. Keep in mind that the type and intensity of the channels you use to represent information will affect the noticeability of that information. For instance, a sudden sound effect is more noticeable than static text, and a very large icon will be more noticeable than a very small one. Using intense sensory cues for something trivial can both annoy players and reduce their sensitivity to communications for information that is genuinely important. Conversely, if communication never really grabs players' attention, then critical events can easily be missed. We'll explore these pitfalls together a bit later. For now, you should understand that more important information should be more noticeable, and less important information less so.

4.1.5 *Sometimes the right choice is—everything!*

Redundant encoding is a data visualization concept which refers to the use of more than one channel to represent the same piece of information. As an example, icons in a chart might use both shape and colour to represent their type, rather than just one or the other. Though the term *redundant encoding* is currently specific to data visualization and niche in its usage, it's a nice way to describe an otherwise nameless phenomenon which is, for good reason, incredibly common in games.

In *The Long Dark*, a survival game set in the brutal Canadian wilderness, players need to be acutely aware of their character's current status. One important factor is their character's need for warmth, which is strongly tied to the world's current temperature and weather conditions. This information needs to be communicated continuously, as it is a constant factor in players' decision-making. Players are warned about dangerous temperatures through several different communication channels. Iconography on the game's HUD displays their character's current tolerance and the rate at which it is depleting. Visual effects in the game's world, such as their character's breath fog, snow, blowing tree branches, and colour grading all change in accordance with weather conditions, and consequently, temperature. The breath fog effect, for instance, becomes more opaque, and thus more obvious, as the temperature drops. Sound effects, such as the wind blowing, their character's teeth chattering, and breathing patterns provide further reinforcement. Lastly, the player's character will also remark on the temperature of their surroundings and how quickly they need to find shelter. The use of so many different channels helps to ensure that if players miss any one cue, they will still be cognizant of the information since it is conveyed in other ways. Additionally, the use of many different cues helps to reinforce the information's importance.

Figure 4.10 In *The Long Dark*, players have constant access to information about their exposure to the elements no matter where they look. Weather conveys the harshness of conditions visually, while a HUD gauge displays how quickly player warmth is depleting. An in-game menu additionally provides the current temperature and wind chill.

Credit: *The Long Dark* is the property of Hinterland Studio Inc.

Redundant encoding can also help to make sure players don't miss out on key feedback if their attention is split between different tasks. In the hectic cooking simulator *Cook, Serve, Delicious* and its sequels, players' attention is constantly shifting focus from one dish to the next. In the resulting pandemonium, it is important for players to be aware of whether they have prepared orders properly as they move to the next task. Feedback is provided

Figure 4.11 The *Cook, Serve, Delicious* games offer multiple cues to let players know whether they've thrilled or disappointed virtual diners. Amidst an interface that lets users track all current orders (left), each individual order ticket provides visual feedback for a perfectly executed order (top right) or one they've fumbled (bottom right). This is accompanied by appropriately cheerful or grumbly sound effects, as well as a combo indicator tracking the number of perfect orders completed in a row.

Credit: *Cook, Serve, Delicious! 2!!* was developed and published by Vertigo Gaming Inc.

for individual tasks with both an animated visual effect that uses colour and stylized emoticons to display quality, and a sound effect indicating customer satisfaction or frustration.

You should always communicate important information in multiple ways, to underscore its value and make sure that players won't accidentally miss out on that information. Obviously, it is also important to note that not everything should be communicated through six different modes of representation at once, lest you leave your players in a hopeless state of overload. Nonetheless, using multiple channels is a great way to make communication more satisfying and less likely to fall through the cracks.

4.1.6 *A word on accessibility*

If we did indeed have only one word to address game accessibility, that word would be "important."[2] About 15% of American adults report some difficulties with their hearing. If you're born with XY chromosomes, there's about a one in twelve chance you'll have some form of colour vision deficiency (the odds are much lower otherwise). It is estimated that nearly one third of the global population has some form of visual impairment.

What this means is that assuming all your players will have the hearing of a well-rested bat and perfect visual acuity is, ironically, incredibly short-sighted. There are any number of conditions that can affect someone's ability to play and enjoy a game. Since our current discussion revolves around communicating information to players, here we'll focus on sensory impairments which can interfere with how a player will perceive a game's output.

Various degrees of hearing impairment might mean that players can't discern between similar sound effects, have trouble locating spatial sounds, or be unable to hear any sounds clearly at all. This can be particularly troublesome for in-game speech, especially if that speech is conveying instructions or vital story information, which is why subtitles should always be available as an option.

Visual impairment can affect players' ability to read on-screen text, discriminate between various icons, or see contrast between different objects. HUD scaling can help to alleviate this for more minor impairments, with different picture settings such as high-contrast options serving as additional mitigators.

---

[2] Here's a few sources, current as of this writing, that might help to underscore just how many people are affected by, for example, sensory impairment:
https://www.nidcd.nih.gov/health/statistics/quick-statistics-hearing
https://ghr.nlm.nih.gov/condition/color-vision-deficiency#statistics
https://www.who.int/news-room/fact-sheets/detail/blindness-and-visual-impairment

Due to their high incidence, colour vision impairments, particularly red-green colourblindness, should be something close to the forefront of your mind in communicating with players. Though colour alone is a remarkably effective cue for those with normal colour vision,[3] it might be useless to someone with a colour vision deficiency, depending on the colours chosen.

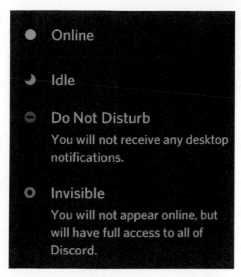

Figure 4.12 Discord uses a red-green colour scheme for publicly visible user status in combination with shape cues to better accommodate colour vision impairments.

Credit: Discord is the property of Discord Inc.

Perhaps the easiest way to instantly make your game more accessible is to never use green and red as indicator colours. In addition to risking associations with garish Christmas décor, red and green pose problems for those with the most common forms of colour vision impairments. For example, the radar screen in *Galaxy on Fire 2* uses green dots for allies, red for hostiles, and yellow for neutral. No other definite indicators are provided, other than who is shooting at whom. While this scheme is instantly understandable and easy to use for someone with normal colour vision, for the nearly 5% or so of people with some form of impairment, the icons may become nearly indistinguishable. Simple settings like a "colourblind mode" using blue and orange, or adding icon shape as an additional cue, can provide a quick, cheap way to reduce such issues.

---

[3] In visualization terms, colour supports "popout"—the instant recognition of an object which differs from its surroundings by its visual attributes. To someone with normal colour vision, a red dot amongst a sea of green dots will "jump out," making it easy to identify, for example, an enemy on radar. For someone with a colour vision impairment, this effect may be entirely absent depending on the combination of colours used.

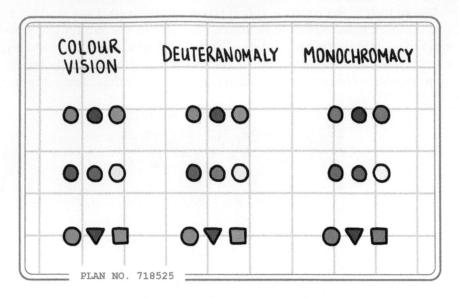

Figure 4.13 Left: Three different icon schemes as seen by someone with unimpeded colour vision (left), deuteranomaly (a form of "red-green colourblindness"; middle), and monochromacy ("total colourblindness"; right). Selective use of colours (e.g., orange and blue as opposed to red and green) can better support users with more common forms of colour vision deficiency. If you want to preserve the green/red "good/bad" association for users with normal colour vision, you should ideally include the option to switch to a different colour scheme. Including another cue, such as shape, can provide more universal accessibility—and probably makes your scheme more understandable in general.

All these points provide further credence to the concept of redundant encoding. A player with severe hearing loss will enjoy your game all the same if no important information is conveyed with sound alone. A player with visual impairments will have a much more enjoyable and usable experience if rich sound design is there to support cues that otherwise rely on sharp sight. Such examples also reinforce the value of giving players options; if you can, include options for large font, high contrast, enabling additional sound effects or verbal feedback, and so on.

In the case of exceptionally severe impairments, it may not be easy or possible with what resources you have available to make your games completely accessible to players who are deaf or legally blind. Nonetheless, there is a lot for us to learn from games that do accomplish near-universal accessibility. *The Last of Us 2* is a paragon of accessibility, packing dozens of options to assist players in reducing any interface-induced frustration.

A high-contrast mode, which turns the environment grey, outlines important objects, and uses a colourblind-friendly blue and red palette to highlight allies and enemies, makes the game playable for those with low vision. Touchpad gestures can be mapped to various text-to-speech options reading out things like the player character's health and whether they are crouching.

Even if resource limitations mean that you simply can't afford to develop every accessibility option you would like, you should at the very least avoid early mistakes that sacrifice accessibility, like red-green colour schemes. Wherever possible, you should also include options for players to customize how they will receive information. Individual players are ultimately different people with different needs; a one-size-fits-all solution is rarely the best one.

4.2 Continuous communication and HUD design

There is a wealth of information that we can communicate to players at any given time. Health, ammunition, stamina, the nutritional value of a packet of virtual crackers, countless other possibilities, and any combination thereof. We have already examined how we can represent these individual bits of information in isolation. But how can we create a cohesive way to continuously communicate everything that players need to know?

Players will have constant access to information in two main ways. First, they can see and hear things in the game's world through their point of view (via a character or otherwise). Second, you can selectively feed information to players through a virtual interface you design—in other words, an HUD and in-game menus. Depending on the game and the situational context, players' informational needs will change, and our designs must adapt accordingly.

Since players will spend a good deal of their time staring at the HUD, its contents can have a significant impact on players' moment-to-moment experience. Too much information can create visual clutter and spoil a game's aesthetic—did *Doom Eternal* make a mistake in the neon-coloured additions it made to the old *Doom (2016)* HUD, or did it succeed in making players more informed? Missing information can cause player frustration—should buffs and debuffs be displayed in *Skyrim*'s HUD, or stay buried in a separate menu for the sake of immersion?

The answer to these questions isn't always obvious or straightforward, and individual preferences can mean that certain decisions will leave some players unsatisfied. Perhaps, therefore, the most critical step in creating these designs is the simplest—selecting which information to communicate in the first place.

Figure 4.14 In "vanilla" *Skyrim*, various effects such as cloaking spells and potions have varying durations—but players can't explicitly tell how long they have until buffs or debuffs wear off just by looking at the HUD (left). The *SkyUI* mod adds a number of indicators for different buffs which indicate their function and display remaining duration (right).

Credit: The Elder Scrolls V: Skyrim was developed by Bethesda Game Studios and published by Bethesda Softworks. *SkyUI* was a mod developed and maintained by an independent team, with core members snakster and Mardoxx with art by psychosteve.

4.2.1 *What do they know, and when do they know it?*

When video game design first established itself, games themselves were re-markably uncomplicated by modern standards. By necessity, classic arcade games like *Pac-Man* and *Donkey Kong* needed to create fun through sim-plicity. Technical limitations meant that games couldn't have save states, complicated physics, or large-scale levels.

As a result of this simplicity, communicating information in classic arcade games is a generally straightforward endeavour. The entire level is displayed on screen at once, so the positions of any obstacles, enemies, and collectables are always known to the player. Most games had only a few other values to track that players could conceivably care about. After sticking the current score up in the corner and tacking on a little counter for remaining lives, there wasn't really anything else to worry about.

Skip forward a few decades and the task of communicating information to the player can be a far muddier process. While some games still find the fun in simplicity, the likes of massively multiplayer titles, management simulations, and in-depth strategy games take the opposite approach. Shaking loose the technical limitations of yore didn't just allow us to make games that look far prettier; it also permitted us to expand the complexity of the systems we design.

Let's take the massively multiplayer online (MMO) shooter genre as an example, enumerating just some of the information that we could communicate to players. Health, armour, ammunition for the current weapon, ammunition/charges for other weapons and tactical equipment, which weapons are available, score of each player or faction, time remaining in the match, geography of the surrounding area, which players have recently been killed and by whom, health of teammates, position of teammates, health of enemies, position of enemies, position of level objectives, progress on level objectives, experience points, achievement progress, active buffs and debuffs, ability recharge times, and of course, the seven-day weather forecast.

This list is a chore to read, let alone try to keep track of while desperately trying to evade the gunfire of a trigger-happy twelve-year-old hurling hurtful insinuations regarding the promiscuity of your close relatives. But how can we possibly go about deciding what needs to be communicated, and what should be ignored? As a player, you want to know everything that you need to make good tactical decisions. As a designer, it is your job to make sure that players can access everything they need to know, while paring down the gargantuan mountain of information that might be displayed at any time into something manageable.

Fortunately, we have multiple options at our disposal for the availability of information. We can identify five different cases for when players have access to certain information:

1. **Always-off:** Players are never given this information. An example is the contents of an enemy's hand in the online card game *Hearthstone*.
2. **Always-on:** This information is constantly available and actively communicated to players. An example is the onscreen display of damage percentage in the *Super Smash Bros.* games.
3. **Contextual:** This information is typically silent, but automatically communicated to the player in certain situations. An example is the health bar in *Skyrim*, which is only shown when the player has taken damage.
4. **On-request:** This information is given to players only when they request it (e.g., by accessing a separate screen or talking to a character). An example is the inventory screen in *Starbound*, or indeed almost any other game with an inventory system.
5. **Customizable:** Players can choose whether (and/or how) information will be made available to them. Examples include games that allow players the option to disable their HUD or play in some form of "cinematic mode," such as *The Witcher 3*.

Figure 4.15 Five options for controlling when players will have access to information, such as an enemy health bar.

Depending on the game, a mix of these choices for different pieces of information is often appropriate. These options are also not mutually exclusive; for instance, some information which is displayed contextually might also be available on request in a separate screen.

Unfortunately, there is no game-agnostic way for us to neatly choose among these options based on the type of a piece of information. While that descriptive seven-day weather forecast from our earlier diatribe might be completely useless in a shooter, it could be essential information in a city-building sim. Even something as basic as character health might not warrant the same treatment in different games. In a fighting game, any health meter is typically always-on. In an adventure game with limited combat, health might only be displayed during a confrontation.

Instead of relying on arbitrary categories like health and weather, we should approach the problem of what to communicate by examining the context and importance of information, rather than its type. Understanding an information's importance can also help us determine the best way to represent it, as discussed in the previous section.

For any given piece of information, we can select an appropriate option (always-on, always-off, contextual, on request, customizable) by answering the following five questions:

1. **Should players be able to know this information?** This question is about balancing what makes sense in the context of a game's world with what information needs to be available for a game to work as intended.[4] Anything a player's character could reasonably know on their own (e.g., own health, ammunition, money and so on) or with in-game equipment or abilities (e.g., position of enemies via radar) is information the player could conceivably have available.

   Information that a character wouldn't necessarily know, such as the exact map coordinates of a previously unvisited location, might still be something that *players* are able to know for the sake of reducing confusion and frustration. Other times, this kind of information needs to remain unknown in the interest of fairness (e.g., enemies' remaining ammunition). If the player does not control a character, similar logic can be applied; if information would be fair to have without "breaking" the game's intent, then it is a candidate for communicating to the player.

   Sometimes, information must be earned by the player before it becomes available. For instance, players must place friendly units to lift the fog of war and view an enemy's terrain in *StarCraft*. In this case, the information might be eventually available to the player, but its reveal is conditional in some way.

   If the answer to this question is a definitive no, then the information should never be explicitly communicated to the player (always-off). If the answer is yes, sometimes, or maybe, then the remaining questions will help to determine the best option for when the information should be available.

---

[4] A related, but tangential concept is the idea of perfect versus imperfect information, a concept which applies to any rivalry between players or players and AI opponents. If you are new to these terms and would prefer to avoid a few hours reading about economic theory, here's a quick rundown: In a perfect information game, all parties have access to the same information (e.g., chess, where both players can see the entire board). In an imperfect information game, some information is hidden at least some of the time (e.g., poker, where you can only see your own cards).

2. **When do players need or want this information?** Certain pieces of information are always needed, and should thus be always-on by default. Examples could include things like score or time remaining in an arcade-style game, or current ranking in a racing game. Even in games with minimal or no persistent HUD, multiple pieces of information are typically always-on—for one, everything visible through the player camera.

   Players might need to know something in certain situations to decide on their next move. For instance, in combat, knowing their character's current health is necessary to select an appropriate fighting strategy and decide when to heal. In games where combat is infrequent, the ever-looming health bar might prove to be no more than a visual nuisance. In such circumstances, contextual availability should typically become the default option: make the information available only when needed.

   For something that players may want to know from time to time, but is not strictly necessary, information should be available on request. An example would be something like progress in completing collections of items; players will likely wish to check in occasionally, but filling their HUD with a clutter of always-on lists would be nightmarish. Another option in these scenarios is to contextually display information when it changes, for instance, a small notification informing players they have completed a collection upon retrieving the last item.

   If players would not conceivably ever find information valuable in some way, whether for utility, interest, amusement, or otherwise, then it should be always-off.

3. **How important is this information to the player?** If you are on the fence after answering the previous two questions, considering the importance of the information at hand can help make the decision. More important information should be more readily available—for instance, a critically important value, like total cash in a management simulation, might be always-on, even if it is not always strictly necessary for player decision-making. Less important information may be kept at bay to avoid overwhelming the player with clutter.

4. **Can this information be conveyed outside of the HUD?** In *World of Warcraft*, players can install custom addons to strip down its HUD, or more commonly, stack additional information on top of it. As anyone who has witnessed one of these abominations can attest, the adage of "less is more" certainly applies to HUD design. At the very least, the default HUD you offer up to players should minimize the amount of information being bombarded at them. Remember that the HUD is not the only channel for continuously communicating with players; players will also constantly take in information from a game's world. In other words, if you can reasonably convey something through what

players will see in the world rather than on the HUD, you should. Consider hiding that minimap by default and putting up street signs; let players feel a little bit more like they're peering into a game's world and not staring at a screen.

5. **Should we give players control over the availability of this information?** The answer to this question is almost always yes from a design standpoint. Practically speaking, it is often treated as no due to the increased work resulting from things like customizable HUD configurations and ever-expanding options menus. While this decision is understandable, the best design possible will give players a great deal of agency in this regard. Some players might like to minimize what they view as intrusions on an immersive experience, disabling HUD features entirely. Others might like to have as much information always-on as possible, accounting for every detail they can before making a strategic decision. As a designer, the best decision you can make is to respect these differences whenever possible: select the appropriate default based on the previous questions, but give players the option to decide what suits their own preferences.

Answering these questions is a relatively simple and straightforward process, and yet, things like HUD design even in well-received titles can be the subject of contention. A quick search for "HUD clutter in Battlefield" (or the appropriately relevant multiplayer shooter at the time of your reading) will yield innumerable threads on Reddit (or the appropriately quirky public forum at the time of your reading) arguing over whether minimaps and achievement ribbons are immersion-breaking. Such debates often make salient points about the merit of options like UI scaling before inevitably breaking down into chaos and vague threats to send various undesirable materials through the postal service.

Trying to appease everyone with some magical set of default options in such cases should be treated as an impossible task. The answer in many of these cases is to invest the extra effort in customization options, giving players control over the availability of information.

Finally, the answer in some cases might be to forego the inclusion of a HUD at all, optional or otherwise. Sometimes, everything that players absolutely need to know is shown through their surroundings. Most games might have some critical value that players need to keep tabs on—health, money, time—but for those that don't, communication can occur through their character and the environment. Indie darling *Limbo* strips down the player's experience to something resembling a black-and-white film, with no HUD in sight. Granted, its gameplay makes this choice relatively obvious, with no lives or hit points to keep track of. Even so, navigational aids could conceivably have been added. In the case of *Limbo*, a game whose core atmosphere is one of feeling lost and alone, such additions would have served to detract from the experience.

4.2.2   Layout, icons, fonts, colours, and all that other jazz

The visual choices you make in presenting a HUD can impact its usability and its aesthetic appeal. We'll have a look at what makes an interface "beautiful" or "ugly" at the end of this chapter. Beyond what we have already discussed in terms of choices for representing information, there are other factors which contribute to the visual gestalt of a HUD and its usability.

There are a great many individual factors that we could identify, but perhaps the best way to quickly grasp the essentials is to review some general design principles.

If you've ever spent more than five minutes in the company of a UX specialist, you've probably heard the name Don Norman, likely accompanied by fervent pointing at the nearest teapot, coffee mug, or poorly designed door handle. Don Norman is an accomplished design researcher, perhaps best known for his book about the design of everyday things, controversially titled *The Design of Everyday Things*. The original edition establishes six design principles, going on to form the first six lectures of every undergraduate class on human-computer interaction created since its publication. Two are of special interest to HUD design: visibility and consistency.[5]

Visibility. If you expect players to process information, that information needs to be readily visible (or audible, in the case of audio cues). Having elements that are too small, lack contrast, or are grouped too closely together can all make a HUD harder to interpret.

One visual choice that can significantly impact visibility is typographic design. Text readability is severely affected by font selection, size, and spacing. If you're one of the people that stopped to read every in-game book in *The Elder Scrolls IV: Oblivion*, firstly, congratulations on your degree in English literature. Secondly, we're sorry that you had to stare at all that crowded text written in a script font that becomes virtually unreadable after the first few words. Except for titles, it's generally a good idea to avoid using overly stylized fonts, no matter how much they "fit" with the theme of your game.

Subtitles are an area where typographic choices are extremely important, especially for players that have difficulty hearing dialogue or trouble with a character's accent. *Life Is Strange* handles subtitles well, choosing a lightly stylized font that is comfortable to read at its default size, and packing options to adjust scaling and toggle a text background to improve visibility.

---

[5] We'll encounter the other four principles in due time. *Feedback*, the notion that a system should communicate the consequences of user action, is essentially the concept of responsive communication. The other three principles are *Mapping* (the relationship between the position of controls and their function), *Constraints* (restrictions on the actions a user is allowed to perform), and *Affordances* (appealing to a user's existing conceptions of how an object should be interacted with based on its design). These three principles will be addressed in Chapter 5, in discussing the design of game controls.

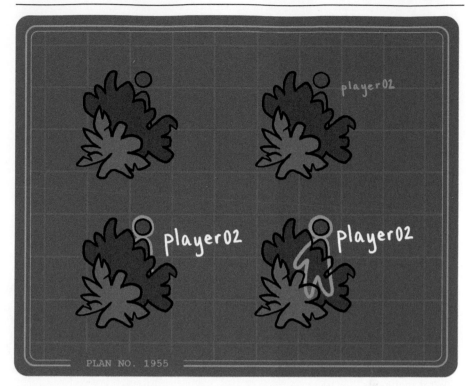

Figure 4.16 Visibility means that information is easy to perceive. Let's say you want players to be able to spot their comrades for easy coordination and avoiding friendly fire. Rendering another player as a normal character might provide poor visibility in certain conditions (top left). Adding a simple label adds some form of visual distinction (top right). Adding an outline and more contrasting label improves visibility (bottom left). Many games will opt for an outline on teammates which is visible through world geometry to further boost visibility (bottom right).

Such settings don't just improve the game's quality-of-life; they also make it more accessible.

In discussing HUD visibility, positioning is another important factor to acknowledge. HUD elements should never obscure a player's view of the game. Aside from a central reticle or aim indicator if necessary, HUD components should be pushed away from central vision. Existing in the periphery means that these elements will usually be outside of a player's focus: in view, but with far less detail perceptible than through central vision. As a result, they should be easy to interpret at-a-glance as players look away from the action, and positioned in such a way that players know exactly where they need to look for a certain bit of information. Take *Minecraft*'s relatively simple HUD as an example. Everything is accessible at quick downwards glance along the bottom centre of the player's view. The player character's status (health and hunger) is displayed at the top of the HUD group, making it easy to monitor

97

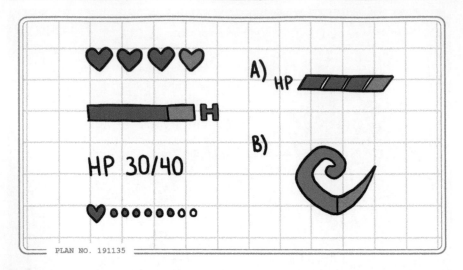

PLAN NO. 191135

Figure 4.17 Given the four health displays at left as examples players may have been exposed to in the past, A) is a design which is externally consistent. Using a bar shape, the "HP" label, and red colour, it's obvious what this gauge is meant to represent. If B) is meant to represent health, it has poor external consistency; the blue colour and swirl shape doesn't exactly scream "health bar"[6]. This isn't to say it's a bad design, but depending on context, you might want to be careful in making sure players know what it represents.

both at a glance. The player's armour indicator is grouped with their health bar, since armour will affect how much damage they take in combat. Below the needs bar is an experience bar that fills as resources are mined and enemies are killed, and finally, a hotbar of currently equipped items is shown for reference. This grouping makes it easy for players to quickly find and interpret different pieces of information.

Consistency. There are two different types of consistency: external and internal. External consistency is the idea of obeying conventions established by other games. An example is the ubiquitous red health bar common in role-playing games. From the *Zelda* games to *Divinity: Original Sin* and (nearly) every RPG in between, if you see a red bar without context, you assume it serves as a health indicator. A game with a blue health bar and a red magic

---

[6] One thing that does scream "health bar" is the eponymous red cross, which you may notice is conspicuously absent from this diagram. There's a very good reason for that: the symbol is protected by the Geneva Convention, and is not to be used outside of very specific and very serious contexts. This is something we discovered during writing, necessitating changes to the initial version of this diagram and joining the likes of *Stardew Valley* in removing the red cross symbol by way of update. But based on the number of games that depict it in some way to represent healing, a shocking number of developers are technically in violation of the Geneva Convention.

bar would be externally *inconsistent*: violating the expectations players have based on past experience and taking a lot of time to get used to.

This isn't to say that going against the grain is always a bad idea; the relatively unique and convention-defying HUD of *Dead Space* has drawn admiration from players and critics alike. We'll talk about *Dead Space*'s HUD and others like it towards the end of the chapter. For now, it's sufficient to note that straying from convention can be a good thing, if it is done for good reason and executed well.

Internal consistency is, as you might expect, whether a game adheres to its own established conventions. Mismatches in internal consistency are almost universally bad, unless done intentionally for comedic effect. There's a reason the *Elder Scrolls* games, and in particular *Skyrim*, always seem to crop up in discussions nitpicking UI design; despite their immense popularity, they are terribly flawed in some respects. Look at *Skyrim*'s character status bars, for health, stamina, and magic. Each bar appears only if it is not full; this is good internal consistency. However, while the stamina and magic bars deplete from the left-hand side, the health bar depletes from both sides towards the centre. In addition to making it more difficult to accurately assess the player's current health, this creates inconsistency between the different indicators for no good reason.

Good internal consistency can make it easier for players to navigate a game's HUD and use it effectively in different contexts. In *Team Fortress 2*, players can take on the role of several characters, each of which has different weapons and abilities. As a result of these differences, the HUD needs to display different information depending on the character chosen by the player. Shared elements, such as health and killstreaks, are displayed identically between different character HUDs. Differing elements, such as recharge timers for special abilities, are grouped consistently depending on their function. Buffs that provide some temporary bonus are always shown in the bottom left; recharge meters for unique weapons are always shown in the bottom right. This consistency allows for players to switch between characters more easily, without having to acclimate to many different layouts.

4.3 Responsive communication

In *Stardew Valley*, one of your in-game tasks is to gather specific items and complete in-game collections of crops, minerals, fish, and so on. Upon harvesting that last precious turnip and depositing it in the appropriate box, you'll be met with dancing forest sprites, cheerful music, and a bouncing little gift box containing your reward.

Unfortunately, stowing away root vegetables in real life carries no such fanfare, which is merely one of the things that makes reality a crushing disappointment in comparison to video games.

In our lives, we find ourselves waiting for feedback on what we've done. An email from the boss letting us know that we're off the hook after that last meeting. A review from a customer who didn't turn out to be all that upset about the extra olives on their sandwich. A note from our mother informing us that we, once again, neglected to buy the apricot preserves, because the strawberry just doesn't work with the new raisin toast, and don't we have any respect for the pantry in this house?

Sometimes, we'll receive contradictory opinions on what we've done. Sometimes, the assessment we've been waiting on never arrives. We balance enough precarious uncertainty to make Damocles himself blush, all exacerbated by the ever-entangling web of modern communication channels.

Games, or at least well-designed games, let us escape this hellscape of unresolved tension through carefully crafted feedback, or in other words, responsive communication. When we do poorly, we can know of our failure immediately, and get some encouragement or advice if applicable. When we do well, we can receive a clear indicator of our success. This helps us keep track of our performance, helps us decide what to do next, and can even be rewarding.

4.3.1 *A quick primer on feedback*

Feedback is another one of Norman's design principles, applicable to the whole of software and systems design. It's a simple idea: any time a user takes an action, the system needs to provide an indication of its consequences. If you hit a button to print a document, you'd hope that some system dialog would pop up informing you whether your printer will eventually decide to do something about it. Failing this, you'll be relying on the printer itself for feedback, left alone to interpret the demonic beeping and flashing lights of a machine obviously designed by denizens of the underworld. This is, of course, a fate far worse than death, and the only evidence anyone should need or want to justify the importance of system feedback.

Another important part of responsive communication is informing the user of relevant events, like the lonely message notification from that one person you know that still uses Skype. There are a lot of different terms for these different flavours of communication, but for our discussion, we'll just use "feedback" as shorthand for any kind of responsive communication in games.

Just as in the previous examples discussed, games need to provide feedback on a player's actions, as well as any events that affect them or their character.

If you hit a button to fire a weapon, the game needs to provide feedback on that action. Maybe there's a muzzle flash accompanied by sound effects if you fire successfully. Maybe there's a clicking sound and a voice line if you're out of ammo. Maybe there's a grinding noise and a curse word or two if your gun is jammed. Even if you as the player don't *do* anything, events that affect you also require feedback, such as a notification that a teammate's character has died.

4.3.2 *Creating effective feedback*

In the first-person shooter *Valorant*, one of the side effects of being shot is that your character will be temporarily slowed down. The magnitude of the slow-down effect is such that it is hard to miss; however, when standing still, the remaining feedback for taking damage is lacking. A faint red indicator near the centre of the screen shows the direction of any fire taken, but its visibility is reduced by a fade-in effect and often poor contrast with the game's environment. The player's character can grunt after a significant hit, but audio feedback for taking a hit is otherwise absent. The only other indication of damage is for players to check their health on the HUD, which is shown as a number only and relatively subtly animates its text colour when critically low.

The outcome of this design is that it's entirely possible for a player's character to take a great deal of damage, or even die, without the player noticing. This is especially problematic for new players accustomed to games that use much more obvious damage indicators. It's worth noting that, as of this writing, *Valorant* has received several patches, some of which aim to address these issues and make damage feedback easier to spot.

Another game that makes hit feedback more obvious while avoiding overzealous screen-shake effects is Valve's zombie-themed FPS *Left 4 Dead 2*. Like *Valorant*, *L4D2* uses directional indicators to alert the player of damage sources. However, the use of a more saturated colour against the much darker environmental design of *L4D2* improves contrast a great deal. Additionally, the markers appear instantly when the player takes damage, rather than fading in, and are located closer to the player's crosshair, making them easier to spot. A translucent red overlay quickly flashes in and out whenever a hit is taken, ensuring the player will notice damage no matter where they are looking without obscuring their view. It's also worth noting that continuous feedback on health also makes it easy to understand character status at-a-glance, with a health bar on the HUD that changes colour as it lowers in addition to a numeric display.

Of course, much of the damage in *L4D2* comes from enemies close to the player, so hits from the front are easily recognizable from the animated

Figure 4.18 In *Left 4 Dead 2*, the player is met with obvious damage indicators including sound effects and splashes of colour (left). This also includes an on-screen message when they are incapacitated and require assistance from a teammate (right).

Credit: *Left 4 Dead 2* was developed and published by Valve.

zombie snapping its lifeless jaws an arm's length from your character's face. Nonetheless, during what can become easily hectic fights with lots of enemies in all directions, all that feedback helps you to pick out when you've actually taken damage. What's more, characters automatically trigger descriptive voice lines during combat to plead with teammates for help and warn of the danger posed by specific enemies.

Naturally, feedback for different events and actions requires different considerations. Nonetheless, we can establish a few general rules of thumb for what makes feedback effective, learning from the previous examples and others like them. In general, feedback should be:

1. **Immediate.** Feedback needs to happen as soon as possible for players to understand what's going on around them, prevent frustration, and inform future decisions. Imagine trying to execute a difficult button combo in a fighting game like *Marvel vs. Capcom* and having to wait several seconds to see whether you were successful. Instead, feedback on the success of an action, event, or otherwise should be immediate; if players don't see or hear anything, they will naturally assume that nothing has happened.

2. **Distinct.** Different actions or events should map to different cues that are easily distinguishable to avoid confusion. Think of the variety of visual and sound effects used in games that feature magic systems to highlight different spells. In the JRPG *Bravely Default*, for instance, casting different types of damage, healing, and support spells are accompanied by unique sounds, visual flair, and bursts of colour. This makes it easier for players to keep track of what's going on without having to constantly second-guess their actions or pay more attention to text indicators.

3. **Easy to interpret.** Unsurprisingly, feedback should be clear, lest players be left scratching their heads, or worse, resorting to searching for something on an abandoned wiki forum. This is also where our friend consistency comes back into play. The same type of action or event should trigger the same type of feedback to remain internally consistent. Existing conventions should be noted to maintain good external consistency as well; for instance, a red halo at the edges of player vision says, "you're taking damage," not "you've just earned in-game currency."

4. **Appropriately attention-grabbing.** If the previous point relates most to consistency, then this one relates most to visibility. If players are likely to miss out on feedback, it will become a source of frustrated confusion—as we have already noted. Conversely, obtrusive feedback can annoy players, or create something akin to sensory overload if taken to the extreme. Creating the ideal middle ground is challenging, but can help make sure that feedback is both effective and satisfying. Striking the right balance between these extremes is so difficult, in fact, that it warrants some discussion of its own.

Figure 4.19 Feedback in *Galaxy on Fire 2* when killing an enemy ship is immediate (audio and visuals trigger when the ship's health reaches zero), distinct (very different to the effects corresponding to normal weapon firing), easy to interpret (recognizable as destruction) and attention-grabbing (sound effects are appropriately loud, and an explosion triggers a flash of light within a certain radius).

Credit: *Galaxy on Fire 2* was developed and published by Deep Silver Fishlabs.

4.3.3 Packing a punch (or holding one back)

When you successfully strike a monster with your sword, the feedback can be as simple as a number floating out of the enemy accompanied by a ding to their health bar, and you'll understand exactly what's happened. It's probably not an experience that will stick in your head, though, and it's likely you'll be thinking in terms of numbers rather than reveling vicariously in the bloodlust.

Now imagine that when you strike that same enemy, something different happens. The blade makes contact. A gurgling sound effect rings out as it tears through demon flesh. The monster's body shrinks away, springing back after the hit. Instead of a number floating out, a spray of blood flies from the wound, coating the ground and splashing onto your character's boots. As the creature roars in protest, your character stumbles, your view shaking from the sheer power of its battle cry. Your sword takes on a crimson hue as you land hit after hit, blood pooling on the ground. As you walk away from the monster's corpse, its blood sloshes at your feet, reminding you of your victory.

There's a word for this sort of exaggerated feedback, and that word is *juice*, popularized in a 2012 GDC talk and the subject of many video essays and blogposts since. Adding rich feedback that exaggerates a game's intended tone—or "juicing up" its interactions—can make players feel more immersed and rewarded for their actions.

Juice is a tactic that has been applied in some form or another since the inception of digital game design. The act of "juicing up" interactions has become even more relevant in the past decade or so; one of the things most drastically affected by advances in technology is audiovisual effects. The feedback on a jump in the original *Super Mario Bros.* or a gunshot in *Commandos* is still certainly satisfying. However, modern games can make the same types of interactions far more engaging in terms of feedback. In the indie platformer *Super Meat Boy*, for example, the titular meat boy leaves a literal trail of juice wherever he goes, his elastic body responding to every moment and landing with a satisfying flop whenever he touches the ground. In the top-down shooter *Hotline Miami*, every fight yields an appropriately gory spray of blood across the level, accompanied by some appropriately 1980s flashing text indicating points earned for the kill.

To an extent, every effect you add can make an interaction feel more satisfying, within reason. That last caveat is an important one, too; overdoing something like screen-shake can make your game feel less like a juicy experience and more like a targeted attack on players with epilepsy. The line between too little and too much feedback isn't always clear, though, and sometimes that line can shift depending on the context.

Overwatch, a multiplayer shooter with a diverse roster of playable characters, is a game with incredibly satisfying feedback. Each character's unique abilities, particularly their "ultimate" ability, carries a maelstrom of particles, rays of light, sound effects, and animation. Even regular combat is filled with splashes of light and colour, generally making the game a feast for the eyes. However, being a competitive game that can pack lots of players in close quarters, sometimes these effects can be overbearing. When six players are all visible on screen, all triggering different abilities in a relatively confined area, *Overwatch* suffers from undeniable visual clutter. It can be difficult to tell what's going on, and even more challenging to try and aim at a character silhouetted between five different bursts of particles and auras of coloured light. With the amount of action on screen during typical play, *Overwatch* could benefit from an across-the-board reduction on the intensity of visual effects—or at least some contextual trigger that tones down particle counts and brightness in crowded areas.

Like everything else, the level of attention-grabbing that feedback demands should correlate somewhat with its importance. Making a big deal out of something players find unimportant can detract from more memorable moments, or even become frustrating. The initial release of *No Man's Sky*, for instance, stole control from players for earning so-called milestone achievements, taking ten seconds to pan out, display some cinematic bars, award the achievement, and play some heroic music before focusing back in on the player. The issue here was that the milestones include things like covering a certain amount of in-game units on foot (first at zero, then five thousand, then ten, then twenty...), something players would accomplish

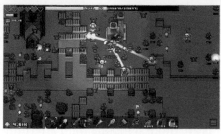

Figure 4.20 *Forager* offers a great deal of "juice" including particle effects, cheerful foley, and succulent bits of visual flair on collecting resources, leveling up, or unlocking items (top). This can become overwhelming when the player has sufficiently powerful gear (bottom), but the game's settings offer options to tone things down if players so choose.

Credit: *Forager* was developed by Hopfrog and published by Humble Games.

quickly with no significant challenge. Every single achievement carried this sequence, which felt akin to being given an Oscar for brushing your teeth. Fortunately, after players complaining of the constant interruption to their gameplay for seemingly no reason, the fanfare was made optional in a later update.

When feedback is done just right, the result is something that feels punchy and satisfying, pulling you further into the game's core experience. The indie idle-action-adventure hybrid *Forager* captures the notion of "juice" with its every interaction. Buttons are elastic, springing like soft rubber at every hover and press. Every interaction in game sparkles with particles, cheerful foley, and (optional) screen-shake where warranted. Though the visual spectacle can verge on cluttered at times, options to disable certain effects can help tailor the game's appearance to players less fond of its bouncy animations. And as a game with no competitive elements, sitting back to watch your drones take out a wave of enemies in a flash of light and sound is nothing short of glorious; all that juice makes the game all the more satisfying to play.

4.4 Brief thoughts on creative direction

In *Persona 5*, navigating menus feels more like leafing through a bombastic manga comic. Text varies in size, colour, and even font, with letters from five or more different typefaces appearing in a single word. Labels and buttons can appear at skewed angles, animating in and out of a stark black and white theme with attention-grabbing red highlights. Compared to traditional game typography, it can be difficult to read. And it's absolutely beautiful.

The thing about *Persona 5*'s menu and HUD design is that it fits exceptionally well with the tone and narrative themes of the game. Our edgy, quite literally heart-stealing protagonists are set in a world that might be described as punk, or vibrant angst. Their comic action-hero RPG battles are supported by an appropriately comic action-hero UI and bold feedback. And sure, some of the text can be tricky to read at first glance, but the aggressive styling is used sparingly. Titles and top-level menu items are given the full ransom note-esque treatment, while larger blocks of text such as character dialogue and lists of items are rendered in a clean, easily readable font. Those top-level items are more symbolic than anything else; iconic and recognizable, the fact they're made of text at all serves as just a reference. In a way, parts of the *Persona 5* UI are meant to be felt, not read. Games in the JRPG genre are infamous for packing a plethora of menus to wade through. *Persona 5* embraces its interface, using it as an opportunity to create great art instead of treating menus as a boring layer atop its gameplay. It turns a purely functional perception of HUDs and menus on its head, and the result is something wonderful.

Examples like *Persona* demonstrate the subtle compromises between form and functionality that can have a striking effect: bending rules like visibility and consistency just enough to make something distinctively alluring without sacrificing its usability. Steadfast rules like text readability and obeying the conventions of other games aren't always so clear-cut, providing room for experimentation in the interest of creativity.

Art style, and more broadly a game's creative direction, is another one of those pesky subjective things that players with equally valid arguments can love or hate. Some people see photorealism as the pinnacle of good game art, while others prefer minimalist pixel work. Regardless of individual preference, what is generally considered "good" game art and creative direction is a matter of not only artistic skill, but cohesion.

The most artistically appealing games are generally those that lean into their own themes, creating a visual style and soundscape that support the tone of gameplay and narrative elements. Take *Okami*, for instance, a game almost universally praised for its creative direction. *Okami*'s story is adapted from Japanese mythology, and its core gameplay mechanics allow players to change the world around them by painting over it with special brushstrokes. Fittingly, the game's art style is one that mimics watercolour, with thick, dark accents and outlines and dreamy washes of pastel colour forming its tranquil landscapes. Its music uses traditional Japanese instruments and styles, supporting the game's visuals and its mythical narrative elements, while mixing in sound effects that call back to gameplay, such as the sound of ticking clocks ringing out during a battle with mechanical demons.

Figure 4.21 *Okami's* Japanese watercolour style (left) is connected deeply to its narrative, which frequently references art and the use of a "celestial brush" to manipulate the world. Aspects of its environmental design often tie into the story as well. For instance, the player encounters a village filled with windmills (right) on their quest to restore a divine wind and extinguish a monster bearing the destructive power of fire.

Credit: *Okami* is a trademark of Capcom Co., Ltd.

Another game with astounding creative cohesion is *Ori and the Blind Forest*, with its lusciously painted backdrops, ethereal music, and fluid character animations. The central theme in *Ori* is one of optimism amidst strife—returning happiness and light to a depleted world, holding out hope for a lost loved one, and seeing a glimmer of promise and love even in your enemies. An appropriately rich atmosphere emphasizing the harmony of light and darkness is established early, and maintained throughout. Even the titular character reflects this ideal; Ori is a brilliant speck of light in the game's world, embodying the spark of optimism and hope that underpins its story.

It's clear that cohesion, in combination with skill and polish, creates an appealing aesthetic. As one would expect, dissonance in this regard can thus spark a negative reaction. Unless a creative disconnect is in service to some other goal, such as parody or a thematic crisis of identity, it should be avoided. If you're skeptical of this notion, try pasting the hearts-and-flowers UI style of a dating sim like *Hatoful Boyfriend* onto *League of Legends* with complete seriousness, set it all against the music from *Candy Crush*, and enjoy sitting in the smoking ruins of your reputation.

A far less severe example is the perceived aesthetic disconnect of the default UI in *Doom Eternal*, particularly in terms of HUD design. The *Doom* series has brought us nearly three decades of visceral gameplay and gritty demon-slaying. Alongside that grit came an equally gritty aesthetic, with levels full of fire, brimstone, and everything in between. This brings us to the mild controversy of *Doom Eternal*, which ships with a HUD featuring neon greens, oranges, pinks, and purples that feels a bit less demonic and a bit more disco. This certainly achieves the goal of visibility, but its juxtaposition with the game's overall aesthetic is jarring, generating exactly the sort of complaints you'd expect from long-time fans of the series. Luckily, the game includes a plethora of options to customize both the contents and colours of its interface, though one is left wondering why 80s Kaleidoscope seems to have been chosen as the default palette. Cohesion can be the key to building a successful atmosphere; discrepancy can risk eroding it away.

4.4.1 *Authenticity and the value of in-world information*

In *Dead Space*, your health isn't displayed as a bar overlaid on the screen. It's displayed physically on your character's armour, as a meter running along his spine. Menus like the inventory and upgrade screens are shown as holographic projections originating from and visible in the game's world. In addition to the novelty of holograms and fancy armour, this creates a special kind of immersion. Anything you can see is visible to your character or other inhabitants of the game's world. You have no special prescient knowledge as *the player*; you yourself feel more a member of its world than an outsider.

This type of interface design is referred to as *diegetic*, tracing its origins from the Greek word for narration. An element is diegetic if it originates in a game's world (i.e., could be perceived by its characters) and non-diegetic otherwise. Mario's characteristic wail as he fails into lava is a diegetic sound. The musical riff that plays when he reaches the end of a level is not.

Games that embed their interface in an entirely diegetic fashion like *Dead Space* are relatively rare. Indeed, it can be incredibly difficult to create an appealing, thematically appropriate, and effective interface without relying on common tropes like the overlay minimap. A more common approach mixes both diegetic and non-diegetic elements to create something that feels more immersive compared to a wholly non-diegetic interface without having to work in anything that might come off as forced.

The spaceflight and combat sim *Elite Dangerous* executes this blend rather stylishly, with your spaceship's holographic cockpit screens serving as a HUD angled to mimic a pilot's point-of-view. Menu interfaces like the mission board and ship customization are displayed more traditionally, accommodating the wealth of information and different items players need to sift through without sacrificing any screen-space to accommodate the gimmick of a screen or projector in-world.

Other examples of blending diegesis with "traditional" interface elements and sound effects can be found peppered quite liberally throughout recent releases. In *Subnautica*, the basic HUD is shown as a non-diegetic overlay, but the game's inventory screen, along with several other menus, is shown on a PDA that the player's character pulls from their belongings. A similar setup is used in the *Fallout* series via the Pip-Boy, a device worn by the character that the player can view to accomplish things like inventory management. While music is typically non-diegetic in games, originating from some invisible background source, the Pip-Boy can also be used as a radio. Should players

Figure 4.22 In *Elite: Dangerous*, the HUD functions as a (diegetic) holographic overlay in the player's cockpit, an in-world projection that feels believable and looks beautiful.

Credit: *Elite: Dangerous* was developed and published by Frontier.

choose to tune in, they'll be getting a diegetic soundtrack—and there's a special sort of feeling that comes from knowing your character is hearing the exact same thing that you are.

Diegetic elements can help to make a game's communication feel more natural, though they are by no means necessary to its efficacy or its creativity. *Dead Space* has rightfully earned a great deal of praise for its entirely diegetic, innovative interface design, but the entirely non-diegetic comic-book HUD of *Persona 5* is equally enjoyable for completely different reasons.

Regardless of how you choose to go about communicating information to players, and irrespective of the creative style that communication follows, remember that it is inseparable from a game's core experience. An interface isn't just a layer on top of a game; it is a fundamental *part* of that game. Interaction is about communication, and that communication is inextricably linked to the enjoyable, functional, beautiful, memorable experiences that games can be.

Expert Profile: Cherry Thompson—Accessibility by design

Accessibility Project Manager at Ubisoft Montréal

Ask someone to define "accessibility," and they'll probably say something about accommodating the needs of individuals outside the norm. Ask them about accessibility in games, and you'll be flooded with visions of settings menus, high-contrast icons, and switchable colour schemes. After all, accessibility means adding on plenty of disability-friendly features, right?

For Cherry Thompson, accessibility in games is far more nuanced. While many see accessibility as a layer on top of a game, Cherry sees it as an integral part of the design process. They note that defining accessibility in games is challenging, but describe it as "understanding that satisfaction, that experience, the fun [. . .] and understanding it for more people." And Cherry isn't just speaking in general; they're speaking from experience as a player with disabilities.

Before joining the games industry, Cherry worked as a freelance artist and creative in film, photography, and comics. But when their physical disability progressed as a result of a genetic condition, Cherry grew more interested in accessibility. They directed that interest to games after realizing how powerful games can be for rehabilitation and pain management. After working as a subject matter expert and consultant on the likes of *Horizon Zero Dawn* and *Dreams*, Cherry eventually settled at Ubisoft Montréal, joining a budding centralized accessibility team.

Cherry views their role as contributing to a long-overdue shift in how we treat game accessibility. As Cherry describes it, the typical view of accessibility is "a back door into a building," or "a ramp around the side of the building"—something that gets added on. For games, this mentality conjures up an options menu and little else. Accessibility becomes the job of a consultant, or perhaps a UI designer, and can become an afterthought for the rest of the team. Looking at this separation, Cherry asks why accessibility isn't approached like other aspects of game design.

We all agree that games should be fun. The thought of needing a "fun consultant" to remind your game director of this seems ludicrous. And yet, though we all agree that games should be inclusive, accessibility consultants are still very much needed. Cherry wants to see accessibility become more ubiquitous in design—after all, it's about understanding fun for more players—and cites a few reasons why this hasn't happened yet. In education, the relegation of accessibility to the occasional UX design lecture leads to a lack of knowledge and critical thinking on the subject. Common perceptions of disability also introduce problems. As Cherry puts it, "We think of disability as *other*, or *different* [...] but it's really not. It is part of the human experience." They note that anyone can face barriers to their enjoyment in a game, regardless of whether they identify as "disabled." It's critical, therefore, that accessibility becomes more central in our design thinking.

The question becomes, how can we build a more holistic view of inclusion throughout development, or as Cherry puts it, "accessibility by design"? Historically, they describe the biggest challenge as "buy-in": the need to convince developers that accessibility is important, or more cynically, worth the investment. Luckily, the industry today needs little more convincing, and accessibility has gained a great deal of respect and resources. But Cherry emphasizes that today, the new challenges that have arisen are far more difficult to contend with.

First comes the task of dismantling misconceptions, not just in how we think about disability, but in learning to think more critically about widely accepted designs. Cherry offers UI as an example, noting a wave of flashy cursor-driven menus in mid-2010s console games, seemingly inspired by the runaway success of *Destiny*. While visually appealing and quick to navigate for most players, the precision of gamepad-controlled cursors introduces barriers for players with motor impairments. Meanwhile, the parallax (relative motion) of menu elements that has become popular for its visual flair induces motion sickness in some players. Cherry notes that *Destiny*-type menus, like many other design patterns, aren't inherently bad; they simply illustrate that no design should ever be accepted without question.

Even more challenging are half-truths, where designers recognize barriers, but make incorrect assumptions about addressing them. If players express that part of a game is impossible for them due to disability, the first solution that comes to mind might be a difficulty setting. But, as Cherry puts it, the notion of an "easy mode" carries a bit of stigma, and the idea that players with disabilities just aren't looking for a challenge is condescending at best. Instead, designers need to be more inquisitive about what players are experiencing, and what types of challenges can include different players. The trouble with typical accessibility solutions, Cherry says, is that "No one really stops to think, is this the best way to do it? Is it the right way to do it? Can we do this in a way that's more flexible for players, or more customizable?"

The road to better game accessibility is also replete with procedural challenges. Production and culture shifts are necessary to accomplish that "accessibility by design" that Cherry hopes to achieve. All of these challenges demand substantial investment of time and resources, but to Cherry, the most crucial problem that remains is far simpler, and more human.

Cherry underscores that designers need to recognize that games aren't just systems, but *human* systems: "You have to [design] with empathy." But many people confuse empathy, the ability to understand the emotions of another and view things from their perspective, with sympathy—feeling pity for those who are suffering. And true empathy, as Cherry puts it, is "a two-way street." Before we can understand players and make our games inclusive to them, we need to understand and accept ourselves, and the people we work with.

(Continued)

111

(Continued)

To achieve this understanding, Cherry notes that creating an open and honest atmosphere is critical. They share stories of how openness can help disarm communication in the intense collaboration between team members. Through open discussion of their experiences, like how a stroke in 2013 changed the way they interact with games and the world, Cherry encourages an honest environment free of stigma. With this honesty comes a critical degree of introspection, which designers need to recognize as necessary and potentially painful emotional labour: "You're hearing about people having very difficult lives because of the things we [designers] have done [. . .] That can weigh heavily on someone, when they realize they've excluded someone."

Successful designers need to deal with realizations like this and use them to improve. While many attribute good design to technical skill, Cherry sees emotional intelligence as the most important trait. Grinning, they describe their younger self, like many eager young creatives, as "a bull in a china shop." A deep understanding of people comes with experience, which Cherry uses to guide their design thinking: "You have to [design] remembering that these are people [. . .] Having had firsthand experience of being excluded allows me to remember that."

As for what they hope to accomplish in the future, Cherry says they're shooting for one where their current job doesn't exist—a world where every creative has developed an innate understanding of accessibility. As they exclaim with a chuckle, "I just want peace!". Hopefully, that's a future that we can all work to achieve: one where games are more inclusive, more satisfying, and more fun for more people.

Further reading

Visualization Analysis & Design by Tamara Munzner (A.K. Peters, CRC Press). ISBN: 978-1466508910.

A thorough volume on the creation of information visualizations, with insights applicable to visual communication in general. Chapters 5 (Marks and Channels), 6 (Rules of Thumb) and 10 (Map Color and Other Channels) are especially relevant to the types of visual representations you might develop for game feedback.

Game Sound by Karen Collins (MIT Press). ISBN: 978-0262033787.

One of the more comprehensive volumes on sound in games. The first few chapters focus on history; sound designers will find the most value in Chapters 5 (Game Audio Today), 6 (Synergy in Game Audio), 7 (Gameplay, Genre, and the Functions of Game Audio) and 8 (Compositional Approaches to Dynamic Game Music).

The Design of Everyday Things by Don Norman (2013 ed., Basic Books). ISBN: 978-0465050659.

One of the most famous books on design, and for good reason. After learning many of the concepts presented for the first time, you'll never look at the things you interact with in the same way.

A Primer in Game Theory by Robert Gibbons (Pearson). ISBN: 978-0745011592.

An older work that gives an overview of information in games. If you found the division of perfect and imperfect information games to be interesting, check this one out.

Juice it or Lose it, talk by Martin Jonasson and Petri Purho (GDC, 2012).

A short and sweet discussion of how feedback enriches player experience; must-watch material for pretty much anyone in game design.

Exercises

Port-A-Game: HUD edition

Pick a game you have played on any platform. Think about how you'd port that game to a different platform (e.g., PC to mobile, mobile to console and so on). Focusing on feedback, and particularly HUD design, what adjustments would you make to better accommodate players on the new platform?

Make some sketches or edit screenshots to re-design the game's HUD for your hypothetical port. Include notes on how you'd adapt other forms of feedback in the game as well. Here are some thoughts to get you started:

- Remember that screen size and viewing distance can make a big difference.
- Users might expect different "standards" in things like icons to match other games on the platform (e.g., flat UI design in mobile games).
- Players on mobile might be playing with sound off, while PC/console players might benefit from more complex audio design or spatial audio cues.
- You don't have to confine yourself to replicating bits of the experience; you can also try to improve on it!

Diegenesis

Take any game with a non-diegetic HUD and think about how you could turn elements of that display (or the entire thing) into a diegetic interface. Make a sketch illustrating your idea. Reflect on whether you think the game benefits from having diegetic HUD elements or if they're unnecessary, and why.

Prototyping juice

Using a game engine like Unity or Unreal, set up a very basic interaction, such as collecting a pickup. Experiment with adding various levels of "juice" to that interaction using assets you find online or make yourself. Some of the things you might consider adding are particle effects, sounds, animation, post-processing effects, and so on.

As you layer on more effects, try to play around with how noticeable each one is. How much juice is too much? How can you make a routine interaction feel special without going overboard?

Fantasy sense draft

Using things like taste, smell, and touch in our games might be science fiction for now, but it's still an interesting design prospect. Take a game you enjoy and imagine how

(Continued)

113

(Continued)

you might add feedback for one of these "non-traditional" senses. Why do you think this type of feedback would complement the game you have chosen? What would you use it to communicate? Come up with one or two specific scenarios where you'd use this sense to communicate with players, and explain how that communication would fit in with the existing game.

5

Control Freaks

The year is 2007. In the previous December, Nintendo had unleashed the Wii onto a ravenous holiday market. Gleaming white boxes adorned entertainment centres across the world, illuminating their surroundings with a soft bluish glow. Parents and children alike gleefully swung their arms about, discovering the glorious potential of motion controls amidst a flurry of athletic minigames. Families reconnected over nights spent bowling and boxing by way of the Wiimote and Nunchuk controllers' onboard accelerometers.

And then an overenthusiastic Wii tennis player lost their grip on the Wiimote, flinging it at their television and immediately destroying the screen.

As it turns out, use of the included wrist strap was hardly an unnecessary precaution. Whether the first incident truly sprung from a game of Wii tennis or some other unfortunate mishap, reports of Wiimote-induced destruction began to spread. Screens smashed. Wrist straps snapped. Light fixtures were accidentally punched and shattered. People unwittingly beat one another on an aggressive backhand, leading to a few lacerations and a black eye. Supposedly in one occurrence, a shoddy wrist strap broke and launched the previously attached Wiimote out the window of a twelfth-floor apartment. The apparent danger was real enough to merit the launch of *wiihaveaproblem.com*, a site exclusively dedicated to chronicling Wii-related property damage and injuries.

While *wiihaveaproblem* is now long defunct, it is still accessible by way of web archives. Undoubtedly many of the anecdotes contained therein are embellished, if not fabricated entirely, though there were some very real class-action lawsuits lobbed at Nintendo on account of those shoddy wrist straps. Nothing overly substantial came of those lawsuits, as Nintendo had already launched a voluntary recall, issuing thicker straps on new units and offering the newer straps as replacements for existing customers.

The Game Designer's Playbook. Samantha Stahlke and Pejman Mirza-Babaei, Oxford University Press.
© Samantha Stahlke and Pejman Mirza-Babaei (2022). DOI: 10.1093/oso/9780198845911.003.0005

Nonetheless, the damage had been done, so to speak, and thicker wrist straps didn't entirely halt the destruction of those pricey flatscreens.

Figure 5.1 A) Intended use of the Wii remote. B) Artist's rendering of typical Wii remote usage.

2007 may have been a terrible year for televisions, but it served as a breakthrough for mobile devices. In January, Apple revealed the first iPhone, sparking the evolution of communication tools from colourful boxes riddled with buttons to nondescript black rectangles more featureless than the existential void itself. Perhaps the most remarkable thing about the iPhone was that it didn't rely on any sudden technological breakthrough. Touchscreens, cell phones, mobile internet, and portable music players all predated the iPhone by well over a decade. It was the combination of these technologies, and the design of that combination, that set the mobile market ablaze.

Along with the explosion of social media and endless data-tracking apps that followed, this moment also more or less marked the birth of modern mobile gaming. Smartphones provided not only a new form factor for games, redefining the meaning of "portable" gaming, but also birthed a slew of new ways to interact with games. With no physical buttons, mobile controls rely on touchscreen schemes that vary from dead-simple tapping and swiping to intricate arrays of virtual buttons and joysticks, occasionally complimented by gyro movement. From the breakout hit *Angry Birds* to later titans like *Candy Crush* and *Clash of Clans*, efforts in mobile gaming proved to be not only innovative, but incredibly lucrative.

Apart from their memorable launches and commercial success, the Wii and the iPhone have another thing in common. Both devices revolutionized the way we experience games, having lasting effects on the field of game design. Though the type of motion controls popularized by the Wii were somewhat of a gimmick and far from standard, their echoes live on in the gesturally focused controllers typically used in VR systems. The magnitude of the iPhone's impact, on the other hand, is hardly arguable. As of this writing, the mobile gaming space is still experiencing meteoric growth, with no sign of slowing down.

Much of this innovation is down to the devices that sparked them, and the development challenges that arose as a result. The devices we use to play digital games shape the means of our interaction. Whether that interaction occurs through joysticks, buttons, or the movement of our bodies, its conceptualization and refinement plays a substantial role in a game's design.

Just as we used the terms "continuous" and "responsive" to describe the ways that games communicate with us, we can also identify two major categories delineating the ways that we communicate with games. The first is *direct input*: the immediate mapping of a player's actions in the physical world to an action in the game world. In other words, you press a button, and something happens. Many of the actions available to a player are commonly defined in this way; character locomotion happens as a direct result of moving an analog stick, gunfire erupts from your weapon at the press of a button. Not all input is given directly, however; a virtual interface may serve as an intermediate between physical input and in-game action. Instead of directly resulting in action, player input manipulates a virtual interface which then causes some in-game effect. For instance, managing a character's inventory might be supported through a virtual interface where the mouse can be used to move icons representing carried items. We refer to the use of such interfaces as *virtual input*.

In the previous chapter, we explored how the design of feedback defines the way that games communicate with their players. Here, we will examine how the design of control schemes and interactive interfaces dictates the way that players can communicate with games. When coupled with feedback, a game's input schema forms the other half of interaction between player and game, fundamentally affecting the game experience.

5.1 I can't find the "any" key

We have already explored half of Norman's design principles—visibility, consistency, and feedback—in discussing how games communicate with players. The remaining three principles are of special interest to designing both direct and virtual means of player input. Before we investigate how these designs can succeed (or fail), we will briefly examine these principles and their meaning in game interaction.

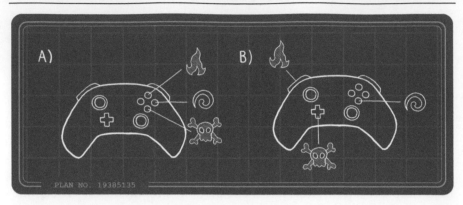

Figure 5.2 If you've got a set of elemental spells to map controls for, it probably makes sense to group those controls together (as in A) so that players can easily access related functions in close physical proximity. Mapping them all over the place (as in B) will be less intuitive in the vast majority of circumstances.

Mapping. In general, mapping is the relationship between the position of controls and their function. The media buttons on a remote often flow from left to right according to their relationship with time; rewind is to the left, fast forward is to the right, and pause resides in the middle. A light switch is most sensibly located in the same room as the fixture it controls. Unfortunately, one of the unspoken rules of modern architecture dictates that each building shall have at least one panel of inscrutable switches for which all sense of logical consequence has been abandoned. This is why those two switches placed oddly to the left and right of your refrigerator control a light in your garage and a lamp in the basement of the Louvre, respectively. The frustration ensuing from the existence of such artifacts is perhaps the best argument for the importance of mapping as a consideration in the design of any interactive system.

In games, mapping describes the layout of physical or virtual controls. While the physical location of buttons on a given controller is constant, different games can assign the function of those buttons differently, resulting in a different mapping. Virtual controls, on the other hand, grant designers total control over both location and function.

The mapping of game controls has a significant effect on the user experience of a game's input system. Awkwardly positioned key-bindings may lead to discomfort; imagine having to rapidly dance your hands over to the numpad every time you need to reload in a first-person shooter. In contrast, a well-designed control mapping will take advantage of ergonomics, leading to controls that feel natural and avoid the hellish metacarpal gymnastics of a lesser design.

Another important note to consider in mapping a game's controls is that, just as with our light switches, the relationship between position and function should be logical. The simplest implication of this is that controls with similar function should be grouped together. A design which exemplifies this idea is the "hotbar," which allows players to assign frequently used abilities or items to a set of controls which are grouped together (such as a row of virtual buttons or the numeric keys on a keyboard). Hotbars are a common pattern in several genres, used for everything from organizing spells in the online multiplayer RPG *World of Warcraft* to arranging frequently used tools in the farming simulator-turned-adventure sandbox *Stardew Valley*.

PLAN NO. 8218

Figure 5.3 To a human, a handle on a porcelain mug "affords" grabbing. Based on design, we know that we can pick up the mug. To a cat, the use of porcelain, like many other materials, affords wanton destruction.

Affordances. Well-designed things usually give you a clue about how to use them based on aspects of their design, such as shape. The presence of a horizontal bar on a door signals that it can be pushed open; we say that the bar *affords* a push interaction. The bar itself is an *affordance*—a clue as to how the object should be used. While a bar affords pushing, a handle affords pulling. When done well, affordances help to minimize error and make things easier to use. When omitted or used incorrectly, affordances help to create comedy in shopping malls and train stations, typically by way of locking people into angry wrestling matches with "push" doors that they tried to pull open.

In games, the concept of affordances usually means mimicking the design of real-world objects to hint at the function of virtual ones. Affordances are also present in the design of gaming peripherals; the triggers on a gamepad or many handheld VR controllers mimic the trigger of a firearm. Having a "shoot" action bound to another button simply wouldn't make as much sense, or be nearly as satisfying. This thinking also applies to the design of virtual interfaces; buttons must signal that they can be pressed in some way (e.g., borders, shading, colour), lest they be mistaken for plain text.

Proper use of affordances can help to guide players while minimizing explicit instruction. The presence of a lever, switch, or wheel in an environment, for example, hints at some machinery that can be interacted with. In virtual reality or any game with gestural controls, the design of such objects can tell players how to interact with them. A lever must be grabbed and pulled, a switch flicked or pressed, and a wheel turned.

Using affordances to convey information was often heavily relied on in classic point-and-click adventure games, which peaked in popularity and infamy around the 1990s. Finding a key in the world usually meant that you should look for a locked door or lockbox. Many adventure games from this period became infamous for the obscurity of the assumptions they relied on. Many puzzles beget a solution that went something like "get matches, melt child's ice cream, child drops toy and runs away crying, grab toy, use to taunt guard dog, steal dog's bone, use bone to distract dragon." One particularly notorious puzzle in *King's Quest V* required that players collect a custard pie to defeat a Yeti in the style of the Three Stooges. As of this writing, the *King's Quest* puzzle and others like it are still the subject of journalistic fodder in the gaming community. Let this be a lesson on the use of affordances in general; a simple assumption like "handles afford pulling" can be a great way to minimize obtrusive instruction. In exploiting an assumption based on a rarer occurrence or cultural reference, you are asking players to make a larger logical leap. As players need to make larger leaps, the risk of misunderstanding grows; arguing that "pie affords throwing at sasquatches" is simply a bridge too far.

Constraints. In using a piece of software, or playing a game, not all actions are always available. You can't copy text to your clipboard if nothing

Figure 5.4 The same action might be allowed or disallowed depending on certain contexts. For instance, on precarious platforms, many games will add invisible collision boxes to keep players from falling to their doom, unless the threat of actually falling to said doom is an intended part of the challenge.

is selected; you can't make your character jump if they're already in the air. Constraints impose contextual limitations on the input that can be accepted at any time.

There are several reasons why you might want to impose such limitations on players from time to time. Constraints can help to prevent player error; if the player is walking their character along a narrow beam, you might make it impossible for them to accidentally move left or right and fall off. During a tutorial, you might successively "unlock" different inputs as players learn one action after another (though as discussed in Chapter 3, this mentality can lead to poor first-time user experience if applied improperly). Constraints like the previous jumping example also serve to enforce a game's rules by disallowing actions if they would be logically impossible in-game at the time input was made.

Another application of constraints in games is to guide a player's experience according to a narrative or predetermined sequence of events. Some games impose relatively few, if any, of these constraints on players. Many games which heavily feature survival or sandbox elements, such as *Minecraft* and the *RollerCoaster Tycoon* series, fall into this category. Others, particularly those featuring strong narrative elements, will periodically rob most or all control from players to keep their experience "on rails" during cutscenes. While many cutscenes in the *Uncharted* and *Tomb Raider* series incorporate limited interactivity via quick-time events, other input, such as moving the player's character directly, is disallowed. These limitations can allow narratives to adhere to strict timelines and cinematography that is completely under the designer's control.

5.1.1 *Consistency, comfort, and customization*

As with so many other things, good player input can be effectively summarized in a quippy alliteration evangelizing three facets of successful designs: consistency, comfort, and customization. Executing just one of these aspects well does not promise the praise of game critics, but falling flat on any of them does all but guarantee that you will incur the wrath of your players.

Consistency, a design principle we previously discussed in relation to feedback, is also of paramount importance in the design of controls. External consistency—that is, consistency between different games—prevents conflict between your design and players' existing expectations based on their prior experience. Good external consistency generally adheres to the accepted conventions of a genre or platform, whereas poor external consistency violates these conventions without suitable reason. As a basic example, consider controls for player movement in a first-person shooter. On a gamepad, FPS games typically map character locomotion to the left analog stick, and camera movement or aiming to the right analog stick. Using this mapping as a default setting represents good external consistency. Arbitrarily switching the binding of the two so that movement is controlled with the right analog stick and aiming with the left would violate established conventions for no good reason. Being different for the sake of being different is a recipe for terrible external consistency, and will only lead to player confusion.

While external consistency will help to make sure that the onboarding process is as painless as possible for new players, internal consistency—consistency *within* a game—is equally important. Imagine a kart-racing game with a variety of vehicles to choose from. While you'd naturally expect the handling of different vehicles to vary, changing the control scheme of different karts would likely serve little purpose other than irritation. One kart maps acceleration to forward on the analog stick used for steering (good luck turning at full speed). Another maps acceleration to the opposing analog stick, throttle-style. Yet another maps it to holding a button, while a particularly exotic variant uses one of the gamepad's rear triggers. Performing the same fundamental action in different ways makes a system internally inconsistent, with no real justification for the disparity. Just as with external consistency, poor internal consistency breeds frustration and little else.

The second entry in our triumvirate of good control design is comfort. Executing inputs should feel comfortable, both in terms of physical handling and how these inputs feel in-game. The latter point is largely a matter of technical fidelity; controls should be responsive, and never evoke the word "mushy." On the design side, tweaking things like the acceleration of a character's movement can help to ensure snappy and responsive controls.

Comfort in physical handling is obviously related to hardware design, though it is also dependent on how our input mappings are designed. For instance, on most standard controllers, the directional buttons (or "d-pad"), are located on the left side of the controller, next to the left analog stick. An input scheme that requires simultaneous use of the d-pad and left analog stick is uncomfortable because it necessitates that players stretch over the right side of the controller with their right hand to reach the d-pad, while their left thumb is occupied by the analog stick. An alternative that uses the d-pad and the right analog stick, or simply both analog sticks at once, would be preferable.

While an uncomfortable action lasting a few seconds probably won't make players toss a game for good, we must remember that players might be experiencing our games, and by extension, our controls, for hours at a time. What seems like a passable, occasional awkwardness may quickly grow untenable, especially for players who are particularly vulnerable to physical discomfort (e.g., players with arthritis or carpal tunnel syndrome).

Our last concern is customization, an element which can, perhaps unsurprisingly, compensate for shortcomings in consistency and comfort. All commands for direct input should be customizable wherever possible; for instance, any action requiring a button press should give players the option to remap that action to any button that is available. There is no exception to this rule; while selecting a good set of default controls is an important decision, controls should simply be customizable without question. It is possible that such settings may be rendered unfeasible by the constraints of a particular platform, or a lack of development time. However, customizable controls can make or break an experience for players based on their prior experiences, preferences, or accessibility concerns. A player who has had one of their fingers amputated, for example, may simply be unable to play comfortably with a "default" control scheme. Customization will be the factor that determines whether a game is inclusive to their needs, or excludes them from being able to enjoy the experience.

Where players perceive a game to be externally inconsistent based on some mismatch in prior experience—think of the flipped layout of XYAB buttons between Xbox and Nintendo controllers—customization can allow them to make a game reflect their expectations. When a player finds default control bindings uncomfortable, perhaps because they have smaller hands, customization can eliminate physical discomfort during play. Customization is not a panacea for every flaw in a game's input design, but it makes all the difference in a game's ability to suit the needs and preferences of different players. For this reason, it is arguably the most critical of the three qualities discussed here.

5.1.2 *Input modes, or a vision for peripherals*

Just as there are many different sensory channels that games can leverage in communicating with players, there are several different means through which players can communicate their intent to a game. Before we dive in to examine the specifics of designing both direct and virtual input in more detail, let's take a moment to briefly review the communication methods at our disposal.

"Traditional" input. Here, the word "traditional" refers to input methods that have been established in digital games for the past several decades. This includes the button- and stick-based input you'll find on gamepads and arcade cabinets, in addition to more exotic peripherals like racing wheels for controlling virtual vehicles, or the specialty joysticks favoured by players fond of spaceflight sims. For PC games, this classification also includes mouse and keyboard controls. The primary advantage of designing for this category is that most devices have long-established conventions (e.g., on a keyboard, WASD to move a character), helping to ensure a basis for external consistency. However, some interactions can feel lacklustre when mapped to a button press (as opposed to a gesture), such as the player's character picking up objects.

Touch input. Touch input is the only form of input available for most games played on smartphones and tablets, though it is not relegated exclusively to mobile platforms. Consoles and handheld platforms like the Nintendo Switch often feature touchscreens. In PC games, trackpads can provide some limited support for touch gestures, and pen tablets typically used for digital art also find a niche use in games like *Osu!*.

Touch input can be a blessing for games that rely heavily on menu interaction (e.g., inventory management), making it easier for players to quickly select and manipulate interface elements without having cursor movement as an intermediate step. The fluidity afforded to certain motions—such as the classic slingshot fire in *Angry Birds*—can help to make input feel more natural. However, touch input is also prone to points of frustration, such as faulty gesture recognition or poor palm rejection leading to erroneous inputs. Furthermore, on small screens, touch input can be frustrating for players with larger hands trying to manipulate miniscule UI elements.

Motion-based input. This category includes both accelerometer-based motion controls, such as tilting a smartphone or swinging a Wii remote, and recognizing player movement directly through a camera, such as the now-defunct Kinect or VR hand tracking on the Oculus Quest platform. We also define this category as including haptic input, such as grip strength on a VR controller. Historically, motion controls are notorious for sparking somewhat of a divide in the gaming community, acquiring a reputation for their often-gimmicky design.

Poorly implemented motion controls can be a source of immense frustration; look no further than the few motion-control shrine puzzles in *Breath of the Wild* for an example. Nonetheless, motion controls have become indispensable for one platform in particular: virtual reality. Well-done motion controls have the advantage of unparalleled realism; in-game actions can be mapped directly to their real-world counterparts. Looting an enemy with a button press in *Borderlands* is surely gratifying, but the interaction quality can't be compared with the ability to pluck ammunition directly off an opponent's corpse in a VR title like *Half-Life: Alyx*.

Other forms of input. The three categories discussed previously comprise the majority of game input, though other forms of novel input do exist. Physiological sensors for things like heart rate and skin conductance (i.e., sweat) can be used as a form of input, though they have not seen widespread use in commercial games. Specialty hardware, such as eye-trackers and headsets that provide indicators of brain activity, have seen niche applications, especially related to the goal of improving accessibility.

Another input method distinct from the previous categories is voice control, which is surprisingly underused given the ubiquity of microphones and their usage for team communication in multiplayer games. Though rare, the use of voice control is not unprecedented. The ghost-hunting game *Phasmophobia*, for instance, has players call out commands to communicate with paranormal spirits.

Although this category of input is not commonly employed, it does provide interesting design opportunities. Novel forms of input can be a point of interest for players, though in designing such games, a lack of familiarity or widespread access to needed hardware can prove troublesome. At any rate, game development is hardly constrained to the buttons and joysticks that once defined the entirety of the options available.

5.2 Rules of thumbstick

Direct input is just that; input which translates directly to in-game action, without the need for interaction with some intermediary virtual element like an on-screen button. What makes a good direct input system varies, to an extent, based on its intended application. While there are many ways to distinguish applications of direct control, perhaps the most straightforward method of doing so is to ask what the player is controlling.

Figure 5.5 Three different perspectives of controlling a human character in defeating the local goblin invasion: first-person (top left), third-person (top right); "omniscient" control of a troupe (bottom).

Games where you control a character. Irrespective of mechanical diversity, most games, particularly in the realm of PC and console titles, have you moving a character (or vehicle) of some sort. To be clear, though, our definition of *character* here is quite loosely a "thing" that the player controls, whether human, animal, vehicle, robot, baked good, or otherwise. Shooters, action-adventure games, platformers, racing games, and RPGs are practically dependent on the concept of character control, with rare exception. A well-designed character controller goes a long way towards pleasing players; the *Mario* series practically founded a franchise on satisfying controls. Legacy entries like *Super Mario 64* hold up surprisingly well. *Super Mario Galaxy*, a game which is practically a relic at 15 years old as of this writing, is still a paragon of good design, in large part due to its smooth and snappy controls. On the other hand, shoddy controls may not manage to put players off entirely, but can riddle a game's reception with words like "sluggish," "floaty," and "unpredictable."

Controlling a character comes down to designing for a few key inputs: character locomotion, camera movement, and actions performed by the character (like shooting, opening doors, and talking to NPCs). We can further subdivide character controllers into three main variations: first-person, third-person, and controllers for unconventional character locomotion.

First-person character controllers. In a first-person game, the player views the game world through the eyes of that character. This includes games like *Counter-Strike*, *Doom*, and *Portal*—and, of course, any first-person shooter you can think of. First-person control schemes link character movement with camera movement: in context, moving the camera means moving your character's head. This makes mapping locomotion rather straightforward; deciding what "forward" means is a no-brainer when your character is constantly facing the direction you're looking.

Seeing the world through your character's eyes means that you might not be seeing very much of them, apart from a pair of hands floating around the lower third of the screen. In a way, this is a sort of blessing; in a single-player title, this shaves off precious time otherwise spent on full-body animations. Hand movement and sound effects can make something like taking damage or rifling through cupboards feel realistic without necessitating a suite of complex animations.

Sharing a pair of eyes with a virtual character comes with its share of unique design challenges, though. Things like mouse acceleration, y-axis inversion, and field-of-view (FOV) can make an experience annoying or even nauseating if set improperly. Default values for these attributes inherently encode assumptions about the player and their gaming setup. For instance, a small FOV is generally more comfortable for longer-distance viewing (e.g., on a TV), whereas for players sat closer to the screen, this same narrow view might induce feelings of claustrophobia.

Consequently, supporting customization in this respect is practically non-negotiable, and yet some first-person games, particularly on consoles, have historically excluded the ability to change field-of-view or related settings. The *Far Cry* series, as of *Far Cry 5*, has yet to include FOV sliders on console, a subject of much consternation in online forums. There are obvious technical reasons why these settings are trickier to support on console than PC; reduced hardware capability means that the extra rendering overhead incurred with high FOV would require other graphical sacrifices. Developers can argue all day that this is an unfavourable compromise, or requires too many additional options to support. From a UX perspective, though, spending six months to make a game's settings more inclusive is far preferable to investing in next-gen raytraced HDR reflections for physically based puddles in a game about shooting zombies.

Unburdened by the need for secondary camera controls, the mapping between player intent and game action in first-person games is, in a way, less complicated. At the same time, this can leave a razor-thin margin for

Figure 5.6 Two screenshots of the player's view standing in the exact same place in *Deep Rock Galactic* with an FOV setting of 80 degrees (left) and 120 degrees (right). An increased FOV has an effect similar to "zooming out." An FOV that feels too high or too low for the viewing distance and screen size can make players feel uncomfortable, so providing settings to control it is advisable in all first-person games.

Credit: *Deep Rock Galactic* was developed by Ghost Ship Games and published by Coffee Stain Games.

errors in timing; the frustration of input delay or jittery movement is made worse when it affects a player's entire view. *Mirror's Edge*, and the subsequent *Catalyst*, are first-person parkour games whose core appeal is essentially "controls that will never irritate you." Faith, the game's protagonist, runs, climbs, and vaults through the game's environment effortlessly. Snappy controls mean that players always feel *in* control, and yet the game manages to seamlessly blend in tweaks that help to sell the feeling of locomotion, such as a subtle downwards tilt applied to the camera over the course of a long fall. In marrying quick responses to player intent with tricks like this that help to boost realism, first-person controllers can provide an immersive and satisfying locomotion experience.

Third-person character controllers. Third-person titles position the camera such that players can see their character's body, ranging from over-the-shoulder views to situations in which the character's entire body is visible. Third-person controls are the norm in several genres, such as platforming and action-adventure, and can be seen in games like the *Witcher* series and mainline *Mario* games. It should also be noted that many games, such as the *Elder Scrolls* series, allow for players to switch between first- and third-person view.

Unlike first-person games, third-person games decouple character and camera movement. Camera movement may be mapped to its own input, such as the right stick on a character controller, or left to be handled automatically. Automatic camera controls are often preferable in 2D and 2.5D games, where the character can simply be kept centred in view, or else the camera can be fixed to look at one "room" or section of a level until the character ventures off-screen. In full 3D, most games rightfully opt to allow players freedom over camera movement. Fully automatic cameras in such games can wrest away the oft-needed ability to line up one's view, for example, before a particularly delicate platforming manoeuvre.

Another challenge introduced in separating the player's view from that of their character is what it means to move "forward;" when the player nudges the left stick upwards, does the character move forwards relative to the game's camera, or in the direction the character's model is currently facing? The latter option, referred to as *tank controls* for its similarity to the steering of actual tanks, was not altogether uncommon in older games. Early installments of the *Tomb Raider* and *Resident Evil* games, for example, featured tank controls. However, this approach can feel clunky, especially when quick movement is required, since turning instantly is either impossible or relegated to a separate series of button presses.

Tank controls ultimately failed the test of time in many games that used them, with a pattern of locomotion relative to the camera taking over in modern titles. One of the reasons *Super Mario 64* has aged so well is that its controls are shockingly modern in this regard. Although the camera suffers its share of collision issues and questionable pre-ordained animations, movement occurring relative to a player-controlled viewpoint in 3D was practically revolutionary at the time.

Another feature differentiating first- and third-person controllers is that a third-person perspective typically puts a character's entire body, or at least most of it, in the player's view. As a result, animation on the player character is brought to the forefront. Fluid animation makes characters feel more alive and at home in their respective worlds, from the graceful tumbles of Ori in *Ori and the Blind Forest* to the heavy weapon arts of the *Souls* games. At the same time, animation introduces several questions related to timing. Ultimately, watching an animation is waiting for something to happen, and character animation invariably produces a slight delay in the journey from input to results.

While this hardly poses significant issues in general, waiting for lengthy animations in the name of realism can be frustrating. In the initial release of *Red Dead Redemption 2*, whenever players search the body of a fallen enemy, their character stoops down to rifle around. This bit of added realism comes at the expense of padding out an otherwise unremarkable interaction to a grating extent. The lengthy loot animation was ultimately patched out in favour of a quicker, albeit more generic, grabbing motion, allowing players to get on their way faster.

The input delay incurred by third-person character animations isn't just a question of eating up precious moments in between bursts of action. Even a second or so of delay on something like a jump can make precision movements downright infuriating to perform. In the very first *Prince of Persia* game, for instance, elegant sprite animations meant that lining up a jump required timing one's button presses to be abnormally early. The prince leapt gracefully, to be sure, but the difference between that graceful leap and an unbecoming death was an undoubtable sense of lag that took a fair amount of getting used to. Contrast this with the controls in a beloved 3D platformer like *Super Mario Galaxy*, where Mario's anticipatory crouch occupies just a few frames betwixt the player's button press and his becoming airborne. By allowing players to see their character, and opening up the possibility for well-timed animations, third-person controllers can provide a boost to the main character's sense of personality and charm.

"**Unconventional**" **character controllers**. While the first- and third-person categories do cover all relevant possibilities for character control—perhaps excepting edge cases where a camera resides pinned to a character's ankle—it is worth placing "unconventional" controls into their own category. Most character controllers follow from established patterns; players control a humanoid or vehicle of some sort, or perhaps a horse their character is riding. However, this is not always the case, and the task of sensibly handling locomotion is further complicated by the relative dearth of examples for controlling snakes (*Snake Pass*), cephalopods (*Octodad*), fleshy eldritch abominations (*Carrion, Inside*), vaguely spherical clods of lawn furniture (*Katamari Damacy*), and baked goods (*I Am Bread*).

Even with a humanoid character, the scheme for directly controlling a character may be so far removed from a typical first- or third-person controller that its design cannot be exceptionally well-informed by conventional examples. In *What Remains of Edith Finch*, for instance, players control many different characters. Though each of the characters players control is human, the controls used in each case are unique and frequently depart from what one would expect. Whereas a standard character controller might concern itself only with locomotion and combat, playing as different members of the Finch family comprises managing momentum on a swing, turning through a flipbook, and beheading salmon in one world whilst piloting an imaginary boat in another.

Designing effective character controllers in these unconventional situations is challenging for a few different reasons stemming from their lack of precedents. First, players' learning of controls cannot be supported as strongly by prior experience in other games. Furthermore, without an abundance of conventions to use as potential templates, development will become more costly as increased efforts in prototyping and testing are warranted. Lastly, it is harder to find examples which can be worked from in tweaking the subtleties of how a character's controls should feel.

If working towards a more common archetype for character control, it is typically possible to find several near-perfect analogs for the system you wish

Figure 5.7 Non-traditional locomotion. In *Carrion*, players click to move, while the amorphous mass of sticky bits they control contorts to squeeze through openings and lets out tendrils to move around. Players have to consider the path their character will cover as they embark on a quasi-slither through the environment.

Credit: *Carrion* was developed by Phobia Game Studios and published by Devolver Digital.

to design. If you're developing an action-adventure game in a fantasy setting, you might look to any of the entries in the *Witcher*, *Elder Scrolls*, or *Legend of Zelda* franchises, for instance. On the other hand, if you're developing a game where players control a sentient ocean capable of dividing itself and leaping between planets, finding successful examples which map one-to-one with your design is no longer feasible.

Without dozens of relevant examples to work from, designing a successful input paradigm within this category is a matter of some creative thinking and falling back to more general axioms. In games like *What Remains of Edith Finch*, where players are successfully introduced to one or many exotic control schemes, a few considerations can help make players' transition into the unknown feel a bit more natural. A lack of previous experience means that initial difficulty curves should be further softened. Each new control scheme also warrants its own tutorialization period; preferably in-world and with minimal instruction (see Chapter 3). Additionally, though a given scheme may be unconventional, this does not mean that it should disregard convention entirely. If players are controlling a robot in third-person view with all manner of buttons mapped to different parts of its body, the player's camera can still have its motion mapped to the right analog stick (or mouse), reducing the amount of new information that has to be learned. Above all, naturally, special attention should be paid to early-stage testing of such control schemes to validate their usability before too much effort is invested in refining a particular design as the final iteration.

Games where you don't control a character. Despite the endless stream of gun-wielding figures in a state of perpetual ennui adorning the covers of AAA games, direct character control is far from universal in games. Strategy, simulation/management, and puzzle games often eschew character control entirely in favour of an omniscient perspective giving players purview over a military fleet, construction sandbox, or mysterious set of geometric objects. It should be noted that the boundary between games with and without character control, like so many other aspects of game design, can be rather fuzzy. After all, strategy games typically allow players to issue commands to their troops—a sort of authoritative character control—so perhaps a better term for this classification would be "Omniscient games," or the cheekier "Infinite-person games."

Many titles in this category rely mostly on virtual input, discussed in Section 5.3. In these cases, direct input is sometimes used as only an alias or shortcut to accomplish something achievable through a virtual interface. For instance, in *The Sims* series, on-screen buttons provide a means to change the game's current timescale, with numeric keyboard shortcuts assigned to provide an alternative form of control.

The abundance of virtual input in games like *The Sims* or *Civilization* arises from both practical necessity and usability concerns. What these games have in common with each other is the large possibility space which exists in normal play. Stepping back, consider a game that features *direct* input heavily in moment-to-moment gameplay, such as a first-person shooter along the lines of *Rainbow Six Siege*. While there are certainly a great deal of strategic decisions to be made during play, the basic interactions available at any moment boil down to a fairly small set: move, aim, shoot, crouch, cycle weapons, and so forth. It is the aggregation of many small decisions and adjustments over time that creates complexity; when to move, how far to move, which direction to face, when to reload ....

Contrast this with *The Sims*, where the player is issuing commands to a household of virtual people that can range from "eat that pizza" to "paint this photograph of the neighbours' toilet rolls I just forced you to take." At a moment's notice, players might flip to an entirely different set of interactions allowing them to customize their digital family's house, expanding the possibility space even further. Part of the complexity in a game like *The Sims* is the sheer number of actions available to players at any given time.

Relying entirely on direct input for something like interior decorating or raising a small army of toilet roll painters presents an obvious practical concern: there aren't enough keys, buttons, sticks, or combinations thereof to

Figure 5.8 You try coming up with a sensible keyboard shortcut for "Make organic Brain Freeze à la mode" when you've got dozens of other foods to handle on top of interactions with sinks, couches, televisions, and bear shrines.

Credit: The Sims 3 was developed by Maxis and published by Electronic Arts.

encode every desired action. From a UX perspective, even if such a task were possible, it would be ludicrous to expect players to memorize an arcane and untenably large system of control mappings. In something like a grand strategy game, relying entirely on direct input is most likely either impossible, a bad idea, or both. For these situations, direct input is best left as a shortcut for players' most frequent actions (like the timescale manipulation mentioned earlier), rather than providing a mapping for every possible in-game action.

General lessons. Regardless of game context, a few key questions guide the design process of any control scheme. First, you must determine which actions players will have direct control over. For instance, most modern shooters employ player-controlled reloading, while the concept of reloading is abstracted completely in the classic arena shooter *Unreal Tournament*. Paring down the inputs available will typically increase the perceived pace of a game, at the expense of realism and mechanical complexity—which can be a good thing, to an extent.

After deciding that an action will be under the purview of player control, you must also decide on the granularity of its representation. In the case of reloading, most shooters (think *Battlefield* or *Call of Duty*) use a very coarse representation, reducing the action to a single button press. In VR shooters, a more detailed representation is often favoured. *Pavlov VR* and *Half-Life: Alyx* both require players to perform actions like ejecting spent magazines, grabbing a new clip, and handling individual shotgun shells to reload different weapons.

Increasingly fine representation of player input is a double-edged sword of sorts. Consider the case of character locomotion, typically controlled with an analog stick. This is a coarse definition to be sure; complete physical agility reduced to a single input. In a sense, you might call this unrealistic. And yet, a game that divided this singular input, asking players to perform painstakingly synchronized button presses mapped to a character's muscle contractions, would be maddening. Naturally, such a game does exist, it's called *QWOP*, and as anyone with access to a school computer lab around a decade ago can tell you, it is in fact maddening. Overly fine representation often begets cumbersome or needlessly obtuse controls. At the same time, such representations can also be part of the fun, whether by means of intentional frustration (*QWOP*) or by creating a satisfying sequence of actions that is ultimately immersive and rewarding (reloading in VR).

Figure 5.9 This game ruined keyboards, recess, the Olympics, and the gradient tool for everybody. And it's beautiful.

Credit: QWOP was developed and published by Bennett Foddy.

By this point, for any given action, you'll have a list of how many inputs you'll need to represent it. A "coarse reload" might only need one input, whereas a "fine reload" might need something like four (eject, grab ammo, insert ammo, chamber a round). Your next step is perhaps the most critical: deciding on a control mapping for each (direct input) and/or designing a virtual interface element (virtual input). Up until now, our discussion has been scheme-agnostic; the decision of whether an action should be player-controlled, and the fidelity to which it is represented, is necessary for both direct and virtual input methods. Deciding *how* players act is where the distinction emerges, giving rise to the obvious question of which method is most appropriate.

A few moments ago, we contemplated the absurdity of selecting a direct mapping for every possible action in a game like *The Sims*. Following this logic, we can extract a rule of thumb for when direct versus virtual mappings are suitable for a given action. As illustrative examples, we'll consider both a game where you control a specific character (*The Witcher 3*) and a game where you do not (*Planet Coaster*).

Direct input has a limited number of reasonable mapping possibilities, but is quick to access. Thus, it is best to identify a manageably sized set of actions that players will perform regularly, and represent those actions directly. In *The Witcher*, an action RPG, these are actions such as moving, fighting, and using the currently active rune (magic ability). In *Planet Coaster*, a sandbox theme park simulation, this includes basic controls like camera movement and pausing/unpausing the flow of time.

Virtual input, on the other hand, offers a near-limitless possibility space on account of things like nested menus, but usually incurs some additional time to navigate and select actions. Virtual input can be awkward for frequent actions (imagine needing to use an on-screen control panel to walk around), but ideal for infrequent actions or those with too many options for an effective direct representation. In *The Witcher*, inventory management and selecting a rune are examples of interactions that use virtual input. Similarly, the number of construction and management options in *Planet Coaster* means that things like managing rides and selecting building materials are left to virtual interfaces.

Figure 5.10 Left: simple, frequent actions like swinging a weapon are best served by direct mapping. Right: more complicated actions, like inventory management, typically require the creation of a virtual interface.

Credit: *The Witcher* 3 was developed and published by CD Projekt Red.

Settling on a suitable direct mapping or virtual interface design is largely a question of respecting the advice discussed earlier, such as prioritizing player comfort and providing customization wherever possible. The design principles of mapping, affordances, and constraints further play into this decision, though perhaps the most crucial consideration is for consistency, discussed at length in Section 5.2.1.

Before moving on to discuss how convention can dictate our designs for better or worse, there is one final stage to acknowledge in the process of control design. Even after every action has been selected, broken into its constituent parts, and mapped, our work is far from over. While these qualities define how an interaction works on paper, they neglect to specify how it feels. Depending on the game context, all sorts of factors can contribute to this feeling: how quickly a character accelerates into a run, the sensitivity of a camera pan, whether the input triggers any "juicy" feedback and after how long, the rules for cancelling or overriding an action in progress with a different input.

All of these factors require design thinking, and careful attention in playtesting. Handing off a list of labelled buttons to a programmer will not give you much success, unless said programmer is also a skilled designer being paid for their time to flesh out how those controls will end up feeling. We would also be remiss to ignore the importance of technical quality in this regard; while this is a book about game *design*, input is a place where poor *implementation* and bugs can leave an irreparable dent in user experience. Well-done controls often blend into the background, but buggy controls practically scream at players when encountered—nothing will ruin your day quite like witnessing physics itself take a vacation as your spatula accelerates uncontrollably to flip a much-needed steak onto the floor in *Cooking Simulator*.

Tragically soiled cuisine aside, the journey discussed here is something you will embark on time and again in designing player input. Having an idea of the complete process, let us return to that most essential factor guiding our decisions: consistency.

5.2.1 *The role of conventions and consistency*

Take a seat in front of any popular game developed within the last ten years. Skip the intro, don't check the menu, just give your friend a shove aside and lay your hands on their keyboard (or controller). Chances are, assuming you've played a game at any point within those last ten years, you'll figure out more than half the keybindings on your first try. If you're staring at a crosshair, you know what to do. WASD to move, mouselook to aim, left click to shoot, right click to aim down sights, R to reload, left shift to sprint, left control to crouch. Without missing a beat, you'll be blasting away at everything in sight, and you'll have wrecked your friend's save file in no time. There's a simple reason for this ingrained knowledge, this instinctual, delicate hover as the left hand gracefully prepares its assault on the far end of the keyboard. That reason, simply put, is convention.

Convention, as we call it, is essentially an alias for external consistency, our old friend describing the persistence of meaning between distinct entities. This is contrasted with internal consistency, or the persistence of meaning *within* something. Internal consistency, to a large degree, is obvious. If you're responsible for setting an expectation, you're responsible for maintaining that expectation. Respecting external consistency is a little more nuanced. Why, after all, should you follow someone else's rules? Your game is your business, and game design is a place for innovation. If someone else sets an expectation, maintaining that expectation is not your problem.

Except, maintaining that expectation *is* your problem, because you cannot and should not be designing your game in a vacuum, as much as you might prefer the quiet and calm of doing so. Most importantly, one of the more useful and simultaneously annoying things about people who play games is that they bring the summation of their past experiences with them wherever they go. Helpfully, this knowledge helps minimize the need for instruction. Less helpfully, it also represents habits born from all the suboptimal design decisions in ghosts of games past. There is a time and place to break away from these conventions to be sure, but before we address the more problematic aspects of blindly following "the rules," let's take a moment to appreciate the value of convention in general.

Legend has it that the proper invention, or at least popularization, of WASD can be traced to a *Quake* tournament in the late nineties,[1] where champion Dennis Fong favoured the scheme over other alternatives lobbied at the time (ASDX, EDSF, and some more exotic combinations involving mouse buttons). While Fong's skill would almost certainly still have shone through with different keybindings, his performance provides some evidence for a simple conjecture: you'll play better with WASD than other movement controls. WASD is appropriately lain out for the resting position of the hand, it keeps modifier keys within easy reach, and assuming you're also working a mouse, it keeps the hands at a comfortable distance apart. In short, the convention of WASD didn't *just happen*, it emerged with solid justification from a period of experimentation.

This sort of rationale is something you can point to for many design conventions. Game development can be an excruciating process, with most titles

---

[1] Source: PC Gamer, accessible as of this writing at https://www.pcgamer.com/how-wasd-became-the-standard-pc-control-scheme/

falling into the "labour of love" category. Design decisions are (usually) not made lightly, and when those decisions are repeated to become convention, it is (usually) because they contribute to a positive player experience. By and large, design conventions represent the agreed-upon best discovered and available solution to a given question: WASD to move, click to shoot.

Even if we can't give a convention the benefit of the doubt in terms of representing an objectively good decision, we may still have good reason in obeying them. Imagine a world where ASDX had become the standard controls for keyboard-based character movement. Objectively, for most people, this is likely a bit less comfortable than WASD, requiring them to crane their middle finger backwards to reach X, rather than relaxing it forwards to reach W. In this hellish reality, though, sticking with ASDX would likely provide more value than breaking convention to ship your game with WASD.

By their very nature, conventions will be embedded in the experience of your players. Following conventions means that you can count on players to learn faster. It means that you can capitalize on muscle memory, creating harder challenges for players with the knowledge they will have practised the skills that your game demands before even starting it for the first time. In a world where ASDX is king, WASD will introduce a bit of confusion, wobbling, and a tendency to hover over an ever-so-slightly wrong part of the keyboard, at least temporarily. Lastly, even in cases where a solution is objectively better, as the stubborn creatures that we are, humans will tend to prefer what they're used to, particularly if potential improvement is relatively minimal. Most people would be aghast if you switched their office keyboard from QWERTY to Dvorak, leaving only a sticky note that says, "it's a bit faster, trust me." Likewise, without a very good reason, you're often best to avoid making players grumpy by deviating from expected keybindings.

Another useful source of conventions, albeit with the caveat of needing to go outside and experience things, is the real world. Making a game externally consistent with non-game contexts can help to make interactions feel more natural, and make the learning process easier for less game-savvy players. Our favourite property destruction device from earlier in the chapter, the Wii, showcased this type of thing masterfully. Nintendo's *Wii Sports* and other games of its ilk were accessible and easy to pick up because they stepped beyond gaming conventions to capitalize on the real-world analogs of various interactions. With the barest amount of in-game context, the Wiimote itself became an affordance. You hold it and "do a thing" as you would in the real world. In golf, you swing; in boxing, you punch; in archery, you draw back and release; in swordsmanship, you slice. This type of thinking rested in the background for a bit before being brought back to life in VR, where the conventions of PC gaming and the real world blend to create a satisfying mélange of immersion and smooth interaction.

Happily pasting a rulebook together from established conventions and following it to the letter is far from a golden path, though. Flamed-out attempts to use the arrow keys as a standard for movement because they have directions painted on them tend to be a bit irritating to return and visit. Some design trends, like slipshod attempts to disguise a slot machine that gives out confetti instead of money as a fun surprise in the form of lootboxes, are just plain harmful. Where the argument against convention gets interesting, though, is in some of the subtler issues that can arise.

Bias is a problem everywhere; disappointingly, game control design is no exception. Standard keybindings are only standard in the sense that they're the result of experimentation to find the best possible compromise. That is, the best possible compromise for able-bodied, right-handed players. There's nothing wrong with the fact that these conventions exist; having rules of thumb to support a positive player experience is a good thing. But, having picked up this book, as someone with a far above average interest in the field of game design, could you confidently list any conventions for left-handed or one-handed controls off the top of your head?

A relative lack of convention to support players falling outside of the able-bodied, right-handed categorization is one of the things that damages the accessibility of games in general. This isn't just a burden that falls on game designers, either. Unfortunately, hardware alternatives for the non-able-bodied and/or left-handed swaths of the world are frustratingly uncommon, perhaps surprisingly, given that a full ten percent of the population is left-handed. Nonetheless, the absence of convention is not an excuse for complacency. Take the time to develop an optional one-handed set of keybindings that players can start with. Ask yourself if handedness would make a significant difference (if you're using gestural controls, the answer is probably yes), and provide a reasonable set of defaults for both right- and left-handed players. Help contribute to establishing conventions where the cruelty of ignorance has failed to do so.

Another tricky element of working with conventions is that those conventions can be at odds with one another, like the Xbox versus Nintendo button layouts discussed earlier. In the realm of mobile games, for instance, what players expect for the case of something like piloting a vehicle can easily differ based on past experiences. Some may be firmly in the camp of accelerometer-driven controls, others may expect a virtual joystick on screen, while still others might prefer some sort of auto-drive with swipes to steer. This is another area where customization can help to remedy any disconnects. Even without explicit customization, giving players multiple options out of the gate can prevent confusion and ensure a smoother experience. In

Plants Vs. Zombies 2, for instance, players can collect items by either tapping on them individually (as you might expect coming from a PC), or continuously swiping across them (faster, and not altogether uncommon in flashy mobile games with lots of shiny things to pick up).

Irrespective of potential pitfalls, sticking to convention as a template for control design is often worth it for the benefits it provides (quick learning, muscle memory, the comfort of familiarity). Maintaining awareness of flaws such as inherently encoded biases and potential conflicts means that they can be mitigated with strategies like providing players with sufficient alternative options. That said, breaking convention in the interest of creating something interesting or pleasant to interact with, so long as you can validate the pleasantness of that interaction in playtesting. Where would we be without the *Octodads* of this world, or the latest oddball Nintendo hardware to challenge our notion of what controlling a game "should" feel like?

A break in convention, whether by necessity or experimentation, is frequently the innovation needed to bring about a better standard as the new normal. Let's return to the example of reloading in VR; a straight port of the desktop "shooter experience" would map reloading to an unremarkable button press (look no further than the VR version of *Fallout 4*). With the relative ease of gestural controls on the platform, though, there's no good reason why this unremarkable button press should hold onto its status as the de facto reloading solution. Fumbling for a new magazine with your hands and jamming it into your weapon while under fire adds a dimension of realism, and most importantly, it's fun. Reloading a gun in *Boneworks* after tossing a new clip into the air is a lot more engaging than tapping a button in *Fallout 4 VR*. That spark of enjoyment doesn't come from obeying a convention; it comes from recognizing that rules are made to be tested and sometimes broken.

Having made it this far, you may have settled on an immaculate control scheme, begging yet another new question—what if you need to take that control scheme somewhere else?

5.2.2 Some notes on porting

Porting is the act of taking software (in our case, games) between platforms. The verb *port* in this sense comes from the Latin for "to carry;" hence, porting is carrying a game from one platform to another. Colloquially, the term port is generally used when a game is adapted for a system it was not originally designed for at some point after its release. Thus, if a game launches simultaneously on PC and consoles, different builds are usually referred to as "versions" of the game for each platform. If that same game is later adapted to a different platform, the build for that new platform is referred to as a port, though the term port and version are often used interchangeably in this case.

Today, porting a game as an indie developer can be as simple as shifting around your HUD, remapping your controls, and hitting "build" with a different target platform selected. But before the widespread use of engines like Unity and Unreal that could readily deploy to PC, Mac, mobile, and console, porting was a far more daunting endeavour. Porting a game often meant re-creating it in a completely new development environment, translating scripts into different programming languages and gutting references to the original platform's API (application-programmer interface). Often, part or all of this work would be outsourced to other development studios. Mismanaged communication might muddy a game's creative vision, leading to (re)design missteps. Today, for developers using in-house tech, such as the proprietary engines commonly used in AAA development, creating a port can still demand this kind of collaboration and massive technical overhaul.

Creating a successful port might seem like a task which comes down to good programming, rather than good game design. The notion of a good experience is hardly platform-specific. Ergo, making sure that a good experience stays good is really a matter of not ruining its performance or introducing bugs. And indeed, technical issues have been responsible for the critical death knells of several ports, at least on launch day.

The PC version of *Batman: Arkham Knight* was initially locked at 30 frames per second, making it feel choppy; while standard on consoles, PC games typically aim for 60 FPS with an "unlocked" framerate allowing users to push faster rendering on superior hardware. Likewise, the PC version of *Mortal Kombat X* suffered similar issues with framerate inconsistencies, and a port of the first *Dark Souls* was locked at a resolution of 720p, leaving owners of 1080p screens unhappy. Three beloved games, becoming three reviled ports out of shoddy optimization and technical shortcuts.

The reality, though, is that while technical issues can certainly break a game on their own, technical fidelity does not guarantee a good experience. A new platform doesn't just mean a new developer API. It means different peripherals, different screen sizes, different viewing distances, and different contexts of play. Sitting in a quiet space several feet from your television with a gamepad is vastly different to standing on a crowded subway car, staring at a phone screen a few inches in front of your face. Successfully adapting your core experience is a matter of suitably redesigning the things that support it. Control schemes need to be adapted to different peripherals; UI elements might need to be rescaled, simplified, or enhanced to suit different screens. Porting a game isn't just moving a game's code between platforms; it's moving a game's experience from one context of play to another.

Resident Evil 4, one of the most critically acclaimed horror games ever released, has been ported about a dozen times since its original launch on the GameCube in 2005. Some of these ports are heralded as improving on the original experience, while others, particularly the first PC port, see regular use on listicles chronicling the worst ports of all time. This makes *RE4* a perfect case study in illustrating how the same experience can succeed or fail as a result of critical design decisions on different platforms.

That first PC port of *RE4* in 2007 suffered from technical and especially graphical issues to be sure, but several of the biggest complaints stem from the handling of keyboard and mouse support. *RE4* is a third-person shooter, and yet using the mouse to aim was not natively supported, requiring users to patch in support via community-made mods. Keyboard control defaults were an unruly mess violating most every convention established in the space of PC shooters, mapping weapon switches to the Shift keys of all things. Although customized keybindings were supported, those customized bindings were not reflected in onscreen quick-time event (QTE) prompts, effectively turning such events into a bizarre game of *Simon*.

The fundamental issue with ports like this iteration of *RE4* is that they seem to disregard the new context of play; while it is fine to recommend that players use a gamepad, the reality is that PC players might not have a gamepad. More likely, they may have a strong preference for mouse and keyboard controls, *especially* in a shooter. This means that any PC game needs to offer a sensible option for mouse and keyboard players. Creating such an option isn't just a matter of mapping each button from a gamepad one-to-one on a keyboard. It demands that the process of designing controls must be revisited, paying particular attention to established conventions in the new context of play. Had this been the case for *RE4*, we might have expected controls which respected the expectations set by behemoth PC shooters like *Half-Life*.

While some ports are hailed as the worst versions of the game, one is often touted as the best, surpassing the original and creating a uniquely memorable experience. That version is the Wii port, also released in 2007. While the later Xbox One and PS4 iterations of the game brought increased graphical fidelity, the Wii edition boasted something special: motion controls that players actually liked. Aiming the Wiimote meant aiming your weapon, a natural mapping that was fun to interact with. A thrust of your knife was achieved through swinging the Wiimote. Taken together, and given the game's focus on zombie-crushing combat, these simple interactions made for a shockingly enjoyable experience in a game whose same-year PC release didn't even support standard mouse aim.

In comparing these two ports, the difference is obvious: where *RE4* on PC seemingly ignored its new play context, the Wii port embraced it. Gyro aim and swing was a uniquely Wii-focused design decision. Had the Wii port been treated with the same design ethos as the PC version, one might expect aiming mapped onto the D-pad of the Wiimote, and melee combat as just another button press. Using point and swing as proxies for aiming and combat were already established on the Wii; thus, this decision both respected platform conventions and leveraged the console's distinctive features to improve the experience.

These trends of adhering to player expectations and exploring new opportunities to iterate on an experience are something that can be seen in several ports regarded as successful. Ports that fail to innovate are just fine; described with words like "serviceable" and "straightforward." Those that do everything well and pause to try something new, on the other hand, are more often remembered in less lukewarm terms. The Switch port of *Alien: Isolation*, for instance, like the Wii version of *RE4*, capitalized on a couple of Nintendo gimmicks to support gyro aim and HD rumble for improved haptic feedback. A mobile port and remaster of *Sonic the Hedgehog* in 2013 embraced virtual joysticks while adding in mechanics from more modern *Sonic* games to the delight of fans.

From these examples, it becomes clear that successfully porting a game hinges on both technical concerns and design decisions. Besides a few common-sense technical recommendations—don't lock framerate or resolution, provide appropriate graphical settings, make sure you have enough budget to optimize—what separates a great port from a terrible one can come down to its design. A different context of play means different hardware, different conventions, and different player needs, demanding consideration for a port to become serviceable at all. Beyond achieving mediocrity, though, ports shouldn't be treated as just moving an experience from one place to another. Instead, they are an opportunity to refine a design, pushing it further, and ultimately creating something to delight new and returning players alike.

5.3 Virtual input and two-way interfaces

So far, we've focused primarily on direct input, where in-game consequences are a direct result of the player acting in the real world (e.g., pressing a physical button, making a gesture). Virtual input adds a layer of abstraction to this concept, with in-game consequences resulting from the player acting on some virtual element. In this case, there is an intermediary betwixt action in the real world and action in the game world. You might call this *indirect input* in a sense, whereby a player's physical action only directly influences a virtual element which eventually leads to the desired action. For instance, the player presses on their left mouse button, depressing an on-screen button which then purchases a piece of gear for their character. This intermediary—a button, slider, quickwheel, et cetera—is an interactive, two-way interface.

In Chapter 2, we first introduced the concept of *interfaces*, facilitators of information exchange between players and games. Our primary focus until now has been on one-way interfaces for both game-to-player communication (Chapter 4) and player-to-game communication (by way of direct input). Interfaces supporting virtual input are somewhat unique in that they support both forms of communication simultaneously. Virtual input elements don't just let players *do* something; they frequently *tell* the player something as well. That big red button bearing the image of an electrified skull doesn't just let you press it; its very qualities of bigness, redness, and skull-ness give you a hint as to what might happen when you do.

As mentioned in the previous section, virtual input is ideal for situations with a significant possibility space which renders direct input infeasible. It also works well in cases where conveying additional information to the player is preferable. For instance, if a player is to select from multiple weapons with mouse and keyboard, an obvious solution might be a direct binding for each through the number keys. This is a perfectly fine solution, particularly if shortcuts are customizable. However, the eponymous "weapon wheel" seen in games like *Grand Theft Auto V* provides a virtual alternative that not only gives gamepad users a comfier experience, but lets players view their arsenal while making a choice. This can be especially helpful when players are still learning which weapon is which in a new loadout, or have yet to settle on the hotkeys they prefer.

Virtual input sees many different applications, spanning the gamut from options menus, to HUD widgets, to sprawling shop interfaces, and the complex construction tools of city-builders like *Cities: Skylines*. Just as with HUD elements, we could define a few different categories for virtual input based on when elements are made available. For our purposes, though, it's easiest to simplify this distinction and talk about the degree to which virtual elements are embedded into gameplay.

Loose integration. Loosely integrated virtual input is that which is divorced from moment-to-moment gameplay. Most game menus fit this definition, serving as a vehicle for players to choose a game mode, save their progress, or configure game settings. A more loosely integrated interface is one which provides functionality that does not directly impact what the player is doing in game. Typically, accessing these interfaces interrupts the flow of gameplay in some way.

Tight integration. When a virtual input interface does have a more immediate impact on gameplay, it is usually more *tightly integrated*: it "lives" close to gameplay, and it is less disruptive to access during gameplay. For instance, an always-on weapon hotbar is more tightly integrated than an inventory management screen, which is in turn more tightly integrated than an options menu. Interfaces which are more strongly integrated will typically have elements or imagery which are highly specific to gameplay, and may necessitate tutorialization depending on their complexity.

Irrespective of how strongly a virtual input interface asserts itself as part of gameplay, it is important to remember that all interfaces still affect player experience. Regardless of whether players are accessing something once or it becomes a part of regular gameplay, interactive interfaces need to support interaction which is both usable and enjoyable.

5.3.1 *Finding pleasure in button-pushing*

Just like HUD elements and sound effects, we can ascribe the quality of *diegesis* to elements of virtual input. Recall that, if something is diegetic, it originates in a game world and is something characters in that world would be able to perceive and/or interact with. Anything which exists outside the context of a game's world is said to be non-diegetic. For instance, the tech tree in *Civilization* is a non-diegetic interface, while buttons and switches in the cockpit of *Microsoft Flight Simulator* form a diegetic interface. Diegesis of virtual input elements can also be achieved by "disguising" them as in-world devices, like a character's smartphone. Examples include the PDA in *Subnautica*, or the Pip-Boy in the *Fallout* series.

The decision of whether to make an element of feedback diegetic is almost entirely aesthetic, as we examined previously. The same cannot be said of the choice for virtual input elements; here, there is an argument to be made that diegesis is sometimes necessary for an interaction to feel authentic. In games where a tightly integrated virtual interface is necessary to support gameplay, making those interfaces diegetic serves to boost immersion. Certain interactions might not make as much sense, or feel just plain unsatisfying, if achieved indirectly by interacting with non-diegetic interfaces.

In the bomb defusal simulator and guaranteed party livener *Keep Talking and Nobody Explodes*, players defuse a bomb by interacting with a variety of minigame-like panels on its surface. These panels feature "tactile" elements like buttons and keypads, all of which are physically present in the virtual world. This is tightly integrated virtual input at its best, with every button press and snipped wire contributing to a very real sense of urgency.

Another example featuring diegetic and tightly integrated virtual input is *The Witness*, a game with hundreds of puzzles based around drawing lines on panels placed throughout the world. Often, these puzzles play heavily into the game's environment, with players inspecting the surrounding areas

Figure 5.11 Diegetic virtual interfaces. In *Keep Talking and Nobody Explodes* (left), tactile design makes wires and buttons supremely satisfying to interact with. In *The Witness* (right), in-world puzzles have a more minimal interface, but their placement in the world makes interactions feel rich and rewarding.

Credit: *Keep Talking and Nobody Explodes* was developed and published by Steel Crate Games. *The Witness* was developed and published by Thekla.

to look for clues. The game's core experience would be tarnished if those physical panels were replaced with prompts saying "Press E to enter puzzle mode" before being confronted with a minigame overlay.

In general, tightly integrated virtual interfaces are likely to benefit from diegesis if it can make sense for those elements, particularly if players are taking on the perspective of a character in the game's world. When a player controls a character, their intent guides that character's action. If the player spends a good chunk of time acting through interfaces that their character could not reasonably see or manipulate, it is harder to believe that the player's character is accomplishing anything. It is harder, though obviously not impossible, to maintain that sense of *being* one's character. Incorporating diegesis into the design of virtual input is one way to help prevent this from occurring.

Whether or not virtual input is diegetic, though, its design is plagued by a few common challenges; chief among them is handling complexity.

5.3.2 Tricky waters

Navigation can be a perilous thing, in both maritime journeys and game interfaces. If you're looking to substantiate this claim, look no further than your nearest sea captain, or anyone who's ever found themselves in the personal slice of pocket-management Hell that is virtually any survival crafting game. Wading through the menagerie of bobby pins, reclaimed wood, hamster food, and inexplicably immaculate greatswords that video game characters have been known to carry is a daunting task. Between inventory management, perk trees, and sim control panels filled to the brim with every camera operation known to humanity, virtual interfaces can easily become almost unsustainably complex.

There is arguably no better case for the potential pitfalls of such complexity than the humble crafting menu, a bastion of sandbox games and a favourite addition to shooters that have no business implementing a crafting system. Crafting menus usually serve as an added layer of customization, giving players strategic choice in how they use their resources. They can also help promote a sense of accomplishment; finding flint and sticks to make a spear can be much more rewarding than looting one from an enemy or buying it in a shop. The nature of crafting systems, though, is that they provide players with a great deal of options, all of which are usually managed through some virtual interface.

If the options given to players via crafting are managed inelegantly, they can make navigating a game's crafting menus somewhat of a nightmare, or at least an exercise in memorization. Take the crafting system in *Don't Starve*, which bins craftable items into categories represented as icons on-screen. Clicking each category brings up a sub-menu showing the items in that category, only displaying a few items at a time. While some helpful cues are provided to improve navigation, such as highlighting items the player has the resources to craft, finding what you want to make can be frustrating. Categories are treated as mutually exclusive, although many items arguably belong to more than one—armour is classed a "Fight" item, but not a "Dress" (clothing) item. Compounded with the lack of a "view all" tab or a search function, it's easy to spend an unnecessary amount of time looking for an item's icon, even if you've been playing for a while.

The challenge here is to distill a lot of information into a more easily navigable format. *Minecraft*, a game largely responsible for the crafting system craze, does a pretty good job of this. The in-game recipe book provides a grid view of craftable items, browsable by category, which players can filter to only display items they currently have the resources to craft. Additionally, it can be searched by recipe name, letting you quickly find exactly what you're looking for. For players that have memorized different crafting recipes, you're still free to click and drag resources around manually, enjoying the tangible feel of arranging your sticks and stones into the shape of various tools. This design gives players plenty of options, while search and filtering abilities help to manage complexity and minimize frustration.

From these examples and others like them, we can derive a few key rules of thumb to guide the design of virtual input interfaces, whether expansive crafting menus, tiny HUD widgets, or otherwise, for optimal usability:

1. **Element visibility.** When feasible, all the elements of a given virtual interface should be visible; this reduces the cognitive demand of memorization. For instance, a weapon wheel is preferable to a scrolling list with only a few elements visible at a time. In situations where not all

Figure 5.12 Two hats, two categories: a miner's hat in *Don't Starve* falls into the "lighting" category but not the "apparel" category, while the warm beefalo hat falls into the "apparel" category, but not "survival."

Credit: *Don't Starve* was developed and published by Klei Entertainment.

possibilities can be reasonably displayed at once, like the crafting menus previously mentioned, two practices should be employed. First, complexity should be organized as much as possible, with clear ways to navigate. Both *Don't Starve* and *Minecraft* separate items by category via tabs/icons, a welcome quality which is absent from crafting menus in many other games, like the PC version of *Terraria*. Second, you should display as many elements as you comfortably can at once, without overloading the player. Both *Minecraft* and *Terraria* offer grid views in crafting to help players view multiple options simultaneously, while *Don't Starve*'s shorter list view is lacking in this regard.

2. **Searchability.** Interfaces where everything is visible at once are easily searchable from a quick visual scan, assuming reasonable element density. For more complex interfaces, where players must navigate to see every option, some functionality should be added to help players quickly find what they came for. Ideally, this should include a full text-based search like the crafting recipe book in *Minecraft*. However, to better support gamepad players and quicker searches, filters and sort functions are also useful. For instance, the shop interfaces in games like *Planet Coaster*

often allow players to filter items by their visual theme. The *Skyrim* mod *SkyUI* offers multiple options for sorting inventory items, allowing players to accomplish tasks like quickly selling off their heaviest equipment. In this respect, game designers can learn from UI design outside games. While you (probably) don't want your game to look like the next entry in Adobe's endless slew of subscription services, things like the customizable toolbars in Photoshop might be something you could learn from in designing a control panel for a construction-heavy sandbox.

3. **Frequency vs. integration.** The more frequently a player will need to perform a particular action, the more tightly integrated its virtual inputs should be. Remember that we say an interface is more tightly integrated when it exists "closer" to normal gameplay, and is thus quicker to access. Actions that need to be performed all the time need to be accessed all the time, so if the interfaces supporting these actions are not integrated well enough into gameplay, players will be made to waste their time—which is generally not something they'll be happy about.

4. **Shortcuts.** Following similar logic, shortcuts via direct input or very tightly integrated virtual input should be provided for players' most frequent actions. This can include something as simple as hotkeys, or buttons pinned on the HUD for quick access. In situations where different players might have a completely different set of frequent actions, customizable hotkeys are practically a must, like the configurable "hotbars" for quick access to tools or items in *Minecraft* and *Stardew Valley*.

5. **Follow the rules of good communication.** Remember that virtual inputs both allow players to communicate their intent while also providing some information about their function. Thus, their design should respect the tenets of good feedback discussed in Chapter 4; elements should be sized appropriately, things like icons or text should be clearly interpretable, and you should be careful to respect any association that might be made because of how something is presented. In other words, the big red skull button should probably do some damage, and the little green button bearing a question mark should probably not launch a nuclear warhead in the player's direction. Lastly, a virtual input element should *look* interactive; between two things on-screen, if one is clickable and one is not, there should be a clear differentiator between the two; consider putting borders around icons to show that they are clickable, for example. In all likelihood, players frustratedly tapping on something because they're not sure if it's a button or not is an experience you'd rather not create.

5.3.3 *The form of functionality*

If you've been around long enough to remember what software looked like before 2010, then you're probably well acquainted with the concept of *skeuomorphism*, even if the word itself feels like a type of genetic disorder found only in alien mushrooms. Skeuomorphism is the concept of making the digital representation of something resemble its real-world counterpart as much as possible. If you've heard the term before, hearing it almost undoubtedly conjures up images of calculator apps, virtual synthesizer instruments, and Steve Jobs.

The reason Steve Jobs tends to come up in any discussion of skeuomorphism is that Apple used to be especially infatuated with it; the original iteration of iOS is a classic example illustrating the concept. Its original app icons, and consequently App Store icons in general, practically dripped with the stuff. Everything high resolution, packed to the brim with subtle variations in colour and texture that mimicked physical objects. The original Newsstand icon boasted a subtle wood grain; Passbook displayed colourful tickets in a fabric sleeve, and Instagram was an old-timey camera graphic packing an ultra-realistic lens and viewfinder.

Skeuomorphism is also associated with the notion of so-called *jelly buttons* and the like; while interactive jello is not quite so common in the real world, overt highlights and gradients make things look distinctly pressable— "I am a physical button, please push me." In this way, skeuomorphism can directly support affordances; an element which looks 3D suggests that it can be pressed. Today, this look has largely been eschewed in favour of a much flatter style often associated with the *material design* popularized by Google. Instagram ditched its old-timey polaroid sprite for a minimalist white outline atop some abstract neon fever dream. Apple capitulated as well, swearing off all but the subtlest gradients and drop shadows.

Flat design is also the norm in plenty of games, from the minimalist weapon wheel of *Doom (2016)*, to the crafting menu in *The Last of Us*, to most new mobile games. Skeuomorphic trends haven't completely died out in game UI design, though; even a game like *Civilization VI*, released well into the 2010s, retains jellylike buttons begging to be pressed.

The emulation or exaggeration of physical qualities, passé as it may be in graphic design circles, can still serve a purpose in games. This is particularly true for diegetic elements. Returning to a couple of the examples mentioned earlier, *The Witness* uses relatively flat design for its puzzle panels, but interactive modules on the bombs in *Keep Talking and Nobody Explodes* are meant to resemble their real counterparts, down to analog radio displays. Were the modules in *KTANE* little touchscreens with flat-shaded buttons and minimal diagrams of perfectly straight wires, the game's aesthetic would be ruined. Styling virtual input isn't just a matter of following design trends; it's also about maintaining cohesion with the rest of a game's art and providing players the necessary cues (affordances) to recognize and use that input effectively.

Designing virtual input interfaces is often about creating a clear and simple way for players to accomplish something, with a focus on functionality. However, thinking outside of these limits can help to create a positive, memorable experience. Take the example of a game's main menu. Most menus are effectively little more than a few buttons overlain on a screenshot, with varying degrees of minimalism. Whether you're playing *World of Warcraft*, *Dark Souls*, or *Candy Crush*, you probably see this sort of menu constantly. Another popular design is the "dashboard" style found in multiplayer games, particularly shooters like *Rainbow Six Siege* and *Call of Duty: Warzone*. Like a slightly less disturbing version of the Windows 8 Start menu, these interfaces typically serve double duty in providing players options and advertising various game modes or seasonal content.

There's nothing *wrong* with this kind of design. Like many of the ports we mentioned earlier, you might describe it as "serviceable." Or "adequate." But a game's menu is still a space where some creative innovation can occur, providing players with a bit of delight before they even get started playing. *Brütal Legend* is a game often referenced purely on the basis of its menu design, which used a combination of real video clips and "standard" graphic design to visualize its menu as living on a vinyl album. Some games mash up direct and virtual input for their menus, like *Psychonauts*, which has you controlling a character running around on a three-dimensional brain to select different options. More simply, integrating little easter eggs can give players a treat for idly playing around with interactive elements, like the alien that pops out to say hello if you knock on one of the "E"s in the *Stardew Valley* menu.

Functionality is, of course, king in the design of any interface. To achieve real enjoyment, something first has to be usable, whether that something is a HUD, a control scheme, or a menu. However, just because something is chiefly functional, does not mean that it cannot be playful. As in designing game mechanics, art, or music, sculpting the way in which players interact with our games provides us with an opportunity to create an even better experience.

Expert Profile: Jason Avent—Changing Tides

Studio Head at TT Games

In his 25 years of experience, Jason Avent has seen one constant in the games industry: ironically, or perhaps fittingly, its continual propensity for change. Jason chatted with us about this change, chronicling the evolution of game design, monetization, and player expectations over the past two decades. In that time, his career has seen a lot of change as well.

Jason set out into the workforce in the late nineties, with a degree in civil engineering, but the games industry quickly caught his eye. Following up on a connection through a friend, Jason got a gig as a level designer for *XCOM: Terror from the Deep*. Shortly thereafter, he briefly returned to engineering, but the games industry would soon win him back for good.

In the years since, Jason has worked at all manner of studios and publishers, not to mention starting his own. After a stint at Electronic Arts, Jason eventually landed at Disney's Black Rock Studio as a game director for big-budget console titles. Although Jason loved his work, he describes the mentality of console development at the time as "insular," with an instinct to dismiss other platforms like mobile or VR. But when Black Rock closed its doors in 2011, Jason looked past that dogma and founded Boss Alien, a studio focused on mobile development.

Looking back, there was no shortage of clues ten years ago to suggest that mobile gaming might be the next big thing. But Jason says his biggest motivator was the rapidly growing popularity of the iPhone, which was serving to unify an ecosystem previously split between several different operating systems. With iOS emerging as the market leader, Boss Alien set its sights on creating a game to take the new platform by storm, and so started work on *CSR Racing*.

From the beginning, *CSR* was designed around the newly established free-to-play (F2P) model, intending to land in as many pockets as possible. Jason says that respecting players who choose to stay free is crucial; without any spending, the game would take a bit longer, but wouldn't dangle a competitive advantage behind a paywall. Of course, the hope was that players would eventually convert if they enjoyed the game for long enough.

Early versions of *CSR* started with a core that was all about the racing. Players loved the gameplay, but retention—according to Jason, the most important metric of all—was lacking. So, the team created a campaign featuring races against tiers of increasingly difficult AI enemies and bosses. Reactionary design was key as Boss Alien figured out what *CSR* should look like to attract and keep as many players as possible; as Jason puts it, mobile games were a blank canvas, with little precedent for the F2P features that have become ubiquitous today. *CSR* wasn't just a game; it was a service. Consequently, changes weren't just about the theory of design, but about "responding to player needs as they come up."

In the months following its initial launch, the team made several other additions. Asynchronous multiplayer was one of the first, giving players a chance to race against the recorded "ghosts" of others. Another major addition was a season system, giving players a new set of objectives every few weeks to try and unlock cars before they hit the in-game shop. Without realizing it at the time, the Boss Alien team was helping to pioneer the now-commonplace mobile trend of limited-time events. Each new addition gave players something to strive for, and a path to get there. Fittingly, Jason eloquently describes his view of interaction design as "laying out a trail of motives for players to follow, and tools suitable for players to meet the needs those motives create."

For Jason and his team, this design strategy paid off, and *CSR Racing* became a smash hit, raking in a cool $12 million a month shortly after its launch in 2012. Boss Alien was swiftly acquired by British developer NaturalMotion, which was in turn acquired by Zynga for over half a billion dollars two years later.

As the mobile industry took off, the games that drove it were constantly changing. Outside the microcosm of *CSR*, Jason described Finnish giant Supercell's line of hits as emblematic of these changes. *Hay Day*, the studio's first major release, effectively ported the "social singleplayer" of games like *Farmville* to mobile. Next came *Clash of Clans*, which added asynchronous multiplayer into the mix, and *Boom Beach*, which largely served as an iteration on the *Clash* formula. With Clash *Royale*, that multiplayer became synchronous, with fire-and-forget interactions that minimized the impact of lag. By 2018, Supercell had released *Brawl Stars*, which took things a step further with full-on shooter action in real time.

The stories of Boss Alien, Supercell, and even the industry at large are those of rapid change. If Supercell had pushed for *Hay Day 2* instead of *Clash of Clans*, they might have become long forgotten. Were it not for CSR's many additions, it may not have landed among the top ten iPhone games of 2012. And were it not for his foresight to change gears toward mobile, Jason would never have started Boss Alien in the first place.

So, what's the cause of all this change? Jason attributes some of it to technology, but sees people as the driving force. Innovations in hardware only shape the market because of how people respond to those innovations. Jason notes that "as [players] live with a device for longer, [they] become more and more sophisticated." In this sense, "sophistication" means the ability to handle, and the expectation of, engaging with more complex interactions.

Designing these interactions effectively is a matter of understanding players, and the market in which they participate. Jason notes that looking at what other designers are doing and improving upon it is key. But the ultimate determining factor for him is the player. To Jason, a good interaction designer is one who is *curious*, to find out what players think, and *resilient*, to use feedback no matter how ego-bruising it may be. Jason views the concept of profit with a simple and user-friendly ethos: "If it satisfies the player, it will satisfy the company." All that change, then, isn't really driven, but more so guided by designers, under the direction of players.

What's next for Jason, or the mobile industry at large, is anyone's guess. After NaturalMotion's acquisition by Zynga, Jason stayed on for a while before leaving to help fund indie developers. Eventually, he was approached by Warner Brothers to lead another studio. Today, he's working with that studio on *Lego Star Wars Battles*, a multiplayer tower defence game for iOS and Android.

When Jason spoke to us, he looked toward the future of mobile games with a sort of curious optimism, while his Darth Vader portrait looked on in the background. He sees the future of the mobile industry as focused on creating richer experiences, looking to experiment with what's been left unexplored on the platform. No matter what that looks like, we can be sure that the constant flow of change isn't stopping anytime soon, and it's something designers will need to welcome. As Jason puts it, "You have to embrace change, or you'll miss out on the biggest opportunities."

Further reading

Interaction Design for 3D User Interfaces by Francisco R. Ortega, Fatemeh Abyarjoo, Armando Barreto, Naphtali Rishe, and Malek Adjouadi (A.K. Peters, CRC Press). ISBN: 978–1482216943.
A review of interfaces for input and output, with both games and more general applications in mind. Contains some interesting history and hardware details for the devices we've come to know and love.

Level Up: The Guide to Great Video Game Design by Scott Rogers (2nd ed., Wiley). ISBN: 978-1118877166.
A great book on game design in general, though Chapters 5 through 7 (Character, Camera, and Controls) are particularly relevant to the discussion at hand.

Exercises

Port-a-Game: Controls edition

Pick a game you've played and imagine porting that game to a new platform. Come up with a new control scheme to support players on that new platform. Write/draw out your new control scheme, keeping in mind what we've talked about in this chapter. Here are some thoughts to get you started:

- Remember that actions don't have to be mapped 1:1—a button press on one platform doesn't necessarily have to be a button press on another.

- Keep player comfort in mind, and keep some hardware at hand if you have it to think about hand positioning and so on.

- Put some thought into whether your new controls can be not only functional, but incorporate some kind of fun movement.

If you completed the "Port-a-Game" exercise in Chapter 4, feel free to extend on what you've already done.

Prototyping input

Using a game engine like Unity or Unreal, set up a basic interaction (e.g., jumping)—if you completed the "Prototyping Juice" exercise in Chapter 4, you can use that same interaction as a basis.

Experiment with setting up lots of different control bindings for your action using whatever peripherals you have available. Don't confine yourself to directional input and button presses; think about how you might use different ideas. What about mouse movement? What about analog stick "gestures," like the semicircle input combos you might find in a fighting game?

Compare how different control mappings feel. Think about comfort, novelty, and player expectations. Which controls work well, and which don't? In your own projects, don't be afraid to play around with different input designs while prototyping, instead of settling on an existing convention without modification or question.

Virtual interface mockup

Think about a favourite place that you visit (e.g., restaurant, park and so on) and imagine a simulation game where you build, manage, and expand on that place. Design a rough mockup of a virtual interface for managing day-to-day operations and monitor your progress. Here are some questions to get you started:

- What, if any, camera controls will you need?
- How will you control/display the flow of time?
- How will you lay out an interface for building or buying new things?
- How will players access different bits of information about their progress?
- Will you opt for a design that mimics other software, real-life elements, or both?

6

The Play's the Thing

It was a dark and stormy night. A young man dashed across the street, denim work overalls clinging to his body from the downpour. The torrent had only just started; when he'd left home ten minutes ago, the night had been far more welcoming. Shivering, the man retrieved a keyring from his left pocket, glancing up at the sign above. *Castle Furniture—Where your home is your Castle.*

The door emitted a familiar chime as he stepped inside, rattling as it closed against the hostile wind.

"Lou?" the man called out.

A gruff foreman, likewise, clad in overalls, emerged from behind a stack of crates. "Mario? What are you doing here? Your shift's not till six."

"The boss emailed me, he said they found her here. She must've tried to follow me to work." Mario held up a leash and smiled weakly. "I still can't believe she snuck through the fence."

"Oh yeah, I think I remember hearing about that. I'll check the loading dock; you check the show floor." Lou jogged off to the back of the store.

"Here, girl!" Mario said softly. "I brought your leash. Maybe we can go for a walk together next time?" He pulled a small bag of treats out of his overalls, holding one out as a promise. "Here, Princess! Come here, please. I'm sorry about the fence!"

Hearing a rustle from the loading dock, Mario turned to see Lou gesturing from the back. "She's not here, buddy. I just checked in chat; boss sent the address for this location by mistake."

"You mean they found her at the store on Park?" he replied, confused.

"Yeah. I'm sorry Mario, but your Princess is in another Castle."

The Game Designer's Playbook. Samantha Stahlke and Pejman Mirza-Babaei, Oxford University Press.
© Samantha Stahlke and Pejman Mirza-Babaei (2022). DOI: 10.1093/oso/9780198845911.003.0006

Stories are powerful things. Great novels can make us laugh or cry. Great films can surprise us, or prompt us to reflect on ourselves. Mediocre textbooks can make us groan with the realization that we've wasted precious minutes of our lives to set up poorly conceived satire.

The stories that games tell us are also powerful. Just as we might bemoan the death of a favourite television character, we can also grieve the loss of a treasured virtual companion. The lore of a mythical world can be just as complex in a game as in a Hollywood fantasy epic. The allure of a good story is far from platform-specific, and a good character can charm their audience irrespective of the screen or page they call home. No matter the medium, a meaningful and well-told story will always be something that humans can appreciate.

Game stories are especially curious, by the very nature of gaming as an interactive medium. For thousands of years, stories were told *to* us. The only way to experience a story firsthand was to live through its events yourself. Movies and television let us relay stories more viscerally, though the audience remains a passive observer. Games break down this barrier betwixt audience and story even further. We, as players, participate in the story that a game creates. If we do nothing, the story cannot move forward. Our actions, our decisions, and our failures may affect how the story plays out, with varying degrees of subtlety. With enough freedom, the story becomes our own. Through our interaction with a game, our stories can be told *by* us.

In crafting a story, we might start from a singular idea for an interesting scene or journey and look to literary structures like the monomyth. We might pick out elements common to any story—plot, characters, setting, premise, themes—and pin down any that our initial idea might be missing. Maybe we'll start jotting out a storyboard, or just sit at our keyboards and write until the keys seem to melt together.

This isn't a book about creative writing, though, and this chapter will focus less on the process of crafting a good story and more so on how games can make the most of their interactivity to tell stories in a compelling and immersive way. Not every game requires a narrative to succeed, but every game designer needs to understand the connections between narrative and gameplay. Storytelling is part of game design. Even games without a "real" story will leave players creating stories out of their own trials, successes, and failures. For those games that do employ a traditional narrative, the characters and world that live within can have a lasting impact on the players that come to know them.

6.1 What's in a feeling?

There is no precise universal definition for emotion, and it is meaningless to dwell on this lack of absolute certainty. One way to describe emotion is as a biological state, involving both physiological and psychological components. Our emotions manifest physically, as an alteration of brain chemistry and expressions like smiling, posture, and fidgeting. Our emotions also manifest psychologically, shaping our outlook on life and our attitude towards others. A change in emotion can affect us profoundly. Critically, these changes are largely dependent on outside factors; while our neurological state is internal, it is influenced by everything we sense and experience.

Games evoke emotion by making us experience things in a visceral way. On top of their interactive nature, games deliver many sensory and experiential components at once. Games can combine the rich audiovisual content of film with the intoxicating competitiveness of sport, or the experience of reading a story with listening to a moving piece of music. Occurrences during play can feel consequential enough to warrant a substantial emotional response, even if they are of no importance in the physical world.

Players can have emotional reactions to gameplay resulting from in-game occurrences (e.g., the death of a favourite character) or external factors (e.g., personal satisfaction after finally beating a difficult boss fight). Although these reactions can certainly overlap, if you are particularly interested in one category over the other, Section 6.2 is more focused on narrative, while Section 6.3 centres on player action.

Regardless of what prompts players to feel something, our goal is to shape that emotional response in a way that benefits experience. There are a lot of different approaches we might take, many of which would depend on a specific design context. You may want to push a given response to be more of a positive or negative feeling. You may want to intensify a reaction, or maybe even reduce it. But since we're in the business of engagement and not disengagement, we'll focus on the former—understanding how we can create moments that resonate with players and stick with them even after the adrenaline of gameplay has faded.

Ultimately, this comes down to a question of emotional investment. Getting players interested in what's happening inside a game, and more importantly, keeping that interest alive. Making players' actions feel valuable in the moment, and following through on the consequences of those actions. Beyond telling them they've won, or handing over some shiny achievement, how do we make players *feel*?

6.2 Act I: Narrative and characters

The question of what role story should have in games can be a divisive one. Some argue that gameplay is the undisputed king of experience, and that stories always come second. At the extreme end of this argument is someone who's never missed the opportunity to skip a cutscene, and throws around the phrase "walking simulator" as if environmental storytelling is a bad thing. On the opposing side, you have those players that will sit in rapt attention whenever a character opens their mouth, stopping to pick up every journal littered throughout a game's world. These types of players might be so attached to narrative that they'll find little satisfaction in a game without any explicit story to tell.

Both sides are correct in their assertions. Some players will never find the slow burn of exploration in a game like *Firewatch* to be all that fun or compelling, while others appreciate the chance to drink in a story without stopping to shoot up a room full of baddies along the way. For those players that much prefer the shooting of baddies over hearing about their backstories, a game like *Hotline Miami* pushes story to the back burner, handing the spotlight over to fast action with less narrative significance. In the middle, games like *BioShock* or *The Witcher* balance plenty of that fast action with telling a complex story.

In any case, the important thing is that any story elements need to contribute positively to the player's experience. Our earlier question isn't about how prominent a game's story should be. Instead, it's about the role stories have in supporting the game experience. The answer is simple: a game's story should be satisfying for the players that consume it.

How successful a game is at creating and delivering a good story depends on several different things. Coming from a perspective of other storytelling media, the common thread and obvious answer here is writing quality. Our enjoyment of media can come down to the mettle of its writing. An intriguing premise can be ruined by a shoddy script, and even the simplest of stories can come alive with interesting turns and great dialogue. What we read (or watch) is defined by its writing.

Except players don't experience a game by reading or watching it. They experience a game by *playing* it. Something that is fun to read, or watch isn't necessarily fun to play. Likewise, something that might be incredibly compelling to play might not make for a particularly riveting film— perhaps explaining the endless tide of what can charitably be described as aggressively mediocre "video game movies" in the early 2000s. While books and film have only the language of the senses available to communicate, games have the language of interaction. This fundamentally changes both how we experience narrative in games, and how we design those narratives in the first place.

6.2.1 *The story and the game*

As a player, you are an active participant in a game. You are interacting, you are *doing something*, and every part of a game's experience needs to integrate with that act of *doing*. A game might have compelling gameplay. That same game might have a beautiful soundtrack. But if the two were treated as entirely separate, the experience would be ruined. It would be ridiculous if you had to stop playing for five minutes whenever you wanted to listen to a song, and then return to your gameplay in total silence.

Following this argument, the idea of cutscenes as the de facto standard for delivering narrative content in games starts to feel somewhat misguided. This isn't to say that cutscenes are terrible; in the right circumstances, they can be fantastic. The problem is that our default understanding of delivering story in games is a tennis match between cutscenes and gameplay. Title after title, particularly in the AAA space, players arrive with the expectation of alternating between 30 minutes of shooting at alien zombie police terrorists and five minutes of watching the protagonist on the phone with their wife. And a lot of the time, that's exactly what they get.

The trick to circumventing these expectations, and hopefully creating better stories in the process, is to avoid seeing "the story" as some magically separate entity from "the game." Back in Chapter 3, we talked about the importance of treating learning as part of gameplay. This same holistic attitude applies to narrative as well. A game's story isn't just a layer on top of gameplay; it's something that needs to bleed through in a player's moment-to-moment experience.

Before exploring how this idea can benefit a game's narrative, we should examine what happens when a game's story is treated as a separate layer. The most obvious consequence of this treatment is the near-inevitable spawning of conflict between story and gameplay. This conflict can arise in several ways, some of which are more detrimental than others, and we will explore a few different examples throughout this chapter. One of the simplest instances of this discrepancy is when characters are shown to do things in cutscenes that substantially over- or under-state their abilities when compared to their role in regular gameplay. Such choices might be made in service to a particularly cool-looking action sequence, or to move the plot forward without the interference of gameplay rules.

Depending on the extent and consequences of the conflict in question, this can range from amusing to irritating. The titular character of *Bayonetta* heavily favours the game's default starting weapons in cutscenes even against powerful enemies, but this is hardly enough to destroy a player's suspension of disbelief. Although the default guns can't be used as effectively as later-game weapons during play, this disconnect is a relatively minor sacrifice for the sake of pleasant choreography.

Contrivances designed to move a plot forward during a cutscene can be much more frustrating, where the player is robbed of their interaction in a situation that would be substantially different if occurring during gameplay. In *Uncharted 2*, player-controlled Drake is shown to hide behind a wall and watch while the story's villain stoops to drink mythical invincibility-granting resin. A few moments later, the villain calls out to Drake, who steps out from cover and starts shooting at his newly near-immortal foe. Naturally, if this exact sequence happened during gameplay, players could have taken the opportunity to shoot *before* their adversary gained superpowers.

Given its niche popularity as a buzzword, we would be remiss to exclude the phrase "ludonarrative dissonance" from our discussion. Initially coined in response to a perceived conflict in *Bioshock*, the term is used to describe a conflict between narrative and gameplay. As the argument goes, *BioShock*'s gameplay encourages you to be selfish by "harvesting" mutated young children to gain resources, while story elements require you to help another character in moving the plot forward. The argument here is flawed, though. Valuable gameplay rewards are still given for the less selfish choice of saving the children, and the assistance you provide to another character is presented as a mutually beneficial transaction. These factors make the situation far more nuanced than "story protagonist good, game protagonist bad." On top of this, in a game where players can perceive harvesting child mutants as a viable option at all, that sense of internal conflict contributes to a more intense emotional experience. The situation here isn't one where story and gameplay disagree, it's one where story and gameplay together contribute to something intentionally unsettling.

Despite the phrase's dubious origins, ludonarrative dissonance is still a helpful catch-all term for cases where story and gameplay fail to be at peace with one another. One of the most irritating consequences of disconnecting story and gameplay, though, is a far more obvious problem requiring no identification of inconsistencies in logic or ideology. To put it simply, cutscenes really can be boring sometimes.

In games where action is the priority, overly long or frequent cutscenes can feel like interruptions, rather than intermissions. For all the fascinating mythos explored in *Okami*, the game's cutscenes tend to drag on, exacerbated by written dialogue that often moves forward at a fixed, excruciatingly slow pace. Even in smaller indie titles, relying on the formula of sticking narrative dialogue exchanges at arbitrary gameplay milestones can damage otherwise enjoyable experiences. The arcade-style fun of *Super Motherload*, a game about mining on Mars, is interrupted far too frequently in parts for mostly useless exposition sequences with little relevance to its otherwise satisfying gameplay. Leaning on auto-triggered cutscenes and written dialogue sequences will typically prompt players to lean on the skip button in return.

The idea of making cutscenes unskippable has gained well-deserved notoriety for completely robbing players of control to sit through expository dialogue punctuated by the occasional explosion. The real horror of unskippable cutscenes, whether the 20-minute opening sequence of *Far Cry 4* or the cutscenes in *Destiny*'s story missions, is when they are *always* unskippable, even on replaying the game. In the most always beneficial vein of giving players options, the decision to make non-interactive content strictly and permanently mandatory is almost never a good idea.

If it is best to refrain from relying entirely on the cutscene formula to tell our stories, the question becomes: What are we supposed to do?

6.2.2 *The story is the game*

One of the oldest adages in creative writing is "show, don't tell." This says that conveying information through demonstration is more engaging than conveying it through description. Describing someone as "an angry person" is an adequate way to label them with a character trait, but it isn't particularly engaging. Showing that person's anger, by having them snap at others or become violent, is both more effective characterization and more interesting to read about. In the jump from books to movies, we gain the ability for our audience to see things directly, instead of imagining what characters and places look like. In film, the axiom of "show, don't tell" is applied more literally; heavy voiceovers and expository dialogue are usually inferior to visual sequences that show characters' interactions with each other and the world around them.

In the jump from films to games, we gain an even more distinct advantage—the ability for our audience to *do* things firsthand from a character's perspective through their gameplay. In terms of engagement, this form of storytelling is hard to beat. Demonstration via *showing* an event is certainly more effective than just *telling* the audience about it, but neither can come close to the engagement resulting from participation in that event yourself by *doing*. We previously talked about the idea of doing, showing, and telling regarding game instruction in Chapter 3, though it is even more pertinent here. In games, we might push that old aphorism forward a step, and instead say "do, don't show."

To understand why this is the case, let's consider an event that is especially impactful: a character's death. If we are only ever told about a character's death, we might not feel much attachment. Oftentimes, protagonists with a tragic backstory involving deceased family members will merely recount their perishing as a sort of exposition. Lara Croft's father being presumed deceased is a source of uncertainty and angst for her character, but as a player of the *Tomb Raider* series, you don't particularly ache for his loss.

Even for a character of significant importance to a game's lore, hearing about their death second-hand can serve to minimize its impact. In *Skyrim*, you hear about the death of the former high king Torygg from his widow, among other anecdotal accounts. In the context of the narrative, this event is monumentally important, literally igniting a civil war. In practice, though, hearing about Torygg's death isn't particularly engaging, and quite forgettable in comparison to the deaths you'll witness (or cause) firsthand.

Figure 6.1 A much more engaging example of character demise in *Skyrim* is told through Frostflow Lighthouse, an in-game location where the player finds the remains of its residents and slowly uncovers the heart-wrenching nature of their deaths.

Credit: *The Elder Scrolls V: Skyrim* was developed by Bethesda Games and published by Bethesda Softworks.

Watching a character die instead of just hearing about it is one way to help raise emotional stakes and memorability. In *The Last of Us*, players are introduced to the protagonist Joel and his daughter Sarah in the opening moments of gameplay. In a cutscene shortly thereafter, Sarah is killed by gunfire and dies in Joel's arms. Although Joel's story still would have been tragic had we only been told about Sarah's death after the fact, *seeing* and *hearing* it happen helps to make this event more memorable, and thus more effective in characterizing Joel as a bereft father.

Directly watching a character die, and the immediate reactions and interactions of other characters surrounding that individual, make their death more impactful. This tactic can create remarkably memorable moments, such as the death of Eli Vance, father to the player character's NPC companion Alyx at the end of *Half-Life 2: Episode Two*. Both the timing of this scene—after we've gotten to know Eli—and our ability to see the events firsthand make it far more powerful than if Alyx had been an orphan from the start and simply recounted her father's passing.[1]

Players can become further engaged in a character's death if given the opportunity to take a more active role in the key events surrounding their demise. In the third act of outer-space action ARPG *Mass Effect 2*, referred to as the "Suicide Mission," several of the player's NPC companions can die because of poor strategic decisions. This includes both in-the-moment decisions, like who the player selects to accompany them into final battle, and previous choices, such as whether the player upgraded their ship's defensive capacity. Your actions as a player directly determine the fate of these characters; if one of your teammates dies, you bear part of the responsibility through your actions. While the environment of a game allows for a "redo" to potentially change outcomes like this, the player's direct involvement helps to make those outcomes more powerful, particularly on a first run.

Direct player involvement can also intensify the experience of witnessing an inevitable death. In *What Remains of Edith Finch*, player interaction is essential in understanding how each character of the Finch family succumbs to their eventual fate. Even though there's nothing players can do to save these characters, experiencing their death firsthand leads to moments that aren't easily forgotten. Certain vignettes—like seeing through the eyes a toddler who drowns in the bath surrounded by toys, or controlling the maladaptive daydreams of a character as they transform his work into suicide—are particularly powerful.

The takeaway here is that deeper levels of interaction produce greater emotional investment. This is not to say that a written account of an event will always be inferior to a visual or interactive one; merely that in general, more interaction means a richer experience of a given event or piece of information.

This notion is far from exclusive to the example of character death; all storytelling can benefit from richer integration with what players are *doing* when they play a game. Narrative content shouldn't be relegated to the occasional expository dialogue exchange, and perhaps a few cassette tapes bearing suspiciously documentary-like soundbites. A game's story should come through in its environment, in its characters, and in its mechanics.

Environmental storytelling, the practice of communicating lore or the past events of a game's world through its contents, can be a compelling way for players to experience story through actively exploring their surroundings. The *Portal* series, particularly *Portal 2*, frequently conveys lore tidbits

---

[1] Naturally, its timing at the end of the game is also necessary to support the timeline-bending shenanigans in the follow up *Half-Life: Alyx* over a decade later.

or larger narrative messages through the environment. Murals throughout the facility explored by the player hint at its mysterious background, and introduce them to the desperation of Douglas Rattman, a former employee whom the player never meets in person. In the mid-game of *Portal 2*, a series of physics puzzles is punctuated by long exploration segments filled with decades-old, recorded exchanges between characters, conveying years of history (and comedic character development) while giving the player awe-inspiring industrial environments to explore. Abandoned places are used as an opportunity for the player to peek into the past undisturbed; this type of environmental storytelling is a common and effective tactic seen in everything from *Subnautica*'s vacant underwater bases to abandoned lighthouses and animal dens in *Skyrim*.

Figure 6.2 Visual design choices in *Portal 2* that connect to its story. Left: a mural depicting the events of the first *Portal*, now overgrown with ivy, that players can see when they first acquire the dual portal gun. Right: after crazed AI Wheatley takes command of the facility, his incompetence and frivolity shine through in the "frankenturret" walking cubes he creates to serve as proxies for the player in their absence.

Credit: Portal 2 was developed and published by Valve.

A game's mechanics can also communicate story details and reinforce narrative themes. *Celeste*, for instance, is an indie platformer about climbing a mountain. Just below the surface, it's an exploration of learning to cope with anxiety and depression. The environmental and mechanical gimmicks used in each chapter of the game reflect the events of the story. As the character faces a tumult of motivation and self-doubt, for example, the player experiences a shifting wind mechanic that can serve to literally push them forwards or hold them back. *Celeste* communicates a great deal through its mechanics and environments, without constantly relying on written dialogue to explain its themes or what the protagonist is experiencing internally.

When a game can integrate its narrative seamlessly with a player's interaction, the result can feel almost unsettlingly satisfying. One game that builds its core on the idea that "the story *is* the game" is *The Stanley Parable*. It opens on a voiceover, much like any other opening cutscene. The narrator describes a character—evidently the player's point-of-view character—and outlines his actions. Except players are in control of the character, and perfectly capable of defying what the narrator says. As they choose to defy, obey, or refuse to act, the narration changes in response to players' interactions. The result is that, on your first experience with *The Stanley Parable*, you'll end up with a parable quite different to many other players. While such an absurd degree of narrative freedom isn't appropriate for every game, the delightful experience of *participating* in rather than simply *perceiving* a story is something that all game narratives can strive to achieve.

6.2.3 Creating likeable characters

One of the more appealing quirks of humans is our tendency to personify things other than people and animals. Maybe you've nicknamed your favourite houseplant. Maybe you've drawn a smiling face on a sticky note to keep you company at your desk. Maybe someone in your household affectionately refers to the family car as Lily, because "that's just her name."

Perhaps it is this ability to so easily empathize with anything that makes us so fond of a good story. If we can personify *things* unprompted, when we are introduced to a character and learn about their experience, it is easy for us to become attached. Even though characters in books, films, or games aren't real, we can still care about what happens to them. In constructing a narrative, it is our hope as storytellers that our audience will care about the characters we bring to life. To make our imaginary folk relatable, likeable, and memorable requires good *characterization*: the process of developing a character's personality through their past and present actions. Before addressing what constitutes effective characterization, though, let's take a moment to understand how character design can fail.

Examining flawed characterization in games is trickier than it first appears. While it is easy to rhyme off a dozen or more characters that players love, it is hard to identify game characters who are disliked without exception. For every player that dislikes a villain being evil for evil's sake, you can usually find someone who's won over by the cool factor. Plenty of players despise Kai Leng from *Mass Effect 3* for his shallow motivations and cutscene power creep, but some players love to hate the arrogance of a brutal space ninja. There are some characters who are shunned more unanimously—Navi from *The Legend of Zelda: Ocarina of Time* springs to mind, the notoriously shrill tutorial fairy constantly imploring the player to "Listen!". However, Navi demonstrates less a failure of characterization and more a severe misjudgement of how much instruction players need (and perhaps the direction of voice actors).

PLAN NO. 19888

Figure 6.3 If you were around in the nineties, you can hear this picture.
Credit: Link and Navi are characters owned by Nintendo.

The reason it is so difficult to name characters who are famous for being badly developed is that poor characterization doesn't cause infamy, but instead the far worse fate of forgettability. Mention the *Metal Gear Solid* series and you'll likely be met with cries of "SNAAAAAKE"—referring to the protagonist—even from people who've never played the game. Ask someone to name the main character from any single player *Call of Duty* campaign and you'll probably be met with a blank stare.[2] There is literally a cardboard box in *Metal Gear Solid* with more personality and name recognition than many characters falling under the gritty action hero archetype. A common thread that we can identify about many unremarkable characters is one-dimensional design that eschews depth in favour of adhering to a formula.

---

[2] They can probably guess exactly what that character looks like, though: a tall thirtysomething white guy with stubble is a safe bet.

To issue a blanket condemnation of archetypal character design would be misguided at best. Even our most beloved heroes and companions tend to rely at least partially on amalgamating well-known tropes. Snake (*Metal Gear Solid*), Gordon Freeman (*Half-Life*), and Nathan Drake (*Uncharted*) all fall into that same gritty action hero bin. And yet, these characters are so memorable that they've become just as recognizable, if not more so, than the games that spawned them. So, what saves a character from the fate of forgettability and pushes them into the public consciousness?

A well-developed character is a memorable one; good characterization, then, is about creating strong memories. The challenge with games in comparison to other media is that our relationships with characters are much more personal. A clever NPC has to work extra hard to win the title of lovable quipster when the *player*, not just their character, is on the receiving end. And while a comic book superhero might win us over by saving the world, it's tough for a game's protagonist to skate by on their skill and heroics alone when we've been controlling them the whole time. The medium closest to games in terms of how we interact with characters is, arguably, reality. To effectively develop our characters, we should take some inspiration from how we create memories with real people.

Our relationships are built on moments.[3] Mostly insignificant ones, in fact. Watching someone walk away from an explosion is cool, but it doesn't make you like them, or really remember them as a person. Your best friend might have won the Nobel Prize, but it's not what made them your best friend. The thing that made them your best friend is all the little things, all the memories you've made together. It's sitting at work together debating the merits of the new breakroom couch. It's singing terrible karaoke at a party. It's watching them stir honey into macaroni and playfully berating them for their understanding of what constitutes "food."

Creating truly great characters in games is about orchestrating these little moments. In *Undertale*, an indie phenomenon beloved for its characters, characterization is typically independent of heroics, despite its loosely fantasy-inspired setting. Take Sans the skeleton, a character so beloved that he made it into Nintendo's *Super Smash Brothers: Ultimate*. Sans is eventually revealed to be powerful, sure, but snags players' hearts by telling them incessantly groanworthy jokes, sharing his love for family, and spotting the player for a plate of fries.

Even the most serious and thoughtful characterization doesn't require sophisticated backstories or painstakingly crafted lore. *The Last of Us* is

---

[3] There is no definitive and simple way to sum up how us complicated beasts get to know one another. But you opened this book for some guidance on a topic that frequently veers off the cliff of subjectivity, and that's exactly what you're going to get.

famed for its relationship between Joel and Ellie, the girl he effectively adopts years after the death of his biological daughter. Their relationship emerges from a collection of small moments that become meaningful. Car rides, arguments, caring for wounds, admiring an abandoned city together— these characters develop through *interactions*, not big events. In creating likeable and memorable characters for us to interact with, it's the little things that count.

6.2.4 *Stale stories and wobbly writing*

Games have accrued somewhat of a reputation for bad writing, though that reputation often feels like it's far more popular among people that haven't played very many games. Sometimes this reputation is deserved, and often-times it's not. Games are certainly not uniquely remarkable as a medium for having some badly written apples. For every *Anna Karenina*, there's a *Twilight*. Cinema gave us *The Godfather*, but it also gave us *The Room* (and *The Godfather III*, for that matter). Likewise, for every dull FPS whose idea of story is a char-acter shouting "And that's how it's done!", we get a game like *BioShock* that toys with our ideas of free will and self-interest.

The real issue with most poorly written game stories, like most poorly written characters, is that they are thoroughly unexceptional. A story that's so-bad-it's-good is preferable to some repetitive pablum that's hardly discern-able from its predecessors. Part of the reason game stories are often seen as subpar is that many, if not most, games neglect or completely ignore story until after other parts of the game have been significantly developed.[4] In *Uncharted 3*, action set pieces were chosen *before* the story beats that sup-ported them. This technique can still yield an engaging experience, built on interactive moments instead of some grand mythos. However, this treatment can easily make story feel like a less valuable shellac on top of gameplay.

Mirror's Edge didn't bring on a writer until over six months into its just over two-year development cycle, and the separation between "game" and "story" is painfully obvious at times. Gameplay is filled with plenty of intense moments and bits of environmental storytelling, but the cutscenes and dia-logue conceived to glue everything together feels like a distracting veneer. It leans on tropes, with voice lines ripped straight from the movie adaptation of a dystopian young adult novel. This certainly doesn't spoil the game, but it does make you yearn for something more.

---

[4] If you're curious to know more, here are a couple of articles (links current as of this writing) on the examples discussed for *Uncharted 3* and *Mirror's Edge*:
(Mirror's Edge) https://web.archive.org/web/20131103152620/http://www.newsarama.com/1896-looking-at-the-mirror-s-edge-with-rhianna-pratchett.html
(Uncharted) https://www.cnn.com/2011/10/30/tech/gaming-gadgets/uncharted-3/index.html

Other annoyances in writing can bring down the overall quality of a game's narrative. Plot holes and logical inconsistencies aren't the tragedy that some online critics make them out to be, but such errors can certainly diminish how a story hangs together. At the end of *Fallout 3*, for instance, the player character is asked to sacrifice themselves by entering a highly radioactive control room. The player can also ask one of their companions to complete the task for them. Human companions will, sensibly, refuse this request. However, the players' other companions, who are either immune or incredibly resistant to radiation, will *also* refuse, even going so far as to insult the player for asking. This contrivance is frustrating, implying that loyal companions immune to the danger would happily stand by and let the player's character die rather than step in unharmed, even when asked. Fortunately, this decision was reversed in an add-on for the game, allowing hardier companions to willingly step in without berating the player.

Dialogue is another area where writing can succeed (or fail miserably) in making a story and its characters more memorable. Lines that feel canned, like Faith's constant reiteration of something resembling a melodramatic "She's my sister!" in *Mirror's Edge*, typically don't do much for a story. Conversations can be remarkable because of their banality, shaping the humanity of the characters that share them. There is little in *Half-Life: Alyx* that establishes the plucky Russell as a caring mentor more effectively than his in-depth description of a club sandwich to the player's character as she asks for something to alleviate the terror of navigating a building infested with hostiles. Good dialogue serves to complement the events of a story and develop the characters that deliver it, not push forward an offscreen plot or provide some constant verbalization of a character's motivations.

This sort of general writing advice—conceptualize early, avoid tropes, write interesting dialogue, avoid lazy plot holes—is certainly relevant to the construction of game stories. But, as with everything else in games, the core of our narrative experience comes down to our interactions as a player.

6.3 Act II: Player agency

Imagine that you're at work right now. You're stuck in a meeting, listening to your boss drone on about half-margin eased inventory scaling, whatever that means. And there's nothing you can do about it, except stare longingly out the window and envy the pigeons for their inability to participate in this meeting.

Most everyone either has or had a job they hated, and a large part of that frustration stems from a lack of freedom. You're not doing what you'd like

Bread
Lettuce
Tomato
Turkey
Ham
Bread
Bacon
Lettuce
Tomato
Bread

PLAN NO. 141513

Figure 6.4 Artist's rendering of a club sandwich as described by Russell in *Half-Life: Alyx*.

to be doing, and you don't really have a choice. You're dealing with rude customers, or stuck pushing papers you'd rather not push, and you can't just wheel the boss out of the room and order pizza for your equally fed-up comrades.

One of the many appeals of gaming is the ability to feel in control of your actions. Regardless of where you're stuck in real life, in games you are the dragon slayer. You can vanquish the goblin invasion. You can architect the city of your dreams. You can order that pizza.

This feeling of control is referred to as *agency* in the social sciences. Formally, agency is the ability of an individual, or agent, to act freely and independently in their environment. Less formally, agency means that you can decide what you want to do, and then do that thing. Essentially, agency combines the free will to make choices, and the power to act on those choices. Games grant us a sense of agency in terms of gameplay pretty much effortlessly. As players, we choose when and where we want to run, shoot, move stuff around, and so on—we are in complete control of how we use the mechanics available to us. To grant players agency, games need to fulfill two basic requirements:

1. **Players feel like they can make decisions**. This relates to the free will part of agency, and means that players can make meaningful choices about what to do. For instance, in gameplay, players might be able to pick which weapons they'd like to use against a particular boss. In the context of story, players might be able to choose whether they'd like to obey or disobey the wishes of a certain character. The feeling of free choice can be compromised if players do not feel like multiple viable alternatives are available for a given situation. For instance, players' sense of agency will diminish if routinely faced with ultimatums, or pigeonholed into decisions that present one reasonable option amongst others which are clearly ineffective.

2. **Players feel like their decisions have consequences**. This relates to the power component of agency. After a choice has been made, players should feel that their decision was important, and that their actions had a tangible effect on the situation at hand. Fulfilling this requirement will make players feel like their actions matter, and provide at least the illusion that someone who acted differently would have a different experience with the game. In gameplay, this might be as simple as different weapons having different efficacy based on how players use them and what they are used against. In a story context, the choice to obey a character might result in their loyalty, while the choice to disobey might eventually turn them into an enemy.

While having agency in moment-to-moment gameplay is practically a given, ensuring player agency in the context of a game's narrative is more complicated. Technologically, we are limited in our ability to simulate cause and effect in things like social situations. Artistically, we may have pre-set story beats or set pieces that we want players to experience regardless of how they play. These factors constrain our ability to give players truly free choices, and to follow through on the consequences of those choices in a realistic manner.

The question of agency is further complicated by the fact that it may not be appropriate for players to have agency at every moment in every game. In something like an RPG or strategy game, a strong and constant sense of agency might be a core part of the desired experience. In tightly scripted linear stories, though, you'll likely need to force players into certain decisions or actions to hit the desired dramatic moments. Much of the time, you might be interested in how to maximize a player's *perception* of their agency, while working within constraints that severely limit your ability to provide decision points that influence the course of the game.

Throughout this section, we will explore how agency can be nurtured in a game's narrative and gameplay, balancing player freedom with a designer's creative vision.

6.3.1 *Finding yourself*

A player's journey through a game belongs not only to them, but to their character, should they control one. As the player works through any series of decisions during play, they exert their will through their character. To preserve immersion and lend these decisions an increased sense of importance and meaning, players need to be able to relate to, or at least have a deep understanding of, their character. This brings about a challenging design question—how do we develop a compelling protagonist, when their actions will ultimately be controlled by someone else?

There are two primary approaches to this task, varying in the degree to which a protagonist's personality, backstory, and motivations are developed. Naturally, not every solution lies neatly in one category or the other, though most games will comfortably rest on one end of the scale created between the two.

Blank slate (silent) protagonists. The goal of this approach is to create a character who is inherently relatable through a lack of definite features, giving players a "blank slate" on which to project their own motivations and personality. A true blank slate protagonist would have absolutely no characterization. Their physical appearance and backstory would be unknown, with their motivation coming externally from some instruction, or simply from the player's will. Most games with blank slate characters won't go to quite these lengths, though. The real defining quality of a blank slate protagonist is simply their silence.

Silent protagonists don't speak; at least, not in a way that players can understand. Even in a game with a significant narrative context, this choice can work without disrupting the story. One of the most famed silent protagonists resides in a universe with one of the most deep and convoluted collections of lore: Link from *The Legend of Zelda*. Like many other silent protagonists, we can also see Link as proof that "silent" doesn't have to mean bland or devoid of personality. In everything from cutscenes to combat animations, Link is given an affable charm that showcases his bravery, wonder, and a touch of clumsiness. While these traits make Link likeable and fun to control, they are generic enough to preserve a player's ability to easily see themselves as Link.

Figure 6.5 Despite never saying a word (unless sighs and yelps count as "words"), Link has plenty of personality. Whether playfully emoting during a shield surf, or cheering in delight at his latest culinary creation, Link exudes childish optimism throughout gameplay.

Credit: The Legend of Zelda: Breath of the Wild was developed and published by Nintendo.

Aside from the occasional yes/no choice, which is never voice acted, these protagonists observe a complete vow of silence. In games where a total lack of dialogue is inappropriate, other characters may remark on the player character's reluctance to speak, or act as if the protagonist has communicated without acknowledging anything other than a general sentiment. Another common choice is to provide some companion characters which speak for the protagonist in a sense, commenting on the situation and interacting with the player's character (and by extension, the player themselves). Link had Midna in *Twilight Princess*, Chell has GLaDOS (and later Wheatley) in the *Portal* series, and Gordon Freeman had Alyx Vance in the *Half-Life 2* era. In a game where the main character is primarily a vessel for players to inhabit, companions can help to provide some extra personality and opportunities for dialogue.

Characterized protagonists. At the other end of the spectrum is a main character whose personality, backstory, and motivations are fully developed. Characterized protagonists aren't afraid to speak, and often have existing relationships with characters the player is meeting for the first time. Together, this collective comprises some of the most recognizable and beloved characters in gaming—Geralt of Rivia (*The Witcher*), Lara Croft (*Tomb Raider*), Kratos (*God of War*), Cloud Strife (*Final Fantasy*), the aforementioned Snake (*Metal Gear Solid*), and Nathan Drake (*Uncharted*), and the list goes on.

The wrinkle with characterized protagonists is that someone who is compelling and interesting as a character might not be enjoyable as a protagonist. No matter what traits or intricate backstory you ascribe a protagonist, players will still try to see themselves in that character. Crucially, their motivations need to reasonably align with the motivations of their character. If the protagonist acts for the sake of hitting a particular narrative beat, their choice needs to be one the player would reasonably make. Otherwise, players may become frustrated, feeling that the character they control is no longer in their control and thus becoming deprived of their agency. This can happen relatively easily when a protagonist is strongly characterized. In *LA Noire*, for instance, protagonist Cole Phelps chooses to have an affair despite being otherwise portrayed as incredibly straitlaced. While this twist of his character is objectively interesting, a lack of sufficient motivation on the part of the *player* to support this decision, coupled with an obvious potential for disaster, creates frustration.

This is not to say that characterized protagonists can't have strong personalities or flaws; most well-loved protagonists possess both. Take Geralt in the *Witcher* franchise; he is often gruff or rude with inhabitants of the world, and reluctant to take on the burden of slaying a monster unless there's some coin in it for him. This demeanour is justified, though, and probably shared by the player, since Geralt is often treated as a monster himself by villagers ready to hurl slurs about his genetic abnormalities. A characterized protagonist may come with their own baggage, but they still serve as the player's surrogate in a game's world. If your protagonist is prepared to make a decision, you need to be prepared to justify it in the player's eyes.

A note on character customization and dialogue options. Providing players options in the identity or appearance and narrative choices of their character can be used to support individual expression, both for blank slate and characterized protagonists. Typically, more extensive choices are present for blank slate characters, such as character creation and interaction with NPCs in role-playing games. In either case, these options can be a valuable way for players to identify more strongly with the characters they control. Some form of character creator can prevent blank slate characters from feeling bland, or allow players to recreate themselves if they so choose. Customization options for characterized protagonists—even something as simple as choosing a new haircut or piece of armour—can help players to see themselves in an otherwise predetermined character.

Neither a blank slate or characterized approach is a guaranteed success (or failure) in creating a compelling narrative that preserves player agency. Blank slate protagonists are generally easier for a wide variety of players to easily and immediately see themselves in their character, while characterized protagonists are generally easier to work into a linear narrative where strong relationships are needed with other characters. Typically, either choice *can* work to create a good experience. The fact that Geralt can talk doesn't make *The Witcher* any less compelling as a fantasy experience than *The Legend of Zelda*. Likewise, Link's silence doesn't make the *Zelda* games boring by comparison. The choice of a characterized protagonist simply means that more of the story in *The Witcher* can explore Geralt's relationship with other characters, while the *Zelda* games are focused on developing lore for the kingdom of Hyrule more than Link himself.

One thing that can completely make or break the choice to characterize a protagonist is the desired degree of player freedom. In games where the "do anything" mantra is paramount, a blank slate protagonist is usually the correct choice. *Minecraft* just wouldn't be the same if you had a spouse, three kids, and a designer-imposed fear of birds to worry about. When players are afforded a huge amount of customization and choice in a game's world, a heavy-handed backstory can detract from the overall experience. In *Fallout 4*, an open-world game selling itself on the concept of "go anywhere, do anything," your custom character is voiced, widowed, and saddled with a missing child in the opening sequence of the game. This creates an inherent disconnect between the motivation of the player to play in a post-apocalyptic sandbox, and the motivation of their character to find their son. This choice becomes an especially perplexing thing to force on player-created characters when a substantial portion of the game's target audience are young, unwed, and childless.

The lesson here is relatively simple: don't hedge your bets. You can create a characterized protagonist who might be quite different to your audience on first look, give them compelling motivations, and create an interesting story. You can let players create their own character and set them loose in an open world where they can save the world or wreak havoc and ignore the chaos around them. Alternatively, you can create something in between. But mashing up a voiced protagonist with a world that begs players to ignore the main storyline practically forces them to detach from their character's motivations entirely, losing a bit of immersion in the process.

6.3.2 *Choose your own adventure*

Once players are comfortable with who (or what) they are, they will constantly be making decisions that shape their path through a game. As we addressed in the introduction of this section, gameplay decisions are a given for players to exert their will over a game. Choices which impact a set narrative are a different beast entirely. Presenting these decisions effectively and dealing with their consequences is both a design and technical challenge. In the absence of a feasible way to simulate complete narrative freedom, how do we effectively present players with choices?

One approach is to trick players into thinking they have a choice when none exists. In theory, this provides all the emotional weight of a real decision, without the need to account for divergent consequences. Ridiculous as it may seem, situations that create this illusory choice, at least temporarily, can be an effective way to leave players with lingering questions (at least on a first playthrough), or an uncomfortable realization of inevitability.

In *Portal*, the player reaches a point where they are asked to incinerate their companion cube, a box bearing a small heart icon, before moving on. Having been "accompanied" by the companion cube for part of their gameplay, and suspiciously reassured that the cube is not sentient, most players will not want to incinerate their boxy friend. Many may try for a few minutes to find a way around the task, or to trick the system.[5] In reality, there is no choice to be made, and the cube must be destroyed. Coming to this realization creates dread and grief for players that take the time to explore other options, while players that obey without question might feel a twinge of guilt wondering if they acted too hastily. Killing your faithful companion isn't a real choice, but its presentation as a voluntary, player-controlled action makes the moment far more powerful.

This moment of overestimating one's free will is not always handled so deftly. We need only to reach back a few paragraphs and drag *Fallout 4* back into the spotlight for such an example. For a game in a franchise whose earlier entries would often let you outright kill main characters, sacrificing swaths of story in the name of good roleplay, many of the narrative "choices" you'll encounter in *Fallout 4* are laughable. Choosing between dialogue options is typically an anti-choice which controls how the protagonist will *phrase* a response, rather than what the substance of that response actually is. This amounts to little more than window dressing, birthing memes in the community of the player's dialogue options in response to yes/no questions often boiling down to "Yes" or "Yes (but sarcastic)."

The design thinking here does make sense in a way; only so many different conversations can be reasonably voice acted. Moreover, if players decline a request or shoot an important character in the face, they'll be missing out on some precious quest or another. However, this is an ethos that prioritizes quantity over quality, and feels like a slap in the face to player agency. If a player could reasonably decide to do something that would deprive them of some extra content, let them. Feeling the power to do something like kill off an NPC is usually worth losing out on that later side-quest—in addition to creating the potential for substantially different experiences on subsequent

---

[5] So loved is the companion cube, in fact, that the internet is filled with guides to save the cube via glitches or respawn it via console commands.

playthroughs. In situations where players don't have this freedom, it's usually better to be upfront about the inevitability of something. A thinly veiled anti-choice won't fool players for long, and can be far more irritating than no choice at all.

The task at hand then evolves into a question of how to handle "real" decisions that do impact the course of a game's story. Simply put, branching narratives are hard.

Life is Strange is a game about actions, consequences, and exploring the power of choice. The game's gimmick is a time-travelling power granted to protagonist Max, who can rewind time around her and make decisions with the power of hindsight. While the game's narrative has its fair share of contrivances, it does a more than serviceable job of making choices feel impactful for a first-time player. The main story arc of the game is fixed, which diminishes substantial feelings of consequence on later playthroughs. However, the player is constantly presented with choices that affect their interactions at a micro scale; other characters' immediate emotional reactions and treatment of the player reflect their decisions appropriately. These reactions are believably different between different choices as well, a vital boon when players can rewind time and explore other avenues at a moment's notice.

While the main plot beats of *Life is Strange* are fixed to preserve the integrity of the intended story experience (and keep development scope feasible), several impactful events can vary depending on the player's choices. For instance, Max's classmate Kate Marsh attempts to take her own life in the game's second chapter. With her time travelling powers suspended, it's up to the player to counsel Kate by recalling important things about her character. Whether Kate chooses to jump or step down from the ledge she's perched on will depend on their exchange, in addition to her previous interactions with the player. Kate's survival or death is echoed in later chapters of the game, giving the player a strong sense of meaningful consequence without creating a technically infeasible degree of branching in the storyline.

Another game following the strategy of mostly fixed plot points with several smaller decisions of immediate consequence is *Undertale*. *Undertale* leans even further into the idea of a branched narrative by having three main paths for the player: one which results from killing all monsters/characters they encounter, one which is predicated on complete mercy, and one which falls in between. The game reflects which path the player is on in a few ways; for instance, minor NPCs can disappear from around the world if enough monsters are killed. Characters may act in fear of the player, with dialogue shifting if they cross the line into violence. Consequences are both immediate (such as hearing the dying cries of a murdered monster) and contribute to larger shifts in the overall gameplay (taking the player from one main path to another). The fallout from player action feels even more important given how

Figure 6.6 Before encountering her on a rooftop the player can interact with Kate and learn more about her character by spending time with her in her room (left). Later, the player can recall this information to help remind Kate that she is loved (right).

Credit: Life Is Strange was developed by Dontnod and published by Square Enix.

effectively the game forces players to love its well-developed characters, from quirky reptile scientist Alphys to nap-addicted Sans the skeleton.

From these examples, we can derive some general advice for handling choices with narrative consequences. Sticking to a relatively simple overall story structure can help to keep complexity under control. To make decisions feel impactful under this constraint, immediate reactions to player action from other characters can help provide emotional weight. Lastly, the quality of a given interaction should be prioritized over the *apparent* abundance of choice. Being able to say yes to something four different ways a thousand times is worthless next to the ability to save the life of a treasured companion just once.

6.3.3 Do the right thing

It is a crisp autumn morning, and you've just stopped for a coffee before work. With only a few minutes left until your shift starts, you're second from the register, staring at the back of a very expensive flannel shirt. The shirt's owner is occupied interrogating the poor barista on the exact caloric content of each beverage on offer. His cell phone rings, and he answers it, turning away from the barista but maintaining his position in queue. The barista whispers out the first half of an "excuse me" before Flannel Shirt angrily shushes them and returns to his call. You notice a rubbish bin a few metres away, and quietly contemplate suplexing him, fedora and all, into the garbage where he belongs.

There are several things stopping you from giving Flannel Man his comeuppance: the threat of retribution, the rule of law, the thought of disappointing your mother, and hopefully a sense that it would be wrong to throw someone in a trash can, no matter their impoliteness. Though ethics vary between individuals, there is a widespread understanding of basic right and wrong in modern society.

Video games are a different story entirely, and the only thing stopping you from shoving an NPC into a trash can is often, well, nothing. Part of the appeal of games like the *Grand Theft Auto* series is the ability to run around shooting people in the face willy-nilly before stealing their cars and running them off a cliff into a big pile. In *Skyrim*, the player's iconic "fus ro dah" dragon shout can launch enemies into the air, but its real value is in conscripting unwitting city guards into the Tamriel space program. Anyone who's played *The Sims* has forced their Sims to light fireworks indoors, and anyone who claims not to have done this is lying.

The truth is that acting like a complete monster can be fun, and provide a harmless outlet for expressing the rage incurred at coffee shops across the globe. Nonetheless, it is often preferable to enforce some basic sense of right and wrong in games, and not just to keep our inner beasts in check. Moral or legal consequence helps to make a virtual world and its inhabitants feel more alive. In games with heavy roleplaying elements, a sense of allegiance to the moral code of a particular group or society can be an important part of immersion.

Serious players will often choose their behaviour based on their personal understanding of right and wrong, or an understanding of their character's ethics. Nonetheless, reflecting some sense of morality in a game's writing or mechanics can help to reinforce this idea, improve realism, and make less serious players think twice about their actions. Since the days of alignment charts in *Dungeons and Dragons*, morality systems have helped govern player choice in games. Sometimes, these systems sit at the forefront of gameplay, while others rest just below the surface.

Explicit morality systems. Many games, particularly AAA games with the effervescent label of "role-playing elements," employ some form of explicit morality or reputation system. Sci-fi games seem to be especially fond of the notion, as if every game with a spaceship needs to have a litany of alien races with independent legal systems in binary opposition with one another. These systems permeate the subgenre, from the Paragon system in *Mass Effect*, to Reputation in *Elite: Dangerous* and the *Galaxy on Fire* series, and even faction friendship values in *Spore*. You can scarcely kick a rock through the vacuum of space in such games without consulting your reputation meter to check if you've accidentally declared war on the Rocklover Empire of Andromeda-6.

These mechanics are far from limited to the interactive spiritual successors of *Star Trek*, though. Karma is a word used to describe the explicit morality systems in both the *Fallout* and *InFamous* games (though not all entries in each series use the mechanic or treat it in the same way). *InFamous 2*

Figure 6.7 In *Galaxy on Fire 2*, a reputation meter accessible via an in-game menu lets players know where they stand with the game's four major factions. In addition to affecting the behaviour of AI ships, faction loyalty changes mission payouts and affects the appearance of certain NPCs.

Credit: Galaxy on Fire 2 was developed and published by Deep Silver Fishlabs.

gives you choices in whether you'd like to fight or support crime with your character's superpowers, unlocking additional hero or villain-themed powers according to your place on the karma spectrum. Similarly, in *Fallout 3*, terrible karma will get you liked by big bad villains and hunted down by the goody-goody police. Naturally, excellent karma will get you liked by the good happy nice guys and hunted down by the having-a-bad-day police. Terminology aside, this is not an exaggeration of how binary these systems tend to be.

Thus, a pervasive problem emerges with explicit morality systems in general; they tend to feel like cheap dichotomies. These systems can be *fun* mechanically, of course. Shooting up a cargo freighter in *Galaxy on Fire* to get in good with the aliens that have cheaper space liquor is an enjoyable thing to do. However, these systems rarely exhibit political, ethical, or narrative nuance. Explicit morality systems tend to offer choices that reduce to hilarious extremes in keeping with their binary nature: Would you like to extinguish the fire in the village, or throw kittens into it? And for situations where any semblance of moral ambiguity is preserved, players can always consult the karma meter to double-check how many good boy points their last dialogue choice was worth. The act of reading a number or a fancy little icon replaces the much more interesting potential of reflecting on your own actions, or experiencing a little doubt.

Implicit morality systems. Getting players to actually think about what they've done for more than a few microseconds—perish the thought!—can be as simple as foregoing a reputation meter. Internally, that same value can tick away, still an oversimplification, but an easy way to track players' actions and shape the behaviour of NPCs accordingly. Without the crutch of an icon to peek at, players will be forced to take their decisions more seriously, perhaps left wondering as to whether they've done the right thing in the eyes of different characters. An example of such an implicit system is *Undertale's* handling of player mercy, determining whether they're on a good or evil path. The world changes around you depending on your actions, and characters act differently, but there's no magic number telling you whether you're good or bad.[6] This keeps you more immersed in the real consequences of your actions, instead of babysitting a UI counter.

BioShock also uses an implicit system to track the player's treatment of Little Sisters strewn throughout the world. The number of sisters killed or saved affects which ending the player receives, but there's no karma bar letting you know how far you've dipped into the bad guy side of things. What's more, other characters don't agree on the right choice; the game makes a point of providing an argument for killing the sisters that goes beyond "you'll get more stuff." Indeed, the more stomach-turning option does net the player more immediate reward. Somewhat unfortunately, the game not-so-subtly gives away that rewards will balance out if the player does the "right" thing instead. Without this detail, the situation becomes more interesting: a player planning to do the "right" thing might be turned by selfishness and come to feel guilt, while a player that turns down that initial reward might be left wondering if the clean conscience was worth it.

Sometimes, games present a moral choice without any implication of lasting consequences or definite rewards. In *FTL: Faster than Light*, the player can be confronted with a fellow ship in distress, and asked to spare some nominal amount of resources to help. They might receive a reward for their efforts, or nothing at all—and for first-time players, there is typically no indication of reward when such choices are presented. This makes these choices far more ideologically interesting than if they were presented as transactional. Once players get used to the outcome of different events, some uncertainty helps to preserve interest from a gameplay standpoint.

---

[6] One of the brilliant things about Undertale, at least on a first-time playthrough, is that there is in fact a magic number telling you whether you're good or bad. However, you're not told that's what it is—it masquerades as a regular old RPG experience bar, with EXP earned from killing monsters—until you face the reality of your actions later in the game. If the cute monsters weren't enough to push you towards pacifism, you'll learn that EXP stands for "Execution Points," and if you've accrued any significant amount, the game will proceed to give you a really bad time.

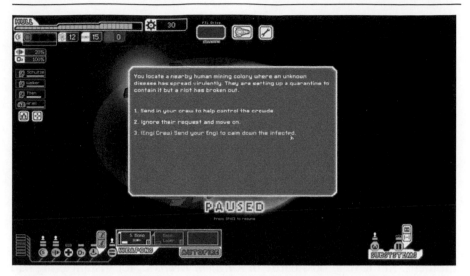

Figure 6.8 In *FTL: Faster than Light*, dilemmas are presented to the player text-adventure style. Special options can be offered based on the player's past choices, such as how many resources they've preserved or their crew composition.

Credit: *FTL: Faster than Light* was developed and published by Subset Games.

From this, we can learn that a heavy-handed approach is an easy but largely uninteresting option if you're planning to enforce some form of player morality. While explicit reputation meters have their place in spicing up the gameplay of intergalactic trading and interacting with roving NPC gangs, encouraging a little bit of grey will usually make choices feel more engaging.

6.3.4 *The player is the star*

No matter the grand plans you have for a story, or a certain key event, you must always remember that you are designing for a *player*, not an *observer*. Wherever possible, players need to be an active participant in important events, as we discussed earlier. A more active (and interactive) role for the player serves both to bolster engagement and make their actions feel more meaningful, thus contributing positively to player agency.

A simple way to promote this mentality is to avoid yanking control away from the player wherever possible. In *No More Heroes*, every single boss fight is ended with a cutscene. That cutscene shows the player's character finishing off the boss, accompanied by some dramatic back-and-forth dialogue. This effectively removes the power of the killing blow from the player, swooping in at the climax of every fight to make the player a passive observer in the most critical moment. This is inherently dissatisfying; what's to say these dialogue snippets couldn't be played during battle? Any cutscene beats difficult to orchestrate in gameplay could be left for the aftermath, perhaps showing their foe's dying breath after the player is able to deliver a finishing move themselves.

Relegating the "real" final moments of a battle to a cutscene is a frustratingly common pattern, though more preferable alternatives exist. One common solution is to insert quick-time events into a boss' death cutscene, giving the player some interaction while watching a more tightly scripted sequence. An example is the player's fight against eight-headed menace Orochi in *Okami*, where killing moves are dependent on their ability to quickly execute a few precise inputs.

An even more effective approach is to employ a strict interpretation of "do, don't show," making sure the player has full control in the most critical moment. In the final boss battle of *Kingdom Hearts II*, for instance, big bad Xemnas is ultimately killed by the player. A cutscene after the main fight shows a bit of combat, returning to gameplay for the player to execute the killing move themselves before playing a final cutscene showing Xemnas evaporating into the ether. This does a better job of preserving tension and giving players a sense of accomplishment, while preserving the insertion of some flashy animation and VFX via cutscenes.

Figure 6.9 In *Okami*, the player controls a wolf goddess, though her most fearsome rivals are sometimes defeated with the help of the lazy, brave, and sometimes-pesky human warrior Susano (pictured swooping in to assist you in battle).

Credit: *Okami* is a trademark of Capcom Co., Ltd.

In this specific instance, we can say that players should be granted the agency to land the final blow against a boss during gameplay. More generally, the player needs to have an active role in important events; they need to be the star of their own experience.

A straightforward way to accomplish this in structuring a game's plot beats and narrative events is to understand the unique challenges of game writing from the outset. A game story is unlike any other story in that it happens *to* its audience, not in front of them. In writing a game, you shouldn't just be writing what happens in terms of plot. You should also be writing what the player experiences, with careful considerations for the consequences of their actions and what they will personally witness in a game's world.

Consequently, the player's experience needs to react to their actions. For every guard that you can intimidate after becoming a guild leader in *Skyrim*, you can find an NPC from that guild who will talk to you like a petulant child. And if you complete the quest where you literally assassinate the sitting emperor, you'll be shocked by how little impact your actions have. Aside from a few new voice snippets among townsfolk, the death of a world leader has virtually no impact outside of ticking a box in your quest journal. When a game's world or story doesn't react appropriately to a player, their agency is compromised. A player's sense of meaning, accomplishment, and immersion is strongly tied to how well their role in a game's world is realized.

As a final note, it should be reiterated that not all stories players will experience are written by developers. The term *emergent gameplay* is used to describe play which isn't explicitly planned by designers, and rather "emerges" from a player's interactions and experimentation with game systems. We can also speak of emergent stories in this regard. In strategy games like *Civilization*, narratives can emerge from a player's interactions with AI.[7] Games with sandbox elements or physics-based combat systems like *Just Cause*, *Grand Theft Auto V*, and *Metal Gear Solid V: The Phantom Pain* can create zany scenarios through player experimentation. For all the months spent on beautifully realized cutscenes, a player's favourite story might be one that comes from their own gameplay. That final action sequence you've so carefully crafted can pale in comparison to "that time I rode a cow, attached explosives to a hot air balloon, and almost killed myself."

This point brings us back to an insight we've reached time and again in the preceding pages. Players don't watch a story alongside a game, they live a story through a game. Whether orchestrated by designers, created through gameplay, or something in between, some of our dearest gaming memories can come from the stories we experience.

---

[7] One of the most widespread and memorable occurrences of this is "Nuclear Gandhi"—referring to Mahatma Gandhi's AI abruptly transforming from peace lover into nuke-happy supervillain. (While originally thought to be a bug, designer Sid Meier has since claimed that this was an intentional decision, presumably to provide a hilarious surprise in the stories players would create for themselves.)

Expert Profile: Osama Dorias—Something for everyone

Lead game designer at WB Games Montréal

Any game developer who's been at it for a while will have at least a few solid stories about their specialty. Osama Dorias isn't just any game developer, though, and when we sat down to chat with him, he treated us to a preview of the dozens of stories he's collected over the years.

Osama started his professional life as an agent in the shipping industry, and while he liked the people, the paperwork quickly lost its lustre. And after constant travelling made him miss one milestone too many, he decided to do something a bit more local. He took odd jobs in graphic design and tech support, all the while learning how to make games in Flash in his spare time. Not long after becoming a freelancer, he watched a friend break into the games industry full-time, and decided to try out the same path. Portfolio in hand, Osama says he applied for a hundred or more positions, and got a single callback, from mobile developer Gameloft.

At his interview, it became clear what Gameloft was looking for. One line on his CV in particular had piqued their interest: mention of a poker hobby with friends. Osama recounts the dialogue like something out of a sitcom: "So they're like '*Hey, we need a poker expert.*' I'm not a poker expert, [but] I'm like '*I'm a poker expert!*'" Pleased with his enthusiasm, the interviewer informed Osama that he'd be asked back for a poker knowledge test two days later. The next 48 hours whirled by in a montage of panic and excitement, buying up rulebooks and learning everything he could. If nothing else, Osama had demonstrated that he could pull off one hell of a bluff.

The day of the test came around, and Osama put forth his best effort. Achieving a perfect score, that effort surpassed the other candidates, and he got the job. On that first gig, everything was new, and he was learning on the fly. Despite doing quality work in everything from menu to AI design, Osama recalls a severe case of impostor syndrome. Three years and many projects later, he still felt guilty about fibbing during the interview, and invited his boss out for lunch to confess that he was never a poker expert. With a chuckle, Osama was reassured that nobody thought he was, or expected him to be. His boss said that what the studio really wanted was a quick learner who'd be useful on lots of projects, not just poker—and in Osama, they had found exactly that.

In the years he spent at Gameloft, Osama worked on lots of games for lots of platforms, including smartphones, the Nintendo DS, and the Wii. He says that he liked to "jump franchises" at the end of a project whenever he got the chance, to challenge himself and learn something new. Osama carried a similar attitude about his disciplinary focus, working in many different specialties including UI, gameplay, narrative, mission, and cinematics design. A decade after the poker interview, he's now a lead designer at WB Games, but describes himself as "a junior designer in 12 different fields."

Osama's varied interests and diverse expertise reflect his view of game design as a multifaceted domain. "Game design is not one discipline. It's like 20 disciplines layered on top of each other that are interconnected in very interesting ways. We are architects, and psychologists [. . .] We're worldbuilders, and storytellers. Game design means everything and nothing at the same time." Laughing, he mentions the caveat that game designers are "not necessarily really good at all of these things," but that diversity of interests strengthens the field, nonetheless.

When talking about interaction design, Osama says the first thing that comes to mind is the actions a player takes in a game's world through their character. He says that a good designer in this regard is "someone who can put themselves in the player's shoes," espousing empathy as a critical trait. He looks for this quality in new recruits, presenting them relatively simple scenarios with many possible resolutions and looking at whether would-be designers can think from a player's perspective. Creating good user experience, Osama says, is about designing a whole collection of satisfying interactions and feedback, which depends in turn on understanding players' needs and priorities.

On the subject of UX, Osama describes how game design as a whole has improved. In earlier days, he says that UX was "a thing that happened in between art and design, and it wasn't very clearly defined." He recalls artists and programmers he worked with who integrated user-centric thinking before the industry collectively realized its importance, noting that "people are more than just the role they have on paper." Today, he's noticed roles becoming more specialized and diverse, allowing the diverse subdisciplines of game design to earn the recognition they deserve. He notes that simultaneously, playtesting has gained a more solid footing, instead of stagnating in its early status as "a thing you did when it was too late to make any real changes to the game."

Unfortunately, not everything he's witnessed during his time in the games industry has been positive. Recently, he was asked to participate in a panel of industry veterans, noting that he hardly thinks of himself as a "veteran" after 12 years. But the reality of the games industry is one of high turnover, with many developers burning out entirely and switching careers after just a few years. Osama says empathy, that critical trait of a good designer, is something that's all-too often lacking in positions of higher management.

Games take a lot of time and skill to make, and finding highly skilled developers (or poker experts) is hard. The worst consequence emerging from these challenges is *crunch*, a word that will give any developer a pained expression. For the uninitiated, "crunch" describes a period of often mandatory, and often unpaid, overtime imposed on developers, often during the final stretches of a project. Osama describes the phenomenon as vicious and cyclic: "A lot of the studios crunch because they have a hard time hiring talent. So, they're trying to squeeze the most out of the talent that they have. But by squeezing their talent, they're losing them. So they have to repeat the cycle, endlessly."

The burden of fixing crunch, he says, can't be forced on its victims, particularly new employees and students entering the workforce: "If you're in a position where you're choosing between jobs, or even able to speak up within a job, that's a privilege. And a lot of the time, students don't have that privilege. It's rare that they do." Instead, he says, "the responsibility lies on people like me." In addition to making sure that his own team has a healthy working environment, he says that the security of his seniority allows him to publicly advocate for industry-wide improvements with less fear of being cast out. Besides crunch, Osama says that inclusion is another thing the industry needs to work on, with affirmative action as an important, if imperfect, first step towards moving past the problems we see today. He views his advocacy on these issues as an important step, noting that "the way to fight systemic things is to educate people." Taking action will benefit the industry in many ways; ultimately, Osama says that "happier people will make better games."

(Continued)

(Continued)

In his current role, Osama says he's shifted recently to learning more about management and communication than game design, on a path to becoming the best leader that he can be. Since his days of post-interview cramming, Osama has come a long way, but he's always looking for new challenges, and seems to have cemented himself as a generalist. For him, the beauty of game design is that there's always more to discover: "I love learning new things. This is my favourite thing."

Further reading

Slay the Dragon: Writing Great Video Games by Robert Denton Bryant and Keith Giglio (Michael Wiese). ISBN: 978-1615932290.

A good introductory volume on game writing and understanding what sets the structure of interactive narratives apart from regular storytelling.

The Gamer's Brain by Celia Hodent (CRC Press). ISBN: 978-1498775502.

An examination of the psychology of playing games, and consequently that of designing good games. Contains fascinating connections between cognitive science and user experience.

Video Games and the Mind edited by Bernard Perron and Felix Schröter (McFarland). ISBN: 978-0786499090.

A collection of essays on the emotional impact of games. (You might find a familiar name in the list of contributing authors.)

Authors' Note: Although hardly a formal resource, the site tvtropes.org catalogues a number of narrative archetypes throughout film, TV, literature, and games. It's an interesting rabbit hole to fall into, from which you'll always emerge with an ever-so-slightly more complete understanding of what makes stories tick in popular media.

Exercises

Anti-Hero complex

Take a game whose story you are familiar with and reimagine it if the player played as the game's current antagonist (i.e., the antagonist becomes the protagonist). Write out the game's main story beats from the perspective of your new protagonist. Jot down some notes on how the game might change to accommodate this new perspective. Here are some questions to get you started:

- How does your new protagonist become aware of their nemesis (the former hero)?
- Will you stay true to the game's original ending, or re-write it so that your new player character comes out on top in the end?

- Does the original protagonist play a significant role, or are they merely a side character in your new hero's journey?

To inform your ideas, try and pick out bits from the original game that characterize the (former) villain in a relatable or understandable light. If there are lots of details missing, try to fill in the gaps and imagine what motivates your character to act the way they do.

Paperback memories

Write out a short choose-your-own adventure story with at least four distinct decision points. You can outline your story by hand, or use a prototyping tool like Twine to help you. Try and find a way to make some different decisions eventually reconnect to one or two main plotlines—think about how you'd control scope if this narrative was to be used in a game. Insert notes on how you might use subtle cues to reflect past decisions, even if main story beats stay the same.

7

Rejecting your Reality

Virtual reality is an experience radically different from any other gaming platform. The jump from arcade cabinets to home devices was certainly something, but it pales in comparison to leaping from any other screen to one that's right in front of your face. VR is the ultimate first-person perspective. Slip on a virtual reality headset and you don't just have a window into a game's world; you become a part of it. Nothing can really compare to it—as much as the manufacturers of overpriced bits of cardboard for "smartphone VR" may want you to think otherwise.

Your first time in virtual reality isn't something you're likely to forget. Maybe you were at a crowded trade show, wondering if the 30-minute line to try the first Vive headset was really worth it. You watched one stranger after another bounce out of the booth grinning and gesturing to their friends. Eventually you found yourself at the front of the queue, and pondered for a moment whether you wanted the uniquely eclectic blend of sweat inside of that headset coming anywhere near your face. But, with the scent of alcohol wipes strong in the air, and yet another grinning patron emerging from the demo, your apprehensions lifted. And as soon as the visor descended, blocking out all the lights and chatter of the show floor, you knew something amazing was about to happen.

The displays in front of your eyes blinked on to reveal your virtual surroundings. Maybe it was a relatively simple space in an early demo of *Tilt Brush*, prompting you to create some 3D art. Maybe it was a game like *Beat Saber* that had you flailing around and out of breath in the first two minutes, giving the alcohol wipes a run for their money. Maybe it was a custom demo of a rollercoaster ride, a submarine journey, a forest clearing, or the far reaches of outer space.

At any rate, that first brush with a world outside our own is something that sticks with you. Barring any negative side effects (we'll get to that), it's something you'll want to do again. VR can wrap any of a hundred different

The Game Designer's Playbook. Samantha Stahlke and Pejman Mirza-Babaei, Oxford University Press.
© Samantha Stahlke and Pejman Mirza-Babaei (2022). DOI: 10.1093/oso/9780198845911.003.0007

worlds around you. To interact with that world is an experience of play which is engaging and immersive like no other. From the second that display comes to life in front of your eyes, you'll be treasuring every moment.

The cool factor of VR is undeniable. Its promise is seductive, offering a piece of the technological utopia that science fiction has promised us for the past century. And yet, if the current state of virtual reality lived up to this promise in every sense, adoption rates would be far higher.

At the time of this writing, just shy of 2% of users on Steam, the largest digital distribution platform for PC, own a virtual reality headset.[1] VR hasn't quite taken off in the mainstream, and understandably so. Headsets are still expensive, with even budget options running about the same price as a console. Those low buy-in rates combined with comparatively few dedicated multiplayer titles mean there's little peer pressure to take the plunge. Setup is a nuisance, with every headset having some compromise or another in the form of cumbersome wires, bulky tracking stations, or lesser screen quality. Most importantly, with a few notable exceptions, the VR release schedule isn't packed to the gunnels with over-marketed and over-hyped upcoming titles like those driving the console exclusive wars or the race to upgrade one's graphics card.

These compromises along with other factors contribute to a number of design challenges endemic to VR. A lack of widespread adoption means that regular VR use is still new to the vast majority of users. Much of the background knowledge and intuition built up from a lifetime of gamepads and keyboards doesn't necessarily apply in VR, which can make onboarding difficult. This is compounded by constantly evolving and wildly diverse hardware, demanding accommodation for different controller variants (or in some cases, relying on a user's hands alone). Design standards for VR are still being established, and with a relative dearth of existing titles in comparison to other markets, developers have less of a chance to learn from the successes and failures of others.

Some additional problems arise from the very nature of VR. A lack of proper force feedback limits our ability to make interactions feel natural, relying on tricks to accomplish something like making an object feel heavy. Making users feel comfortable can be tough, with many susceptible to a phenomenon similar to motion sickness. While design choices can help to mitigate or even prevent this effect depending on the user, these choices are not always obvious from the outset. Even for users that eventually gain their "VR legs," it's easy to become disoriented with respect to the real world. The internet is replete with videos showing exactly what happens when some

---

[1] Source: Steam's official hardware survey, accessible as of this writing at https://store. steampowered.com/hwsurvey/

headset-clad rube forgets where they are and full-on headbutts a credenza (or their roommate).

Balancing the enticing possibilities of this platform with the complications it poses is the challenge of designing for virtual reality. VR isn't just a generational leap; it represents a fundamental change in the way we think about understanding game interaction.

7.1 Designing for VR

The use of the term "virtual reality" has shifted somewhat over the years, and has further contextual nuances to boot. Here, we use a colloquial interpretation of the term, referring to the wearable headsets[2] available to consumers. The defining feature of VR is placing the user in a digital space, where they can look and move around by physically moving their head and typically their body. In pure virtual reality, the real world is made to be unseen and unheard, only keeping track of boundaries to prevent accident and injury while moving around.

A cousin of virtual reality is augmented reality (AR), which refers to the superposition of digital elements on a view of the real world. Most AR applications run on smartphones, using the device's camera to provide a live feed on which additional graphics are overlain. An example is 2016's cultural behemoth *Pokémon Go*, which let users chase down and capture cuddly and not-so-cuddly creatures in their own neighbourhoods.

Yet another term related to VR is mixed reality (MR), which has a frustratingly muddy interpretation lying somewhere in between virtual and augmented reality. Usually, this means wearing a headset like you might for VR, but seeing something akin to AR instead of a fully digital world. Mixed reality demands a more advanced form of AR, which can appropriately respond to changes in the physical world and the interactions of the user. In a mixed reality application, you might transform your area rug into an ocean, able to push around physical odds and ends which turn into digital battleships. As appealing as this proposition is, mixed reality isn't yet widely available, and presents technological and economic challenges even beyond those of VR.

To put it bluntly, augmented reality isn't all that interesting when held up next to virtual or mixed reality, and mixed reality isn't here just yet. VR, on the other hand, is both quite interesting and already here, though it has resided perpetually in its status as "the next big thing" for the last ten years.

---

[2] As of this writing, popular commercial examples include the PlayStation VR, Oculus Rift, HTC Vive, and Valve Index headsets.

Our discussion here will focus on VR as a result, though many insights regarding naturalistic interaction and immersion in Section 7.2 apply to its exotic siblings as well.

7.1.1 What VR gives us

A typical VR headset uses a combination of microelectronic sensors including gyroscopes, magnetometers, and accelerometers to determine the orientation of a user's head. In theory, an accelerometer alone can also allow for positional tracking. In practice, the data from an accelerometer is too noisy to provide any acceptable level of accuracy in this regard, so it is combined with the use of cameras on a headset's exterior to track user position. This can be done with optical recognition of surroundings like walls and furniture, or more commonly, measuring the time discrepancy in receiving synchronized flashes of infrared light emitted from stationary beacons. Similar systems are used to track the position and orientation of the handheld controllers featured by most commercial headsets.

In a PC or console game, the game's "camera" renders to the user's screen. The camera is positioned either automatically (e.g., fixed top-view), by the user (e.g., rotated around their character with an analog stick), or with a combination of both user input and automated adjustments. In VR, the game camera is posed based on the known position and orientation of the user's head. The view from this camera is rendered on two displays, one for each eye. Strictly speaking, each eye usually has a separate camera, with a slightly different view providing stereoscopic vision. Just as in the real world, stereoscopic vision allows users to perceive fine differences in depth based on the position of elements in the virtual world relative to each eye.[3]

Of course, what we have described here is a high-level summary of what the "average" modern VR headset does. Some headsets differ in their application of these features, but regardless of implementation, VR gives us some interesting things to keep in mind and play with in designing interactions. Both in terms of how we communicate with games and how games communicate with us, VR is a unique beast in comparison to traditional digital gaming.

Visual immersion. Inside virtual reality, the real world effectively disappears. VR headsets block out light to prevent bleed-through from ruining visual quality, serving also to minimize distraction. This serves to force immersion, sticking the game world an inch from the player's eyes with nothing

---

[3] Unfortunately, if like one of the authors you are partially sighted or blind in one eye, VR will not magically fix your depth perception, and you can continue to enjoy misjudging basketball shots and incoming projectiles in the virtual world as you do in reality.

else in sight. If given the chance, players can appreciate much smaller details in their environment, holding an object up to their face or crouching in a corner to examine some curiosity on the ground. The act of looking around in VR is much more engaging than manipulating a camera with a mouse or analog stick, breathing new life into gameplay that involves searching your environment, aiming a weapon, or other tasks involving visual perception and hand-eye coordination.

Spatial audio. On other platforms, players might use all sorts of solutions for audio. In a game where spatial audio is particularly important, you can probably persuade users to put on a headset. In general, though, console and PC players might be using any number of external speaker configurations. Mobile players will frequently have their devices muted entirely, unless they decide to become everyone's least favourite person on the train that day.

In VR, on the other hand, it's a safe bet that players have speakers jammed right up against their ears. Several headsets come with inbuilt speakers, and most all offer an onboard jack for users to plug in their own headphones. Provided that users want sound, with the rare exception of showing something off to friends, they'll be wearing their audio instead of piping it somewhere else. This further reduces the impact of external stimuli, blotting out noise from the real world. It also pretty well guarantees that you can use precise spatial audio cues to provide players with richer feedback, without worry that a large portion of your user base will lose out as a result of their speaker setup.

Gesture-driven controls. All popular commercial headsets offer some way of tracking the player's hands, typically by way of handheld controllers. Some controllers, like those that ship with the Valve Index, provide even finer information on the position of a user's fingers, allowing you to point or make a fist in the digital world. Even basic hand position tracking offers the possibility of replacing what would otherwise be a button press with gestural controls. This can make interaction more natural, intuitive, and fun.

Potential for full-body movement. The combination of head and hand positions, in combination with some old-hat development tricks like inverse kinematics, is already enough to approximate a user's full-body pose. Additional position trackers, though not widely popular, can provide further pose information, such as sensors that can strap onto your feet. Regardless of how precisely we can estimate the fine details of a user's position, even basic information provides us with some interesting opportunities. For instance, a headset's distance to the ground in comparison with a user's height gives us jumping and crouching—combined with hand position, this is everything we need to get users dancing, dodging obstacles, or taking cover in a shooter.

The crux of all of this is that we as designers need to take advantage of these features to succeed. This isn't as simple as slapping a new coat of paint on a successful game, mapping the camera to the headset, and calling it a day. As much fun as *Skyrim* is in all its many iterations between PC, console, and PalmPilot, its VR port is mediocre in capitalizing on things like gestural control. Compare this to one of the many successful games designed for VR first (or exclusively), like the physics-based madness of *Boneworks*, and it is obvious that good VR design is about far more than adjusting to a new paradigm of camera movement. A memorable experience in virtual reality is one that thoughtfully integrates the unique features it offers—and plans ahead to compensate for its shortcomings.

7.2 What we don't want VR to give us

The feelings you want your game to evoke depend on your design intent. Maybe you're looking to make players laugh, give them suspense, or strike fear into their hearts. Irrespective of your design intent, it's probably safe to say you would prefer that your game doesn't evoke headache, dizziness, sweating, and nausea.

Unfortunately, these symptoms are a relatively common complaint among new VR users, and can persist for many people even after having a fair bit of experience. Termed "simulation sickness" or even "VR sickness," this unpleasant ailment is something akin to motion sickness.[4] There are a few different theories as to what causes VR sickness, but the prevailing explanation is that it results from a mismatch between the vestibular system and other sensory stimuli. In other words, your vision says "motion," but your inner ear says, "you can't fool me, we're standing still, and now it's time to vomit." More precisely, your vision (and/or hearing) indicate an acceleration of some sort, but that acceleration doesn't match with your movement in the real world. For instance, you push forward on an analog stick to move in VR, and your viewpoint starts to move forward, but you stay standing still. Other factors can exacerbate the effect of VR sickness as well; mild symptoms can become worse after an extended period in a headset which is typically heavy and quite warm.

We have three options in addressing VR sickness. First, we could tell players that VR isn't for them, or to only play games that don't make them sick. Second, we could assume that anyone susceptible will play clutching their Dramamine, and self-moderate to prevent serious discomfort. Lastly,

---

[4] While still a relatively nascent area of research, some estimate the incidence of VR sickness to be quite high; in this article (link current as of this writing), kinesiologist Thomas Stoffregen estimates that 40–70% of players experience motion sickness after spending 15 minutes in VR: https://insidescience.org/news/cybersickness-why-people-experience-motion-sickness-during-virtual-reality

we could do our jobs and find ways to make our games more accessible by eliminating or providing options to reduce factors associated with sickness.

Since this is a book about game design and not a web forum, we'll opt for the third approach. Although designing for VR is still a relatively new challenge, there are already a few things we can do to drastically limit the likelihood that players will become sick, and reduce the severity of symptoms experienced.

Performance. Low refresh rates and high latency can potentially induce VR sickness, or make it much worse. Most commercial headsets offer a fairly high refresh rate, though the current standard of 90 Hz is likely to increase as technology improves. To reduce the chance of sickness, games should keep up with the headset they're played on, maintaining a stable framerate (i.e., 90 frames per second for a 90 Hz display). This already exceeds the performance target of most console or PC games, which typically aim for 30 or 60 FPS on average hardware. However, the demands don't stop there—assuming you're going for the stereoscopic effect, you'll need to render separately to each eye, hitting the equivalent of 180 FPS.

Even on very high-end hardware, meeting these requirements is hard for a graphically complex experience. While performance is a technical problem and not a design one, you might find yourself in a position where you'll be choosing between visual fidelity and a higher or more stable framerate. With incredibly rare exception, for a VR game, that choice should favour performance. Quality assurance (QA) testing should also focus on identifying potential framerate drops or latency spikes, which can be significant annoyances on any platform. In VR, these issues can quickly induce nausea, and are thus of vital importance to identify.

Locomotion systems. In a designated "standing VR" experience, players can be largely stationary while they play. In a strictly "room-scale" game, the game world is only as large as the physical space players have available to move around in the real world. In any other game, the game world will be larger than the player's physical play-space, and players will have to be able to move around somehow. This presents a conundrum: how do we let players move around virtually in a way that mismatches their physical movement *without* inducing VR sickness?

A naïve implementation of player locomotion in VR is a straight port of standard first-person movement. You hold forward on an analog stick, and your avatar moves in the direction the camera (i.e., your head) is facing. To spin around, you can spin around in the real world, thus re-orienting the headset you're wearing. Alternatively, you can use another analog stick to turn smoothly without spinning around yourself. The problem with this approach is that it can easily and rapidly make players feel sick, by creating those sensory mismatches we discussed earlier. When your avatar starts to

Figure 7.1 Four options for moving from point 1 to point 2 in VR. A) Walking forward in the physical space mapped to walking forward in the virtual world. B) Using a controller to point at location 2 before triggering a teleport. C) Moving an analog stick to move smoothly forward in the virtual world. D) Triggering an automatic fade out of the player's view in location 1 and fade in of their view in location 2.

move forward, you visually perceive a change in speed from stationary to moving; it looks like you're accelerating, but you're not physically moving. Turning around using the analog stick presents the same problem: you visually perceive angular acceleration, but your orientation hasn't physically changed.

There are a couple of things that we can do to improve on "standard" locomotion in VR. Players should also have the option to move in the direction their hands are pointing instead of the direction they're currently looking. Though it may sound strange at first, this allows players to look around while walking, using their body to control the direction of movement rather than their head. This is a more accurate reflection of locomotion in the real world, and prevents subtle unintended changes in direction if players are locked to moving in the direction they're currently looking. Additionally, if your head is turned relative to your body, moving in the direction you're looking creates a feeling of strafing, which will feel less natural for most players in comparison to moving in the direction their hands (and feet) are pointing.

Another improvement is the implementation of "snap" turning. While many players may prefer to physically spin themselves around, repeated turning can become a nuisance when dealing with the tether cable that most VR headsets still require. Snap turning lets players rotate their viewpoint instantaneously by some increment (e.g., 45 degrees), all but eliminating the perception of angular acceleration while allowing players to turn around quickly in the virtual world with a few flicks of an analog stick. With support for snap turning and controller/hands-relative movement, smooth locomotion can become a viable option for players who would otherwise become sick. One last thing you can consider is applying a light blinder-type effect to the periphery of the player viewport during smooth movement—effectively reducing field-of-view—which some academic work has suggested may further reduce discomfort.

Even with these changes, smooth locomotion can still be sickening for some players. The best option for accessibility here is to offer an optional teleportation-based mode. Teleportation systems allow players to point at a desired location, typically within a certain radius of their current spot, and press a button or flick their analog stick to instantly arrive at their destination. This removes the sensory mismatch created by smooth forward movement, thus reducing the likelihood of serious VR sickness.

Teleportation is, at least currently, the ideal locomotion solution for people especially prone to VR sickness. It can also provide a bridge for players who are new to VR to gain some experience and acclimate over time before eventually moving to a smooth locomotion system. However, implementing teleportation can require a bit of extra thinking on the part of designers. The ability to teleport a few metres away at a moment's notice can provide an unintended gameplay advantage. For example, in a shooter, a player could teleport behind cover or away from a grenade. When faced with an environmental puzzle requiring players to build some sort of ladder or bridge, teleportation might allow them to skip it. These problems are not unsolvable; for instance, if players are required to solve a puzzle, you could simply remove the ability to teleport beyond that point until they complete it.

Any gameplay advantage which is trickier to account for, like teleporting behind cover, is typically worth it for improved accessibility. The question here becomes "Can I really let a few players get away with cheesing the mechanics for improved accessibility?" The answer is yes. Preserving bragging rights for achievements over the ability of certain people to play your game is ridiculous. Even with that cover issue we mentioned earlier, Valve's VR shooter *Half-Life: Alyx* offers a slew of movement options, including teleportation. Teleportation doesn't lock you out of earning any achievements, either—in a single-player game, having a slight "competitive edge" doesn't impact anyone else's experience.

Alyx's contemporary physics-based cousin *Boneworks* doesn't offer a teleport option, with the official word from the developer being that it would "make much of the game physically impossible."[5] This is disappointing; while teleportation can certainly break some puzzles dependent on climbing or similar, providing players with accessibility concerns a way to enjoy the game at all should take priority over preserving the "purity" of the experience. The only argument here is that additional options incur a resource cost developers can't realistically afford—which is certainly valid. However, given the prevalence of players prone to VR sickness, investing in the option is likely worth it for the majority of projects.

In a multiplayer game, allowing this compromise can be trickier. Competitive shooter *Pavlov VR* no longer offers a teleport option, which would provide a distinct advantage over players using smooth locomotion. However, in such scenarios it would be beneficial to offer a game mode which enables teleportation for accessibility, giving all players the advantage up front.

Camera design. Another source of sensory mismatch comes from how a game handles its camera. On any other platform, you wouldn't think twice about doing something like taking control of the camera for a cutscene. In VR, yanking control of a player's viewpoint away from them, especially unannounced, is a recipe for disaster. If you need to "move" the player, you should prompt players to move themselves, either with explicit instruction or by providing a point of interest at the desired location with sound or visual effects. Alternatively, you can move some of the action to them, for instance, by having a character walk over.

Should neither of these options work for your desired experience, consider moving things *around* the player, providing some stationary references to prevent them from perceiving their avatar as accelerating through the world. For a complete scene change, you should never "cut" unannounced, as a jarring change in viewpoint which isn't controlled by the player (e.g., via snap turn or teleport) can be uncomfortable. Instead, prefer a fade to a neutral colour like grey or black before fading back to a new location or viewpoint.

---

[5] Official developer account response to a player question on the Steam forums: https:// steamcommunity.com/app/823500/discussions/3/1660069015247587262/

If you're wondering how to mimic something like a dramatic landscape panning shot without making players sick, the answer is that you can't, really, at least not universally. Fading to the interior of a vehicle already moving slowly might work, reducing the perception of acceleration. But, when architecting cinematic sequences in VR, try to ask yourself if you can replicate the *purpose* of a given shot or scene without trying to visually imitate it. The point of a dramatic landscape pan is to let players take in the beauty of an area, provide a sense of scale, and maybe a moment of relaxation. All of these things can be accomplished by placing the player on a hill and letting them look around for themselves, while greatly reducing the risk of VR sickness.

Other commonplace camera manipulations can also cause problems in VR. In non-VR first-person games, a degree of head bob is often added to the camera to give the impression of a character walking or running. This effect can be quite nice if you're sitting in front of a screen, but can easily cause queasiness in VR, since the motion is *added* on top of the player's actual head movements. Another thing that should be avoided is zooming the camera; giving players an object they can manipulate like a rifle scope or binoculars is usually just fine, but zooming their entire field of view, especially unannounced, is unadvisable.

The last thing to be careful of here are visual effects and post-processing like screen-shake, motion blur, varying chromatic aberration, and flickering lights. Any effects which are traditionally used to create a sense of motion or disorientation on other platforms—like using screen shake to emphasize a nearby explosion in *Battlefield V*—simply work *too well* in VR. These effects can be suitable for someone who is not susceptible to VR sickness, and/or has a lot of experience. However, if you're planning to include any form of post-processing which induces a sense of motion or flickering, you should opt to disable these effects by default and present first-time players with a prompt to enable them if confident in their "VR legs."

Play habits. VR sickness usually isn't all or nothing; some players may feel sick immediately, but many will be able to play comfortably for short periods, while still others can play for hours without ill effect. Anecdotally, players often report building up a tolerance, being able to play comfortably for longer after having more experience in VR. Nonetheless, you should not assume that all players will be able to comfortably play for long stretches.

There are several ways to design around this. For both single- and multiplayer titles, you can design play to occur in bite-sized chunks, which players can choose to experience one at a time or back-to-back if their tolerance is higher. In *Beat Saber*'s campaign, for instance, like other rhythm games, players can experience the game one song at a time. Longer-form games can compensate for this with save systems, by allowing players to save at any time (e.g., *Half-Life: Alyx*) or providing a checkpoint system which creates natural stopping points (e.g., added in an update for *Boneworks*). The ability to pause for a quick break to take a drink of water or cool off is also vital; while infeasible in general for multiplayer, providing the option for hosts of a friendly game to pause the action for less experienced players is a welcome design choice.

You might also consider an optional, timed prompt reminding players to drink water, rest their eyes, and take a break. For those prone to VR sickness, a customizable reminder can help them to regulate their play sessions and pause *before* unpleasant symptoms set in. You can also recommend some tips for players new to VR about their physical play-space, such as setting up a cooling fan if they have one, which can help to alleviate nausea and counteract the heat given off by a VR headset.

Regardless of whether players experience some form of VR sickness, these considerations can also help to alleviate the universal concerns of fatigue and repetitive physical stress. Many VR titles require players to stand, walk around, and make heavy use of gestural controls (for good reason). However, this can be strenuous, particularly if you're used to the more traditional paradigm of sitting down and not moving around much during a game. Sufficient playtesting to make sure that the gestural interactions demanded by regular play are not too taxing, and giving players the opportunity to tackle a game in short bursts can help make your game a more comfortable experience for all players.

7.3 Putting the "real" in reality

VR gives us plenty of compelling features out of the gate: a true first-person perspective, support for gestural controls, and near-perfect sensory immersion. Almost any experience in VR will be cool for at least a few minutes to a first-time user. To make a more captivating creation with some longevity, though, we cannot rely on the novelty of the platform alone. A VR headset by its very nature promotes total immersion, but making players feel fully present in a game's world is more complicated than just wearing that headset. Gestural controls are always a fun gimmick, but making an interaction feel satisfying is more complicated than taking a problem and throwing motion sensors at it.

Certainly, what we have discussed in the preceding chapters in terms of feedback and control design still applies in VR. However, interaction design in VR demands additional considerations for the unique opportunities it offers, particularly in terms of control design. In creating entirely new experiences for VR or adapting our existing ideas, three main factors can help to shape our understanding of how players should interact with the digital world: intuition, tangibility, and the novelty factor.

Intuition. It is three o'clock in the morning, and your smoke alarm's battery is low. Naturally, to let you know, it is kind enough to start screaming at you. You startle awake, run downstairs, wrest it from the ceiling, and get a new battery ready. But now is the time you've been dreading. You need to slide the panel off the battery compartment. First you have to find the panel, which is tricky enough as the entire thing looks like a smaller and more impenetrable version of the Pentagon. After you find the panel, you can't remember how it slides off, because it exhibits eight degrees of lateral symmetry and there are no markings anywhere on the damned thing except for a tiny picture of fire. You try sliding it in each of the cardinal directions five times with varying amounts of force before cursing and chucking the thing across the room, at which point the panel pops off and your bleary-eyed spouse peers in to inquire about the racket.

Intuition is our ability to understand something without or having to spend time reasoning about it. Something is intuitive if we can use it without getting instructions or having to think about it very much. Most things aspire to be intuitive. A save button bearing the image of a floppy disk (to those of you born after the turn of the millennium, a "floppy disk" is that thing on the save icon) is intuitive. The panel on your smoke alarm is not.

The design principle of affordance, discussed in Chapter 5, is essentially an ethos of capitalizing on intuition. Affordances tell us how to use something without explicit instruction. The evolution of affordances in design from physical products to video games is interesting. In the real world, the design of a cup's handle suggests how it should be held based on your experience and the shape of your hands. This is an affordance. In a digital game, we can describe "perceived" affordances based on experience specific to the medium: the presence of a cup on a table suggests that you can probably liberate that cup into your inventory by pressing a button. Here's the catch—in VR, we can (and should) return to physical affordances in many cases. If you see a cup on a table, your first instinct won't be to press a button. Assuming it's within arm's reach, you'll reach out for the handle and try to grab it instead. In a world where you look around by moving your head instead of a mouse, the intuitive choice is to pick things up by moving and grabbing with your hands instead of pressing a button.

Looting is a good example of how perceived affordances on other platforms have evolved into physical affordances in VR. On any other platform, if you see a dead enemy or stack of items, the expected interaction is that you will walk over and press a button to collect supplies, perhaps with an intermediate menu to select what you'll take. *Borderlands, Destiny, Red Dead Redemption, Fallout, Dishonored*—pretty much every game that you can touch with some action subgenre has some form of "Press X to loot." In VR, the paradigm is different. If you find an ammo crate in *Boneworks*, you walk over and pick it up instead of pointing and pressing a button. In *Half-Life: Alyx*, you can pluck grenades and weapon clips off of your dead adversaries. On top of being incredibly satisfying, this choice is also more intuitive. In designing interactions for VR, we can't blindly follow the conventions established for other digital games; we need to consider the conventions of the physical world.

Figure 7.2 In *Boneworks*, grabbing any object—prop, loot, or otherwise—is a matter of physically grabbing it, not just pointing and pressing a button.

Credit: Boneworks was developed and published by Stress Level Zero.

Gestural interaction makes this type of design "easy" to an extent for basic interactions. If something can be reasonably mapped to its analog in the real world, then it should be. This serves to lower the cognitive demand of onboarding by relying on the real-world experiences common to all players, reducing the need for tutorial prompts and giving players fewer key bindings to memorize. Moreover, most VR controllers have just a few buttons, so this thinking will help you to save those buttons for actions that are less intuitive to map gesturally, like toggling menus.

Mimicking less obvious nuances of real-world interaction can further boost intuitiveness while providing players with a satisfying sense of attention to detail. Aiming a weapon by moving your hand and shooting by using a controller's trigger is intuitive. Taking this a step further to mimic some context-specific behaviour of real guns—or things players might have seen in action movies—juices up those interactions further. In *Pavlov VR*, for example, players can mount a virtual stock on their weapon to (pretend) brace it against their shoulder, stabilizing their reticle and reducing the impact of shaky hands. Some guns are also made for two-handed play, with aim stabilization if both hands are positioned properly. Another example is the favoured reload technique for shotguns in either *Pavlov* or *Alyx*: after inserting new rounds, you can flick your wrist backwards to secure the barrel, gunslinger-style.

Tangibility. One of the many reasons why it is fun to throw rocks at things is because rocks are heavy, which makes them feel satisfying to pick up and launch like the big strong person that you are. Unfortunately, no matter how heavy a rock, gun, frying pan, or captive sea slug should be, in VR, everything is exactly as heavy as the controller you're holding. At least for now, VR is still a little too V for its own good. High-fidelity force feedback is one thing currently out of reach alongside comfortable omnidirectional treadmills and affordable full-body tracking with decent precision. Despair not, though, for there are a few design tricks we can employ to make interactions feel weighty, even with only basic VR controllers (or a player's hands) at our disposal.

Our first course of action is to seek out the one bit of force feedback that we do have: haptics. Applying a bit of vibration at the right time and with the right intensity curve can give players an effective impression of resistance. This is commonly used to simulate recoil in VR shooters like *Onward* and *Robo Recall*. Though the intensity of controller vibration doesn't measure up to a real weapon, it's certainly better than nothing. Haptics can also shine in other contexts; in *Beat Saber*, for instance, whenever the player's sword slices through a block, a vibration curve matching the speed of the virtual blade is applied, giving a pretty convincing impression of resistance lending weight to player's rhythmic strokes.

Other tricks rely purely on our design prowess to give the impression of force feedback without any real ability to do so. A commonly employed strategy to make objects seem heavy is to limit the speed at which a player's virtual hands can move while holding a heavy object. This might seem like an objectively bad idea; having your virtual hands lagging behind your real hands is surely frustrating. Furthermore, as a mismatch between proprioception (bodily awareness) and vision, you might have concerns about wooziness. Unfortunately, there is little evidence that we could find as of this writing to thoroughly validate or debunk virtual hand latency as a contributor to VR sickness. However, since it doesn't involve latency in head movement (and thus viewpoint) or imply full-body acceleration, you're probably safe from sensory mismatch-induced sickness in this case. This leaves the question of frustration: how can what amounts to deliberate input lag possibly be a good idea?

If we step back to consider how weight is applied to interactions in the real world and other games, it starts to become clear why this might be a workable solution. If your character is dragging away a body in *Dishonored*, you move more slowly; it would be immersion-breaking if you could haul away a human at full sprint. If Link is using a heavier weapon in *Breath of the Wild*, it takes him longer to swing. Slowing things down on purpose is sometimes exactly what you need to do to meet player expectations. In the real world, if you're lifting something heavy, it's going to take you longer to raise your arms than if you weren't holding anything at all. And since we're unable to physically force players to move more slowly, mimicking this with their virtual hands is one of the only options we've got.

In practice, this technique works pretty well. *Boneworks* employs this liberally to give its physics-based world more weight with props and weapons. Unburdened, the player's hands in VR map exactly to their real-world position. When trying to move something heavy, they'll be artificially limited, lagging behind if players try and move quickly in reality. The effect of this as you play can work surprisingly well to change player behaviour. If something looks heavy, based on both your real-world expectations and the knowledge that the game will limit you, you'll instinctively start to move more slowly when picking it up. Instead of flinging your hands around and sighing in frustration at lag, you'll feel a sense of weight, even though the controllers in your hand haven't changed. This tactic carries through in swinging melee weapons, giving them a satisfying physics-y punch when biting into enemies. The ability to pick up a heavy crowbar, perceive its weight through virtual fakery, and crack someone over the head with it is terrifically visceral.

One last thing we can do is rely on other forms of feedback to help things feel more tangible. In *Keep Talking and Nobody Explodes*, the bombs players are made to defuse feel like wonderfully complicated fidget toys. Irrespective of other tricks, visual and sound design helps bring players' interactions with the bomb to life. A tangle of gnarled wires lets you cut them with satisfying little snips, while every big red button delivers through on the promise of a tactile click. In combination with other tricks, regular old feedback does a lot for us in this regard; the weightiness of that crowbar in Boneworks is further emphasized through the satisfying *thunk* you hear when flinging it around.

Novelty. Your first time in VR is especially entertaining for the same reason that first learning the word "defenestrate" is amusing—it's novel, and rather odd in comparison to your usual experience in game-playing or word-hearing.[6] Preserving that novelty can be a challenge, though it ultimately comes down to applying the same sort of innovative thinking you'd strive for in any game's design to the unique features offered by VR.

To understand this strategy, it's best to consider the implications of the opposite. Taking a page out of Chapter 5, we'll take a look at an unimaginative port, the design space where innovation goes to die. We've already alluded to some disappointment with the VR version of *Skyrim*, and a complete lack

---

[6] If this happens to be your first literary encounter with defenestration, it is the act of throwing someone out of a window.

of novelty is one reason the game can't hold itself up as a system seller à la *Beat Saber* or *Alyx*. Take switching or putting away weapons, a simple interaction fundamental to the combat loop. In *Boneworks*, you can put away a melee weapon by letting it go over your hip (or shoulder), and you can retrieve it by grabbing on your person where it was stashed. *Alyx* uses a radial menu activated with touchpad and a flick of the wrist to switch between the available weapons and tools, while grenades and ammunition are stashed on the player's body. *Skyrim VR* makes you pause the game and scroll through a menu to switch weapons, while sheathing is mapped to a button press. This is a direct mapping of what you'd expect from a console game (albeit even worse from the lack of quick-select), failing to have any semblance of the novelty that can make VR interactions particularly fun and engaging.

Figure 7.3 In *Half-Life: Alyx*, players can interact with pretty much anything that isn't bolted down. But instead of just walking up to things and grabbing them, Alyx's "grabbity gloves," known to foremost experts as Russells, can be used to fling objects around. With the smallest bit of practice, players can wing objects across the room into their waiting grasp with ease.

Credit: Half-Life: Alyx was developed and published by Valve.

Those system-selling games we mentioned take a more innovative and platform-considerate design approach to heart. An excellent example of this thinking is the so-called "gravity gloves" in *Alyx*. Like any shooter, playing *Alyx* requires you to be on the lookout for resources strewn about the game's world, like ammunition, health boosters, and explosives. Except instead of relying on boring button presses or even walking over and picking things up, Valve has a far more engaging solution for most of the looting you'll be doing. In *Alyx*, you can point at something, depress the trigger, and flick your wrist backwards to beckon it in a graceful arc into your waiting hands. Naturally, this only works for objects light enough to pick up, and you actually have to catch the thing when it sails into your arms.

The gravity glove interaction is expertly designed for a few reasons. First, it's easy to learn, taking advantage of the pre-existing standard of laser-like point-to-aim that most VR games use for in-game menus. Second, it helps prevent fatigue and motion sickness by reducing the need for players to physically move around in the game's world. You can accomplish a lot (if you so choose) by standing in place and flicking things around with your wrist. It's also largely optional, so any players who find the repetitive wrist motion uncomfortable are free to move about and loot as normal. The best thing about this interaction, though, is its novelty. At the time of release, it wasn't quite like anything else in VR, and gave the player a fun way to grab things that called back thematically to the gravity gun of earlier *Half-Life* games. After a long play-session, you might find yourself pointing at things in reality and flicking your wrist, like some telekinetic embodiment of the Tetris effect.

Novelty doesn't have to depend entirely on VR-exclusive features like hand tracking, though. Ghost-hunting fun in *Phasmophobia* is compounded by inventive interactions like using voice input to have players call out questions to troubled spirits. This doesn't *require* VR to work, though it does leverage the fact that the majority of VR headsets have inbuilt microphones—meaning players won't be rifling around for a mic like they might in a console or PC game. Like any other underused form of interaction, this provides a bit of a pleasant surprise which lends the experience some flair.

7.3.1 *Amping up immersion*

Having addressed considerations for one side of the game interaction equation, our next step is to examine the other, looking at how a VR game can communicate effectively with players. Here, we're not just concerned with functionality; what we've already discussed in regard to the sensory representation of information still applies. More specific to VR is how a game communicates its intended atmosphere, and contributes to players' sense of presence and immersion. With the right approach, VR experiences are exceptional at making you feel acutely focused on both the present moment and of your place in a game's world.

Combined with the right level of challenge, this sublime sense of presence is a recipe for the enigmatic state of *flow*, a term coined by renowned psychologist and bearer of objectively awesome surname Mihaly Csikszentmihalyi. Flow describes the phenomenon of total absorption in the task at hand. In games, this is achieved when the challenge offered by a game matches perfectly with a player's skill level, and the player is able to focus completely on play. The ideal flow state is sometimes described as trancelike or "zen."

Players have a sort of intense serenity as they nimbly work through obstacles that demand enough attention to inspire total focus without resulting in anxiety. In the reduced-distraction, increased-presence environment of virtual reality, achieving flow is a truly magical thing to experience.

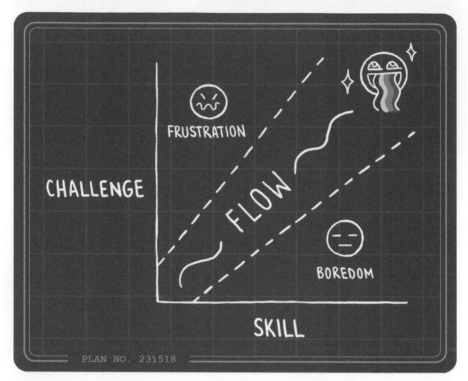

Figure 7.4 The flow state occurs when the challenge offered by a game is in balance with the player's level of skill. If the player's skill is high and challenge is low, a game can become boring. If challenge outpaces a player's skill, a game can become frustrating.

Our conversation then pivots to how we can boost immersion, making our worlds seem as real as possible, and presence, ensuring players feel their place in those worlds. While a great deal of artistry is involved with such an undertaking, there are a few general tactics we can identify in service to this goal.

Consider limited-scale design. Having a larger-than-life world as you might find in a title like *Jet Island*, or the incomprehensibly massive landscapes of *No Man's Sky* (playable in VR), can be breathtaking. Due to their size, these worlds necessitate a locomotion system on top of players' physical movement. Using an analog stick to walk around or teleporting from place to place is a perfectly fine experience, but being able to move around in the real world is even better. To map players' physical movement to their virtual movement 1:1, we need to design for a virtual space no larger than the physical space we can reasonably expect, usually a couple of metres on edge.

SEATED   STANDING   ROOM-SCALE

PLAN NO. 18151513

Figure 7.5 Three different paradigms for experiencing VR with varying levels of freedom to move in the real world.

This might sound incredibly restrictive at first, but "room-scale" (playable with a small area of free space) and "standing" (playable with only head and slight arm movements) VR experiences can some of the most memorable and engaging. As is often the case, constraints can serve to enhance rather than diminish creativity.

Superhot is a game adapted remarkably well to VR, playable in a standing or room-scale context. Its gimmick of time only moving forward when the player moves physically feels especially powerful in VR, but level design is what really makes it work. Locales are varied, with each short segment giving the player an interesting vantage point to fight from before teleporting them "forward" in the setting of a loosely structured story. Plenty of cover and interactable objects are given within arms' reach, and enemies are always moving toward you. This brings the action to you, providing ample opportunities to engage and defend without needing a massive space to roam around.

Games designed from the ground up with room-scale or stationary play in mind often have a unique feel. With traditional locomotion removed, a core component of the "typical" play experience is lost, bringing the focus onto things usually overshadowed by the promise of open worlds and fast action. *I Expect You to Die* is a game for seated VR, with environments about the size of a small room that let players manipulate objects out of reach in a similar manner to the gravity gloves from *Half-Life: Alyx*. Part escape room and part Bond movie, *I Expect You To Die* is a game that zeroes in on puzzle-solving and quick thinking, giving all the mental thrill of espionage with none of the running away. Inventive environments, like the interior of a car trapped aboard a plane or a submarine about to implode, create a tense and intricate puzzle without making players feel limited by the space available.

Even if constant motion is needed to support play, a game (or part of it) can be kept at a smaller scale to keep players feeling anchored. *Beat Saber* keeps its onslaught of slashable blocks constantly moving towards the player, while a stationary stage reassures that they are standing still, helping to reduce feelings of motion sickness. Even in a large-scale game like *Subnautica*, piloting a vehicle can be used as a surrogate to prevent a sense that the physical space around you doesn't match with the virtual one you're inhabiting. Players can explore the ocean depths while their small room full of air is canonically grounded in the context of piloting a submarine like the room-sized Seamoth in-game. Naturally, if you're going to take this approach, VR sickness will become a pressing concern.

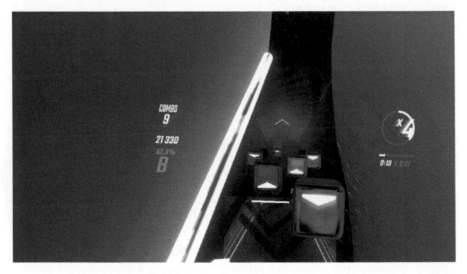

Figure 7.6 To preserve the motion essential in many rhythm games, *Beat Saber* has elements of the environment move toward the player, rather than the other way around. Letting players stand still while props move toward them helps to avoid motion sickness. Larger elements of the backdrop stay stationary, or move as lights around a stage—never giving the player the impression that they are moving through space.

Credit: Beat Saber was developed and published by Beat Games.

Sense of scale. The ability to look around and perceive depth in VR means that players can more easily appreciate drastic changes in scale. Small objects can be inspected more closely, with subtle details easier to appreciate. They can also exude adorability, like the player-guided mouse in *Moss* or the toy dog in Valve's VR demo playground *The Lab*. Conversely, massive landmarks can leave players awestruck, suspending their sense of the limited space around them. In *Boneworks*, players explore a museum with huge, open exhibits where every glimpse over a railing makes you want to stop and admire the space. Over the course of *Half-Life: Alyx*, players move toward a massive "superweapon" contained in a neighbourhood-sized structure suspended over a city. In outdoor segments, the weapon looms ever-closer overhead, instilling a sense of dread and removing any awareness of a ceiling or restrictive space.

Figure 7.7 In *Moss*, the player is placed into spaces that emphasize a sense of scale, making even a seated VR experience feel like it's taking place in a grand world. A grand cathedral (left) and woodland grove (right) use clever scaling and arrangement of props and visual effects to emphasize their perceived size.

Credit: Moss was developed and published by Polyarc Games.

These moments make worlds feel more real, and larger than life, but they aren't limited to worlds that let you roam around. With a bit of care, room-scale and standing experiences can also create this effect, helping players to shed the restrictions of their physical environment. In *Moss*, for example, segments in between gameplay are set in a church complete with vaulted ceilings and golden dust drifting through the air. Although players find themselves seated in front of a book with nowhere to go, the scale of their surroundings makes the game feel more open. During play, you focus on a level laid out in miniature for your mouse companion to navigate. Looking to the distance, you can observe a sprawling forest which opens the virtual space further. This extreme contrast in scales serves both as a point of interest and as a way to make players feel freer even when confined to a seated experience.

Bodily presence. Seeing your own hands (and potentially arms) in VR can be a tricky task involving lots of smoothing and inverse kinematics, but it's generally worth the technical effort. Some games render other objects in place of your hands to show you their position in a game's world, as in *Moss* (orbs of light), *Tabletop Simulator* (models of your handheld controllers), or *Beat Saber* (unsurprisingly, lightsabers). Other games, like *Pavlov* and *Half-Life: Alyx* show an actual pair of hands, while still others including *Boneworks* and *Blade + Sorcery* attempt to render hands and arms.

The decision here is tricky; hands incur a larger expense to support animation of things like grabbing, but help increase the sense of presence in a game's world. In general, hands are preferable to include, since their orientation can be deduced almost exactly based on controller position and standard grip. For controllers with individual finger tracking, support for this feature will help to further ground players in the world. Whether to include arms is a different quandary entirely. Without elbow trackers, arm position is a best guess of sorts, which while mostly accurate, may occasionally break player immersion by misjudging orientation. Other parts of the player's body, like their feet, are *generally* unadvisable to render without full-body tracking, since seeing your VR feet move while you stand still serves little purpose other than to break you out of your character.

One area where full-body estimation is often necessary is multiplayer experiences, whether full-body tracking data is available or not. In some contexts, this estimation might be mostly for show. In *VR Chat*, a casual social app, seeing other players' avatars walk around and animate creates a more dynamic atmosphere, and the opportunity for self-expression via custom animations. A similar impetus drives the VR avatars used for streaming or recording gameplay in titles like *Beat Saber* or *Pistol Whip*, where seeing a players' movements in context instead of mirroring their first-person perspective can make for a more engaging show.

In other contexts, the positioning of a player's avatar can be far more important. In a multiplayer shooter like *Pavlov* or *Onward*, incorrectly estimating a player's pose or arm position can be the difference between getting shot and staying unseen. In VR, taking cover is a matter of physically crouching and dodging, an interaction which is intuitive, engaging, and feels natural. In such an experience, investing in good pose estimation is critical, lest players complain of ill-formed character models that let a leg or arm jut out of cover and put them at an undeserved disadvantage.

Adapting feedback to VR. On other platforms, the typical always-on method of communication is the heads-up display, pasted in "screen space" as a constant overlay of helpful information. In VR, the usual approach of pinning bits of information to the edges of the screen is undesirable. While it's perfectly fine for players to glance at the corner of a screen at arm's length, when that screen is barely an inch in front of your face, focusing on an extreme corner can be uncomfortable. Furthermore, at least as of this writing, visual quality in the periphery of headset displays is often degraded in comparison with a player's central vision.

The most common way to adapt any "screen space" interface to VR is to display it in "room space" or "player space," fixed in position relative to where a player is standing or the centre of their physical space. Thus, players can move their *head* to look at or away from the interface, rather than relying on only moving their *eyes*, which can cause frequent and uncomfortable straining if elements are positioned improperly. Elements should still be drawn on top of gameplay to create the effect of an overlay, but without the uncomfortable sensation of having a barrage of text and icons taped to the extreme edges of player vision. Alternatively, elements can be fixed in a comfortable position without straying too far from a player's central view. Examples include the pause menu in *Beat Saber*, which presents an aim-and-fire menu just in front of the player, or the HUD in *Pistol Whip*, which lays out health and level progress just below their resting eye level. *Pistol Whip* takes the additional step of displaying an ammo counter on the back of the player's gun, allowing them to make the critical decision of when to reload without having to even glance away from the action.

Figure 7.8 In *Pistol Whip*, HUD elements are overlain on the player's view, allowing them to keep track of things like their armour and ammunition (shown on the back of the player's gun).

Credit: Pistol Whip was developed and published by Cloudhead Games.

This is also an area where our old friend diegesis returns to shine, as embedding that always-on information in-world is both a comfortable and more immersive way to communicate in VR. Minimizing the presence of overlays and menus helps an experience to feel more realistic, in addition to reducing visual clutter and helping to avert eye strain. *Alyx*, like *Pistol Whip*, needs to keep track of health and ammunition, but accomplishes the task by way of in-game LCD panels on players' gloves and weapons. This ensures that information is comfortable to access and easy to see—residing right in front of a player's face, in a manner of speaking. Its presence as an in-world element also makes the game feel more immersive; you're not babysitting a character with information they don't have, and tilting your gun to see the number of bullets left in the clip is just a fun interaction. This type of thinking can also benefit utilities, as the performance tool FPSVR opts for a widget that pops up when players turn the inside of their wrist upwards, like a sort of utilitarian holographic sci-fi watch display.

Wonder, horror and everything else. This is where the artistry part comes in. All the opportunities that VR offers—total sensory immersion, presence, sense of scale, a supreme feeling of freedom—can greatly amplify our emotional response to games. That is, assuming we achieve competent control design, comfortable feedback, and a locomotion system that doesn't send players running for anti-emetics.

VR excels especially in supporting horror games that play to our fear of the unknown. If you have a fear of the dark, your character's flashlight going out is always a tense moment. But when that failure blacks out your entire field of vision instead of just your computer screen, the terror is magnified. Likewise, a sudden noise behind you is even scarier when you can literally glance over your shoulder to peer at its source. Horror games like *Dreadhalls* and *Phasmophobia* are incredibly effective at instilling fear as a result.

Another uneasy sensation magnified in VR is the fear of being hunted. In the mid-game of *Half-Life: Alyx*, one segment has players trapped with a blind mutant bent on destroying anything that makes noise. Hearing the beast lumber around keeps tensions high, while any misstep or sound in the player's immediate vicinity instantly makes your heart rate skyrocket. This is paired with a fantastic bit of intuitive and novel interaction design, where players need to physically cover their mouths to keep their character from coughing in response to airborne spores.

Outside of the horror niche, perhaps the most notable emotional impact of VR is its potential to be awe-inspiring. *Subnautica VR* gives players a sense of thalassophobia, and of being hunted by its many leviathan sea monsters, but its predominant tone is one of wonder. Wonder at the scale of the ocean, at the beauty of its mostly peaceful denizens, and at what the player has yet to discover. Just as the unknown can make us afraid, it can also give us an unending and desperate curiosity which is incredibly rewarding to satisfy.

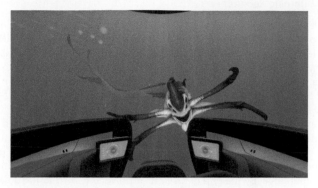

Figure 7.9 It's terrifying enough having this come at you on a regular screen. *Credit: Subnautica* was developed and published by Unknown Worlds.

VR gives us the chance to explore that which is beyond our physical reach, in a way that is more engaging than any medium other than reality itself. Learning about the solar system in a documentary or museum is fascinating, but standing in the middle of outer space, even in a relatively simple demo like *The Lab*, is nothing short of bewitching. A game like *Elite Dangerous*, which sees you piloting a ship through an incomprehensibly vast galaxy, is an even more remarkable experience. Virtual reality isn't just a tool to make our experiences of play more engaging; it's one that lets us create entire worlds within our own.

Let us not get swept away completely by our optimism, though. VR still has its problems, and most systems are priced out of non-enthusiast budgets. Technology has been in the process of catching up since VR first tried to steal the spotlight ten years ago, and in many ways it still is. VR development is exciting, and interesting, but fails to capture anything close to the market share of PC, console, and mobile games. It isn't a given that our current era is the one in which VR will find its footing, or whether it will fall in and out of favour as a niche until affordable and portable solutions break through.

In spite of its drawbacks, the promise of virtual reality is still ever so alluring. The platform may be imperfect and incomplete for the time being, but the challenges it presents should serve to embolden our creativity as game designers. Great VR experiences already exist, pushing the boundaries of interaction to the delight of spellbound players. If that spark of interest can stay alive, so long as market forces don't choose to abandon the platform before it can finally find its footing, more of these experiences will come—it's simply a matter of time.

Expert Profile: Mark Laframboise & Steven Smith—Partners in Play

Founders of Lightning Rod Games

If you've ever looked for a job in game development, you've probably noticed that most every posting, regardless of role, demands something along the lines of "strong teamwork, leadership, and communication skills." And while these qualities are essential in any capacity, if you're looking to start your own studio, you've got to have them—particularly teamwork—in spades. Friendships can keep a team going, or sometimes tear it apart. In the case of Mark Laframboise and Steven Smith, it was friendship that created their studio in the first place.

The duo met in university, both studying computer science as a path into game development. For Mark, the early years of the program had been enjoyable, while a disinterest in later years led him to switch majors and finish his degree in psychology. Steven's experience was starkly opposed, having struggled early on with little programming experience. By the end of his time at university, he'd found a new passion, and thrived in his final year.

During their studies, the pair had discussed the idea of starting a studio together, but graduation shifted their plans. Steven went to art school for a brief period to explore a different side of development and earn some extra credentials, while Mark considered a graduate degree in interactive technology. Disenchanted with the idea of studying games instead of building his own, Mark quit academics in favour of working for a few different studios as a designer and associate producer, before landing at Disney Interactive in California. Steven, meanwhile, had forays in app development, game engine development, bartending, and contract work before ending up at Electronic Arts (EA) working on *FIFA* and later on motion capture technology. After a time, Steven and Mark had settled into their industry roles. But neither had forgotten their dream of starting an independent studio, and both were growing restless. Deciding that it was now or never, they gave notice to their respective employers, and moved back home to start Lightning Rod Games.

The road to this point had been challenging, to say the least. Steven had chosen Canadian studio Silicon Knights over EA for his co-op placement in university. On top of witnessing some early turmoil that would later lead to the studio's legal battle with industry giant Epic Games—a battle it wouldn't walk away from—it was a decision that hardly ingratiated him to EA when he applied a few years later. Meanwhile, Mark's move to California had made his long-term relationship a long-distance relationship, putting a strain on both him and his partner. This experience would inspire the studio's first commercial release *A Fold Apart*, a narrative puzzle game where players fold a world made of paper to literally bring two characters closer together. With this project, the studio solidified their identity as creative, family-friendly, and full of heart.

When we sat down with Mark and Steven, it became clear why the two work so well together. Mark presents as affable and outgoing, which Steven complements with a more reserved, reflective tone. Mark is a writer, preferring to explain and understand in words, while Steven is a visual thinker. When one has trouble explaining something to the team, the other is ready to translate, drawing from their years of experience working together.

Their favourite aspects of development, much like their personalities, seem to be in symbiotic opposition with one another. Steven is fascinated with how tools shape the game development process: "The tools that you have at your disposal help you structure thoughts, and how you're going to approach a program." This fascination translates into a love for building tools, perhaps matched only by Mark's enjoyment of exploring how those tools can shine in the studio's games. While Steven is fascinated by the creation of underlying systems, Mark prefers prototyping, describing his favourite aspect of the development process as "having that high-level design idea and being able to write it in code really quickly. And not having to worry about coming up with [systems or tools]."

For all their complementary qualities, Steven and Mark always seem to come to-gether when it matters, and both share a view of interaction design centred around shaping players' actions. Mark describes interaction as a loop of input and feedback, with the role of a designer being to tweak that loop and serve as an interpreter of player input. "Taking literal inputs is probably almost always bad [. . .] I think the best feel-ing games are the ones where you take what the player is literally telling you and then give them what they're actually expecting. And that gap is the core of good interaction design." He offers up the example of 2018's *God of War*, which includes a generous buffer in terms of combat accuracy to avoid punishing players whose precise inputs wouldn't yield a satisfying result.

Steven shares a similar view, adding that he thinks of it as setting up a space for players to act, have experiences, and express themselves. He sees the challenge of design as shaping the way players understand what they can, or should, do, "ideally [. . .] without thinking too hard about it."

In talking about the evolution of game design over the past several years, Mark in-sists that the pillars of what make a game feel good, like strong feedback and responsive input, haven't changed. But the field of design as a whole has gained more poten-tial, and thus more complexity, from the introduction of new technologies. Steven, meanwhile, points out that as more games live on and sustain player communities for many years, we can observe the evolution of a game's design within its own lifetime, as it pivots from prioritizing learnability for new players, to quality-of-life for existing fans. Mark worries that in some cases, positive design changes are artificially held back by market forces. He argues that the dominance of free-to-play models, for example, has stifled creativity in the mobile space, rarely allowing titles with an upfront cost and no microtransactions to succeed. He sees haptics as the next interesting area of technological development in games, pointing to devices like the PlayStation 5 and Nintendo Switch as experimenting with more sophisticated touch feedback in their controllers. Irrespective of what comes next, though, both are eager to explore the frontier together with their growing team.

When we asked them about any growing pains their studio has experienced, a mo-ment of silence preceded Mark's answer, which quickly trailed off into a sheepish grin: "Money . . .?" With a chuckle, the two underlined the challenges of funding for any indie studio in a crowded marketplace, particularly early on when direct sales aren't an option. Now that they've released a title and are thinking towards their next, new hires are also a challenge. With less than half a dozen team members, just one person can completely change both work and social dynamics for the entire studio. But in spite of these challenges, the pair says that running their own indie studio, which also happens to be fully remote, is a great experience.

As their team continues to grow, Steven and Mark say that administration and lead-ership are becoming more important. This is another area where their friendship has

(Continued)

(Continued)

helped them to succeed. "You need candor," Steven emphasizes, recounting instances where he and Mark have navigated challenging situations with a level of honesty that might be considered brutal outside of a close friendship. With the studio getting bigger, the two have transitioned from developers to leaders, now viewing the success of their employees as an instrumental part of their own work. Through their complementary working styles, honesty, and friendship, Mark and Steven have developed a common leadership style: one where their team succeeds, and so do they.

Further reading

The VR Book: Human-Centred Design for Virtual Reality by Jason Jerald (ACM, Morgan and Claypool). ISBN: 978-1970001129.
A fantastic overview of designing VR experiences, including an in-depth look at player perception in Part II and VR design patterns in Part IV.

Virtual Reality by Steven M. LaValle (In Press, Cambridge University Press, available freely online as of writing).
If you're curious about the technology behind virtual reality, this book takes a wonderfully deep dive into that technology.

Designing to Minimize Simulation Sickness in VR Games, talk by Ben Lewis-Evans (GDC Europe 2015).
A succinct overview of design strategies for minimizing ill effects in players. If you're looking to develop a VR game and would prefer not to make half of your players clutch at their bellies, this comes highly recommended.

Exercises

Claustroludia

Think of a VR game concept where the player never has to move their body in the game's world (only head and hands). In other words, room-scale VR, but with no teleporting between different spaces. The entire game should take place in a single room/with the player in a single position. Here are some prompts to get you thinking:

- What about a very small escape room?
- What about a game that explores small physical oddities, like wooden puzzle boxes?
- What about a game that plays with a job, like working at a desk or restaurant counter?
- What if the player were a giant presiding over a miniature world?

Think about how players would interact with your game, paying special attention to how head and arm movements would keep players engaged in a limited space.

Generation leap

Pick your favorite franchise and imagine a new installment in VR. How would the game's mechanics need to change to support VR controls and movement? Do you think that moving to VR would be a good or bad thing for the franchise, and why?

Motion mapping

Imagine you're designing a fighting game for virtual reality, with the headset/control combination of your choosing. You want to integrate the types of intricate combos you might see in other games like *Street Fighter*. How would you adapt complicated control inputs, like mixing partial analog stick circles, directions, and button presses, in VR? What perspective would the player have? Keep comfort in mind, and try to use gestural controls as much as you can. Can you think of a system that would consider combinations of gestures, or specific timing of those gestures, to capture the spirit of arcade-style fighting games in VR?

8

The Audience is Listening

On March 1, 2014, the unthinkable happened. A crowd of around one hundred thousand people controlling a single game of *Pokémon Red* defeated the game's final gauntlet of battles, and crowned their character champion.

Twitch Plays Pokémon, or (TPP), started out as a social and technical experiment. The idea of TPP was simple; a Pokémon game would be broadcast online, except instead of being controlled by a streamer, it would receive all input via chat commands from the audience. On February 12, it launched to humble viewership via the online streaming service Twitch. In the days that followed, that crowd grew to thousands, and then tens of thousands.

The stream's opening hours were relatively tame. Since any valid chat input was fed directly to the game as a button press, factors like varying viewer latency meant that chance had a substantial influence, even with a unified goal to progress. As the viewer count grew, so too did the chaos governing the stream. With more inputs coming in than the game could process, many were effectively lost. In any given frame, the input which "stuck" was effectively random. Besides latency, another element had taken over, causing the pandemonium to spiral out of control: the human factor.

Unsurprisingly, not all ten thousand viewers maintained that unified vision of progress. Plenty of participants valued the chaos of the stream over anything else, doing things like spamming the "start" input to bring up a menu and interrupt gameplay, or suggesting inputs in the exact opposite direction the player should be walking. To mitigate this, a new feature was added allowing viewers to continuously vote on which input system they wanted to use. The new "democracy" system would poll chat commands over a short period and input the most-requested command, while the "anarchy" system would represent the existing anything-goes model.

In the ensuing days, the stream snapped back and forth between anarchy and democracy. The change had caused a (mostly) playful rift among participants, sparking debate over which alternative represented the true spirit of

The Game Designer's Playbook. Samantha Stahlke and Pejman Mirza-Babaei, Oxford University Press.
© Samantha Stahlke and Pejman Mirza-Babaei (2022). DOI: 10.1093/oso/9780198845911.003.0008

TPP. This quickly became embedded in what was already an intricate mythos being woven by the community[1].

For a game which was already 18 years old at the time, and a play mechanism only allowing nine commands—one for each valid button plus "democracy" and "anarchy"—the lore of TPP was pathologically intricate. Fans chronicled the events of the stream, spinning narrative interpretations of key events (like "Bloody Sunday," where a dozen Pokémon were accidentally released) and creating an in-universe religion.

The so-called Church of Helix established a pantheon with a nautilus Pokémon at its helm, dubbed Lord Helix by the community. Alongside Lord Helix were "Bird Jesus" (a bird) and "Battery Jesus" (also a bird), together representing anarchy as the purest embodiment of TPP. The forces of Helix were opposed by the "False Prophet," a Pokémon that players had accidentally evolved with a fire stone instead of following the unofficial plan to use a water stone. Canonically, this event was interpreted as the progenitor to a number of misfortunes, including Bloody Sunday.

TPP's new religion drove the lore machine going forward. Fans generated elaborate written accounts of gameplay events contextualized in the Helix belief system. Ornate artworks were created. *Old School Runescape* even included a reference to the stream as part of a 2017 update, adding the flavour text "Praise Helix!" to a fossil creature.

As the Twitch hivemind persisted onward, TPP soon found itself nearing the end of the game. Before victory could be declared, participants had to clear the Elite Four, a final set of Pokémon battles against the game's most powerful AI opponents. With a team of six Pokémon, including Lord Helix himself, the stream set off to meet their final challenge. After twenty-one failures, participants finally managed to secure a win in the last battle, with Battery Jesus dealing the final blow. Twitch chat had won—fittingly, their victory had come in anarchy mode.

Twitch Plays Pokémon was the epitome of lightning in a bottle, sure, but it also represented a growing interest in the streaming medium and highlighted its interactive potential. TPP was one of several factors, alongside esports and the rise of popular streamers, that helped cement Twitch's status as the de facto site for game streaming.

The streaming behemoth that Twitch would become can trace its lineage back to Justin.tv, a website founded in 2007. The site hosted an always-on livestream broadcasting the everyday life of one of its cofounders, attracting a host of curious viewers, pranksters, and media attention. By 2008, the site had expanded, giving users the ability to host their own streams in a number

---

[1] For the curious, a fanmade wiki can be used to peruse this lore, accessible as of this writing at https://helixpedia.fandom.com/wiki/TPPedia_Wiki

of categories. Three years later, the site's gaming category was spun off into its own website: Twitch.tv.

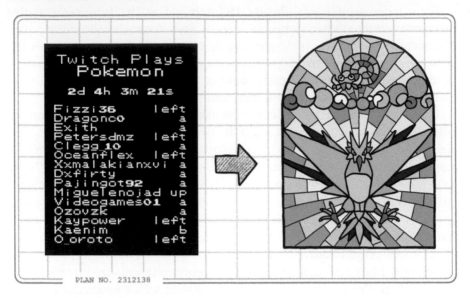

Figure 8.1 It started out with a keypress, how did it end up like this?

After a period of meteoric growth over the last decade, Twitch sits at almost two million concurrent viewers on average as of this writing. Other services like YouTube and Facebook Gaming have since made a push to compete with Twitch through their own live content. Naturally, short-lived competitors have sprung up as well, using a wall of corporate money and little else to push themselves straight into obscurity, acquisition, or closure, like Microsoft's Mixer platform. At least for now, Twitch maintains its status as the cultural locus of streamed gaming content.

Within the ecosystem of services like Twitch, there is a constant competition to secure viewers in the onslaught of eyes searching for game content. Content creators strive to be the best at playing, providing commentary, engaging with viewers, or creating humour and interesting situations. But this contest isn't just for the people who are streaming games; it's for the developers of those games. In the streaming economy, the success of a game is dependent on the experience it creates for both players and an audience of potentially millions.

8.1 The ratings war

The race to attract all of those eyeballs starts with an understanding of why people watch gaming streams in the first place. As a designer, you might already have a solid understanding of several reasons contributing to the appeal of *playing* games. Among others, you could list escapism, curiosity, achievement-hunting, social interaction, dominating other players, and the vague, ever-elusive "just for fun."

Some of these factors still certainly apply in the motivation to *watch* gaming content. For escapism, watching another player's journey through a fantasy world can help to psychologically transport you away from the hum-drum tribulations of reality. But this sense of fantasy would arguably be much stronger if you experienced that fantasy firsthand as a player. And, surely the vicarious accomplishment of watching someone else earn an achievement pales in comparison to the pride you'd feel in earning that achievement yourself. In a way, the question becomes, why would anyone watch games when they could choose to play games instead?

Answering this question requires that we pin down viewer motivations. To do so, we have a few options. We can seek out research that examines audience statistics, surveys, and interviews specific to game streaming. We can learn from our existing knowledge of why people engage with similar content like sports, or "Let's Play" videos, the prerecorded ancestor of game streaming. Of course, we can also draw on our own experiences, breaking down the factors that might compel us to make stream spectatorship our activity of choice in the moment.

One of our most useful tools here is to examine what type of content is most popular within the space, identifying commonalities that can help us verify and expand on the reasons that people watch. Services like Twitch cate-gorize streams based on content, letting us understand which games draw the most viewers. Over the past several years, you can pretty reliably summarize the top ten games on Twitch as follows:

- A few multiplayer shooters
- A couple of MOBAs (multiplayer online battle arenas)
- An MMO (massively multiplayer online game)
- A sandbox game or two
- Flash-in-the-pan viewership of a highly anticipated new release

Recently, the battle royale, a subgenre featuring the free-for-all competition of a large group of players, has worked its way onto this list as well. Battle royale modes have been worked into all manner of games, though the typical entry will see something like a hundred players competing to be the last one standing in some flavour of a multiplayer shooter with survival elements.

As of this writing, the regulars on Twitch's top games are *League of Legends* (a MOBA), *World of Warcraft* (an MMO), *Fortnite* (a battle royale shooter), *Counter Strike: Global Offensive* (a multiplayer shooter), *DotA 2* (another

MOBA), and *Minecraft* (a sandbox game). Maybe the most remarkable thing about these games is their longevity. Aside from *Fortnite* (2017), these games are practically senior citizens by software standards. *DotA 2* (2013), *CS:GO* (2012), and *Minecraft* (2011) are a decade old at this point. *League of Legends* (2009) recently celebrated a tenth anniversary, and *World of Warcraft* (2004) would be old enough to drive if it were a person, an objectively terrifying notion.[2]

The vibrant communities who support these games, driving their developers to provide regular updates years after release, provide the viewership to sustain their continued domination on platforms like Twitch. In combination with our existing knowledge of why people *play* games and the appeal of things like watching sports, we can look to these games and others like them in understanding a few different motivations key to the appeal of game spectatorship.

Diversion and escapism. Just like playing games, watching gameplay can provide a welcome escape from everyday obligations. A high-stakes competitive match presents a tense conflict, while a casual stream of a single-player game can allow viewers to experience a fascinating world and story alongside the stream's host. Simply put, watching someone else play a game can be fun, interesting, and relaxing.

Watching a game instead of playing yourself can have several advantages in this regard; in several ways, streamed content is easier to consume. You can't play games while working at a computer or folding laundry (not effectively, at least), but watching a stream can provide a welcome background to your work. Streams in general demand less attention than a movie or television show, meaning that they can be an effective diversion, like music, without distracting too much from the task at hand.

To pile on the convenience aspect, the vast majority of streaming game content is free to access, while many of the games streamed are not free to play yourself. Streamed content has a low barrier to entry in many ways. In addition to lacking financial cost, it also eliminates the skill barrier associated with enjoying a game's content. If you like the idea of something like intense competition, speedrunning, or a certain extremely difficult game, streaming can let you engage with this type of content without running into gatekeeping or offering up the immense investment of time and effort required to participate yourself. Spectating can preserve much of the appeal and fun factor of playing yourself while removing the pressure of playing well.

---

[2] Readers in the know will note that Leeroy Jenkins could have secured a learner's permit by now as well. Lord Helix help us all.

Vicarious competition and accomplishment. Watching games offers some of the same draw as watching sports or other athletic competitions. If you play sports, you might enjoy watching sports to admire the strategy and skill of players at a highly competitive level. A big part of the appeal might also be cheering for an individual or team that you associate with. Just as you might tune in to the World Cup or the Olympics to cheer for your country or a favourite athlete, you might enjoy watching a stream to cheer for a favourite *StarCraft* player.

Of those five games we mentioned earlier as regulars in Twitch's top games list, all except *Minecraft* are primarily competitive multiplayer (and *Minecraft* supports player-versus-player combat). All five see regular tournaments organized, with some more or less official than others. *DotA 2*, *League of Legends*, and *Fortnite* have especially sizeable tournament scenes, streams for which draw millions of viewers.

Figure 8.2 A stadium of spectators at *The International DotA 2* tournament in 2019.

Credit: Image by Yrrah2 (CC BY-SA 4.0) via Wikimedia Commons.

Part of why the vicarious competition and victory of gaming streams can be so intense is down to the at-times ludicrous stakes involved. In 2019, *DotA 2*'s annual tournament *The International* saw a total prize pool of a cool $34 million, with the top team of six players taking home over $15 million. Watching a favourite team or player work their way to the top spot in a tournament makes for an intense viewing experience. Irrespective of stakes, any competitive match can provide the excitement of tension and a sense of camaraderie in shared victory or defeat.

Another thing that makes competitive games watchable—or perhaps more importantly, *re*-watchable—is unpredictability. Injecting strategy and competition into a game creates uncertainty. Without any uncertainty, watching the same game over and over again can easily become boring. In a competitive environment, though, the course of a match and its ultimate outcome are subject to all sorts of variation. Even though the content of the game itself hasn't changed, your experience watching one match compared to the next might be vastly different. Which characters will players pick, how will they play them, will the other team be able to anticipate "our" strategy? These types of questions help to keep viewers watching, and explain part of why competitive multiplayer games tend to dominate streaming platforms.

Social interaction. One of the reasons you might pick up a game is because your friends are playing it. Likewise, one of the reasons you might watch a stream is because your friends are watching it, and you'd like to preserve the illusion that you're a sociable extrovert and not a recluse who spends 90% of their leisure hours swaddled in a blanket eating popcorn in front of re-runs of *Law and Order*.

Though *Law and Order* marathons have very few drawbacks, one disadvantage is the inability to interact with other be-swaddled and be-popcorned viewers around the world if you so choose. Game streams, on the other hand, do allow for real-time audience communication. Depending on the platform, viewers can chat with each other or even send messages directly to content creators. In this way, streams can provide a casual, low-pressure way to interact with some like-minded folk. Though the chat amongst larger audiences can easily descend into chaos (see Twitch Plays Pokémon), a smaller group can have a meaningful side conversation while enjoying the show.

Even disregarding situations with active participation in something like chat, streamed content can provide a sort of second-hand fulfillment to social needs. The term *parasocial relationship* is used to describe the phenomenon of an audience feeling social bonds with performers, even when that bond is completely one-sided. In other words, you might come to think of a favorite streamer as something like a friend, even if you've never talked to them.[3]

This effect explains why the most popular content on Twitch, at least for the time being, isn't a game at all, but the "Just Chatting" category, a catch-all for streamers broadcasting conversations with their audience or other "everyday" content. Outside this category, a streamer's personality and interactions with their audience are a vital part of game-related content. Things like quality commentary and jokes can make a stream far more interesting, and on smaller streams, players might engage directly with their audience by responding to chat messages or taking requests for games.

---

[3] For the most part, this kind of attachment is healthy and normal, so long as you recognize yourself as a member of the crowd. However, this type of thing *can* lead to unhealthy and obsessive behaviours, and it is important to remember that a performer's engagement with their audience is not the same thing as a personal relationship. This is not the focus of our discussion, but it should be noted nonetheless.

Some social appeal can also come through in gameplay. In competitive games, players' interactions with each other can create interesting social dynamics. This is especially true in games where deception, cooperation, and communication style play a large role in gameplay, as in the breakout streaming hit *Among Us*. Outside of multiplayer interactions, a sandbox game like *Minecraft* lets streamers express parts of their personality through their creations, and how they choose to experiment with the game's mechanics. In addition to supporting social engagement with content creators, much like competition, this contributes to the re-watchability of a game by injecting uncertainty.

Curiosity and learning. While entertaining, streams can offer value to viewers beyond being a playful diversion. Just by virtue of watching skilled players in a game with strategic or competitive elements, viewers can take away knowledge to benefit their next play session. Some streamers might offer commentary specifically aimed at educating interested viewers or giving advice on how to improve their own playing. Watching streamed play can serve as an education of sorts in areas like competitive play or speedrunning strategies.

Even more simply, viewers might tune in to a stream to learn the basics about a particular game. This might be motivated by a desire to find out more about a game before making a purchase decision. If you don't have time to play a game or can't afford it, watching a stream of that game might be the next best thing. And when a game first comes out, especially a hotly anticipated one, viewers might flock to streams of that game just to see what all the hype is about—helping to explain why games like *Cyberpunk 2077* and *No Man's Sky* tend to briefly crack Twitch's top ten shortly after release.

8.1.1 *Making a game watchable*

With an improved understanding of what compels people to watch streamed content, we can identify design choices that promote a game's watchability. We can observe these characteristics in existing games popular for streaming, examining how they are leveraged to create content which is easier or more interesting to consume.

It would be inaccurate to suggest that a game having all the qualities explored in this section is guaranteed to become a smash hit in the streaming community. Certainly, it would also be wrong to imply that a game without any of these elements cannot become a streaming hit. However, all of the current regulars to the top ten games on Twitch and Facebook Gaming, at least as of this writing, do possess at least one of the characteristics listed below. Although not a magic formula by any means, we can broadly describe a few design decisions that take advantage of the reasons viewers choose to watch in the first place:

Support episodic content. The role of streaming as a convenient diversion means that viewers should be able to tune in for variable lengths of time, with the ability to jump in or out relatively quickly. When you first join a stream, you'd hope to get up to speed relatively quickly. Conversely, if you're in a hurry or have an unknown amount of time to watch, you don't want to feel like you'll be missing out if you can only watch for a short time.

These qualities are supported by the format of many popular games, particularly multiplayer titles. Relatively short match lengths create digestible segments of content for viewers to enjoy, even if their time is limited. Stats aggregator League of Graphs puts the average match time of streaming favourite *League of Legends* at around 25 minutes, depending on competitive rank. An average match of its MOBA cousin *DotA 2* takes around 35 minutes, according to tracker Datdota. Unfortunately, while most games don't make statistics available regarding match length, anecdotally and based on tournament play, similar figures emerge for other popular titles. *Fortnite's* solo battle royale matches last about 20 minutes, while competitive *Overwatch* games usually come in just shy of 30 minutes.

Figure 8.3 Full of recognizable characters and colourful chaos, an average *Overwatch* match is around 20–30 minutes of near-constant action that's pretty easily understandable even to an inexperienced player.

Credit: *Overwatch* was developed and published by Blizzard Entertainment.

The sweet spot seems to be an average of around half an hour—perhaps it is no coincidence that this is about the length of a sitcom episode. Though match lengths can obviously vary, this type of range gives viewers the ability to sit down for a quick watch and appreciate a complete experience. Matches that are too short offer less potential for strategic depth and interesting conflict; matches that are too long lose out on the convenience factor and may seem to drag on. Of course, designing for this range isn't just good for watchability; it can also support a better player experience overall. Having relatively quick rounds makes it easier for players to fit games into their schedule, resulting in a more reasonable time commitment (at least for casual play). Additionally, shorter match times mean that any negative experiences with other players are over more quickly, and can lessen the sting of loss to reduce the chances of toxic behaviour.

One final thing to note here is that certain features might *detract* from how well a game adapts to being sliced into digestible chunks. In multiplayer titles, the ability of an opposing player or team to stall can kill the flow between games. A long match of *Hearthstone* can be compelling to watch, but if the match is elongated by a player running out the clock on every turn, it becomes frustrating. In single-player games, things like cutscenes and long slow-paced sequences can make for a streaming experience more akin to a period drama film than a sitcom. While this may have some niche appeal, or a flash of popularity after a sufficiently anticipated release, it's not likely to support mass streaming appeal in the long term.

Competition and strategic depth. The majority of games dominating streamed play, and indeed most multiplayer games, favour competition over cooperation. We could probably say something poetic about the human condition here, like "mankind is a society born in fire, and our ever-restless watch prefers to gaze upon conflict even in times of peace". We will refrain from doing that, however, as it would sound incredibly pretentious. Besides, there are plenty of other reasons why competition is appealing to watch, some of which we already dissected in our discussion of viewer motivation. Competitive games create unpredictability and tension, making them interesting and exciting to watch.

This isn't to say that cooperative play isn't interesting. Indeed, cooperation might be an important part of this dynamic in a team competition like *League of Legends* or *Overwatch*. However, purely cooperative play is by necessity a PvE (players-versus-environment) conflict, with any adversary provided by the game. Predefined challenges eventually run out, and procedurally generated levels or AI-driven foes aren't yet quite at the level where they can match the intrigue of human opponents on a massive scale.

The most popular streamed titles involve competition with lots of people—unpredictable, complicated, messy people—keeping viewers on the edge of their seat with the idea that anything could happen. While pure cooperation doesn't seem to be a winning formula for streaming popularity, at least for the time being, pure competition does. Battle royale games with solo modes distill large-scale competition into "everyone for themselves", and the popularity of titles like *Fortnite* and *Warzone* among spectators speak to the success of the format in playing to our bloodthirsty viewing desires.

Strategic depth is another factor to consider. Tic-tac-toe is a competitive multiplayer game, but its small possibility space means that the optimal strategy is easy to understand, games are too short to feel meaningful, and are almost immediately boring to watch. Chess, on the other hand, offers a larger possibility space allowing for intricate strategies and a more captivating spectator experience. Likewise, a game like *Warzone*'s battle royale mode is more interesting to watch than a round of *Agar.io*, although both are one-versus-many competitions.

In addition to making content feel less predictable, strategic depth also appeals to a viewer's curiosity and desire to learn. Part of the appeal of watching chess matches (if you're into that) is the potential to learn how to become a better player from watching the masters. Of course, this also applies to digital games. The existence of or possibility to develop complex strategies creates implicit learning opportunities for the audience, as well as giving creators the possibility of hosting informational content, like tips for improving play.

Together, these aspects might help to explain why some competitive games experience such brief stints in popularity. For instance, *Fall Guys: Ultimate Knockout* drew massive crowds in the month of its release, hitting almost 200,000 average concurrent viewers on Twitch, before regularly falling to less than 10,000 just two months later.[4] *Fall Guys* is amusing to watch, but has relatively little strategic depth. Compare this with a game like *League of Legends*, which has hovered at or above 100,000 viewers or so almost ten years after its release, displaying a slight *increase* in viewership over time. Competition in a game like *League* has more longevity because of its depth, continually presenting interesting conflicts even for players intimately familiar with the game.

Figure 8.4 Like *Overwatch*, *League of Legends* offers plenty of fast-paced eye candy for viewers. Once you know what's going on, there's also a good deal of strategic depth to be appreciated in terms of team composition and strategic play.

Credit: *League of Legends* was developed and published by Riot Games.

Provide opportunities for self-expression through play. Games with sandbox elements, base-building, map creation, and similar features can help satisfy players' creative inclinations. They also serve as another

---

[4] Viewership statistics mentioned here are taken from TwitchTracker, accessible as of this writing at https://twitchtracker.com/

way to expand a game's possibility space, keeping viewers on the hook for a potentially unique experience. Most notably, they give content creators the opportunity to inject personality into their gameplay, which can make a stream feel more personal and engaging. As a consistent streaming favourite, *Minecraft* allows players to build impressive creations with a touch of personal flair. Less creation-oriented sandbox elements, like flexible physics-based combat systems, can hit similar notes with viewers. *Grand Theft Auto V*, another streaming favourite, has plenty of opportunities for zany police chases and over-the-top situations that create humour and suspense in situations of players' own making.

Like competition, creative or sandbox elements boost the variation viewers can expect to see from a single game. Additionally, just as strategic depth can appeal to viewer curiosity and an interest in learning, so too can features focused on creativity. Games like *Minecraft*, which offer a virtually unlimited toybox for players to build with, allow content creators to share experiences that can give inspiration on top of their entertainment value. This might also give viewers an inclination to play for themselves; if you feel that your experience will be distinctly different from what you've just watched, then the promise of firsthand play becomes more interesting.

Provide opportunities for interesting social dynamics. In service to the social motivations underlying our desire to spectate, mechanics that promote social interaction can make for a more interesting viewing experience. So-called *Mafia*-style games, which pit a small team of villains against a larger group unaware of their identity, create opportunities for players to lie, team up, and potentially watch a web of lies crumble around them. Such scenarios have contributed to the runaway popularity of *Among Us*, a game where almost all strategic depth comes from communication rather than gameplay skill. Other titles like the *Jackbox Party Pack* series present a host of situations involving humour, contests of wit, and deception, among other varied social dynamics.

Giving players more chances to interact through gameplay or communication as part of their design can help audiences to connect with creators as well. Heavily social games like *Among Us* are natural candidates for celebrity streamers to collaborate and draw in fans for special events. In 2020, several celebrity *Among Us* games saw viewership in the hundreds of thousands, including high-profile politicians, streamers, and YouTube personalities. A similar appeal can apply to games with an active tournament scene, where viewers can watch their favourite players compete and interact with one another.

All of the qualities discussed here predate streaming by a longshot; in fact, some of the most popular games on live platforms, like *League of Legends* and *World of Warcraft*, released before the popularization of game streaming. This makes sense; there is a significant degree of overlap in the appeal between playing and watching games, just as there is between participating and watching any other activity suited to an individual's interests. However, while many of the design decisions to make a game more watchable are old hat at this point, streaming presents an entirely new frontier in design which has yet to be fully explored.

Players interact with games, and spectators watch. But with a captive audience of tens, hundreds, thousands, or more, can those spectators become active participants themselves?

8.2 Come on down

In the mid-to-late twentieth century, game shows experienced a surge in popularity. While old favourites like *Jeopardy!* and *Wheel of Fortune* still set screens abuzz in the homes of suburban grandparents and people with internet data caps, their cultural relevance pales in comparison to that enjoyed a few decades ago. From *Match Game* and *Password* to *Who Wants to be a Millionaire*, game shows captivated millions across the globe. If you're of a certain age, you might have fond memories of tuning in to enjoy the antics of comedians featured on *Hollywood Squares*, or watching a favourite quiz show with your family every week.

Part of the appeal of game shows is that the contestants are everyday people, either fans who signed up for a chance to participate and win big, or members of a studio audience beckoned onstage. If you're watching a game show, you're thinking "that could be me," perhaps trying to play along and wonder if you might be able to do better in your own five minutes of fame as a participant. In some ways, reality television took over in scratching a similar itch, showcasing the lives of ordinary people—or at least, people who were groomed to be as melodramatically "ordinary" as possible on camera. But all our ogling at the dramatized and sanitized lives of reality stars has lost that participatory spirit that came along with game shows, urging you to play along at home.

Memories of that excitement may owe most of their power to nostalgia at this point, but game streaming offers us a glimmer of that same feeling with its interactive potential. Like sports, competitive streams urge us to cheer along. Like game shows, they can also make us want to play the game we're watching. However, unlike game shows, we are no longer bound by the limitations of traditional broadcasting media. In practice, we can let viewers take part in the action, thanks to real-time communication and APIs offered by services like Twitch.

Why audiences might be motivated to participate in such interactions blend the reasons people have for playing games with those for watching games. After watching a stream for a while, you might feel more comfortable trying your hand at playing whatever's on offer, reducing any barriers to entry in terms of knowledge or skill. Even in a small group, being selected as a participant gives you a few minutes of celebrity, stealing the spotlight for a brief period to impress others with your skills or laugh along with them. In a larger group, being acknowledged by a well-known creator can be a satisfying brush with fame. Lastly, the always-on nature of streaming means that you can always find a community to interact and potentially play with even if your friends are offline, providing much more personal interactions than faceless strangers found through multiplayer matchmaking.

Games that take advantage of these motivators and provide some form of interaction are sometimes a little gimmicky, as you'd expect in any new design area. As of this writing, some titles feel like early Wii games a little too trigger-happy on motion controls, or the first cavalcade of iPod Touch apps released after game developers discovered the accelerometer. Starting sometime around 2015, several games boasted some form of Twitch integration or another, and we seem to be entering the middle of a first generation of forays into the realm of interactive streaming.

No matter how this particular design avenue ends up shaking out, it does present some interesting opportunities. More in-depth viewer interactions may prove themselves capable of drawing a larger audience, and transforming that audience into something more.

8.2.1 *Turning viewers into players (or something in between)*

There are several different ways to facilitate audience interaction with live game content. Such interactions might be as trivial as highlighting commentary from the crowd, or as dramatic as lifting lucky viewers out of the audience to play for a match.

While some of the features we will discuss aren't specific to livestreaming interactions, many of them are. At first, you might wonder how these features could possibly be worth it unless streamers are your one and only target; why invest so much time and effort to enhance the play experience of the select few players who will host streams?

The obvious answer here is that it is not only the play experience of those few content creators that will benefit—it's also their entire audience. For viewers that choose to engage with any interactive mechanics, their experience will become more memorable, and you may convert a few extra players out of it. Even for viewers that don't want to join in, the addition of audience interaction injects uncertainty. Throwing viewer participation into the mix can make for a more interesting show, even if you don't plan on participating yourself.

Another important thing to consider is that these features don't exclusively support massive crowds; you don't have to bank on drawing thousands of viewers to create an improved experience. The *Jackbox Party Pack* series is practically built for playing via stream (or video call), and despite only having a few hundred concurrent Twitch viewers on average, *Jackbox* reports an estimated active player base of over 100 million. Design thinking that supports livestream interaction supports any context where a group of interested people all have their own devices—in the smartphone era, this is known as any group of interested people. Thus, even if you're not planning to become the next runaway Twitch sensation, thinking of an "audience" can inject some social interaction into almost any experience.

Let's take a look at some of these features, starting with the most basic and stepping forward in order of increasing engagement.

Platform features. Services like Twitch and YouTube offer basic features like text chat among viewers. Other game-agnostic interactions include making monetary donations to highlight a message on stream, or paying for a "subscription" to a favourite content creator. These features provide audience members with an easy way to interact with one another, and show support for the content they enjoy. Since you'll be getting this basic level of interaction "for free" with any streaming service, you may want to consider how you might use them as a jumping-off point for more complicated interactions.

Without any additional development investment, something like a donation system can already add in a layer of interaction. Though more of a testament to event planning than game design, speedrunning collective Games Done Quick, or (GDQ), hosts regular livestreamed speedrunning marathons of various games to raise money for charity organizations. GDQ events boast a slew of donation "mechanics," where viewers can vote with their wallets to make decisions like naming a character or selecting a special trick for speedrunners to pull off. Certain choices have practically become landmarks of the annual events, like whether to kill or save the animals in a speedrun *Super Metroid* (a choice which generated almost $300,000 alone in donations during GDQ's 2019 winter event).

Outside of special events, though, basic interactions like text chat *can* factor into your game's design. Development-wise, this is just a matter of finding the right tools, like Twitch's Extensions API or suitable chatbots compatible with the platforms you plan to support. Such tools let you transform things like chat messages into commands, which you might use to support some of the more engaging features discussed below.

Betting or affiliation. Give any group of people a deck of cards, dice, a couple of horses, or literally any spinning object, and they'll find a way to gamble. Livestreaming is no exception, and so long as you're not asking people to buy in with real money, betting mechanics can be a fun and perfectly legal way to increase audience engagement.[5]

SaltyBet, a site founded in 2013, is built around wagering on the outcomes of different competitive events, such as fighting game tournaments. Outside tournament play, users can bet on the outcomes of *Mugen*, a 2D fighting game engine supporting extensive customization, played by AI bots. Although the site's currency has no real value, hundreds of viewers tune in concurrently even outside of tournament season to try their luck at predicting the outcome of AI matches. This is similar to the current status of Twitch Plays Pokémon, though its popularity has diminished immensely since the original run. More than five years later, the channel has evolved to primarily support betting on Pokémon battles via chat commands, though crowd-controlled game runs are still hosted from time to time.

Some games also support viewer bets more directly. Viewers can place bets on how the player they're watching will die in *Clone Drone in the Danger Zone*, earning virtual currency which can be used to participate in other interactive mechanics. This helps to keep viewers invested even when they might not be interacting directly, as the outcome of a round incurs some personal stakes—even if those stakes are fairly low.

A similar tactic to wagers is directly affiliating audience members with competitors in some way. *Marbles on Stream*, for example, is a marble racing game which assigns individual viewers to their own marbles, effectively turning them into players of a sort. Although the outcomes of races are determined by physics simulation, the promise of momentary glory for a win can help make a viewing experience more memorable.

Influencing game content. This is where our use of the term "interaction" becomes much less of a stretch—where the will of the viewer has a tangible impact on gameplay. How viewers achieve this impact, and the degree to which it affects a game, can vary substantially. This might be as simple as collectively voting on something like which map to choose for a round of play (*Marbles on Stream*) or individually having the power to spawn in items or enemies (*Clone Drone in the Danger Zone*). Typically, this is accomplished through chat commands, a tactic which is certainly not unique

---

[5] Before you say anything, yes, some games already have you effectively betting with real money via microtransactions. The loophole seems to be that as long as you can't turn your winnings back into real money, it's legal in most places. Given the state of microtransaction regulations, you can probably get away with this. But these types of tactics are psychologically and financially predatory, and they're not good *game* design. So please do not use them, lest this book burst into flames while you hold it.

to games; musicians, for instance, often use chatbots to take song requests from their audience.

Several games have integrated viewer choice mechanics of some sort. *Clustertruck*, a platforming game that sees players sprint along the tops of cargo trucks, supports audience voting on special events, like exploding trucks, low gravity, and inverting player controls. *Dead Cells*, a metroidvania platformer, has Twitch integration to support voting for areas, character upgrades, and bosses. Some games lean more into the idea as a selling point of the complete experience, like *Party Hard*, a game about breaking up inconsiderately loud social gatherings. In *Party Hard*, viewers can invite crowds of NPCs, summon law enforcement, and otherwise wreak havoc with players' missions of mass desocialization.

A natural challenge that arises with this type of design is that, if a game is *dependent* on audience interaction, it may have trouble reaching the popularity needed to sustain a sizeable audience. *Choice Chamber* is a game built around viewer votes, and while its moment in the spotlight was brief, it took the concept of audience polling to an interesting extreme. Nearly every choice is reduced to an audience vote in the action platformer, from which weapon players will receive to which direction bosses will aim their attacks.

While a perfectly fun game to play and watch, *Choice Chamber* never took off outside of a few short-lived streams by notable content creators. Assessing why it wasn't a larger hit is pure speculation, but one reason could be that the game's content *outside* of audience interaction was fairly run-of-the-mill. *Choice Chamber*'s voting mechanics were a fun gimmick, but they lacked the social depth of a *Jackbox* game among friends. Meanwhile, single-player *Choice Chamber* didn't have the same draw as something like *Dead Cells*, whose voting mechanics were merely a bonus to an otherwise solid and distinctive experience.

From this, we can learn that shallower "viewer mechanics" implemented through something like polls or text commands, are challenging to hold up as the core of a game. Instead, they should be treated as a supplement to a game which is enjoyable *without* them, as an enhancement to a complete experience, rather than a building block.

Viewer-created content. Any game that supports user-created content is a natural fit for streamers to interact with their audience, by playing with content their viewers create. This might include mapmaking, character creation, or active support for mods, all of which are a boon to player creativity in general.

As a designer, assuming you're investing the effort in user creation tools in the first place, helping to support the stream-friendliness of that content is relatively trivial. Providing users with a quick way to share their creations that doesn't involve searching for usernames and level titles is a good start.

Ultimate Chicken Horse and *Super Mario Maker*, games built on player-created platforming levels, both offer a code system as a way for users to easily share levels. A short alphanumeric code can be copied and shared anywhere, and is an easy way to place an audience level request into the chat of a livestream.

One thing to keep in mind here is that a user-created content system should come with some means for players to preview and censor content if need be. This is important in any context, but particularly if you anticipate that a player might be happening upon some content for the first time in front of a large crowd. You should provide a way for players to preview content, for instance, in a browser, game client, or window panel that can be easily obscured by a stream's host. This can both reduce the chance of an unfortunate encounter with malicious or offensive content, as well as deter users from creating ill-intended content in the first place by making it less likely that such content will be seen.

Viewer play-along. The most in-depth form of interaction an audience can have with a livestream is to become players themselves. In its most basic form, this can be accomplished through text commands, as in the original Twitch Plays Pokémon. Some smaller projects have experimented with similar mechanics, like tile-based battle royale *Stream Animals*, though platform-specific interactions through something like Twitch chat can lack a sense of satisfaction. The original run of TPP was fascinating in part because of its novelty; the chaos was unprecedented, and it was in a sense an experiment in what interactive streaming could accomplish. Novelty can only go so far, though, and whether games built entirely around chat commands will establish a sizeable and stable niche remains to be seen. To an extent, these sorts of implementations blur the line between what constitutes as "influencing" a game versus "playing" it.

More direct participation has seen a good degree of success, particularly in the genre carved out by Jackbox titles and their ilk. Games like *Quiplash* and *Drawful*, in addition to sites like *Skribbl.io* outside of the *Jackbox* umbrella, work immensely well for local multi-device games or remote play. These games work by having one player host a party game (which they own), while a small group of others join in via web browser or a (typically free) mobile app. In *Quiplash*, for example, players are given fill-in-the-blank prompts to answer. At the end of a round, players vote on the funniest answers for different prompts, and the player able to best delight their friends' sense of humour wins.

While fun as a local experience in their own right, these games work exceptionally well on livestreams, where audience members can join in first-come first-serve or queue up for a chance to play on larger streams. Naturally, this sort of social interaction demands a way to moderate content in the same fashion as map creation, even more so if drawing or text is involved.

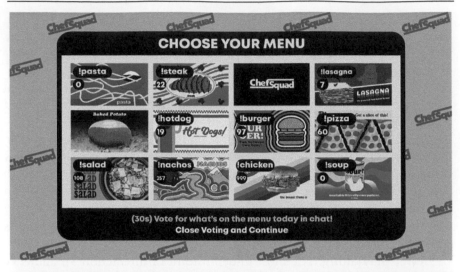

Figure 8.5 *ChefSquad* is an example of a game designed for livestreaming "first," with viewer participation a necessary part of the experience. As a co-op restaurant sim, the game lets viewers, among other things, vote on menu items, vie for streamer attention to get "hired" for the next challenge, and help prep ingredients via chat commands.

Credit: *ChefSquad* was developed and published by Vertigo Gaming Inc.

Sadly, the censoring features in most *Jackbox* games aren't subject to a delay, meaning that strict moderation is impossible without vetting players beforehand.

Perhaps the culmination of audience-stream interaction in the last few years is *HQ Trivia*, the livestream-game show hybrid over which everyone seemingly lost their collective minds in 2017. Boasting a staggering two mil-lion concurrent players[6] and a Time Magazine "App of the year" nod in its heyday, *HQ Trivia* was a live quiz show streamed through a mobile app, which all viewers could play along with. Enough right answers could win you real money, and for a while the app seemed to recapture the game show craze of years past. Though it still technically exists as of this writing, *HQ Trivia* has since lost the majority of its funding and suspended operations entirely be-fore revival through an acquisition. It remains to be seen whether *HQ Trivia*, or another app like it, will make a permanent position for itself in the stream-ing space. Nonetheless, this level of interaction is more akin to betting of a sort than playing, being somewhat impersonal.

In theory, the richer experience of viewer play-along can be accomplished for any multiplayer game with a suitable invite system. *Jackbox* and *Among Us* provide codes for easy join-up that hosts can share with a selection of their viewers. *Human: Fall Flat*, a physics-based puzzler and fairly successful capturer of eyeballs on Twitch, allows players to generate an easily shareable invite link.

While making the leap from viewer to player isn't necessarily for everyone, the possibilities offered by interacting with livestreams further diversity the experiences games can offer. It remains to be seen whether these types of interactions will be a short-lived gimmick that never really takes off or the future of online content creation, but at any rate, streaming is certainly here to stay. In making our games more watchable, or perhaps even playable by those that lend their time to spectate, our designs can adapt to improve the experience of people immersed in this new medium.

Expert Profile: Kris Alexander—Learn to play, play to learn

Assistant Professor at Toronto Metropolitan University & esports competitor

Kris Alexander's fascination with games began when he was 14, just after getting his first job. His parents, two Grenadians-turned-Canadians, had three kids, and money was tight. The family rule was simple: do anything you want, as long as you can pay for it. Kris wanted to play games, play the piano, and go to school, and so he did. Often working two or three jobs at a time, Kris lived at home until he was almost 30, helping to pay down the mortgage and support his siblings while earning several degrees. At the same time, he became a globally ranked player in both *Street Fighter 3: Third Strike* and the digital card game *Lightseekers*. He also trained in classical piano, earning an undergraduate degree in sound engineering and a Master's in media production.

For his PhD, Kris studied the role of games and interactivity in education, firmly in line with his current role as a professor at Toronto Metropolitan University (TMU).

(Continued)

[6] Source: TechCrunch, accessible as of this writing at https://techcrunch.com/2018/08/14/hq-trivia-apple-tv/

(Continued)

Following from his doctoral work, Kris strives to apply game design to the courses he develops, and his interactions with students. "I would love to consider myself as a game designer who is an educator," he says, arguing that the task of guiding players is not so different from that of guiding students.

Kris argues that interactivity in itself is a mode of learning, much in the same way as text, audio, or video. Much of his work is focused on offering students different learning opportunities to suit individual needs. This isn't an entirely academic exercise, either: it's rooted in his own experiences studying at university. Kris says he struggled to focus on assigned readings in school, until he created his own audiobooks of sorts using text-to-speech software and his own hip-hop mixes as background music. Afterwards, Kris says his grades shot up, sparking an interest in multimodal approaches to learning. It's something he's since applied in several settings, including teaching his daughter to read by showing her what she says in real time via speech recognition.

In the classroom, Kris' teaching focuses on multimedia and rich interaction, where the playful influence of game design is prominently on display. Some of his classes are delivered via Twitch, with chat integration allowing students to throw their questions on the big screen. He's created video content summaries delivered by a virtual avatar—a bear given life by his impression of an English accent—to help knock down the barrier of postsecondary professionalism. He's even gone so far as to colour-match his wardrobe with weekly slides and syllabus headings, one of the many "Easter eggs" he likes to include in classes for students to find. Kris sees his actions as part of a larger effort reaching beyond his own class: "It's not for me. It's about bringing awareness to the world about the things outside of video game *playing* that can benefit society."

The potential of games in education, Kris says, is immensely underdeveloped. He offers up history class as an example of unrealized potential, where games like the *Assassin's Creed* series have undergone significant consultation with historians as part of development. Why not ask students to explore virtual worlds and pick out landmarks, artworks, and events to compare with historical truths, thus fostering an interest in history and developing critical media literacy? Kris becomes animated at the prospect of embracing games more fully in education, explaining that a large part of his motivation is to create the classroom he wished he had in his youth: "That could fix school!"

Outside teaching, Kris runs a research lab at TMU called *The Conduit*, focused on educational applications of game design and the development of infrastructure for esports at postsecondary institutions. That second point is a big part of his current role, comprising everything from work with networking hardware to setting up scholarship opportunities. "We focus on everything outside the playing," he chuckles, noting the behind-the-scenes work necessary to set up a proper league.

But Kris says labour isn't the only, or even the most challenging, obstacle on the path to creating professional opportunities for students in esports. He says that his first crack at pitching esports to a university almost a decade ago was met with a resounding and outright dismissive rejection, though general attitudes have improved in the past few years. Since that first rejection, he's started two such programs at different schools, including one in his current post at TMU.

Although games have been mainstream entertainment for some time, Kris says their legitimization in education is still lacking. Many educators have some degree of skepticism as to the value of games, which Kris attributes partially to a generational gulf between students and teachers who may have grown up without exposure to the medium. But that gulf is closing quickly, as new educators come into the field and older professionals get acquainted with games. "What excites me the most is that people are finally starting to listen," Kris says, a sign of change to come.

Change is also overdue in the industry, he says, noting that using games for education depends on developer buy-in. He draws infallible parallels between game design and teaching, insisting that any game designer claiming not to be a teacher of sorts is mistaken. Speaking of both games and classroom development, he describes the task of design as "trying to carefully craft something that somebody can interact with, stay motivated with, engage with, and most importantly transfer learning from." Developers, Kris says, don't always realize the full potential of the things they create, or for that matter, themselves: "They think that they're making fun experiences for entertainment. That's true, but also, they represent the teachers of the future."

This framing of game design as a form of education and vice versa fits nicely with Kris' understanding of game interaction itself, which he describes as "a bidirectional engagement between player and [designer]." "For me," he says, "good interaction design comes from understanding your outcomes as they relate to the audience." He says this true whether those interactions are being designed for a game, a classroom, or any other experience with some semblance of an intended takeaway for participants. To Kris, gaining that ability to understand outcomes in relation to your players (or students) is a matter of learning to analyze why you enjoy certain experiences, and break down the reasons why different groups might enjoy others.

While advances in technology and design have made interaction more complicated, Kris says that all interaction design is still firmly centred around engaging our basic senses. That engagement might be something exotic—here, Kris invokes Smell-O-Vision—or as simple as listening to the description of a new foe in a game of *Dungeons and Dragons*—he excitedly recounts his recent first experience with the game over an online call. At any rate, Kris says that the success of a design is less about technological sophistication, and more about understanding people, giving them a sense of presence and importance in worlds both virtual and real.

For all his time spent in education, Kris says one of the most useful things he learned came from *Street Fighter.* He cites the parry mechanic, by which a skilled player can anticipate and quite literally walk into an attack, as a life lesson of sorts, particularly in dealing with negativity. "That is how I look at almost every interaction. How can I pre-emptively assume that this person doesn't like video games, and walk into it?" He says he wants to fight stereotypes, grinning as he recounts placing as a top *Street Fighter* player globally despite picking one of the "worst" characters, an experience he likens to being a person of colour in academia. As an advocate for the importance of games in and outside the classroom, Kris is pushing for change in more ways than one. Above all, he's working towards a world where games can help us learn to lead better lives.

Further reading

This is Esports by Paul Chaloner (Bloomsbury Sport). ISBN: 978-1472977762.
An introduction to the world of esports from a general interest perspective. If you're a fan of the space or looking for more insight as to their general appeal, this is a good place to start.

Watch Me Play: Twitch and the Rise of Game Live Streaming by T.L. Taylor (Princeton University Press). ISBN: 978-0691165967.
An overview of how game streaming came to be, and has grown: a great primer if you're especially intrigued by the idea of designing for streaming. It's also available online for free, courtesy of the author.

The Fall of the Fourth Wall, open-access research article by Samantha Stahlke, James Robb, and Pejman Mirza-Babaei (IGI Global).
We were collaborators on this article a couple of years prior to writing this book, looking at the design (and evaluation) of interactive game streaming experiences.

Sources on Twitch Plays Pokémon

The bizarre, mind-numbing, mesmerizing beauty of "Twitch Plays Pokémon" by Andrew Cunningham (Ars Technica). https://arstechnica.com/gaming/2014/02/the-bizarre-mind-numbing-mesmerizing-beauty-of-twitch-plays-pokemon/.

Twitch Plays Pokemon conquers Elite Four, beating game after 390 hours by Nick Statt (CNET). : https://www.cnet.com/news/twitch-plays-pokemon-conquers-elite-four-beating-game-after-390-hours/.

Generation 1 Timeline, community-maintained resource on TPPedia Wiki. https://helixpedia.fandom.com/wiki/Generation_1_Timeline.

Exercises

Port-a-Game: Twitch edition

Reimagine a favourite game to be made with the *intent* of being turned into a crowd-driven title in the fashion of Twitch Plays Pokémon. How will the game work? How will its mechanics be any different—for example, how will you replace or tweak sections requiring precise timing?
What commands will you offer to your crowd of players, and how will they input those commands? Will you use a chat system, or design your own virtual web interface?

Field research

Pick a game-playing stream on a platform like Twitch and watch it live—you want a stream with a chat lively enough to have a steady flow of conversation, but not so many participants that you can't follow any of what's being said. Keep an eye on the proportion of messages which are directly related to the game (e.g., suggestions about strategy/what the player should do) versus general chatter.

Take notes on the game-related messages that people are sending; what are people interested in when watching this game/streamer? Pick another stream of the same game if you have time and repeat the process. Can you see any patterns?

Based on your observations in the field, what features would you add to the game to support audience interaction? What does the audience's discussion suggest in terms of what they would find interesting?

9

Rise of the Machines

The *Grand Theft Auto* (*GTA*) series is famous for being a crime sandbox of sorts, where players are free to wreak havoc on its virtual inhabitants. For any *GTA V* fan, a normal day in Los Santos consists of starting fires, beating up random people on the street, robbing banks, and of course, stealing cars.

For all the controversy historically surrounding the *GTA* games' violent roots, there is more on offer than pure wanton destruction. Beneath the veneer of hardened criminals and high-stakes gang missions lie living cities filled with toys for players to experiment with. In many ways, the franchise lives up to the open world promise of "go anywhere, do anything." Theoretically, players can spend their time bowling, window-shopping for new shoes, or stealing a vacant emergency vehicle and pretending to be a firefighter all day.

As you can imagine, this deal of freedom results in a fair number of unusual scenarios making for memorable stories. It also results in a notable amount of internet fodder in the form of videos chronicling players' most oddball half-baked heist attempts, ludicrous ways of getting themselves killed, and other various popcorn moments.

One *GTA V* video from 2015[1] chronicles the seemingly mundane interaction of a verbal confrontation with an NPC. The player walks up to a man and greets him. The man responds in kind, and the player offers up a taunt in return. Enraged, the man throws down his cigarette and the situation quickly descends into an exchange of profanities. "You are dead meat!", the man shouts, advancing on the player with his green polo shirt and soul patch growing ever more menacing. At this point, the player resorts to their last logical option and draws a gun. Mid-animation, the man immediately returns to a resting pose with a deadpan expression, and says in a calm tone, "I want to apologize."

---

[1] Since links for videos tend to vanish rather easily, if you'd like to find this clip for yourself, the search term you'll want to use is "GTA I want to apologize".

The Game Designer's Playbook. Samantha Stahlke and Pejman Mirza-Babaei, Oxford University Press.
© Samantha Stahlke and Pejman Mirza-Babaei (2022). DOI: 10.1093/oso/9780198845911.003.0009

On top of being one of the best ways to spend fifteen seconds of your life, this video is notable for its role in the landscape of fine gaming-focused internet humour. While an admittedly minor blip on a relative scale, it spawned an entire community with over 40,000 members as of this writing on content aggregation site Reddit. The subreddit r/iwanttoapologize catalogues amusing game AI behaviours, mostly consisting of bugs and questionable design decisions. Its selection of clips is an exemplary way to kill a few hours, particularly if you're fond of watching people float away in invisible vehicles or scream at nothing.

In games, our artificial companions and adversaries in games can be a source of humour, to be sure. But for every chuckle-worthy glitch, there's a heart-stopping moment when you know you've been bested by a difficult enemy, or a heartwarming one watching a couple of virtual dogs play together. Sometimes, you'll wonder how a developer thought that two distinct voice lines would be enough for an NPC you run into every fifteen minutes. Other times, you'll remark at its apparent cleverness, or find that it blends into the background as part of the virtual world you inhabit. But before we can tackle the challenge of designing good AI for our games, let's take a moment to pin down what it is in the first place.

9.1 The toaster is sentient now

AI, or artificial intelligence, is a catch-all term for computers exhibiting traits associated with human intelligence. There is no universal definition for AI, though we'll offer one of the more understandable options here: artificial intelligence is the ability of a computer to acquire and apply knowledge or skills to solve problems. The problems we're concerned with can be anything from classifying images, to controlling a robot, to writing a symphony—the idea being that a perfect "artificial general intelligence" could handle any problem that a human can.

There are a number of terms you'll hear thrown around in regard to the field of AI, and while you don't need to be an expert in any of them to understand or use this chapter, we'll explain a few in the interest of demystification. The first is *symbolic* or *classical* AI, referring to techniques which explicitly embed human knowledge. In other words, you outline the problem-solving process in code, defining rules for a system to follow along the way. A simple example might be something like a routine for playing tic-tac-toe, which first examines whether the program can win on its current turn before moving on to assess the best possible move. In stark contrast to classical AI is *machine learning* (ML), which describes algorithms that solve problems without being explicitly programmed for a specific task.

ML seems like an impossibility the first time you hear of it. Even after you've worked with it for a while, machine learning is still magic, and frankly even more of a headache. There are many different types of machine learning algorithms, the vast majority of which work in more or less the same way. You have a problem, and a massive set of already-solved examples. You use these examples to "train" an ML algorithm, and then apply that algorithm to solve new examples for you.

Consider the task of data classification; maybe you want to assess whether a player in an online game is at risk for toxic behaviour based on their game-play statistics like win/loss rate, playing time per day, and so on. You take a collection of player records, for which you've manually flagged any users with a history of harassment. You feed these records, sans flags, into the algorithm of your choosing, like a *random forest classifier*.[2] At first, your classifier won't be any good at guessing whether an individual player was labelled as a troublemaker. By peeking at the labels, the algorithm will tweak the logic it uses to separate players into the "safe" and "trouble" bins—in the case of the algorithm we mentioned, this could be something like swapping out which gameplay statistics it focuses on. After this "training" phase, you can give the algorithm the gameplay records for new players, and it will estimate whether those players are likely to give you grief.

A subset of machine learning is *deep learning*, used in reference to a specific family of algorithms known as neural networks. Neural networks were conceived as a loose approximation of biological brain matter, consisting of artificial neurons or "perceptrons" that output values based on incoming connections from input data or other perceptrons. Each perceptron can have its own logic for how it manipulates the values of those incoming connections. Essentially, each incoming value is multiplied by some number which can be tweaked to change what the perceptron's output will be. Stack a bunch of these together and you have a neural network, the likes of which have been applied to everything from reading brain scans to generating photographs of imaginary humans.

Perhaps unsurprisingly, the nature of AI has given it an air of mystery and power in popular culture. Even when home computers weren't yet achievable, AI had already cemented itself in the public consciousness—from the android in *Metropolis* (1927) to the infamously maniacal HAL 9000 in *2001: A Space Odyssey* (1968). In the current media landscape, AI often fulfills the

---

[2] This isn't necessary by any means for understanding this chapter, but if you're curious: a random forest is an "ensemble" of decision trees. A decision tree, in turn, essentially generates a flowchart through which a particular record is fed to determine its classification. In the case discussed, such a tree might have a nodes which effectively ask questions like "Is the player's win rate below 30%?" or "Has the player ever reported another player's behaviour?". A random forest is like a council of decision trees, considering the output of many individual models to make a more informed decision.

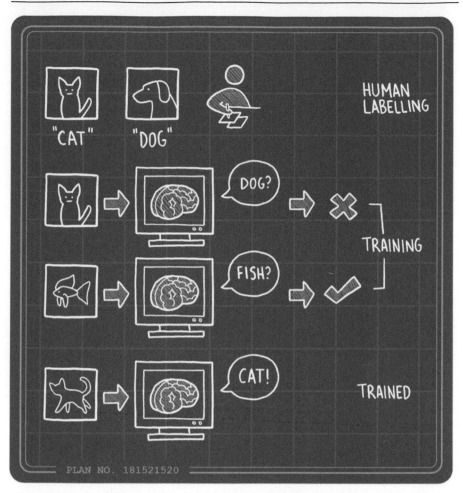

Figure 9.1 A classical task for machine learning is image classification. First, training data is labelled by a human (top). Then, the system is repeatedly tasked with classifying images. Based on its errors and successes, at first tantamount to random guessing, values in the system are tweaked to improve performance over time through training (middle). After training, the system can be shown previously unseen images and classify them, hopefully accurately (bottom).

role of the foreboding big bad that will ultimately lead to ruin, temporarily snatching the crown of world destroyer from zombies, aliens, alien zombies, or zombie aliens.[3]

Impending doom aside, AI also holds the promise of the future. Its potential to create a dystopia is largely outpaced by all the wondrous possibilities

---

[3] An important distinction to note here is that an alien zombie is a human who becomes a zombie after infection by an alien, while a zombie alien is an alien who is also a zombie.

it offers. Maybe AI will cure cancer. Maybe AI will help us solve the climate crisis. Maybe AI will get us out of the solar system. And if you still have a cable subscription or don't have an adblocker installed, I'm sure you know that AI can help you fix your online reputation, improve your credit score, and pick the jeans cut that works for you (maybe). These days, AI is all the rage, and corporate-speak is especially infatuated with machine learning buzzwords. If you're looking for venture capital or a script deal, throw the phrase *deep learning* into the mix and maybe AI will make you an overnight millionaire.

Fortunately for us, AI in games doesn't have to be so grand. Something as simple as a routine for an NPC that tosses a stone at you when you're not looking and then whistles innocently when you turn around can give players a moment of delight. A few if statements that make a character passive if ignored and hostile if shot at can be perfectly serviceable, with no fancy ML or complex rulesets required. Great game AI is just as much design as it is technology, if not more so.

The history of AI in the context of games is an interesting and storied one. Both board and digital games have been used as a testbed for improving AI techniques for decades, while simple AI has in turn proven itself a staple of video games. Today, game technology is advancing forward with the help of AI, by way of things like increasingly marvellous procedural generation and AI-driven development tools. We aim to design good AI for players to interact with, and in a far more sophisticated form, AI can help us produce good designs.

When you think of the phrase "game AI," though, you're probably not thinking of a super-intelligent development assistant that can help you design better platforming levels. You're probably thinking of the guy in the polo shirt from *Grand Theft Auto*. And so that's where we'll start.

9.2 AI that plays with you

Game-playing AI has existed for decades at this point, while the idea of game-playing AI has intrigued people for centuries. In the late 1700s, Hungarian inventor Wolfgang von Kempelen created a machine he claimed to be an automaton capable of playing chess. The machine, which included a mechanical human model, was dubbed The Turk. And indeed, Kempelen's Turk could beat most human players, a fantastic achievement for the time.

Of course, this achievement owed itself to a hoax, as The Turk's cabinet concealed more than just machinery. A human operator sat inside, controlling the "player" via mechanical linkages and observing the board via magnets attracted to the rigged pieces used for the game. A few other chess automatons created in the decades that followed used similar tricks, but suspicion didn't stop them from captivating their audiences.

When computers came along, playing games became a natural demonstration of their ability, with the goal of besting humans in games of strategy serving as objectives for early AI development. Chess was a longstanding problem, from the first true automatons built to attempt the game in the early twentieth century to the grandmaster programs of today. Perhaps the most famous milestone along the way was the victory of IBM's Deep Blue over Garry Kasparov in 1997, the first time a computer defeated a human world champion under standard tournament rules. It would be the first time of many, as the last time a human reportedly won out in such a match was back in 2005.

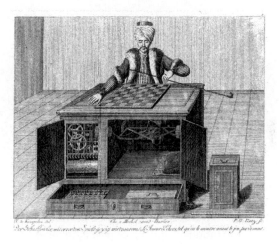

Figure 9.2 A wood engraving print of the original Turk. Many of the mechanisms visible to the audience (e.g., the left cabinet) were largely for show.

Credit: Image from a book by Karl Gottlieb von Windisch (public domain), via Wikimedia Commons.

Since the conquering of chess, other games have found themselves as fodder for AI developers, including both board and digital games. In *DotA 2*, AI team OpenAI Five recently defeated OG, human two-time world champions, marking the first victory of an AI over world champions in any esport. And in the realm of board games, the late 2010s saw Google's DeepMind team racked up wins against world champion *Go* players with the AlphaGo AI. Since then, subsequent projects building on AlphaGo have improved on and generalized its performance to other games, including chess and classic arcade games.

Creating a state-of-the-art competitive AI player is a challenge that demands remarkable technical effort and computational resources. From a game design perspective, though, we aren't usually concerned with creating the *most skilled* AI. Instead, any AI that players interact with should be aimed at enhancing their experience as much as possible. Or rather, as much as reasonably possible given the programming time and performance budget available. This might mean trying to create a skilled challenger for the player, but the AI that you encounter in games isn't always an adversary, and it's almost never trying to call itself the next Deep Blue.

Player-facing AI has a myriad of different manifestations, which we could split up in all sorts of ways from complexity, to behaviour, to the type of entity being controlled. In the interest of keeping our design thinking centred squarely on the player, we'll make our distinction based on the role that AI serves relative to players.

Figure 9.3 Three types of AI characters in BioShock Infinite: The player's companion, Elizabeth (left); an enemy (middle), and a group of ambivalent NPCs (right).

Credit: *BioShock Infinite* was developed by Irrational Games/Ghost Story Games and published by 2K Games.

First, we can speak of supportive AI, which assists the player in some way through direct interaction. The most straightforward example of supportive AI is a friendly companion character, such as Elizabeth in *BioShock Infinite* or Alyx in the *Half-Life 2* games. Another example of supportive AI might be a character that delivers contextual hints, such as the protagonists of the *Trine* games, who remark on potential puzzle-solving strategies if players stay in one place for too long.

At the other end of the spectrum is opposing AI, which works against the player. This includes enemy AI ranging in complexity from goons in a turn-based RPG like *Final Fantasy*, to the practice AI opponents in a multiplayer game like *Overwatch*, to the intricate bosses in a game like *Sekiro* or *Dark Souls*. This is probably the first category that comes to mind when thinking of "game AI," since once of the core functions of AI in many games is to provide the tension and challenge of conflict in the absence of other human players.

Lastly, we can bin other AI controllers into the classification of independent AI, which doesn't have any strong "feelings" about the player one way or another. This includes most drone-like NPC behaviour in a building or management game like *Zoo Tycoon* or *Planet Coaster*, or the more complex behaviour of agents in a god game like *The Sims* series. Independent AI might also serve a sort of decorative function, making a world feel more alive—think of city crowds or herds of animals in an open-world game.

Obviously, these categories are far from mutually exclusive. Some AI might rest in a permanent state of overlap between them (you might think of a shopkeeper character as resting between independence and support), while others can shift depending on context (an independent city guard might become supportive if you do them a favour, and turn into an adversary if you assault them). Nonetheless, when designing an AI that interacts with players, the intended purpose of those interactions should be at the forefront of your thinking.

9.2.1 *What makes a good friend (or foe)*

Irrespective of whether a given AI agent should be helping out, setting things on fire, or just minding its own business, our core goal is the same: to improve the player experience in some way. The assistance of a supportive AI should be seen as helpful, the opposition of an adversarial AI should prove a fair challenge, and any independent AI should be interesting or at least understandable depending on its application. If these objectives are met, players are more likely to perceive the AI in a positive light—on the flip side, players are unlikely to enjoy interacting with a "helper" AI that gets in the way, an enemy that seems to cheat, or an independent AI that's just plain boring.

We can identify several desirable traits in helping any AI that players encounter to improve their experience and perception of said AI as a result:

Believability. Making sure that an AI's behaviour seems feasible is an important part of maintaining suspension of disbelief. Players understand that their treasured companions and vicious enemies are little more than several if statements wearing a trench coat, but you want to preserve the illusion that those trench coats are thinking beings. This is true no matter an AI's intended purpose. When support AI makes sensible decisions, it's easier for players to form bonds with the characters that assist them. For opposing AI, a believable level of skill helps keep combat scenarios feeling fair. And for independent AI, believable actions are critical to player understanding when that AI supports gameplay, such as customers in a management sim.

It might seem like *Skyrim* is our favourite game to rag on at this point; in its decade-long lifetime, the game has given us all many wonderful experiences, but there's no denying that it is rife with opportunities for improvement to learn from. One such opportunity is its AI design, which can damage immersion in places. In combat, for instance, most enemies lack any apparent memory or strategic depth. A bandit can be struck from the shadows and respond, "Is someone there?" with an arrow visibly sticking out of their head. After a brief aggro period and walking ten metres from their post to look for the source of said arrow, they'll happily return to standing against their favourite wall, arrow and all, and start singing a sea chanty.

Bandits are far from the only victims of questionable AI design choices in the world of *Skyrim*. During vampire raids on villages, unarmoured NPCs are keen to draw their iron daggers, run into the action, and die immediately. In combat, any companions you've partied up tend to run in front of you, blocking your shots with their own health bar. The shopkeeper you speak with afterwards might have the same voice actor as six of the goons you just killed. And in the middle of an important moment—attending a funeral, climbing a mountain, getting a beatdown from a dragon—the courier will run up to you and hand over a letter, probably informing you of inheritance from an NPC that just got themselves killed. While amusing, moments like this make AI feel less human (or elven, or whatever the nature of the being

Figure 9.4 The courier does not frolic. He does not eat. He does not sleep. He does not dream. He only hunts his next target, letter satchel in hand.

Credit: *The Elder Scrolls V: Skyrim* was developed by Bethesda Games and published by Bethesda Softworks.

simulated). *Skyrim* being *Skyrim*, it's hard to tell if certain moments are intentional design decisions, oversights, or glitches, but they detract from the intended experience at any rate.

Believability doesn't imply total realism, of course. Something like having wounded enemies eventually calm down can help players recover from hasty mistakes and preserve their ability to complete a combat sequence with their desired playstyle. That said, arrow-in-the-face sea chanties thirty seconds after getting shot cross the line a bit. Stretching the limits in other cases can improve experience, though. Generally beloved AI companion Elizabeth from *BioShock Infinite* will toss the player needed items like health and weapons in the nick of time based on their current status. These items don't have to exist in the world beforehand, and Elizabeth will teleport behind the scenes to a location where she can easily aim at the player. But these supernatural enhancements to her ability impact the experience positively, because they contribute to the ultimately believable experience of a smart companion helping you out with something you need. Since Elizabeth's navigation during combat prioritizes finding cover and staying out of the player's way, it's easier to believe she has time to rummage around and find things while you're occupied blowing away enemies. Plus, this logic minimizes the chance she'll run into your line of fire, unlike some other companions we could mention.

The last thing to note here is that part of believability is often imperfection. Not nonstop wall-headbutting stupidity, but flaws that make behaviour more relatable, interesting, and fair. A simple example is enemy aim or other combat abilities. In theory, enemies can play perfectly; their reaction time is limited to one iteration of a game's update loop, they can aim right at the player, and they can act immediately. But playing against such an opponent would feel unfair. As a baseline, enemies should have some inaccuracy in their aiming. Every pull of the trigger shouldn't be a guaranteed headshot. And for melee attacks or boss rushes, actions should be telegraphed before they happen, lest players accuse an AI of being "cheap."

Adjusting an AI to become more or less skilled in this regard is a good way to provide players with diverse levels of challenge. Difficulty sliders which operate by reducing ammo drops and turning enemies into bullet sponges fall into a category of game design best described as "It's Fine, I Guess." Assuming you have the development time, adjusting aspects of AI behaviour, such as an enemy's probability of seeking cover, or the quality of their aim, can prove a much more interesting and believable way of moderating difficulty.

Context-appropriate complexity. Our use of the term *complexity* here boils down to variation in behaviour. More complexity might mean access to a larger library of combat strategies, more diverse or detailed animations, or just a few extra voice lines. No matter the function of a particular character, more complexity makes an AI more interesting to interact with, ignoring any poor implementation or bad decisions made within those extra behaviours. Having many different behaviours can make companions seem more helpful, opponents feel more devious, and regular denizens of the world more interesting to observe.

Of course, since your design time and performance targets impose restrictions here, you will need to be judicious in deciding how ornate your AI should be. At the extreme end of simplicity are the crowds of hundreds you'll see in a management sim, like so-called "peeps" in the *RollerCoaster Tycoon* series. Any individual peep has a basic set of needs that determine their current target (e.g., a hungry peep will seek a concession stand), and the pathfinding to get there. That's pretty much it in terms of individuality; in the player's typical view, they're a crowd of coloured blobs that dispense money. Simple behaviours work here because most of the player's time will be spent working on building rather than following individual peeps like some sort of nature documentarian.

Contrast this with a case where players get closer to AI, and behaviour needs to be more complex. If you're running around a city in first-person, you'll expect pedestrians to sidestep out of your way, and if there's any hint of RPG mechanics, you'll probably want to be able to talk to everyone there. Unfortunately, having a huge crowd of detailed NPCs in one place can still be quite computationally expensive at this writing. This is why you'll tend to see open-world cities with hundreds of NPCs in their pre-rendered E3 trailers, and maybe two dozen characters in the same place at release (if you're lucky). Quality over quantity in this regard can help to keep things feeling alive; consider the city-dwellers in *Watch Dogs: Legion*, which each have their own defined occupation, relationships, and daily schedules. Having the kind of characters that you *could* follow around like some sort of nature documentarian can keep things feeling alive in the absence of real-world levels of crowding.

Naturally, the AI that players interact with most deeply and frequently should be the most complex. First-person combat engagements are a great example, and there are few games that achieved such landmark progress in this regard (and in general game AI) as Monolith's *F.E.A.R.* Monolith pioneered a novel variation of game AI known as goal-oriented action planning (GOAP), giving designers and programmers alike more freedom in customizing AI behaviours. In a nutshell, GOAP applies a pathfinding algorithm to behaviour. Instead of only using pathfinding to find a route through the world to a geographical destination, the AI in *F.E.A.R.* uses pathfinding to identify a "route" composed of *actions* to reach a particular goal. For instance, if an AI is trying to kill the player, but is out of ammunition, they'll need to use a melee attack. But first, they'll have to move closer to the player to hit them. GOAP will produce a sequence of actions for the AI to execute in service to its goal: first, move to the player, and then, smack them.

The result of applying GOAP in *F.E.A.R.*, along with some other clever tricks we'll discuss later, is a set of AI behaviours which seem incredibly complex and believable. Different characters have different sets of actions and goals available to them, resulting in diverse behaviour. A stealthy enemy might wait in the shadows and strike the player if they're not careful about positioning. Someone toting an assault rifle will dive behind cover, and if the player gets in a lucky shot, the AI will blind fire to try and keep them at bay. This kind of variation in behaviour makes encounters with the AI far more engaging.

Predictability (sometimes). If you're trying to make a character as believable as possible—particularly a human—you might be tempted to make them unpredictable, since us humans tend to have all the reliability of a 1977 Lada with the doors taped on. But while the occasional loose cannon is fun to interact with, it's often best if players have a clear idea of what an AI's behaviour is likely to be during gameplay. For support characters, this will give players someone they can count on. For opponents, predictability can be important to maintaining fairness. And for independent AI, predictability can help players manage their plans (e.g., knowing when a shopkeeper will be around).

Predictability can be an important progenitor of an enjoyable experience, particularly in certain contexts. Part of the fun in stealth games, for instance, comes from learning the patterns of enemy behaviour and taking advantage of those patterns to avert detection or take out enemies unseen. A game like *Dishonored* wouldn't be able to deliver on the desired experience if enemies moved around randomly; predicting behaviour is necessary to careful planning on the part of the player. This isn't to say that behaviours have to be boring or simplistic, either. AI characters might have multiple behavioural options for certain scenarios which players are expected to learn and anticipate as well, introducing more complexity into the process of strategic planning.

Another situation dependent on judicious predictability is boss fights. In any game that features prominent boss fights, from the likes of *Dark Souls* or *Sekiro* to *Cuphead*, *Hollow Knight*, or even *Terraria*, learnable attack patterns are a must for players to achieve a satisfying loop of trial, learning, and failure on their eventual road to success. Consider something like the bosses in *Hollow Knight*; although a grand diversity of fights are on offer, each one includes the factor of predictability in full force. The agile fighter Hornet, for instance, will rear up for each of her lightning-fast directional attacks, giving the player time to reposition or dodge appropriately. Over time, players will see each of her attacks, and these attacks will be repeated time and again, allowing players to improve in dealing with them. In experiences like these, predictability of AI behaviours is instrumental in players' journey towards mastery.

Figure 9.5 A boss "telgraphing" an attack in *Cuphead*. The windup for an attack shows the character leaning back and breathing in (left) before spitting a projectile at the player (right).

Credit: *Cuphead* was developed and published by Studio MDHR.

Interactive. It seems like a given that AI should interact with the player, but this interaction is of little value if players don't perceive it to be meaningful. An AI character should react to the players' actions, and remember those actions, at least for a while. Unless you're writing a controller for a goldfish, you generally want to avoid the situation where any AI close to the player snaps between behaviours with a total disregard for what the player is doing. Our aforementioned friend Elizabeth from *BioShock Infinite* manages to avoid the goldfish problem with a few clever tricks, such as maintaining a shaken-up demeanour after a combat encounter instead of snapping back to her pre-fight state of relative tranquility.

Remembering players' actions is also of narrative importance, as we discussed in Chapter 6. The operation of a dialogue tree might not be the first thing to come to mind when you think of game AI. But characters that the player interacts with purely through speech can benefit greatly from carefully crafted reactions to different events that the player experiences. In the roguelike *Hades*, for example, NPCs that the player encounters will remark on what they've heard of the player's latest exploits in specific detail—specifically referring to areas they've explored recently, rival characters they've interacted with, or how they last died. This does a great job of maintaining the illusion that these characters are far more than a set of text boxes, as opposed to a more traditional strategy of barking the same voice lines with little change in response to what the player is actually doing.

Beyond their relationships with the player, AI agents should also interact with each other. Having enemies that never talk to each other and relentlessly gang up on the player one by one without regard for tactics is uninteresting. Establishing some form of social relationship, strategy, or basic communication makes their behaviour more dynamic and interesting. In the *Metal Gear Solid* games, enemies can radio one another for backup. Rather than being pure window dressing, it's possible for the player to prevent this by destroying radios or communication equipment, giving the impression that characters actually interact with each other. This can come through in (relatively) small touches as well, like the fact that given sufficient time to play out, characters in *Hitman* will bring out a body bag for a deceased comrade instead of standing next to their corpse as if nothing happened.

Figure 9.6 Upon returning to the House of Hades, the player's resting spot in between runs, a friendly character will remark on the player's death (above). In this case, he explicitly references the Wretched Thugs, a type of enemy responsible for the player's last death (below). Most of the many characters the player interacts with will regularly reference the goings-on of recent playthroughs, lending them a great deal of believability.

Credit: *Hades* was developed and published by Supergiant Games.

Creative. Successful AI design is also about injecting personality into a character's actions. In creating game AI, we aren't confined to replicating

257

the same sort of generic soldier AI for every ally and enemy that players will encounter. One way to do this is by toying with an AI's motivations; even subtle changes can make a game feel more alive. For instance, the ghosts in *Pac-Man* each have unique "personalities" resulting in behaviour that keeps players on their toes, and if you pay attention closely enough, might even yield some admiration of their quirks. One ghost rushes the player down, another tries to predict where the player will be, one has an affinity for the first ghost, and the final ghost doesn't particularly care what's going on at all. This prevents boredom by avoiding a scenario where four of the same AI would eventually just follow the player in a line of some sort, while staying within the strict technological confines of its time.

Figure 9.7 Many of the enemies in *Deep Rock Galactic* are classed as different types of "glyphids", spiderlike creatures with varying abilities and levels of threat. Distinct designs and behaviours help make the landscape of enemies feel incredibly diverse. Clockwise from top left: a regular glyphid "grunt"; an armoured glyphid "guard"; the dangerously explosive glyphid "detonator"; the pesky but relatively benign glyphid "swarmer".

Credit: *Deep Rock Galactic* was developed by Ghost Ship Games and published by Coffee Stain Games.

Another thing to experiment with is what an AI character is able to perceive, instead of relying exclusively on logic which boils down to "if the player is in front of the AI, they can be seen." Playing with something a bit more complex can lead to more interesting strategies, and is particularly effective in a horror context. The loveable abomination Jeff from *Half-Life: Alyx* is blind and responds only to sound, while the less loveable abomination of the Witch in *Left 4 Dead* is hypersensitive to light but ignores passing gunfire entirely.

How different characters perform the same type of action, such as moving or attacking, can help bring their design alive as well. A charming example of these behavioural variations can be seen in *Deep Rock Galactic*. The legion of bugs ("glyphids") in *DRG* will quickly win you over, in spite of their relentless attempts to kill you. Regular glyphids will advance on the player, screeching and rearing up to attack. Smaller enemies will launch themselves, while larger armoured enemies will cheekily bring up their plated front legs to block the player from shooting in close proximity. And should you unlock the ability to tame an enemy for yourself, they'll have some added behaviours that could bring a smile even to the arachnophobes among us. They'll patiently plod along next to you, and that screeching animation is repurposed into a purr of sorts as the player pets them.

This type of attention to detail can help to make sure that a player's relationship with AI, whether friendly or hostile, is a positive contributor to their experience. But when it comes to emulating the qualities we have discussed here in practise, we can accomplish a shocking amount with fakery.

9.2.2 Smoke and mirrors

Under the time and performance constraints of game development, we find ourselves quite frequently in a position where our AI leans heavily on the "artificial" part and not so much the "intelligence" bit. To make behaviours seem more complex than they are, or to make sure players appreciate the full extent of what's there, can take a bit of doing. Our design strategy here can involve some trickery to make things work; the basis of our AI should reflect the characteristics we've already discussed, but we can accentuate those characteristics further without too much technical investment.

One thing that we can do is to provide extra communication to the player about what an AI is doing. There are a few reasons why it is beneficial to do this. Understanding an AI's behavioural patterns or plan can support gameplay decisions. For instance, knowing where your guests are planning to go in *Zoo Tycoon* can help you figure out better park layouts by observing their navigation. In something like an FPS, occasionally having a way to glean your enemy's next move feels like a special strategic opportunity. Gameplay value aside, communication can also help players appreciate behavioural details.

The aforementioned AI characters in *Watch Dogs: Legion* have an impressive level of detail in their daily routine, given that there's quite literally millions of characters with procedurally generated occupations and relationships. Without following these characters around for hours on end, though, players might not appreciate the care put into constructing these behaviours. In the absence of unachievably realistic moment-to-moment interactions,

Figure 9.8 In *Zoo Tycoon 2*, players can click on animals (or human guests) and see what they're doing—or planning to do.

Credit: *Zoo Tycoon 2* was developed by Blue Fang Studios and published by Microsoft Game Studios.

players could easily assume that the groups of characters they run across are mindless crowds until the player triggers some mission involving them. Ubisoft's inclusion of a profiler gadget, which players can use to reveal a character's schedule, serves as an explicit communication of character behaviour. If players don't appreciate this detail immediately, in using that schedule as a later reference to track down a character, they'll realize that characters follow their routines to the letter. This might prompt players to follow around other characters, or profile them just to learn about their daily lives. Here, communication helps ensure that players notice the efforts put into AI behaviours.

Communication can also be used to create a powerful illusion that a game's AI is more complicated than in actuality. Remember that impressive AI from *F.E.A.R.* that we examined earlier? On top of its individual planning tech, the game also has a system to coordinate the behaviour of multiple enemies in a given combat encounter. To communicate actions to the player, dialogue barks are used. But instead of just drawing players' attention to thoughtful details, these lines also make characters seem smarter and more capable than they are. For instance, the last surviving enemy in an encounter will call for reinforcements—even though no mechanism for reinforcements exists. However, when players run into the next (already planned) group of enemies, the implication is that these are the reinforcements called in by the last goon. Another tactic employed by the developers is to fake a social dynamic by having one enemy issue a verbal order which others will follow. But in reality, no such system exists; instead, after the group's behaviour is already determined, voice lines are selected to act as if that behaviour resulted from a leader giving orders.

Apart from communicating behaviour, things like voice lines can help improve the believability of AI by lending a character some personality. Calling back to the shanties that bandits sing in *Skyrim*, and ignoring the dubious timing of such shanties among the mortally injured, giving your enemies life outside killing everything in sight makes them feel far more believable as people. This tactic doesn't just apply to human characters, either. In *Breath of the Wild*, for example, groups of bokoblins (for non-Hylian readers, basically goblins) can be seen snoozing together or dancing around their campfires before the player parachutes in and turns their cocktail party into a *Die Hard* sequel.

Adding in these sorts of touches—flavour animations, varying voice lines, and so on—usually won't demand much additional technical work, assuming you have a decent system for managing assets and so much as a basic state machine for AI. Of course, they quickly add up to a great deal of creative labour, so depending on the resources you have available, high-fidelity goblin dance loops might be out of scope. If you can spare the time though, adding some flourish onto AI characters can definitely bolster their believability and a player's interest.

Relatively simple technical tricks to make an entire world feel more alive can also be helpful here. If you've got any kind of biotic environment, hammering home the fact that things live there will make it feel more dynamic. If you can show those living things going about their business, players will appreciate it. And to do that, you don't necessarily have to invest in proper AI for all of them. Faraway creatures might even be relegated to particles, as is the case with *Subnautica*'s schools of fish. The player will encounter individual fish with independent behaviours while swimming around, but faraway groups are effectively a smokescreen, with a particle effect providing the illusion of many far-off fish populating the seas.[4]

A rite of passage for game programmers is the "boids" behaviour, which uses a model of basic forces to simulate a large group of entities, like a flock of birds, without advanced independent controllers. Similar, more

---

[4] The developer, Unknown Worlds, has confirmed this on Steam: https://steamcommunity.com/app/264710/discussions/0/617336568078226610/

Figure 9.9 In *A Plague Tale: Innocence*, characters are frequently swarmed by mobs of rats, which display convincing horde behaviour in spite of some trickery behind the scenes.

Credit: A Plague Tale: Innocence was developed by Asobo and published by Focus Home Interactive.

sophisticated logic was used in *A Plague Tale: Innocence* to simulate its hordes of rats without breaking the game's performance budget.[5] The player might see up to five thousand rats on screen at once. Of that five thousand, four hundred animate individually, while rats further from the player share a synchronized animation to reduce overhead, and those even further back don't play an animation at all. Giving each rat intricate individual behaviours was out of the question for performance reasons, and so as much as possible is abstracted to a herd level. For example, pathfinding produces a map of routes that the rats use, rather than having each rat individually plan their way to a given target. By tactically reducing the technical complexity of individual behaviour, games can achieve greater AI density without sacrificing the overall illusion of a dynamic world.

9.2.3 *Player-centric AI*

After focusing on the design of AI entities themselves, we should step back and re-evaluate our core goal: creating a good experience for the player. Having believable and enjoyable individuals or worlds to interact with is great, but in some situations, it might not be enough. Individual behaviours alone

---

[5] As described in an interview with the game's programmer here: https://www. rockpapershotgun.com/how-a-plague-tale-innocences-rat-hordes-were-made

can't necessarily accomplish certain things, like orchestrating a satisfying combat encounter with many enemies. We've danced around this already by mentioning things like the squad coordination system in *F.E.A.R.* and the simulation of horde behaviours. In many situations, we may need additional machinations behind the scenes to shape AI in a way that suits the player. While a great deal of the development effort needed becomes a technical challenge, the details of which are beyond the scope of this writing, this is an important area for designers to exercise their skills as well.

One such machination is the idea of dynamic difficulty adjustment (DDA), which shapes the challenge of a game to suit a player's current performance. The goal of DDA is to create an experience which is hard enough to preserve a sense of tension, while not being so difficult as to inspire defeatism. DDA is a form of AI in itself, in that it "solves the problem" of players having a boring or frustrating experience based on a set of rules specified by developers. DDA isn't an overwhelmingly common feature, but different forms have seen a fair amount of use over the years. An early example is *Crash Bandicoot 2*, where developer Naughty Dog incorporated tricks to make a player's experience a bit easier if they failed a section, like slowing down a fast-moving obstacle for an individual player if it repeatedly caused their demise.[6]

Many forms of DDA rely on adjusting AI opponents to become better or worse depending on a player's performance. In *Metal Gear Solid V*, the "revenge" system works to counter any tactics favoured by the player, forcing players to diversify their strategy or become better at exercising the strategy of their choice. For example, if the player typically relies on headshots to kill enemies, more enemies will don helmets to prevent being picked off from a distance. In this form, dynamic adjustment can help make sure that a player's play experience won't become stagnant by reducing the potential of certain strategies to become overpowered with practice.

Perhaps most infamous example of dynamic difficulty for AI is the so-called rubber banding employed in the *Mario Kart* series (among other racing games). Though Nintendo is notorious for keeping mum on accusations of cheating AI from frustrated players, a patent filed around the release of *Mario Kart: Double Dash* for a "racing game" with a dynamic place-targeting system to make games "more thrilling" pretty much speaks for itself.[7]

Indeed, the AI in *Mario Kart* does cheat in a sense; not every kart is trying to win. Instead, a couple of rival karts target high-place positions,

---

[6] As described by the developers here: https://all-things-andy-gavin.com/2011/02/07/making-crash-bandicoot-part-6/

[7] US patent 7278913, if you're curious.

Figure 9.10 Gaining ground in *Mario Ka*rt can be tricky enough thanks to the track geometry of maps like Rainbow Road (left). Once you do gain that ground, the blasted AI immediately gets a blue shell, and immediately uses that blue shell to ruin your day (right). (The blue shell is an item which automatically homes in on and slams down on the kart in first place.)

Credit: *Mario Kart 8* was developed and published by Nintendo.

while the rest of the pack intentionally stays behind. If the player is doing poorly, those rival karts can decelerate a little bit, while they'll up their driving game if the player is doing well. The goal here is to create an experience where players won't feel like it's impossible to win, while keeping them perpetually fighting to stay in the lead once they have it. Anecdotally, you'll notice other behaviours that seem to support this goal, like your AI opponents conveniently having a blue shell on hand (an item which seeks out and pummels the leader) as soon as you snag first place.

As you can see in virtually any online discussion of *Mario Kart*'s AI, this type of behaviour can frustrate players, so you'll need to design around it carefully. Consider hiding any obvious evidence of AI skill fluctuations (like suddenly accelerating or decelerating right in front of the player in a racing game), for instance. But for all its potential pains, cursing at the AI in *Mario Kart* is a treasured pastime at this point, and its sense of unending rivalry is one thing that helps keep the game interesting.

Instead of focusing solely on moderating challenge, a sophisticated approach to shaping a player's experience with AI might attempt to moderate *emotion*. This is exactly the goal of the AI "director" in the *Left 4 Dead* games, Valve's co-op zombie-survival series from the first decade of the millennium. The director is a system governing how and where events like zombie encounters occur; not precisely DDA, but sharing some of its goals. Typical DDA will use gameplay metrics to understand how players are doing; things like how much time they take to clear a challenge, the cause of their last failure, and so on. According to Gabe Newell, Valve's president, the metrics used by *L4D*'s AI director are more diverse, including whether players are sticking together or splitting up, and how quickly their mouse cursors are moving.[8] This serves to capture information about how players are *feeling*, giving the AI director the power to push players to their breaking point with tense encounters before finally letting up when they've been stressed out for a while.

Left 4 Dead's director system helps to create satisfying pacing, but is equally important in avoiding unsatisfying pacing. Without responding to players' behaviour, a single level of "difficulty" or pure random generation could create runs that feel boring, or too intense for players to truly enjoy. A tailored system allows for an experience that suits individual groups of players, setting zombie AI loose on them or pulling back accordingly. This can lead to some fantastically tense experiences that still feel fair.[9]

Imagine you're on a team of survivors in *L4D* and encounter an enemy like the Witch, whose light sensitivity and bemoaned cries can be terrifying to deal with. If you lose your cool, split up, and look around erratically, the AI director will associate that with the Witch spawned by the game, and can give your team a brief break after you get past her to regroup. Knowing that particular enemy is a source of stress for the team, the director can re-use this information later—avoiding spawning one in if your resources are low and you're coming off the back of a tough encounter, or throwing her right at you if your team has been doing well for a while.

If speaking of things like DDA or an AI "director" makes it sound like AI can function as a *developer* more than a non-human *player* in some cases, it's because that in a sense, it can.

9.3 AI that works for you

We'vept now crossed into a new domain of game AI, the one where most direct interaction occurs on the development side. Our goal is the same: we're still trying to create a better experience for our players. But the way we use AI to achieve this objective doesn't have to rely on agents in a game's world. Using AI in games isn't just about the AI that interacts with players directly; it's also about parts of the development and design process.

As we shall see, many of the boons offered by AI in this respect are to shave off development time, reduce workload on humans, and of course, save money. This isn't a trivial task by any means—you can't toss a neural network

---

[8] Gabe Newell himself wrote an article for Edge magazine on the subject, archived here: https://web.archive.org/web/20130403031720/http://www.edge-online.com/features/gabe-newell-writes-edge/

[9] Interested readers might enjoy having a look at the interview Kotaku conducted with Valve's Mike Booth on the subject: https://www.kotaku.com.au/2018/11/mike-booth-the-architect-of-left-4-deads-ai-director-explains-why-its-so-bloody-good/

at Unity and order it to make *Far Cry 24* (at least, not yet). Game development relies on highly skilled and specialized work, and developing any degree of automation to a suitable level of quality is challenging. Fortunately, we've reached a point where AI can assist us in multiple points of the development journey, and its contributions have already proven themselves invaluable.

9.3.1 *Creation without a creator*

One of the oldest and most widespread ways that AI is applied in the game development process is via procedural generation (AKA procedural *content* generation, or PCG). PCG is a general term which essentially describes the creation of content by a computer instead of a human. A typical PCG workflow uses handcrafted assets as input with a ruleset defining how they should be recombined. Some randomness is injected, and the output is a previously unseen combination of said handcrafted elements, within the constraints laid out by the ruleset. PCG in games pretty much universally falls under the category of rule-based AI. Though machine learning could be applied, ML systems can take more time to create, produce fuzzier results, and it's much harder to manually tweak their output in a specific way.

Since we're clearly in danger of veering into algorithmic gibberish here, let's explore what this means with an example. Chances are that you've already experienced a great deal of procedural generation—probably mostly in terms of level and world design. Take *Minecraft*, for example, whose worlds are created from millions of individual blocks. Each type of block is created manually, with a texture, name, and crafting recipes defined by designers. Based on a set of rules—rarer ores spawn deeper, water needs containment, and so on—these blocks are used to generate a map without having to manually place them. With an initial random number used to "seed" the algorithm, thus affecting any random-number generation within, it's virtually impossible for two worlds to be alike (unless they have the same seed number).

Generating levels and worlds is the most common application of PCG in the wild. Lots of games bank on entirely procedurally generated worlds, like *No Man's Sky*, *Terraria*, *Minecraft*, *Astroneer*, *Spelunky*, and *Spore*. Other games use a mix of manually and procedurally created levels; while the farm and village in *Stardew Valley* are handcrafted, the caverns of the mines are randomly generated. Procedural level generation can vary wildly in its complexity. At a very basic level, you might have handcrafted geometry or "rooms" that are combined together and filled with random items. A common tactic for creating simple random terrain is to generate random greyscale noise,[10] and then

---

[10] If this piques your interest, looking at Perlin noise is a good place to start.

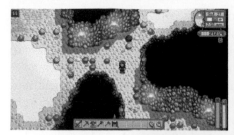

Figure 9.11 Procedurally generated areas in *Stardew Valley* (top left), *Terraria* (top right), and *Minecraft* (bottom.)

Credit: *Stardew Valley* was developed and published by ConcernedApe. *Terraria* was developed and published by Re-Logic. *Minecraft* was developed and published by Mojang Studios.

convert that noise to a heightmap, yielding random mountains, plains, and valleys. At a more advanced level, you might have a multi-pass algorithm that first generates terrain, then carves out caves, adds and "settles" water, places structures, and so on.

The applications of procedural generation hardly end with creating environments. You might apply PCG to create the things that live in those environments, as in the procedurally generated creatures of *No Man's Sky*. In *Spore*, handcrafted creatures are animated procedurally, so that players can stick any number of legs on the vaguely suggestive abominations they create and watch them waddle around with some semblance of realism. Another common application is generating encounters for players; Valve's AI director in *Left 4 Dead* is described as creating "procedural narrative" by shaping the events that players encounter on their journey through cities overrun with zombies. In a similar vein, Bethesda's "radiant" quest system in *Skyrim* and *Fallout 4* generates missions for players to keep them occupied after dozens of hours playing the same character. The possibilities don't end here, either. PCG can be applied to *anything*; obviously, the trick is figuring out an algorithm which isn't too resource-intensive to create and produces results of acceptable quality.

In theory, procedural generation can support any game, though in-your-face PCG is more common in some genres than others. You usually won't find an entirely procedurally generated world in a game with a strictly linear narrative, or in-depth puzzle mechanics. The state of the art in PCG can produce some beautiful and engaging things, but it's not always easy to integrate with other elements of your design.

There are a few genres that are naturally suited to procedural generation, particularly in terms of level and encounter design. PCG is a common sight in games with survival elements, like *Minecraft* and *Don't Starve*. In *Minecraft*, with a focus on exploration, knowing that you'll have a brand-new world to explore whenever you start a new game is a great feeling. Given its building mechanics, starting with a random map can help players feel that their creations are extra special, and anything they stumble upon is uniquely theirs. In *Don't Starve*, players are expected to die many times, especially when they're just getting the hang of things. Since they'll be repeating the same loop mechanically, having a new world to explore helps keep things fresh.

This theme of repeating the same sort of relatively short game loop is also common in the roguelike genre, where players set out on some (perilous) journey where death means a restart from the very beginning. A single successful run in most roguelike games is usually around an hour or less, meaning that early on you might only be playing for a few minutes per round before dying. Procedural generation is one tool that we have to help overcome any potential boredom here, by giving players something they've never seen before for each new run. Many roguelikes use some form of PCG as a result. *Noita* generates a new set of caverns each time the player embarks on their journey to the darkness below, while *The Binding of Isaac: Rebirth* has new enemies and items waiting in its labyrinthian rooms after each restart. In *FTL: Faster Than Light*, the player's trip across the stars is filled with random encounters, generating a story of sorts alongside a fresh bunch of enemies to keep each run interesting.

This isn't to say that full-on procedural generation is strictly necessary for a good roguelike or survival game. Take *Subnautica*, a survival game with a slow burn where players can restore a save after death and experience a linear narrative. Given its environmental storytelling in particular, PCG just doesn't make sense for *Subnautica*, and were it employed, the game would be entirely different. That said, in games that do feature permadeath, some form of randomness is practically a necessity in supporting an experience players want to have over and over again. To have more control over the final experience, the degree to which handcrafted content plays a role can be increased. Consider the roguelike *Hades*, where individual rooms are handcrafted, but sequenced and populated randomly to provide variation through the dozens or hundreds of runs needed to fully complete the game.

The advantages of PCG are substantial. From a player experience standpoint, generated content lends variation to help support longevity in a game like *Minecraft*, or make a repetitive gameplay loop more engaging. With enough diversity, procedural generation can become a game's selling point, as in the billions of planets beckoning players to explore them in *No Man's Sky*. But perhaps the biggest practical advantage of procedural generation is that it can save time, particularly if it's easier for your team to put extra hours into programming rather than art or level design. If you're on a small team, employing PCG might let you create far larger worlds, more diverse encounters, and more for players to discover than you otherwise could. In the right hands, procedural generation can take an experience to the next level.

For all its promise, though, AI-generated content is not the procedural panacea for all our design woes. Getting any generation algorithm just right takes a lot of technical labour, and there might be some wrinkles in the output that you'll need to learn to design around. Consider world generation, for instance. Complex procedural terrain complete with structures and the like tends to generate "impossibilities" depending on your planned navigation mechanics and your definition of impossible. Caves won't always connect nicely to the surface, buildings might spawn atop sheer cliffs. Eliminating specific cases like this can be difficult, time-consuming, and ultimately jeopardize some of the more interesting things the algorithm can generate. Many games that have entirely PCG worlds give you a way to manipulate terrain as a result, like the ability to destroy and place blocks in *Minecraft*.

The biggest design trap with procedural generation, though, is that it's often easy for generated content to feel lacklustre in comparison to that which is handcrafted. In the early days of *No Man's Sky*, for instance, many players complained of discovering planets that felt repetitive and barren, devoid of the variation they'd come to expect from press materials. After several updates injecting additional diversity into the mix through new biomes and structures (and new gameplay mechanics), the game's reputation for engaging exploration in the long term has since improved.

Potentially boring content isn't exclusive to procedurally generated levels, either. The quest generation system we mentioned in *Skyrim* and *Fallout 4* is notorious for its shallowness, owing to what seems like a dearth of interesting "templates" for the game to fill in. Many of these procedural assignments amount to some variation of "go here, grab thing or kill thing, and come back." No matter how often *Fallout*'s Preston Garvey insists that a settlement is in desperate need of your assistance, eventually you'll want to tell him where he can stick those bottlecaps he's offering for yet another gopher mission.

With enough depth, procedural generation can form an engaging core that goes far beyond fetch quests and randomly placing a few rocks. *Dwarf Fortress* is a game built on procedural generation, not unlike *Minecraft* or *Terraria*. What makes *Dwarf Fortress* special, though, and a near-instant cult

Figure 9.12 Landscapes in *No Man's Sky* (above) and *Subnautica* (below). While the vistas in both games are beautiful, procedural generation can lead to "samey" or empty-feeling landscapes (top right). Having control over every element of a landscape, given enough development time, can ensure players never have a dull view. (It needs to be noted that *No Man's Sky*, particularly with recent updates as of this writing, has improved greatly upon the diversity of landscapes generated since its initial release; getting the balance of procedural generation right takes time.)

Credit: *No Man's Sky* was developed and published by Hello Games. *Subnautica* was developed and published by Unknown Worlds.

classic, is how far it takes the concept of the procedural world. The game doesn't just generate terrain, it generates races of creatures, civilizations, and an entire history before setting players loose. Just as you might stumble upon a beautiful terracotta landscape in *Minecraft*, you might stumble into the colourful history of a legendary monarch in *Dwarf Fortress*, exploring their family tree and realizing that their descendants occupy your world to the present day. This type of thought and attention to detail can make generated content feel special, even if the only human touch in its creation was in programming. Ultimately, PCG is a tool that supports and extends our creativity, rather than replacing it.

9.3.2 Work smarter (and probably harder)

Experimentation with AI has given us many other tools to assist in nearly every part of the game development process. The solutions created are imperfect, and those of us who work in the industry don't have to harbour fears of being made redundant by them. At least, not as of this writing, though it would be foolish to assert that we're never in danger of the great automation chopping block. In this section, we'll explore a few ways that AI is already being used in different parts of the development pipeline, and some techniques that might see more widespread use as they improve.

Art. Art is one of those things that reasonably skeptical but still close-minded critics have historically claimed to be "above" computers. *Computers can't create great art. A computer can't write a symphony.*[11] Yet, we've already discussed examples of procedurally generated art assets and animations; perhaps not what those same critics would refer to as "great art," but impressive and helpful nonetheless.

A future application of AI in game art might be the use of generative adversarial networks (GANs). GANs are a flavour of machine learning designed to create, rather than classify or interpret, based on existing examples. Though not yet adopted in game development, in theory, GANs can be used to generate pretty much anything with enough legwork in tweaking architecture and training. In 2017, graphics tech giant NVIDIA famously demoed a GAN that generated photos of nonexistent humans based on a dataset of celebrity faces. The issue with trying to use a GAN for something like texturing assets, at least for now, is the amount of training data required; by the time you had enough textures in your desired style to train with, you'd have more than enough for a whole franchise of titles.

Some other emerging tools that could aid in creative production are AI-driven upscaling and style transfer. Upscaling is the process of increasing the resolution of an image; if done naively, it results in blurriness, blockiness, and other general unpleasantness that comes from blowing up a thumbnail to the size of a billboard. AI upscaling increases image size while intelligently trying to fill in the details, and could be a valuable tool in something like remastering a game where the only source materials available are in the much lower resolutions of the old days. Style transfer, as you might have guessed, is the transfer of an aesthetic from one thing to another. Tools like DeepArt.io and EbSynth let users transfer the visual style of a painting to a photo or video respectively, and might one day find use in creating or processing a game's visuals.

Programming. Automated analysis and code generation are a part of any modern programming workflow, but to call them AI would be a stretch—to grossly oversimplify and anger any programmers reading, these tools typically chalk up to word-matching and very fancy copy-paste. Though one

---

[11] For any readers interested in composing music for games, we would be remiss not to point out that this is already a challenge being tackled by AI. A couple of examples: OpenAI's *Jukebox* project, which among other things generates audio of existing artists covering existing songs that they've never actually sung; and Taryn Southern's album *I AM AI*, which was coproduced by AI.

thing AI is helping us with is identifying potential bugs before they can be introduced. In 2019, Ubisoft and Mozilla announced a collaboration to improve Ubisoft's *Clever-Commit* tool. *Clever-Commit* is a system which employs machine learning to predict whether a programmer's suggested changes to code will introduce bugs, based on past samples of code known to be stable or problematic. In the event that code is flagged as suspicious, the tool presents the developer with an example of the edits used to fix a similar piece of code from the past, giving a basis for the work to be improved.

AI is also helping us indirectly by helping to reduce the need for optimization to achieve increasingly high framerates at increasingly high resolutions. Basically, the higher your resolution, the more pixels your graphics processor has to figure out, and the slower things get. Given that we're clearly on track to all have adopted 16K Ultra-Ultra-Ultra HD monitors at 480 Hz within the next decade if Samsung gets their way, this is every developer's nightmare. Deep learning super sampling (DLSS) is a technology that allows games to render at a low resolution before being upscaled to a higher resolution via machine learning. In other words, push fewer pixels initially, and then have your game upscaled to glorious high resolution by the van Gogh edition of Skynet. While this is more of a consumer-facing technology, assuming that DLSS continues to improve, it may eventually mean that developers can push graphics much farther under the assumption they'll have a helping hand to reach the resolutions that players expect.

Testing. Armed with their GAN-generated textures and bug-free code engineered to render at 32 × 18 pixels thanks to DLSS, the developers of the future will still need to test their creations. Today, this is another area where AI is already helping us to become more efficient and effective. Since game testing has historically been the work of (paid) humans playing in real time, the prospect of an (unpaid) AI that can find issues for us is quite attractive.

In the area of quality assurance (QA), which aims to uncover bugs and other technical issues, AI testing can help root out crashes or unintended behaviour by rapidly executing many different paths through a game. Larger developers have already created in-house tools which use AI agents to this end; at GDC in 2016, mobile studio King shared an AI-driven tool created to help test *Candy Crush*.[12] Among other things, one of the features touted was the ability to identify sequences of actions resulting in a crash, or areas where the game's performance started to lag behind.

QA is distinct from *playtesting*, which is targeted at identifying issues related to user experience, like fun and usability (more on this distinction and testing processes in Chapter 11). Though generally a more complex problem for AI to handle—asking a computer "when does it crash?" is much

---

[12] You can watch the talk here, if you're curious: https://www.gdcvault.com/play/1023858/How-King-Uses-AI-in

easier than "how do you feel?"—this is something that developers are already starting to attempt.

Another goal of King's AI suite is to help designers estimate the degree of difficulty offered by different levels, helping to shape suitable challenge curves. Rovio, the studio behind *Angry Birds*, has also used AI to estimate the pass rate of its levels, giving designers a basis to tweak difficulty.[13] They've also announced plans to make their tool *self-correcting*, making level design adjustments on its own to later pass down for approval. Mobile studios aren't alone in these endeavours, either; Ubisoft employed ML agents to test its combat system in *For Honor*,[14] while Valve used automated testing to help approximate the intensity of encounter sequences generated by its AI director in *Left 4 Dead*.[15]

Community Management. At launch, a developer's job isn't done; at least, it's not done unless they shut down their servers eight months after release because of "poor retention" in an objectively unfinished game that received all of one update (whose sole purpose was to add a few microtransactions). If you've got any sort of player community, it's your job to keep relations running smoothly. Among other things, this includes identifying cheaters and moderating player communications to remove harassment and offensive material. Automated systems have a long history here, like simple string-matching to identify and censor slurs before they can be broadcast. More advanced tools like Valve's anti-cheat detection function in a similar way to antivirus software, identifying the signatures of any software cheats installed by unscrupulous players.

This is another area where AI, by way of ML and natural language processing and machine learning, seems naturally suited to assist our efforts. These solutions certainly aren't something that should be relied on exclusively; having a feature for players to manually report harassment, for example, is always a must. But AI can help us to be more efficient, and manage communities beyond the scope we might otherwise reasonably handle. *League of Legends* developer Riot, for instance, previously shared a few details of an internal system that uses machine learning to validate user reports pertaining to abuse and catalogue them alongside chat evidence before automatically issuing bans.[16] While this type of technology is certainly promising, anyone

---

[13] As discussed in a post on Wired here: https://www.wired.com/brandlab/2019/06/ai-makes-angry-birds-even-more-engaging/

[14] As noted in this GDC talk: https://www.gdcvault.com/play/1026281/ML-Tutorial-Day-Smart-Bots

[15] As discussed in Gabe Newell's Edge article, see Note 8.

[16] Though some of the original information is no longer available on (unarchived versions of) Twitter or Reddit, you can see some of the context in this IGN snippet: https://www.ign.com/articles/2014/07/21/riot-games-dishing-out-strict-punishment-to-toxic-league-of-legends-players

familiar with the *League* community will attest to the fact that Riot's tool has far from managed to eliminate toxicity in the game's player base since its initial use in 2014.

Research. Though not the focus of this book, formal research in the study of games and player behaviour is certainly a contributor to the field as a whole. In games research, the promise of AI help is mostly concerned with augmenting human analysis, making it possible for analysts to crunch otherwise impossibly large datasets. ML, for example, has been used to extract *typologies* of players—classification into groups based on play behaviours and motivations—from the gameplay data of thousands of players. Academically, it's also been employed to try and predict player retention given data after-the-fact, a technique that would obviously prove itself indispensable in numerous commercial contexts as well.

An important topic in AI research, far from unique to game development, is making sure that these tools we create aren't causing any unanticipated harm. Certain facial recognition algorithms have been found to work more effectively for specific races, while automatic resumé scanners have been accused of replicating both gender and racial biases. Google has faced a number of controversies relating to its AI efforts, including allegations that its hate speech detection is racially biased. These types of issues ultimately aren't the "fault" of AI itself; ultimately, we're the ones writing rule-based systems, and providing the data for ML systems to learn. The uglier tendencies of humanity to discriminate and exhibit bias can thus become reflected in the tools we create, risking a perpetuation of systemic problems into the next stage of our technological development.

It might be easy to dismiss these concerns as something for other fields to worry about. Racial discrimination in an automated tool used by law enforcement is terrifying, but is unlikely to pose a problem in using machine learning to make prettier textures. Except tools that us game developers might use for something like banning players on the basis of chat interactions run the risk of exhibiting those same biases. And if we're training content-generation systems based on content from a very homogenous group of human creators, we risk perpetuating the lack of diverse voices that is already an uncomfortable problem in the games industry. We might have other types of bias potentially unique to gaming to consider as well. If we use an AI tool to tweak our level designs based on predicted "average" behaviour, we could accidentally introduce a bias against players with accessibility concerns. Is it acceptable to speed up our process at the risk of making our games less inclusive? Obviously not—but it's something we can't pretend is impossible.

Design. To return to a less concerning contemplation, one might wonder if we can put all of these tools together and create games from the ground up with AI. The largest puzzle piece missing from our current discussion is a game's design: ruleset, mechanics, controls, and all the ideas about what assets and code need to happen to create the intended experience. And while a massive integration of everything we've discussed here glued together with an AI creative director hasn't happened (yet), AI-powered game design is something that people are already pursuing.

Ludi, a system for generating board games, produces its creations via a description language containing definitions for atomic pieces of a game's design, like win states and individual rules around player movement. With some human assistance to convert its generated rulesets into readable language, a board, and pieces, Ludi can effectively author boardgames. Although this might sound like purely a research conversation, two of its games have been published, credited to Ludi itself and creator Cameron Browne. Consequently, you can play "Yavalath" and "Pentalath," two games that wouldn't exist were it not for the AI[17] that came up with them.

Digital game development isn't safe from the rise of the machines, either. The AI system ANGELINA made waves a few years ago for its ability to generate a variety of game demos including platformers, 3D third-person games, and even a few inspired by politics. Angelina is one of the closest things to date of an end-to-end system, picking out assets for its creations from search engines and selecting from rulesets with predefined code implementations.

Thankfully, Angelina isn't coming for our design credentials any time soon, though she might eventually. The games Angelina generates look like terrible asset flips; while impressive and probably enough to get on a digital storefront in today's oversaturated marketplace, they're not exactly winning game of the year any time soon.

But while creating entire games is out of reach for now, AI continues to be an important part of game development, as it has in the past. Even though a lot of what we admire in our artificially intelligent companions and adversaries amounts to design trickery, they are still part of what makes our experience worthwhile as players. And in other manifestations, AI is encroaching on our work as developers.

Irrespective of whether AI will be able to keep up with human players or developers in any reasonable timeframe, it's certainly not vanishing from the development landscape any time soon. Our goal, as it always has been, is creating a better player experience. And AI is becoming better at contributing to that goal, both in fueling the characters that we play with and supporting the creativity that drives what we set out to make next.

---

[17] For readers familiar with the area, Ludi is more specifically an evolutionary computation system—basically an algorithm that repeatedly creates things, evaluates them in some way, and recombines the best ones to create the next "generation" of results.

Expert Profile: Regan Mandryk—The science of fun

Professor at University of Saskatchewan

If you think about jobs that let you work with games for a living, you'll probably start an internal list of industry development positions: designer, programmer, artist, producer, QA tester, and so forth. But if you're looking to dedicate your life to the betterment of play, the industry isn't your only option. Especially over the last couple of decades, a vibrant community surrounding games has emerged in academia, where the science of gaming forms the subject of research.

Regan Mandryk is a member of that community, and as one of Canada's first research chairs focused on digital games, she's helping it grow stronger every day. When we sat down to chat with Regan, she talked about how working in academia has shaped her perspective of design, challenges in both development and research, and how she thinks games can improve our lives.

Despite her prominence in games research, Regan didn't start out studying games. She describes her journey as a "winding path," having completed her undergraduate degree in mathematics and physics before finishing a Master's in kinesiology. It was when she started her PhD that games entered the equation, as she put her previous experiences together to create mathematical models of game experience using players' physiological data (e.g., heart rate). From that point forward, games became Regan's focus, and have stayed that way for the past 20 years.

Although the research community around games is a thriving one, Regan says she still feels the need to help "legitimize" games research, which was often viewed historically with less importance than it deserves. She notes that decades prior, the status of games as a leisure activity diminished their research appeal in comparison to things like how people use computers in business. But with games and play being a universal part of the human experience, understanding our relationship with them is a very valuable course of study.

When we asked Regan what excited her most about working in games research, she paused, leaving us for a few moments under the silent, merciless stare of her prairie dog plushie. "You said there were going to be no hard questions!" she protested with a laugh, struggling to pick from the myriad of things central to her passion. A lifelong lover of learning and creating new knowledge, she settles on the still-understudied nature of games as particularly intriguing: "We don't understand [games] at all [. . .] We're still breaking ground as a research community, but on something that's not niche at all. It's something that's really core to people's lives." Regan mentions several questions that have yet to be answered, such as why we choose to play certain games, how games affect our relationship with others, how they can serve as tools to manage stress, and why we play games in the first place.

Of course, understanding games in general depends on understanding how we interact with them, which is where interaction design comes in. Regan mentions that coming up with a satisfying definition here is tricky, breaking it down with the clinical precision of a lifelong researcher. She describes interaction in this context as, fundamentally, how people work with computers (or games on a computer). From a research standpoint, this is still something we're working to understand, serving as the catalyst for the entire field of HCI: "We know a lot about how people work. And we know a lot about how computers work. But we're still trying to figure out how people work with computers, and how people work with each other over computers."

The second half of that equation, the "design" part, is equally hard to pin down, but Regan describes it as a combination of invention and discovery. First, a designer inventssomething, whether a physical device, interaction, or otherwise. Then, they work to discover how that invention can benefit people, and how it can be improved. Putting the pieces together, Regan characterizes interaction design in games as determining how players execute in-game actions, the tools given to players (e.g., hardware, UI), and how players can interact with one another (e.g., chat, emotes).

This definition of interaction design is an all-encompassing one, with decisions destined to shape every moment of a player's experience. Throughout her years working with games, Regan says she's seen substantial shifts in how these experiences are designed, which she attributes to an overall increase in complexity and the widespread availability of development tools. She describes the growth of engines like Unity and Unreal as a "double-edged sword," providing a strong technical foundation for development while imposing some quiet constraints on design: "We limit ourselves to what the tools could do, instead of our vision of what could be done."

Regardless of how you create games, Regan says that thinking about players is central to good design: "You need to understand how people work." From an education standpoint, she advises that those with an interest in game design, especially an academic one, should work on establishing their knowledge in human-computer interaction. She describes games as a specific case of HCI, emphasizing that a general background in the broader field strengthens one's personal understanding of games.

Regan notes that HCI is just one of many disciplines that help to inform game design and research, saying that one of the most challenging aspects of working in games is their interdisciplinary nature. She offers one of her current research areas, applying games in the area of mental health, as an example. "To make a contribution," she says, "you need to understand games, you need to understand mental health, you need to understand treatment, [and] you need to understand [research methods]." Regan notes knowledge transfer and communication among a research team as key challenges, in much the same vein as facilitating communication between different development specializations such as art, animation, and programming.

In addition to games for promoting and improving mental wellness issues, Regan works on several different projects in her capacity as a professor and research chair. She describes general work in games user research as a standby in her research portfolio, centering around developing new methods to further our understanding of player experience. Some of her work, for example, has explored our physical reactions to gameplay, following from her PhD at the intersection of games and kinesiology. Another recent focus of her research is exploring how games can promote social connectedness, help us form new relationships, and combat loneliness—something which has become especially relevant in light of pandemic restrictions over the past couple of years.

After two decades working in games research, Regan says she's eager to diversify her knowledge further, equipping herself to explore the applications of games in other fields, like treating anxiety and depression. Finding the time to do this can be challenging, she says, with in-depth literature reviews playing less of a central role in her work as a senior researcher in comparison to her time as a graduate student. Nonetheless, she finds these exercises essential to pushing herself forward, as it becomes harder over time to find new surprises without exploring beyond your expertise: "To be able

(Continued)

(Continued)

to go deep into something and really engage with it is a privilege." Indeed, the deep connection that researchers form with their work is something special, and for Regan, there is little more rewarding than understanding the science of fun and games.

Further reading

Artificial Intelligence and Games by Georgios N. Yannakakis and Julian Togelius (Springer). ISBN: 978-3319635187.

   A great introduction to applications of AI in games, providing a high-level overview of many different techniques and some of their design implications.

Procedural Generation in Game Design edited by Tanya X. Short and Tarn Adams (A.K. Press, CRC Press). ISBN: 978-1498799195.

   Authored mostly by indie developers, this book contains a wealth of concepts and techniques related to procedural generation.

Three States and a Plan: The AI of F.E.A.R., paper by Jeff Orkin (available freely online via MIT).

   A short but technical description of goal-oriented action planning as implemented in F.E.A.R. This is a great resource for programmers and systems designers to be sure, but also a fascinating glimpse into the trickery behind good AI suitable for any game designer.

Hands-On Machine Learning by Aurélien Géron (O'Reilly). ISBN: 978-1491962299.

   A practical and very technical introduction to machine learning techniques. If you're fascinated by machine learning and want to learn more about how it works, this is a great volume to work with. If you're a programmer, it has a set of companion examples in Python that will have you up and running with live examples in shockingly little time.

Sources on the history of AI

Campbell, Murray et al. (2002) Deep Blue. In *Artificial Intelligence* 134(1–2), pp. 57–83.

Schaffer, Simon. (1999) Enlightened Automata. In *The Sciences in Enlightened Europe* (eds. William Clark, Jan Golinksi, Simon Schaffer). University of Chicago Press. ISBN: 9780226109404.

Exercises

Atlas rules

Imagine a game where players will be constantly moving through a number of small levels (e.g., a dungeon crawler, roguelike, or platformer with lots of little "rooms"). Pretend that you will be planning to procedurally generate levels for your game. Write out a complete list of rules for how the levels should be constructed, without drawing anything.

Once you have your complete ruleset, sketch out a level following that ruleset. Now try and "break" your design—without violating the rules, see if you can create something that doesn't fit in with what you'd actually want. Note that this is the type of thing you'll have to deal with if you end up going for procedural generation: coming up with rules and tweaks will be an iterative process!

Think about how you might use this type of exercise for designing objects, levels, or other bits of content in general. Even if you're not using procedural generation, could a written ruleset help you to keep your designs consistent?

Build-a-brain

Pick a game with distinct "flavours" of AI—think of different zombie types in *Left 4 Dead* or the four ghosts of *Pac-Man*. Come up with an idea for a new AI to add to this cast of companions or foes, in a way that would complement the game's existing AI (and the player). Focus on behaviour, rather than appearance or lore (though you can come up with a visual design and backstory if that helps you imagine what the character would be like).

Draw a simple *behaviour tree* illustrating a slice of your character's behaviour. If you haven't heard of a behaviour tree, a bit of online research will quickly get you acquainted. In simple terms, a behaviour tree is basically a flowchart with conditions that will tell an AI character what to do at any given time based on things like environment, what the player is doing, and the passage of time.

10

Making the Thing

Starting a project is hard, but with the right idea, finishing one is easy. Every game starts with an idea, and the procedural crux of game development is coming up with a fun idea. Most creators are best advised to work alone in this endeavour. It might take weeks for an idea to land that seems worthwhile to you, and when it finally does, you should always stick with the first one that you like. Avoid changing any aspect of that first idea; if it's what ignited your inspiration, you should hold onto the experience exactly as you initially envisioned it.

From that idea, flesh out your game's design in full. Describe every mechanic, write out your control scheme, and sketch out the details in every last level. Consider each decision carefully, but avoid going back to make any changes; it's a waste of time to waffle on what your design intuition tells you. Only after your design is fully fleshed out should you start to build the game, so that you don't find yourself in a situation where you're unsure of what to do next. With a fully completed design in your back pocket, development time will be much shorter. After your game is completed, make sure to bug-test for at least a few weeks as a precaution—but feel free to cut this short if your planned release date doesn't allow for it.

The process described here isn't a guaranteed recipe for critical acclaim, but assuming that your initial idea is fun, it will guarantee you net positive reception. It also proves something else: game development is simpler than its reputation would have you think. Your process revolves around that first idea; this is why, even at large studios, no job is more coveted or valuable than the role of "idea guy."

The Game Designer's Playbook. Samantha Stahlke and Pejman Mirza-Babaei, Oxford University Press.
© Samantha Stahlke and Pejman Mirza-Babaei (2022). DOI: 10.1093/oso/9780198845911.003.0010

This story, as you can undoubtedly tell, is an abject lie from start to finish. The only truth to it is that the process described certainly won't guarantee critical acclaim. In fact, short of setting your office space aflame, it's pretty much the worst workflow you could adopt. And if you have good insurance, arson might be a better business plan in the long run.[1]

To set things straight, let's start with correcting (almost) everything wrong with the garden path we've just described. First, finishing a project is far harder than starting one, and a "fun" idea on its own is barely worth the cocktail napkin on which it's written. Anyone who self-describes as an "idea person" is usually insufferable. If you're applying this label to yourself, stop it, buckle down and learn, and start calling yourself a designer in training.

That initial ideation process should be collaborative and iterative, like every other aspect of game development. This means that any part of your idea, your design, or your build should pretty well never be set in stone. Exploring alternatives, testing as early as possible, and cutting out swaths of what you thought you were going to do in favour of something better are things that can and should happen.

Simply put, game development (or at least good game development) is far from simple. In the wild, gamedev is messy. Most of the things you come up with—new characters, feature tweaks, or the entire core of your game—will start as random ideas. To make those ideas work, we need a process that helps us transform all of our random ideas into satisfying interactions, solid features, and ultimately better games.

There are a number of development processes that we could explore here, including the truly terrible one suggested at the start. The nature of the process you come up with will depend on your values as a studio. If you prioritize a strict hierarchy, your development might look like this:

1. *Come up with a list of ideas for your current goal.*
2. *Ask your top management which one they like.*
3. *Hack in whichever idea was the manager's favourite.*
4. *Repeat with everything that's left until you're ready to ship.*

If you prioritize making as much money as possible in as little time as possible, you might do this instead:

---

[1] Disclaimer: do not actually do this. If you enjoy fire, the authors suggest a backyard fire pit with sufficient safety measures, an extinguisher nearby, and the number of your local fire department handy. Make s'mores, not war.

1. *Look at top-grossing games on the app store.*
2. *Pick the simplest game in the top 25 apps.*
3. *Copy it exactly.*
4. *Re-skin the game with a theme centred around food, anime, dragons, or interior decorating.*

Obviously, neither of these processes are advisable. The first is a totalitarian regime, and the second is a get-rich-quick scheme of dubious legality. Just like in real life, either option is a developmental disaster waiting to happen. Unfortunately, these types of workflows do exist, and judging by the current state of the mobile market, there are an alarming number of success stories emerging from approach number two. Nonetheless, for every studio that creates the next runaway match-3 success, you can probably find a hundred similar games gathering dust on the fourth page of search results. And in your heart of hearts, do you really want to be responsible for *Sugar Smack 4: Gingerbread Dragon Adventure Casino*?

At any rate, your actual development workflow should, unsurprisingly, prioritize creating a good experience. This isn't to say that respect for your creative management and the almighty dollar should be defenestrated, but they shouldn't drive your every decision. A better approach to game development is iterative, collaborative, informed by other games without verging on plagiarism, and includes player voices. After stitching a few early ideas together, Frankenstein-style, you'll be constantly building on a prototype, at times making additions or cuts (mostly cuts) to the design plans developed along the way. At the end, you'll have a finished product that's been through round after round of polish and testing, and one that's much stronger for it.

Our focus throughout this chapter is exploring how we arrive at these kinds of processes, the methods you can employ to support their different components, and eventually, how you can develop one of your own. But there is one more truth to that first story that we need to address first: every game starts with an idea.

METHOD: Personas. A persona is a detailed description of a hypothetical person representing your target market. Usually, you'll create a couple of different personas reflecting the diversity in experience, play habits, and likes or dislikes of your game's intended audience. The personas you create might be very specific, or a bit more general—though a few barebones sentences won't be enough detail for you to really start understanding who your players are. Some items you might want to include with a persona are things like name, age, occupation, place of residence, cultural background, favourite games/genres, skill level, platforms they own, and time spent playing games in a typical week.

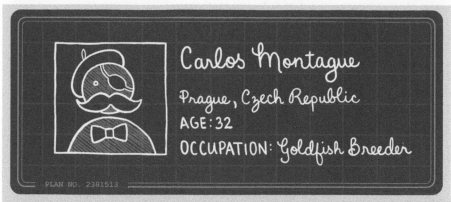

Figure 10.1 If this were a development wiki, we'd go into detail about Carlos' gaming habits, daily routine, and favourite entry in the Metroid series.

Bear in mind that your personas might evolve throughout development, and it's very beneficial to interview real people from your target audience if you can.

10.1 Chasing the lightbulb

Before development starts, you need to have at least a very rough idea of your core experience—or a few different ideas to play with until you find one that sticks. But coming up with ideas is something you'll need to do throughout development, as you refine that core experience into a working game. And when problems arise, as they always do, coming up with creative solutions to those problems will have you back at the drawing board as well.

Sometimes, the best ideas will be the product of chaos. You can spend hours in front of a blank document with only a few bullet points to show for it at the end of the day, and then get struck by something brilliant while you're in the shower. You might find yourself springing out of bed just as you're about to fall asleep, ready to scribble out a few words on a whiteboard that will guide your next four weeks of work.

Despite what self-proclaimed "idea people" might tell you, though, this isn't the only way to hit on a winner. And these types of oddly timed epiphanies usually emerge after you've put in several solid hours of intentional thinking and concept work on your own or with a team. Chalking this up to coincidence is objectively foolish, though mystics might argue that waiting for a breakthrough to emerge from the ether without any prior work is a legitimate strategy.

If you're hoping for a more refined ideation process than clutching some amethysts to your chest and crossing your fingers, then you've come to the right place. There are a lot of different tactics you can employ here, and none of those that we describe are mutually exclusive. Quite the opposite, in fact: in a perfect world, you'd probably use them all.

This isn't to say that this list is exhaustive, or that each and every one of these techniques will be equally useful for every project. Nonetheless, each can serve as both a source of ideas, and far more valuably, a means to refine them into something that will contribute positively to the experience you create.

Meet with your team. Coming up with ideas on your own is fine, but if you can rope in a couple of trusted colleagues, the conversation that emerges will probably be more useful than the one you'd be having inside your own head. Bouncing ideas off of colleagues is a great way to come up with an initial spark or solve a problem you're facing. Especially for indie studios, this can be a good way to select and refine the rough idea defining the core of your experience. If your studio only has half a dozen people, making sure that all of them can be passionate about the game you're making is practically a must. And in this respect, it's perfectly okay to ask yourselves what type of game *you'd* like to play—though you shouldn't rule out creating something for a completely different type of player by any means (more on that later).

There are several "structures," as it were, that you can try to facilitate a team brainstorming session. Plain old conversation is just fine, despite the insistence of internet gurus that unlocking the secrets to their *Holistic Agile Ideation Framework* is definitely worth the asking price of $59.99 a head to sit in a virtual seminar. If you'd like to try something a little flashier, you can adopt a strategy to guide your conversation. The so-called "blue sky" method encourages putting out ideas regardless of their technical feasibility. The thinking here is that any intriguing ideas will eventually be "pulled down to earth"; in the context of game development, bits of a ridiculously ambitious idea might be distilled into a more manageable form. If you'd like to know more about blue sky, we recommend finding an experienced colleague instead of relying on a search engine, lest you become buried in a sea of cloyingly inspirational infographics. At any rate, another aid to your structure will be the tools you use to keep track of ideas—no need for anything fancy here, as a cloud text document, whiteboard, or flurry of sticky notes are all acceptable.

Collaborative brainstorming is relatively easy to orchestrate successfully, assuming you take a couple of necessary steps to make sure that your sessions fall in the five percent of meetings around the globe that actually accomplish something. First, avoid dragging an unwieldly number of people to an ideation session. Sticking twenty people around a table and having them raise their hands to talk will achieve little beyond script material for an awkward sitcom. If you want to include more than four or five participants, split yourself into smaller groups so that everyone has a better shot at being an active voice. Reconvene after you've had a chance to speak in your groups, and try to avoid long sessions with one person summarizing what's already been discussed.

Other key measures to take here are honesty and equality. If you've invited someone to a brainstorming session, it should be assumed that their opinions mean just as much as those of anyone else. Enforcing a strict hierarchy here is a good way to alienate your employees, and turn everyone into sycophants for the highest-paid person in the room. This brings us to honesty, the most critical thing to enforce. There are a number of quotations from motivational speakers and entrepreneurs alluding to some variation of "there's no such thing as a bad idea," usually with some caveat about bad execution. Thankfully, most people have clued in on the fact that this is a blatant lie. There are plenty of bad ideas, such as an idle game about filling out tax returns, a combat system built around quick-time events, or using a two-party system as a basis of government. Bad ideas might be able to eventually turn into decent products with enough finessing, and you might pick something interesting out of a bad idea to inject into a good one. But the truth remains that some ideas are best left to decay in the memories of those subjected to them.

The point here is that your team should feel like they can say that an idea is terrible without hurting anyone's feelings or jeopardizing their future. Being a cynic in a brainstorming meeting shouldn't put you in danger of hushed whispers about your incapability of being a "team player," as long as you're not attacking your colleagues along the way. The best team discussion, and really the only one of value, is an honest one. Most first ideas are outright lousy, or at the very least wildly underdeveloped, and honest reflection is the only way to eventually land on something great.

Look at (and play) other games. One of the best ways to come up with a shortlist of ideas for a new game is to peer at what's already out there. If you have absolutely no idea what to make, return to your favourites, play the games your friends have been nagging you to try, and check out some of the latest indie darlings and hyper-anticipated AAA titles. If you have a vague idea of the type of game you'd like to make, pick out some games in the adjacent space and play those. Identify some moments of play, narrative, or bits of interaction that you find intriguing or satisfying, and note them down as inspiration. Try combining two or three moments from different games in your head, and imagine the type of game that union would birth.

One strategy you can use to assist in divining an initial idea, or fleshing out bits of your experience after the fact, is to create a mood board. Traditionally used in fields like interior design, a classic mood board is a collage of images and bits of text meant to inspire. A mood board for game development might include screenshots, concept art, dialogue snippets, music clips, mechanic descriptions, and gameplay videos from games that inspire you. This can be particularly useful in shaping a game's aesthetics and atmosphere, though it can also serve to collect lots of intel on interactions via descriptions and video to help shape your design.

More formally, looking at other games is the basis for competitive analysis, a technique we'll explore later in the chapter. In short, competitive analysis involves looking at how other games accomplish some goal or another, learning from their successes and failings to create a solution that works for you.

Examine your experience. There's a good reason behind that series of expressions related to the imitation of art and life by one or the other. Many of the most powerful creative works relate to the lived experience of their creators in some way. Looking back on your life and seeing what stories you—or your team, families, and friends—have to tell can provide a wealth of inspiration, particularly if the subject of your brainstorming

---

METHOD: User stories. In general, user stories are short snippets describing the ideal version of a feature from a user's perspective. A soul-crushingly boring example is the save menu in a word processor: "*I want to save different versions of my work, so I can use the save menu to make a new copy of my document.*" Archetypal user stories are often in the form of an "I want" statement followed by an explanation, packaging together a need the user has with the feature that fulfills that need.

In games, we can speak of player stories, quick descriptions of gameplay or features from a player's perspective. This doesn't mean that you should start every player story with "As a player, I want . . ."—the structure can be helpful if you're not sure where to begin, but should you write out dozens of player stories like this, the effect will be dangerously similar to ingesting a bottle of horse tranquilizers. Instead, focus on writing out (or gathering clips and images) of cool moments you want to create. If you wanted to create a fun system for the type of emergent gameplay in *Metal Gear Solid V*, you probably wouldn't start with "As a player, I want to have lots of options in combat, so I can select from ten different types of hollow-point bullets." Instead, think about an interesting moment: "What if you could confuse an enemy by deploying a ridiculous number of decoy balloons all at the same time?"[2]

It's also worth noting that depending on your specialization, you might consider user stories from the perspective of your teammates; for example, if you're programming a level layout tool, think about how your level designer likes to work.

---

[2] Readers in the know will be familiar with the exploration of this scenario in-game by a certain connoisseur of the arts known as Dunkey.

---

happens to be narrative. Drawing on your own experience or that of a loved one (with appropriate permission, of course) gives you greater insight as to what a story about that kind of experience should look like. Consequently, the way you represent bits of your own life, whether mechanically, narratively, or otherwise, will feel more real.

This approach is particularly relevant if you're keen to make a game with themes like introspection, familial relationships, social identity, or basically, anything related to understanding oneself as an individual. Take *Celeste*, for instance, which explores a character's journey in learning to cope with depression and accept the "darker" parts of herself. Designer and writer Maddy Thorson has shared that she was heavily inspired by her own struggles with anxiety and depression, leading to many of the thematic and story directions taken by the game.[3] The result is a story which feels potent and personal, enhancing its emotional impact.

Examine themes or topics of interest. If you have no idea where to begin, looking at a real-life concept can be a great jumping-off point. History, politics, art, science, mythology, rock collecting—virtually nothing is off limits, and anything could form the core of a game, should it strike your creative fancy. If you already have a core idea, exploring relevant subject material can help you flesh out the details of your world, mechanics, art style, and so forth.

If you're planning to make something like a game for change aimed at promoting awareness or perspective on a social topic, looking at history and politics are obvious choices here. However, this type of brainstorming is far from limited to the games for change category. Take *Papers, Please*, a game about immigration. If you squint, you might think you're looking at a somber animation about living in the USSR circa 1970. But despite openly being inspired by the conflict between East and West Germany in the mid-twentieth century, developer Lucas Pope has stated that the game isn't intended to deliver any sort of political message. Instead, the historical and political elements of the game serve the primary purpose of getting players more interested, with any critical thinking they inspire as a side benefit.[4]

Consider your target players. In theory, you can pick a target audience before you have a core idea, and then pick an idea based on that audience. If you have literally no conception of the experience you want to create, this decision will probably be motivated by money, and the idea you come up with as a result will probably lack passion. Kicking off your development with a question like "What experience will yield the highest 1-week retention for heavy smartphone users between the ages of 45 and 54?" isn't exactly the stuff of dreams.

With some existing idea of what you want to accomplish, though, this tactic can be the most effective out of any we've discussed thus far. If you're

---

[3] Maddy has discussed the themes behind *Celeste* in many different forums, but one particularly candid discussion can be found on the development team's AMA ("ask me anything") on the r/NintendoSwitch subreddit.

[4] As discussed in an interview with *The Verge*: https://www.theverge.com/2013/5/14/4329676/papers-please-a-game-about-an-immigration-inspector

making a serious game of some sort, like a training simulation or educational game, reaching out to your target audience to understand their needs early on is a must. And no matter what you're making, so long as you have an idea of your core experience, reaching out to find out what your players like and dislike about other games, and what their ideal experience looks like, will help inform your design.

We should underscore the idea here that all of these tactics can be relevant throughout development, not just at the ideation stage. Interviewing players, looking to the real world for inspiration, or hammering out some ideas with your team are just as viable for developing individual features or improvements later in the production cycle. With that in mind, let's have a look at what the rest of that production cycle is like.

Figure 10.2 Soviet propaganda (left) versus *Papers, Please* (right). The game's visual styling, in addition to its soundtrack, evoke an atmosphere of totalitarian oppression mixed with unbridled patriotism that is somehow aesthetically appealing.

Credit: Top propaganda image is cropped from a 1920s poster by Gustavs Klucis (public domain) via Wikimedia Commons. Bottom propaganda image was a 1940s poster by El Lissitzky (public domain) via Wikimedia Commons. *Papers, Please* was developed by Lucas Pope and published by 3909 Games.

10.2 Follow the rulebook

Game production has evolved quite a lot since the first commercial games were created half a century ago. This evolution owes itself in part to technological advancements, such as cloud computing and the widespread availability of distributed version control.[5] Arguably, a much stronger driving force behind this shift is a change in thinking about how people work. Understanding the human creative process, and how ideas can transform themselves organically over time, has helped to shift the conventions of the industry as a whole.

We won't outline every major production structure here, instead boiling down most approaches into two major descriptors corresponding to more established and modern thinking respectively.

Waterfall development (the old school). If there were one word to describe waterfall development, that word would be *rigidity*. The idea here is that development flows from one phase to another one-way, thus the aquatic nomenclature. In its purest form, waterfall development means that there's no overlap between these stages, and certainly no hopping back and forth. Waterfall is linear, it's easy to understand, and it aims to wrap up the process of development with a neatly tied bow, if one made from exceptionally boring twine.

Now is as good a time as any to formally introduce those stages of development we've been alluding to, since you'll hear them discussed as part of virtually any production cycle:

First is the *Concept* stage, during which you flesh out the initial idea for a game's experience. This includes tasks like brainstorming, creating concept art, and rough storyboarding.

Next is *Pre-production*, where you work out the finer details of your game's design. This includes design documentation, sketching, and lots of heated discussion with your creative director.

This is followed by *Production*, the part where you actually make the game. Programming, art, sound, and the like live in this phase.

After the game is virtually complete, you enter *Post-Production*, focused on things like testing and fixing bugs, ramping up marketing, and last-minute polish.

Following post-production, your studio rides off into the sunset of *Release and Post-Launch*, which is less of a sunset and more of an onslaught

---

[5] In general, version control is a way of tracking the history of changes made to a collection of files, such as a game's codebase or assets. Distributed version control gives everyone on a team access to the full history of said collection locally on their computer. As you can imagine, this is quite helpful for inspecting the history of a file, or rolling it back to its previous state in a panic at three in the morning after you've accidentally broken your prototype. An example of distributed version control is Git.

of responding to critical feedback, providing updates, and handling community management.

Different sources might divide up these phases differently, and we should note that what's described here is vastly oversimplified. In some cases, it's quite misleading in implying what does (or does not) occur in all of those stages leading up to release when following a more modern approach—as we shall see momentarily.

METHOD: Sketches and storyboarding. The utility of sketching is obvious—it's a quick idea to get your ideas on the page (or screen) without spending too much time agonizing over details. Sketches are also useful as a means to share your ideas with teammates; if you've got a picture of something in your head, trying to convey that in words alone is frustrating. There's not much to explain about process here, apart from taking a moment to address storyboarding. You probably associate storyboarding with, well, stories—sketching out major plot points for something like a movie or cutscene in sequence. And while storyboarding is useful for narrative in game development, it doesn't stop there. You can also "storyboard" interactions; if you want to sketch out the flow of interactions for something like fighting a boss or buying new gear, quick sketches of what the player sees at each step can be immensely helpful.

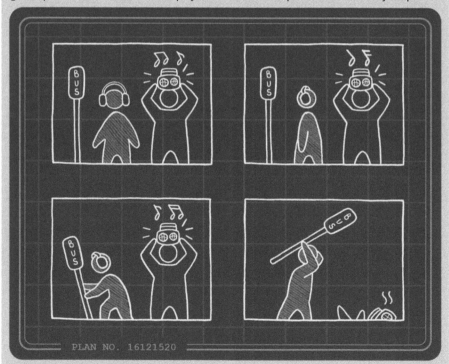

Figure 10.3 A storyboard illustrating the appropriate reaction to an individual playing music through speakers in a public space.

A linear progression between these phases as described would be what you'd expect to see in a "true" waterfall approach to game development. Other characteristics of such a development philosophy typically include a focus on enforcing a strict management hierarchy, and attempting to determine specific timelines long in advance. The result is a development workflow guided by orders from the top, usually with little room for individual voices. A waterfall dogma is also inherently resistant to change, with design activities mostly sequestered to the early stages and testing near the end. When followed to the letter, waterfall development is inflexible, with any substantial design changes practically required to occur in the late stages of development once testing becomes a priority.

If you're thinking that all of this sounds a little too close to the hypothetical example given at the beginning of this chapter, you're right. Indeed, more forward-thinking game development has largely moved beyond the stoic linearity and aged mindset of a strict waterfall approach.

Figure 10.4 A waterfall development process.

Agile development (the new school). If waterfall development embodies rigidity, then agile development's core value is *flexibility*. The underlying motivation of agile game development is to respect the highly iterative and collaborative nature of the creative process. It's hard to give an accurate procedural summary here, simply because "agile development" is itself a very general term. Boasting a litany of non-mutually exclusive subdisciplines with names like *scrum, kanban,* and *lean,* so much as uttering the word agile in certain company will subject you to hours of quasi-motivational speech about 'adopting a value-added people-first teamplay optimization that fits with your company culture.'

As you might have suspected by this point, one of the only drawbacks of agile development is having to listen to people talking about it, so we'll try to keep this brief. For our purposes, it's not exceptionally valuable to dwell on all of the subtle distinctions between different agile methods and management tools with esoteric names like *planning poker*—go read a project management book if you're looking for that. Instead, here's a quick look at a *sprint*, the fundamental unit of an agile development timeline:

First, you spend a short while in the *planning* phase, understanding the problem you're currently working on, what you hope to accomplish, and what you intend to do in service to that goal.

Next, most of your time is spent in *implementation*, where you aim to prototype a complete solution to your problem, and refine it as much as time reasonably allows.

After implementation, you *test* your solution to understand its efficacy and identify potential issues.

Following this, you *review* and reflect on what you've accomplished, noting areas for improvement and any insights about your project's future development.

The trick here is that each sprint lasts somewhere on the order of a week to a month; a full development cycle comprises dozens of sprints, instead of focusing on just a few linear stages. This isn't to say that those production phases we mentioned earlier are absent from an agile-focused approach. It simply means that each of those stages have a heavy focus on iteration, and there is often a far less defined boundary between them. Testing is no longer exclusive to post-production, and emphasized throughout development once any prototypes are available. Barebones prototypes will be developed in pre-production or even at the concept phase, as experiments in feeling out little bits of the desired experience. Essentially, each stage is broken down into more manageable goals (e.g., "Get an initial version of the HUD working") which are tackled in sprints.

There are many different sprint flavours of a sort, each with varying riffs on the basic stages of a sprint. The Google Sprint, for example, proposed in the early 2010s, is a five-day (!) process for solving a problem. "Problem" here will depend on context, but you can think of a suitable game development "problem" as figuring out a way to implement a relatively small feature (maybe something like adding the initial version of a new movement ability for your main character). One day of the sprint is dedicated to each of mapping out the problem, sketching out potential alternatives, developing an implementation plan, prototyping, and testing. Though such a timeline might be a little too compressed for most game development tasks, industry examples like this can certainly inform the approach you take.

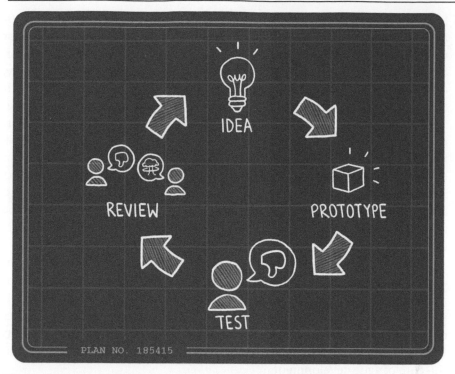

Figure 10.5 Iterative design, AKA the honest revelation that nothing anyone ever creates is remotely acceptable the first time around.

Regardless of which sprint playbook you use for a basis, the core philosophy remains the same: small units of work, highly focused, and completed quickly by a small group of teammates with relevant experience.

> **METHOD: Competitive evaluation.** Looking at other games can be a huge source of inspiration, giving you ideas for core features, or how to address a particular problem. In your initial ideation, look at games that evoke a similar mood or target the same type of player. If you're making a punishingly difficult game with a dark atmosphere, you might look at *Dark Souls* or *Sekiro*. Conversely, you're probably not going to bother with *Animal Crossing*—though sometimes ideas can come from the strangest places.
>
> Similarly, competitive analysis can help you figure out how to implement a certain feature (e.g., a collectible system for a platformer) or solve a problem (e.g., how to port controls for a mobile version). One thing to note here is that you shouldn't limit yourself to games that do something well; dissecting failures is also invaluable in figuring out what design choices you should avoid.

Another aspect of agile methodology is a focus on smaller teams that work together, rather than individual work strictly directed by management.

Different individuals or small groups might have slightly different goals during a sprint—for instance, while a programmer, designer, and graphic artist work are working on refining the HUD, a team with a composer, animator, and 3D artist might be working on a rough cut of the teaser trailer. Usually, each team will have a leader to help steer the ship, as it were, but there's much more room in agile development for individual voices to make a difference.

As you can imagine, this line of thinking is also less structured than waterfall development in terms of timing. Most proponents of agile won't argue for pre-planning the exact order and timing of every sprint at the outset of development; instead, you'll aim to have a fairly precise idea of the next sprint, an understanding of what the next few sprints should look like, and at best a coarse estimate for the total length of the project. Items might be added to or removed from the "backlog" of sprint goals as a project wears on, allowing new problems to be addressed or scope to shrink as necessary.

The rationale behind all of this, and its relevance to game interaction design, is that agile development is naturally suited to address all of that messiness we introduced at the beginning of this chapter. Creative work is iterative, as we come up with better ideas while working on our existing ones or solving problems. It's also highly collaborative, as designers and artists thrive on each other for inspiration and feedback. These two qualities are at the core of agile development.

On top of all of this, another huge benefit of the agile way of thinking is that it provides a clean way to chop the production cycle into manageable bits. Macroscopically, the entire development process is long, slow, complicated, and ludicrously dauting. The notion of a sprint gives us a reasonably simple way to divide this objectively terrifying process into much more understandable and achievable chunks of work.

Agile development is quite fashionable in the tech industry, at least for the time being. In game development, you're usually much more likely to see something that screams agile at a smaller studio, as opposed to a larger one. This isn't to say that all AAA developers stick to their guns with the old ways of waterfall, but you won't usually see the same kind of small, highly efficient and collaborative groups working in sprints on a team of hundreds.

User-centred design (a new wing for the new school). Every designer's greatest fear, aside from bad kerning, is handing their product to a user and hearing the words "I don't want this." User-centred design (UCD) is about preventing that moment from happening, by including users in the process of design and development. UCD approaches chiefly aim to *augment* and *modify* existing processes, rather than attempting to outright supplant them. It doesn't really replace either waterfall or agile development, though it certainly tends to fit more naturally in the workflow of the latter. In this sense, UCD is less of a singular method and more of a philosophy.

In game development, UCD means bringing in representatives of your target audience as early as possible, to make sure your creation meets with their expectations, needs, and desires. At a very high level, user-centred game development will first aim to understand who your target players are, gather requirements from those players, prototype whatever you're working on, and evaluate it with—you guessed it—players from your target audience. Bits and pieces of these steps integrate seamlessly with the stages of iterative agile development. Understanding your players and their needs becomes part of the *planning* phase. Prototyping is already a part of *implementation*. And when the time comes to *test* and *review*, getting feedback from players, as opposed to other employees, gives you a more accurate picture of how a given feature will be received.

Realistically, especially if you're an independent developer, you won't have the money or the time to orchestrate bringing players in for every single sprint. Following a UCD approach, then, you should try and work in real players whenever you can—bring in a focus group to test out your core concepts at the early stages of your project. Interview players in pre-production to see what they love or hate about games similar to yours. And when things really get rolling with your main build, recruit external playtesters who represent your target market instead of relying on in-house QA and designer intuition alone.

All of this being said, you might think you're best advised to print out a copy of the agile manifesto, watch a few speeches from tech leads, pick out a well-renowned set of guidelines for user-centred design with agile project management, and follow it to a tee.

And you'd be completely wrong.

10.3 Re-writing the rulebook

It should be obvious by now that a good development plan will be flexible, embracing the volatility of the creative process rather than fighting back against it. You'll be aiming to manage that volatility by introducing a structure that capitalizes on the natural affinity to iterate and evolve as a project goes on. But beyond this, the exact nature of what you adopt is up to you. We've just finished singing the praises of agile development, but this doesn't mean that you have to pick up and memorize the nearest book on scrum (please keep holding this one instead).

METHOD: Living design documents. Design documentation is a necessity for keeping track of your decisions, setting a course for the future, and communicating with your team. The stuffier variants of design documents serve as a centralized reference for a large team and something to show to publishers, tens of pages mutable only by a studio's creative heads. Of much greater interest to an agile workflow is some form of "living" documentation, accessible and editable by all (with appropriate consultation for any changes). For a small studio, this can be something as simple as a cloud storage folder with some documents, preferably with synchronous collaboration so that everyone can add in bits during a meeting. For larger enterprises and more sophisticated efforts, you might consider setting up something like an online wiki for easier navigation of the complicated relationships between different aspects of your design.

Our official advice here is to avoid getting too caught up in formal methodology, *especially* if you're a small team. Picking out some variation of agile development that seems like it would work well for your team is a great starting point. Learn some exotic jargon unique to the variant you've selected, get your team on board for a daily stand-up meeting where you look at pictures of puppies, and try it. Plan out a couple of sprints, work for a few weeks, and then take a step back. Is your current process keeping everyone on track and focused? Have you made as much progress as you'd hoped to make in the timeframe? And most importantly, is your team happy with how things are going?

If the answer to any of these questions is no, then talk to your team, figure out what is and isn't working, and change your process as necessary. When something goes wrong, look first to your process, rather than jumping to blame something on a team member. If your programmers don't like stopping to talk about their last line of code five times a day, then re-evaluate whatever meeting-happy version of agile you've adopted and make more time for independent work. Remember that not everyone in the studio has to follow the exact same process, either. Continually having five meetings a day is almost certainly unsustainable for programmers. But assuming the meetings aren't all two hours long, it's not so ridiculous for a small group of designers at the start of a project.

The only definite rule to keep in mind here is that you should be figuring out what works from experience, and going with that. If you're looking for a starting point, or some ideas to improve whatever you're already doing, we'll outline our vision for agile game development here. Where appropriate, we've noted the methods that support each part of the process. You can find explanations of these methods scattered throughout this chapter.

If we were a flashy business book given away at weekend corporate retreats, we'd come up with an equally flashy name for the process we suggest, like *Thunder*, *The Labrador Method*, or *Vortex*. But, since we're a humble design book that just wants to be on your desk for a while, we'll go with something innocuous with the sole intent of not saying "process" eighteen times in the next two pages.

10.3.1 *Say hello to the Stumble framework*

As every student, hobbyist, and professional developer knows, game development is one long stumble in a dark basement, stubbing your toe on some unseen piece of furniture every single day. Consequently, Stumble describes a process that you'll follow at a macro scale for your whole game up to launch. It's also something you'll follow on a micro scale for each new feature. In other words, it outlines both the course of development and the layout of a single sprint.

You'll notice that there's no indication of timelines here, and that's by design. Some agile methods do specify a timeline—like Google's five-day sprint cycle—but so complicated is the beast of game development that it would be foolish of us to suggest you need to spend exactly three days on design, six days on programming, and so on. As an estimate, our official suggestion for the length of a Stumble sprint is two weeks, at least to start with. Divide up work into items that take a week or so of labour to implement or create, leaving a few days for the other steps and in case you've underestimated the amount of work needed. When you're starting out, try and keep your team synchronized in this regard; have everyone starting a new sprint every two weeks. Push around work items as needed if anything needs to be added or fixed, but keep everyone on the same timeline, at least for a while. After you've had a little while to see what's working for you, mix things up as needed. You might need to stagger sprints for different kinds of work; maybe your programmers would prefer a longer go of 3 weeks, while your artists could do with cutting the work and time for each sprint down to a weeks' worth for more rapid iteration.

METHOD: Paper prototyping. Creating paper prototypes is all the rage in mobile application design, or at least it was until the likes of interactive GUI mockup tools like Figma and Adobe XD came into being. Honestly, in digital game development you probably won't find yourself using any sort of physical prototypes very often. Occasionally, you might find it beneficial to collect a few things from your desk and move them around to help visualize something—especially if you're a programmer trying to figure out a camera issue. But the real area of game design where paper prototyping shines is in creating board games. While not the focus of this book by any means, creating a tangible prototype for any game that will be played physically is a must.

METHOD: Digital prototyping. This is the most important tool in your little box of methods as a video game developer. The only real way to see if a design decision works is to test it in the form you expect players will experience your game, and that means creating digital prototypes.

There are a few terms to be familiar with here. First, there's *fidelity*, describing how closely a prototype matches a finished game. A low-fidelity prototype uses premade or placeholder assets, probably plays pretty roughly, and only aims to capture a coarse idea of how something will feel. A high-fidelity prototype looks and feels more like the finished game/feature, and a mid-fidelity prototype is somewhere in between. Another term you'll hear in describing prototypes is *verticality*. A vertical prototype has a small scope, but lots of depth. For instance, if you're making a platformer, a "vertical slice" might be a level that's only a couple of minutes long, but has all of your intended movement mechanics, enemies, and so on implemented and working. A horizontal prototype, by contrast, covers a lot of different features, but with limited functionality and depth. An example might be a mockup of your full menu system, but most of the buttons (e.g., graphics settings) don't actually do anything yet.

Figure 10.6 An early greybox of a city for a 3D isometric game. Using basic shapes allows for quick iteration on layout and content.

One last term specific to level design prototyping or scene layout is *whiteboxing*, which refers to roughing out the layout of a digital scene. In its purest form, whiteboxing uses untextured primitives (literally white boxes, spheres, cylinders and so on) to indicate the placement of things like walls, buildings, and so on. Practically speaking, literal whiteboxing might not always be your first step if you already have some assets to work with. Instead, you could set down some of your existing models as part of the process to better understand the scale you're working with, and which props you still need to request from your art department (fittingly, this embodiment is typically referred to as *greyboxing*).

(Continued)

On the whole, your priority during any development cycle should be working towards a vertical slice of your game as soon as possible, so that you can see if your core experience plays as you've hoped it would. Whenever you make the decision to add or tweak something, aim to prototype that functionality as soon as possible. This means that, even if you're making your own game engine from the ground up, you should have a tool that you can use to prototype early in development or as a backup if you're waiting on any key technical features. Download a free commercial game engine (popular ones as of writing include Unity, Unreal, Game Maker, and Godot, for starters) and get to work. Prototyping is the only way to see if something is going to work in a finished game—so you always need to be ready to do it.

With timelines out of the way, let's get to it and look at each step you'll take with Stumble:

Stage 0: The initial idea. We've labelled this as the zeroth stage since it can occur at any time before you start working, and often in the middle of working on something else. At the macro scale, your initial idea for a new game might spring up while you're working on another project, or you might sit down with your studio and brainstorm before taking up resources to start working right away. At the micro scale, the initial idea for a work item might come up early in development (e.g., "We need to prototype the HUD eventually") or while you're working on something else (e.g., "I was working on the HUD and realized just how atrocious our tutorial is").

At any rate, if you're strapped for ideas, try out some of the brainstorming techniques we discussed earlier in the chapter—get your sticky notes ready, organize a blue-sky session with your team, and take a peek at some recent games.

In the interest of keeping things consistent, let's introduce a running example here, representing the work for a single sprint. Let's say that you're making a platformer, something akin to *Super Mario Galaxy*. Your work item—the initial idea behind this sprint—is to create an initial version of a hub world, a 3D space where players can choose which levels to try and spend their time in between playing individual levels.

Stage 1: Understanding your goals. This stage is where you dig into what you're trying to achieve when you're finished with whatever you're working on. If you're a designer, how will you shape the player's experience? If you're a programmer, how expandable should your solution be for future additions? If you're an artist, what will you be contributing to the game's intended atmosphere?

A large part of this is understanding who the intended beneficiary of your work is. Usually, this means understanding your target player, but not always. A programmer, for example, might be working on an interface for your team's designers. An artist might be creating a rigged model for further use by an animator. At any rate, here you should endeavour to understand their needs—consult your player persona, talk to any team members that will use your work, and scribble down a couple of quick user stories.

Returning to our hubworld example, your goals can emerge based on the hubworld's intended function in player experience, and the type of players that you're targeting. Assuming you're aiming for the *Super Mario Galaxy* crowd and not the *Dark Souls* one, one of your goals might be creating a welcoming and friendly atmosphere. From a functional standpoint, you might have objectives like making it clear how far the player has progressed in unlocking different level. By digging in a bit more, you might stop to think about how sometimes, players will be returning to the hubworld after an arduous challenge. To support their downtime afterwards, one of your goals could be giving players a few fun things to interact with while catching their breath.

Stage 2: Come up with alternatives. Here, you'll come up with a few very rough ideas of how you might approach what you're working on based on the requirements gathered in the previous stage. If you're a designer or an artist, you might sketch out some ideas digitally or on paper. If you're a programmer, you could write out a few high-level approaches and different solutions to research before moving on. Your focus will be on identifying and selecting different design choices based on what you're trying to achieve. Competitive analysis is a fantastic tool at this stage to pick out ideas to try (or avoid) from games that have similar features. You might also create some extremely low-fidelity prototypes at this stage (we're talking five minutes' worth of work), depending on what you're working on. By the end of this stage, you should usually select just one alternative to proceed with—note that sometimes, it might be necessary to take multiple ideas to prototype and evaluate before settling on one to develop fully.

For our hubworld case, a brief competitive analysis would be well-advised. Take some screenshots of how other games handle centralized areas, and don't limit yourself to games exactly aligned with your intended creation. Look at the 3D *Super Mario* games, but see if you can learn anything from the basic level selection screens in 2D platformers, or quasi-"hub" areas in other games, like the City of Tears in *Hollow Knight*. Make a few sketches, or very quick 3D mockups if that's more your style. Before moving forward, select the one that you like best, keeping in mind how each idea supports the goals established in Stage 1.

Stage 3: Planning. Make some notes in your living design documentation to convey your intent and your ideas for what the finished product of your work should look like. If you've been sketching, create a more detailed sketch. If you've been working on a low-fidelity prototype, refine that a little bit to better reflect what you hope to end up with. Figuring out how you're going to proceed is important, but don't spend too much time planning—change is all but inevitable as you work.

In our hubworld example, you'd want to create a more detailed layout sketch, perhaps a top-down view that you could import into a level editor as an image plane for reference. As a precursor to the next stage, you could start creating the hubworld in your game's level editor, using whiteboxing to mock up the hubworld layout with basic 3D shapes.

Stage 4: Implementation. This is likely going to be the longest part of a sprint. If you're a programmer, this is where you butt heads with your engine's API and iterate to fix all sorts of bugs. If you're an artist, this is where you sit down with a source of caffeine and/or sugar of your choosing and prepare to give yourself hand cramps. Implementation isn't always the longest phase though; for an important gameplay tweak you might spend a week arguing about design only to program the solution in a couple of hours.

At any rate, this is where you make the thing, which might vary wildly in fidelity from the first iteration of something to a few polished tweaks on an already established part of your game. Prototyping techniques are your friend here, and remember that within this stage, you'll likely iterate on a small scale. If you feel like a small change is warranted, you don't always have to wait for testing to make that change, though you might want to consult with the rest of your team.

Here, our hubworld level would be fleshed out in the game's level editor. Since this is just an initial version, you'd be focused on getting the layout just right. Some assets might be left as placeholders, and you won't finish all of the fancy lighting, effects, and scripting present in the finished product. But, as you work, make sure that what you're creating is in service to the goals set at the beginning of the process. By the end of this stage, aim to have *something* that you could test, or something ready to insert into the current testable build of your game, to support the evaluation and reflection that should occur at the end of a given sprint or development iteration.

Stage 5: Testing. The testing stage caps off your work, validating (or invalidating) the design decisions you've made. More importantly, feedback from testing serves as a basis to determine your future work. Regular testing can and should be a part of your process throughout development—and that includes the time where you've just barely scraped together an initial idea or a vertical slice of your game.

Game evaluation is an entire field of research on its own, though, and at the very least it warrants a chapter's worth of material to explore the motivations and methods that it entails. And so, with our carefully crafted prototypes in hand, let's march on to the next chapter and see how those prototypes fare in the wild.

Expert Profile: Ario Jafarzadeh—Steps from perfection

Head of Design for Player Experience at Roblox

With two decades of UX work under his belt, Ario Jafarzadeh has worked at the likes of Google, Amazon, and King. When we spoke with him, Ario was in the midst of a stint at Postmates X—now spun off as Uber's Serve Robotics—and he's since moved on to become a design head at gaming behemoth Roblox.

Throughout a whirlwind of projects in web design, games, and robotics, Ario says the thing that excites him most is a simple constant: "Creating something that actually improves and delights people's lives. Full stop." He's hardly joking about that full stop; Ario brings a refreshing brevity to discussing the general subject of design. He summarizes his understanding with "design is how it works," a favourite quote from the late Steve Jobs. Interaction design is where Ario says that details of the "how" come into play, referencing everything from the appearance of pixels at the edge of a button, to the specification of active areas where users can click or otherwise interact.

When Ario talks about interaction design, he focuses on how a product can best support and respond to actions taken by users in the physical world. He describes the case of games as a specialization of this core idea, further subdividing game interaction into functional and gameplay components. Functional game interaction, he says, is a combination of necessities outside of gameplay, like menus and inventory screens. Ario describes these elements as comparatively dry, likening bits of the design process to creating a website. However, he notes that the design of functional elements in games is still far more playful, and less constrained, than in a purely productivity-oriented setting. Things like colour, typography, and layout are more flexible, so long as basic principles of usability are still respected. He mentions the use of quickwheels for weapon selection in games like *Horizon Zero Dawn* as an example. At the most basic level, a quickwheel accomplishes the same thing as a dropdown menu—but the quickwheel is more playful, more satisfying, and given that directional input is available, much more efficient.

Setting pure function-oriented design aside, gameplay is where Ario says that "interaction design becomes everything." Worlds away from productivity-focused applications, he remains laser-focused on user action, saying that players' perceived link between controls and in-game action can make or break their experience. To preserve immersion and promote the elusive state of flow, Ario says that games need to ensure that coupling between cause (user input) and effect (gameplay) is as tight as possible. Any perceptible lag or repeated violation of player expectation in the consequences of their inputs can shatter a player's sense of being in a game's world, he notes. Although gameplay itself might chronicle an impossible fantasy, that fantasy is firmly tethered to reality by a player's ability to exert control within it.

For Ario, creating a good experience for players is a matter of iteration, both in successive prototypes of an original idea, and in building on the "prior art" of past games. He argues that, especially today, very few games offer completely new mechanics, with most innovation occurring as iteration rather than invention. "If you've played *Halo*, then it's probably going to be very similar to playing *Doom*," he says. He doesn't view this phenomenon as stagnation in game design, but rather a sort of maturation. Each new entry in a particular genre can introduce new delights and minimize pain points, ultimately creating a better experience, even if little changes in regard to core gameplay. Ario is careful to note that past work should never be accepted unquestioningly, providing plenty of room to challenge the status quo: "You're going to inherit the paradigms established for the genre, but that doesn't mean that you're completely at the mercy of that."

Moving our designs forward, along with the paradigms they reflect, is a matter of devising positive change, which in turn depends on an understanding of UX. Ario says that in his experience, UX is well-established outside of games, but has only become properly stylish in the games industry over the past five years or so. It's not that UX design was ignored in the past—as Ario puts it, "you don't have to have 'UX' in your job title per se to care about the user experience of your game." But with the realization of its importance, jobs focused on UX have sprung up to make the likes of interaction design and user testing far more sophisticated in the industry as a whole.

Despite these changes, Ario says that the basic fundamentals of good UX design are the same: iterate as much as you can, and test as early as possible. The challenge, he says, is knowing which methods and tools to pick, and when to use them. There's a vast difference between sending out a survey to a few hundred users and sitting down with someone in a cafeteria to perform a quick field test, and whether you select one or the other will depend on factors related to the nature of your product, its stage in development, and the resources at your disposal.

Another challenge of UX design is that the goalposts are constantly in flux; that is to say, intended user behaviour and reactions can vary wildly between different products. Ario offers up Gmail and *Candy Crush* as two projects he's worked on which are diametrically opposed in this respect. He describes checking email in itself as a stressor, with the goal of Gmail being to minimize clutter and get users in and out of an inherently unpleasant task as quickly as possible. Meanwhile, the act of play serves as a de-stressor and a form of escapism, and so the intent of *Candy Crush* is to keep users enrapt in casual fun for as long as possible. On the basis of time spent in-app, the two projects are in complete opposition to what constitutes a positive user experience.

Regardless of whether you're trying to keep users in as long as possible, brusquely escort them out of a stressful task, or achieve any other metric, Ario says that one method of constant critical importance is prototyping, along with user validation. Speaking of testing, Ario says "the more the better, and the earlier the better." He pithily advocates for this necessity with a favourite quote from a long-forgotten source: "Every design is wrong. You just don't know how wrong it is."[6] Each cycle in an iterative process is crucial to correct mistakes and push experiences one step closer to perfection—even if a truly perfect experience is unattainable.

In the spirit of promoting a healthy design process, Ario has a few pieces of wisdom for designers, especially new recruits. With a chuckle and apologizing for his informality, he says that designers need to realize they have "permission to suck," arguing that early prototypes need to be put out there for feedback as early as possible. "Being rough is the job. You need to put those ugly things out there in order to get to something that's beautiful." Ensuring you'll get to something beautiful in the end, he says, is a matter of making sure that you care. He's been reading *Radical Candor*, a book about management, and picks out the notion of "giving a damn" as one of the most important things any designer can do. Again, he apologizes for his language,

---

[6] Apparently the long-forgotten source of this quote doesn't have the best SEO, as we couldn't find the original either after a round of sleuthing. If you happen to know, please send us a letter.

(Continued)

(Continued)

which we assure him is in keeping with the intended PG-13 MPAA rating for this book. He eloquently rephrases the sentiment in terms of game design, noting the effect of passion on creativity: "When you care [. . .] your whole world becomes an inspiration canvas for what you're going to do in the game." In the end, he says, picking something you're passionate about is one of the most important choices you can make as a designer.

Further reading

Introduction to Game Design, Prototyping, and Development by Jeremy Gibson Bond (Addison-Wesley). ISBN: 978-0321933164.
A heavily practical primer on creating games using Unity and C#. If you're looking to take that first leap into making something but you're not exactly sure where to start, this book is a good candidate.

Sprint by Jake Knapp, John Zeratsky, and Braden Kowitz (Simon & Schuster). ISBN: 978-1501121746.
A best-seller on the ideology of quick problem-solving through iteration. One of the snappier options for learning about the likes of agile strategies more in depth.

Exercises

Junior cartographer

Pick a game you like that involves some sort of navigation in a virtual world. Using the engine of your choice, or a map editor if the game has one, create a new area for that game. Don't be meticulous in your details, or even focus on using assets that resemble the game; instead, create a whitebox of the level which uses primitive assets to block out the general features of your area. If you want, you can start from a rough sketch before moving on to make a 3D (or 2D) prototype in your chosen tool.

Move through your prototype and try to identify issues with spacing, visibility, and the placement of any important features. Do you think you've inadvertently created any "dead" zones where players won't be compelled to go? What have you learned about your personal workflow in creating a virtual world? What would you do differently next time?

Discount classics

Select a simple arcade game like *Space Invaders* or *Pong*—it can be anything you like as long as it's something very simple.

Using the engine of your choice, try and re-create the game as faithfully as you can. Find assets on the internet, or re-make them yourself. Try and keep to a short timeline and a small scope. What was the hardest part of the game to re-create? What was the easiest?

After you've completed the exercise, think about how you might create a more modern version of that classic game—adding layers of progression and "juicing up" feedback, for example.

Put yourself out there

The best exercise we can recommend for this chapter is to participate in a Game Jam! A game jam is an event where participants have a limited amount of time (anywhere from a day to a month, depending on the jam) to create a game prototype. Look up an event near you, or participate in a large annual event like the Global Game Jam. Game jams are typically very low-stakes, and focused on pushing you to explore your creativity, rather than compete for some prize. They can be a great way to experiment with fun design ideas, test and develop your skills, and meet new people to work with.

11

Test your Patience

Every game developer's third-greatest fear is public ridicule of their game. This horror of universal hostility is supplanted only by the thought of having your game crash at E3, and, of course, big bitey spiders. You certainly want your creation to be remembered, but not for being lambasted by critics and reviled by users.

On any list of terrible games, including one's own memory if you're of a certain age, you'll likely encounter the likes of *Superman 64*, *Sonic 06*, and *E.T. the Extra-Terrestrial*. Each is notorious for its own reasons, and all were critically chastised. *Superman 64* was chided especially for its poor and un-responsive controls. The ambitious *Sonic 06* had a myriad of charges levied against it, including unacceptable technical quality, bad writing, and lacklus-tre level design. Meanwhile, *E.T.*'s unfinished state and unattractive graphics led to a quick slowing in sales and a quick uptick in returns following its release.

The ultimate fate of *E.T.* is one of the most spectacular failures in video game history. For years, an urban legend speculated that unsold copies were disposed of in a mass burial by Atari—a legend that turned out to be true when the site was excavated in 2013 as part of a documentary project[1]. The dig recovered several hundred cartridges of nearly a million estimated to have been buried, including copies of *E.T.* But the developers of *E.T.* certainly didn't intend for their creation to end up sunsetting in landfills instead of players' treasured collections. So, how does a multimillion-dollar project fail so remarkably, and how can a much smaller effort ever have any hope of circumventing this fate?

Failures at this scale usually depend on a number of missteps, not just one. In *E.T.*'s case, licensing negotiations yielded a high price for intellectual property and a massively reduced development timeline, giving less than six

---

[1] That documentary is *Atari: Game Over*, and it reflects on the bemusing details of the complete *E.T. affair.*

The Game Designer's Playbook. Samantha Stahlke and Pejman Mirza-Babaei, Oxford University Press.
© Samantha Stahlke and Pejman Mirza-Babaei (2022). DOI: 10.1093/oso/9780198845911.003.0011

weeks for production from start to finish with only one programmer[2]. This should already be setting off alarm bells; we've just spent an entire chapter talking about managing your creative process, with an ideal pretty much antithetical to that undertaken by Atari. And while the conversation thus far can certainly help you avoid plunging your studio into a legacy on par with *E.T.*, it's far from guaranteed. Your most effective tool in this regard is that last step of the iterative design cycle we've been so ham-handedly sidestepping in anticipation of this chapter: evaluation.

Evaluation is critical because it helps you to understand how successful your design is in its current state, and how it can be improved, both for immediate and long-term play. Short-term appeal is a question of initial impressions; is a game intriguing, and does it avoid any annoyances that would repel new players? This early appeal can help drive sales close to release, and positive reception from critics. And if you can validate a long-lasting desire to play, you can anticipate a player community with longevity and growth potential, driving future revenue and giving you the resources to work on updates or your next title.

Depending on how new you are to game development, when you think of the phrase "game testing", you're probably picturing something along the lines of quality assurance, or QA. QA testing is about finding bugs in your game's implementation: things like broken collision boxes, crashes, collectibles you can't actually collect, and so on. Larger studios all have dedicated personnel for QA testing, while smaller studios might work with a QA service providers or have a few members who test for bugs part-time or hire contractors.

Distinct from QA testing is playtesting, which aims to identify issues with player experience. Cheekily, you might refer to this as finding bugs in your *design*, instead of your code. Issues uncovered by playtesting could include things like an unlikeable main character, hard-to-navigate menus, or a poorly received spike in difficulty. Critically, playtesting needs to be done with participants that represent a game's target audience. Not other game developers, definitely not your employees, and preferably not their mothers. Tuning player experience necessitates that you have the right players to tune with, and trying to playtest with members of the development team is a recipe for disaster. The biggest issue here is that your team knows too much; on top of reducing impartiality, you can't hope to uncover something like a confusing puzzle when the "player" designed it themselves.

There is an entire field of research which revolves around playtesting, called games user research (GUR). Obviously, GUR is more complicated

---

[2] You can read an interview with that programmer, Howard Scott Warshaw, on this and other tales here: http://www.digitpress.com/library/interviews/interview_howard_scott_warshaw.html

than evaluation alone; it's also about understanding player psychology, how games affect us, how we can push the boundaries of game design, and so on. But, if you had to sum up GUR in one word, that word would probably be "playtesting." And even if you have no intent on diving into the research world, you can learn a great deal about playtesting from peering into the realms of GUR, something which we'll be doing throughout this chapter.

As you can tell, our focus here will be on playtesting, rather than QA. This isn't to trivialize the importance of QA by any means, or to imply that QA testers should be ignored if they have suggestions about your design. Quite the opposite, in fact; a professional QA tester will have amassed a great deal of first-hand experience with the impact of different design decisions. To grossly oversimplify things, though, QA finds programmer problems, while playtesting finds designer problems. Since this is a book about design, we'll be concerning ourselves with the latter.

Running playtests well is a tricky business, and a peek behind the curtain will quickly reveal that it is every bit as ugly and complicated as any other part of game development. It's not as simple as sitting someone down, handing them a controller, and asking them if they like your game; although, you will usually find yourself building on some flavour of that scenario as a basis. But playtesting itself is an endeavour steeped in design know-how, even before you bring in your first participants.

11.1 Spend your questions wisely

In playtesting, we have lots of different methods at our disposal: observation, interviews, focus groups, and questionnaires to name a few. Diving into evaluation isn't just a matter of picking a few of these methods out of a hat and hopping in, though. Imagine sparing no expense to bring in a hundred players, spend a few hours with each, and prepare the most deluxe of slides to present your results—only to find out that you've blown your entire testing budget six months into development, and not even managed to investigate the things your team actually cared about.

To be successful and provide some semblance of return on investment, any evaluation needs to consider a number of factors. First, what resources do you have at your disposal? You'll need a dedicated place for playtest participants to play, so either set aside some space, budget for some additional rent, or be prepared to set up a framework for remote testing. Estimate how many hours you'll have available for supervising tests and data analysis, making sure to account for any staff that work double-duty in evaluation and some other specialty. Don't forget about the expenses associated with participants themselves, either. If you don't have a recruit list or community to pull volunteers, be prepared to shell out money and time to find testers from your target market. And bear in mind that you'll need to compensate those testers for their time, as well; honorariums often run at or above minimum wage on top of any local travel expenses.

Another thing to consider is your game's current state of development. If you've just cobbled together your very first prototype, your evaluation strategy is going to look much different than it will when you reach a working beta a few months out from release. As we'll discuss later on, certain test structures are better suited to different phases of production.

Resource availability and project status can help you determine the scope and structure of your evaluation. However, they will somewhat guide the specifics of that evaluation, like which parts of your game participants will interact with and the questions you ask them. This brings us to our all-important final consideration, which will guide both higher-level method choices and those low-level specifics: understanding what you actually want to know.

Fundamentally, game evaluation is about asking questions. Our motivation for evaluation is to assess the experience we've created; in other words, we want to ask, *"Is this game any good?."* Playtesting is merely the sophisticated wrapper around the process of answering that question, in the course of which we'll identify any obstacles between the product we have and an affirmative response.

Of course, the question *"Is this game any good?"* is far too unspecific to be practically useful. Learning to identify a good basis for an evaluation, and distill that basis into a set of helpful *research questions*, is a skill unto itself. Any given playtest should be motivated by a strong core research question, often accompanied by a small collection of related, more specific inquiries. For instance, your core research question might be something like *"How do the controls feel?,"* strengthened by guide questions like *"Do players have a strong preference between our keyboard versus gamepad control options?"* Sometimes, you might have a couple of core research questions which are strongly related, such as combining *"How do players like the art style?"* and *"How compelling is the soundtrack?"* into an evaluation focused on aesthetics.

Taking the time to formulate research questions will help keep you focused both in running your evaluation (e.g., knowing what to watch out for in participants' gameplay) and your analysis after the fact (e.g., which issues will be most relevant to the immediate needs of your team). If these points haven't yet sold you on the importance of research questions, perhaps the inevitability of calamity in their absence will. If you jump in without any particular goal in mind, you might find yourself coming back to a team desperate to know whether the prototype tutorial is effective—only to present them with a list of complaints about graphics that aren't even close to finalized. Coming up with research questions doesn't just make an evaluation "more science-y"; it also provides a vital opportunity to communicate with your team and make sure that the next phase of testing will meet their needs.

Before we move on, we should address a fundamental divide in the types of questions that game evaluations can investigate. Here, we can speak of two major categories: usability questions, and opinion questions.

Our first group of inquiries, usability questions, are concerned with objective issues. Examples of usability questions include "*Do players understand the tutorial?*" and "*Can players use the shop interface effectively?*" These questions aren't dependent on players' individual preferences or tastes; something like a button that's difficult to see is a problem that needs little explanation to justify fixing. There's a bit of an asterisk here, though. Just because usability problems are objectively problems doesn't mean that their solutions are always clear-cut. If players struggle with a game's tutorial, for instance, the solution is rarely as simple as "add more instructions." Nonetheless, most usability problems can be identified effectively with a relatively small group of playtesters. If three participants out of half a dozen have trouble reading your menus, it almost certainly can't hurt to re-examine your text choices to promote better visibility.

The at-times more contentious category is that of opinion questions, which target subjective matters. Examples of opinion questions could be "*Is our main character likeable?*" or "*Do players find the art style beautiful?*" The problem with these types of questions, important as they are, is that it is difficult to answer them effectively with a small group of people. Opinion questions are, unsurprisingly, largely dependent on players' opinions. While you might be able to read over a character's dialogue and come to the objective conclusion that they're a bit rude, real players might find a bit of gruff discourtesy charming, especially if they can relate to the character in other ways. And if you reach that same three out of six threshold for players hating that character, it's risky to assume that half of *all players* will dislike them. Plus, it's a safe bet that your development team—probably more than six people—all like the character, and will be resistant to such large changes on the basis of what could be a fluke.

With our research questions in hand, then, and keeping in mind any caveats they present, let's move on to examine that magical box of methods we keep referencing: how do we actually test a game?

11.2 A crash course in testing

Before we rattle off a list of procedures to poke at the psyches of players, let's take a moment to first clarify a few terms and purge any remaining excessive alliteration from our systems. In describing methods to evaluate games, you'll hear of quite a few distinctions made to help distinguish what each method can accomplish, and how to select a suite of methods that complement one another.

First is the difference between "expert evaluation" and "playtesting" methods. The former category is designed to support evaluation *without* bringing in players. An example of an expert method is heuristic evaluation, where a professional will examine a game according to a set of general rules for things like accessibility, usability, and style. Another popular technique is the cognitive walkthrough. For this, you select a number of tasks (e.g., equipping a weapon, buying something from a shop, etc.) and work through individual steps while attempting to emulate a player's perspective in understanding what to do, and how to do it. Expert evaluation can be an effective way to quickly (and often cheaply) identify problems, particularly with usability. That being said, you shouldn't rely entirely on tactics that don't involve real players in the evaluation process, and so our focus will remain largely on methods for playtesting.

There are a few other divisions commonly used in describing evaluation methods, all of which are conveniently binary and straightforward. One is the question of whether a method provides qualitative or quantitative data. Qualitative data is descriptive, while quantitative data is numeric. For instance, an interview transcript is qualitative data, while the amount of time taken to complete a level is quantitative data. It should be noted that some methods can produce both types of data; for example, in observing gameplay, you might note a participant's reactions to their gameplay (qualitative) in addition to the number of times their character was killed (quantitative).

Another characteristic of any given method is its objectivity. Objective methods reveal facts: things like what weapon a player chose, how far they progressed in their first five minutes of play, or something more exotic like a player's heart rate. Subjective methods, on the other hand, rely on data from players about how they feel: things like why they liked or disliked a game, or how they perceived their own level of skill. Objective techniques produce reliable data, which can lack context: you can be certain of how long it took players to learn a particular skill, but the exact cause of any difficulties observed might be unclear. Subjective methods are all about context: players can tell you why they took longer to do something, expressing confusion or maybe surprising you with the conclusion that they just wanted to try a few things before moving on. The problem with subjective tactics, though, is that they rely on *self-reporting*. In discussing their experience, participants might exhibit bias, forget things, filter out bits of information that would make them sound unskilled, or try to be complimentary at the expense of honesty. It's your job as an evaluator to try and overcome these hurdles, but

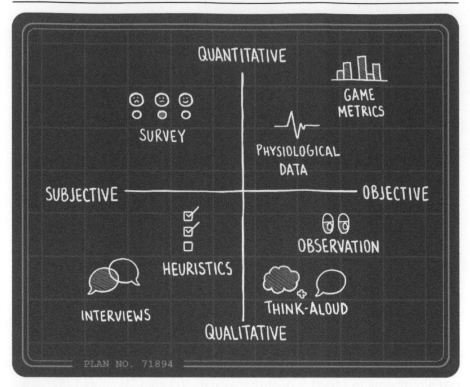

Figure 11.1 Different games user research methods classified according to subjectivity and whether they are quantitative or qualitative. Note that this diagram is meant to separate methods into quadrants, rather than serve as a graph—placement along the dividing lines is not meant to imply relative "levels" of quantitativeness or subjectivity.

the inherent wrinkles of subjective evaluation make them impossible to erase completely.

Our last distinction is that of sampling versus continuous methods. Continuous techniques collect data throughout a player's experience. Attaching a heart rate monitor to a player or constantly recording gameplay information are examples of continuous data collection. Sampling methods, by contrast, capture a "snapshot" of information at a certain point in time. An example is stopping to interview players at the end of their play session.

We should note here that each pair of method characteristics discussed forms is less of a dichotomy and more of a spectrum. While the distinction between qualitative and quantitative *data* is binary, any given *method* might provide both types of data, as we discussed previously. The question of objectivity also has a tinge of greyness to it; timing a player is certainly objective, and asking players which character they'd most like to have a drink with is certainly subjective. Asking players to rate the difficulty of levels, though, while subjective, is arguably "more objective" than the hypothetical bar crawl question. And lastly, the interval at which data is sampled can make it more or less continuous. Asking players to think aloud while they play will produce samples of data far closer together than a single interview at the end of play, but not nearly so close together as the measurements taken by something like a heart monitor.

The reason we have bothered to introduce these terms is not so that you can flip open a volume on games user research without needing to look up every other word, though it is a fringe benefit. Instead, these distinctions are important to understand since they can help you create a more balanced evaluation. In general, you'll want to pick a set of methods that, taken together, cover both ends of each scale. For instance, if you're evaluating difficulty, you'll probably want to collect quantitative data on how often players die and how long they take to complete each challenge. But without qualitative data expressing when and how players failed, your team will have little indication of where any tweaks should be made. This holds true for our other categories as well; objective data without subjective data lacks context, while subjective data without objective data lacks credibility. Relying on continuous data alone excludes methods like interviews, while an approach reliant entirely on sampling would mean that the likes of gameplay recordings would be left out.

Keeping these things in mind, let's go over the methods we've already alluded to in more detail, looking at how you'll practice each one as part of your game evaluation skillset. We can view these methods as helping to support two main inquiries: understanding what players do, and how they feel.

What do players do? Playtesting is about understanding users' behaviours, the reasons underlying those behaviours, and their reactions to gameplay. The first half of this equation concerns player action, and so having a record of that action is vital. This is where perhaps the oldest technique in the book comes in: *observation*.

Observation is exactly as it sounds, watching what players do in-game. This is an objective, near-continuous method (limited by observer error) which can provide both qualitative and quantitative data. During a live playtesting session, you can sit in a position where you have some view of their screen. Here you should be careful not to give participants the feeling that you're breathing down their neck, so position yourself carefully. Ideally, you should broadcast the player's screen to another device (budget permitting) where you can watch from another room or at a comfortable distance. Should you be unable to find local participants, or if you don't have access to a playtesting space, screensharing software still makes live observation possible for remote playtesting.

Regardless of how you watch participants play, you need to have a record of play to consult later. There's no excuse not to record gameplay videos; plenty of free (and open-source!) software exists for screen capture. Combine this with enough storage space, or a free video compression tool and an old USB stick you've had since high school, and you've got a library of participant gameplay videos for reference later. For a bit of extra setup effort, you can record player input and facial expressions as well. If you've got a webcam, and one of the many free utilities for visualizing input, you can simply tack these on beside gameplay in a good screen capture tool.

Even with a beautifully itemized library of gameplay recordings, the most important part of observation is to be vigilant and take notes. Don't tell yourself that you can just re-watch the recording later, or let your mind wander during the test. This will make it harder for you to recall the full context of gameplay, and removes your ability to effectively follow up on key moments with participants right after they play. Make notes on anything that surprises you, any reactions which seem strong from the player, any spots they seem to struggle with, and so on. It can also be helpful to have a timer nearby (e.g., on your phone), synchronized with the gameplay recording, so that you can note down timestamps to easily parse the recording later.

In observation, as with any other method, it's vital that you're mindful of your research question(s), keeping an extra watchful eye for anything related to the focus of the test. Let's say you're working with the following research question: *"Is the tutorial effective?"* Some things you might watch out for might be expressions of confusion from the player, making lots of mistakes when they learn a new mechanic, or seeming frequently bored. Noting these events as they occur would be qualitative data. You might also record some quantitative data here; for instance, how long players take to complete each segment of the tutorial.

Direct observation isn't the only way to record player action; you can also collect data directly from your game. *Game metrics* (AKA *telemetry*) is a technique whereby hooks in your game's code relay specified information to a log file of some sort for later review. Just like observation, telemetry is an objective, continuous method capable of collecting both qualitative and quantitative information. Assuming you have the resources to integrate an existing telemetry tool or implement one yourself, this can be a great way to keep track of events, especially when observation is infeasible. Metrics are less susceptible to error (with the exception of bugs), and work for things that might be hard to track manually (e.g., every time the player character takes damage).

You can certainly implement some form of metrics for small-scale evaluation if you like. Where the tactic really shines, though, is in larger scale remote evaluations, allowing you to collect data from many players without having to beg them for screen recordings or comb through hours of footage. Telemetry data can be as specific or as general as you need or have time to implement (and analyze). Even very high-level data can be valuable in this respect; competitive online multiplayer games can be balanced around metrics as simple as who won a given match. In *Overwatch*, for instance, the win rate of different characters can provide a starting point for balance decisions.[3] If a character has a very high win rate across all levels of skill, this provides a red flag of sorts to indicate that the character should be investigated for being possibly overpowered.

Returning to the research question we introduced earlier, if you were to use telemetry to probe tutorial effectiveness, you might focus on collecting information related to player learning. Keep a gameplay timer in the background, and spit out the timestamp when players complete the tutorial. Remember from Chapter 3 that you probably shouldn't let players die during a tutorial (though you should always give them feedback when they make a mistake). Internally, though, log any events where players would have otherwise died or taken damage, and the thing that damaged them. If testing at scale (e.g., during a beta), this would also be a good opportunity to check engagement and retention. Do players complete the tutorial in a single sitting, or are they quitting and relaunching the game a few times? Do they keep playing afterwards? For how long? Answering questions like these "in the wild" could help you to better understand the efficacy of your tutorial for not only learning, but getting players interested in your game.

How do players feel? The second half of our "playtesting equation" looks at player thinking and emotion. Therefore, we also need a suite of methods tailored to understanding how players think and feel. We have many ways of doing this, some which involve exotic things like heart rate monitors, facial expression recognition, and sensors to measure muscle tension and sweating. These provide objective measures pointing to players' physiological state, from which we can infer things like stress level. However, such tactics require specialized equipment and analysis techniques far beyond the scope of a basic design evaluation. This is where self-reporting (subjective) techniques come in, letting players express what's going on inside their heads.

One such tactic is the *think-aloud* method, where players are asked to speak their thoughts as they play. This can include both the reasons for what

---

[3] *Overwatch* developers have alluded to this process in forum posts responding to player concerns, such as that found here: https://us.forums.blizzard.com/en/overwatch/t/please-nerf-power-creep-instead-of-nerfing-defensesupport/443903/114

they're doing, and their reactions to in-game content. Keep in mind that some players will be more naturally talkative than others, and don't expect every participant to naturally talk constantly while trying to concentrate on play. Again, pay special attention to anything related to your research question; if you're looking at tutorial efficacy, "I don't know what I'm doing" is much more relevant than "That bird looks nice." Think-aloud is like the subjective counterpart to observation, in a sense—a continuous way to obtain qualitative data on players' experience.

Another self-reporting method is the *questionnaire*, a quiz-like set of questions especially useful in getting players' initial impressions. Questions can take any form you like: multiple choice, multiple selection, or written answers. Keep in mind, though, that any attempts to use quantitative rating scales will provide a coarse indication of player favour at best. Don't be tempted to try something like finding a statistically significant difference in players' average rating of different features on a scale of 1 to 10. Different players will have a different understanding of what each rating means to them—to some people, 5/10 is average (it's in the middle), while to others it's almost a failing grade (it's 50 percent). Moreover, arguing that a scale of opinion would be perfectly linear for mathematical reasons is beyond ridiculous. This isn't to say that getting players to distill their opinion into a rating of some sort is always a terrible idea. But, if you're going to make the attempt, take any numeric conversions with a grain of salt and pay more attention to the proportion of players that put their chips on the upper or lower end of the scale. Consider a simple scale with bold options like "I love it," "I don't care," and "I hate it," gently forcing players to pick a less muddy expression of their opinion.

Questionnaires aren't unique to live playtesting; they can also be useful in-game. Many games have a bug report system, but you can also include a system for general feedback in the form of a short questionnaire. *Subnautica*, for instance, uses a form with a small text box and short emoticon-based rating scale. *Deep Rock Galactic* gives players a link to an online survey asking a few questions about their experience alongside an opportunity for free-form feedback.

It's important to note here that questionnaires can also induce something called "survey fatigue." Simply put, questionnaires can get boring quickly. Reading about questionnaires can also get boring quickly, as we're sure you've noticed by now. The lesson here is to keep your questionnaires short and sweet. If you need more detail—and for a live playtest, you always will—that's where our next tactic comes in.

Interviews are, with little debate, the single most useful method at your disposal in understanding players' experience. They're also one of the simplest; just sit down with players and talk to them about their experience. Some evaluators prefer to stick to a rigidly structured set of questions, while others

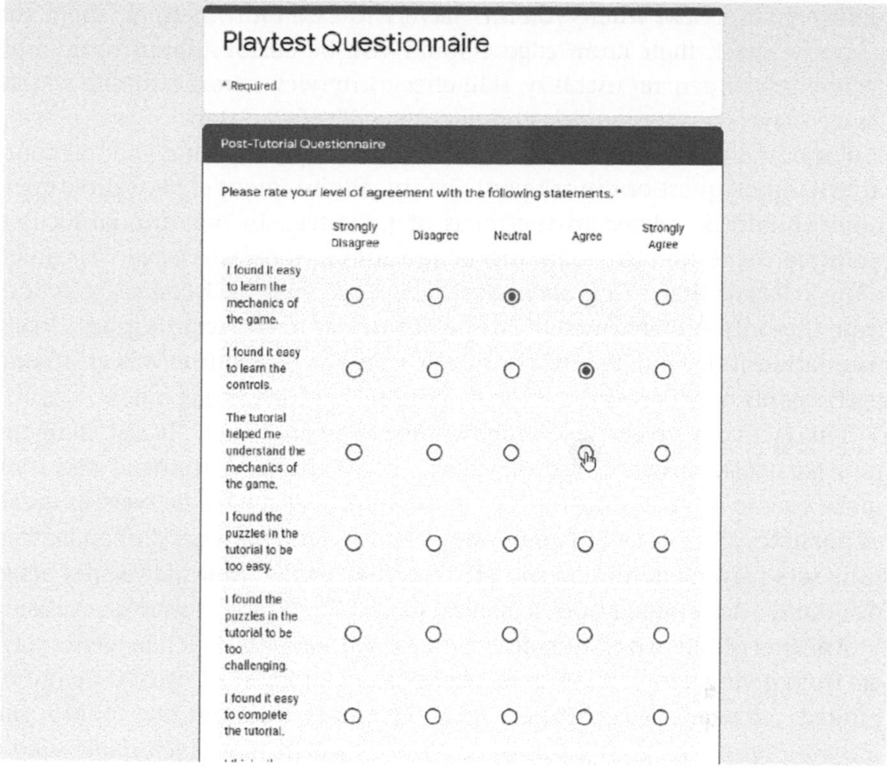
Playtest Questionnaire

* Required

Post-Tutorial Questionnaire

Please rate your level of agreement with the following statements. *

	Strongly Disagree	Disagree	Neutral	Agree	Strongly Agree
I found it easy to learn the mechanics of the game.	○	○	◉	○	○
I found it easy to learn the controls.	○	○	○	◉	○
The tutorial helped me understand the mechanics of the game.	○	○	○	○	○
I found the puzzles in the tutorial to be too easy.	○	○	○	○	○
I found the puzzles in the tutorial to be too challenging.	○	○	○	○	○
I found it easy to complete the tutorial.	○	○	○	○	○

Figure 11.2 Screenshot of a game questionnaire created with Google Forms using Likert scales to assess player agreement with a variety of statements judging a game's quality.

will opt for a free-form discussion. Our suggestion is to rest somewhere in between. Have a set of questions prepared and ask them, but let discussion evolve naturally, and follow up on anything of note you observed during that player's gameplay. Make sure to take notes, and preferably record sessions if you can.

There are a few different "flavours" of interviews, so to speak. Players can be interviewed individually, or as a group (e.g., after a multiplayer playtest). It's worth noting here that there's a difference between a group interview and a *focus group*. Generally speaking, a group interview refers to a setting where an evaluator asks questions answered by everyone in the group, whereas a focus group is more of an observed discussion where the group talks about their impressions of something with little interference.

In terms of timing, you can plan for one long interview at the end of a playtest session, or have a few smaller ones each time players pass key points in a longer gameplay session. One interesting variant on this theme is the *skill-check interview*, where you ask players to explain something about the game to check their knowledge. Should you be curious about tutorial effectiveness or general usability, skill-check interviews are a fantastic way to gauge players' understanding and retention of information.

For both interviews and questionnaires, it's important that you can come up with good questions to ask participants. As you might expect, these questions should be related to the focus of your test. In our tutorial-focused example, a question like *"How easy or difficult was it to learn to play?"* is much more relevant than *"How about that boss music, huh?"* Of course, relevance isn't the only problem with that second question. Its wording, and likely intonation if delivered verbally, implies that the boss music was great, and participants may be swayed to play up their opinions as a result.

This is an example of a so-called *leading question*, which "leads" someone to a particular answer based on aspects of its delivery. To avoid this trap, make sure to use neutral language and temper your verbal delivery as much as possible. Asking *"Did you think the game was great, or what?"* in an excited tone sets players up for a particular response, while *"How did you feel about this game?"* delivered in a polite neutral tone will make an honest reply easier.

Another pitfall in question design is a *loaded question*, which prevents players from giving a fully truthful response based on its wording or the options offered. An example might be a multiple-choice question like *"Which gun was your favourite?"* in a game where players might have exclusively used a sword to play. Such questions are usually more of a concern for questionnaires, which might not give participants the opportunity to clarify that a question doesn't connect with their experience.

One last thing to avoid is the inclusion of any jargon which could make a question difficult to read or understand. Don't use complicated game-specific terms; if you're talking to a first-time player and want to know how they felt using your machine gun, avoid asking *"How was your experience using the G50 20mm MK-37 turret bay autocannon?"* and favour something like *"How was your experience with the machine gun?"*

In general, good questions are understandable and open up opportunities for further discussion. As the starting point for any interview, make sure to ask a few basic questions about participants' overall experience. This will help them transition from gameplay to discussion, and capture initial impressions. Our recommendation, particularly for novice evaluators, is to consider using a basic triumvirate of questions as intro material: *"What, if anything, did you like about this game?,"* *"What, if anything, did you dislike about this game?,"* and *"What, if anything, would you change about this game?"*

11.2.1 *A primer on playtest proctoring*

When the time comes to sit players down for a session, there's a few basic procedural things you should keep in mind. Your top priority needs to be treating players well. Make sure that players are aware of what you'll be asking them to do, and about how long they can expect the test to take. Standard practice for commercial playtests will involve asking participants to sign a confidentiality form, and to provide consent for any data collection. If you're hoping to record something like webcam footage, it's probably a good idea to screen for participants that are open to this before you recruit them.

During the session, make sure that players are comfortable. Tell them that you're evaluating the game, not them—you don't want participants to feel on edge thinking that you're judging their every move. Ask players to be honest, and try to keep a comfortable distance when observing their gameplay. Don't visibly react to their gameplay, and avoid giving hints or stepping in unless you need to push the test along for scheduling reasons.

When asking players questions, don't be adversarial, and don't act like the game is precious to you (as difficult as that may be). Participants will be less likely to be honest if they're worried about getting into an argument or hurting your feelings, so try to stay as neutral as possible. Remember, if everyone hates your game, the time to burst into tears is *after* they leave the interview room.

Apart from how you handle your players, you'll also want to double-check that your setup works well with the methods you've chosen. If you're planning on having an interview or asking players to think aloud, having an easy way to record audio is beneficial. If you're holding an evaluation remotely, make sure to test your software for video calling, recording, or remote play with your teammates beforehand. Always make sure to have a dry run of your test before the time comes to bring in real players, unless you're keen to throw out valuable data when something inevitably goes wrong.

After the test, if you love spreadsheets, this is where the real fun begins. The subject of data analysis is volumes unto itself, some of which you'll find recommended at the end of this chapter. Diving into something like statistical analysis is beyond the scope of our discussion. But even without knowing what it means to violate the assumption of sphericity or run a paired sample t-test, you can still provide your team with valuable feedback. In fact, outside of academic research, the most useful insights will usually come from considerate organization of qualitative snippets rather than extravagant statistical tests.

A good starting point for your analysis is to write out a categorized, point-form list of noteworthy gameplay events and feedback. Keep a tally for each point corresponding to the number of participants that said or did something. How many people struggled at the same level? How many people mentioned the same things when asked about their dislikes? For each item, try to assign a severity based on your own judgement and participants' reactions. A low-severity issue might be something like a participant expressing a dislike for the character who taught them about the controls. A high-severity issue might be watching a participant shout obscenities and describe a boss fight as "total bull that will never disgrace one of my screens ever again if I can help it" before quitting the game.

Taking severity and frequency together, you can assign priorities to each issue that you find. A priority system will help your team to figure out which issues should be tackled first. You can also do this for positive points; if lots of players really loved something, it's worth noting to prevent a well-liked feature from eventually getting cut.

In terms of suggesting solutions, you can try and link issues together to see if they stem from a common root cause. Avoid making lots of inferences in doing so; focus on what players said and did. If lots of players struggled to learn your controls, and many suggested slowing down the pace of instruction in interviews, then slowing down the pace of instruction is a good starting point. On the other hand, ignoring what your players said because you've got a hunch that you just need to rebind a couple of keys isn't such a great idea.

Relying on inference too much can lead to incorrect conclusions. You shouldn't ignore your instincts by any means; if you're reviewing gameplay footage and notice that players consistently miss the same jump in a platforming level, nudging the gap to be a bit smaller is a good bet. However, something like assuming that players dislike a game because they routinely fail can be dangerous. Imagine applying this logic to a roguelike game, where repetitive failure and character death is core to someone's progression as a player. Easing up on difficulty to make failure less likely would ruin the experience. This is part of why paying attention to self-reporting is so important; make sure to always consider the context players have provided surrounding their reaction to a particular event.

On the subject of erroneous conclusions, make sure that you're not falling into the traps that have claimed the credibility of countless junior analysts. Don't get caught up in small differences; a difference of 0.1 between the averages of two 10-point rating scales probably doesn't mean anything. Don't assume that the experiences of one player will apply universally to all; the term "outlier" exists for a reason. By that same token, don't blind yourself to the problems of the few, either: sometimes rare occurrences can point to something like an accessibility problem.

Your biggest enemy in an effective analysis, though, is yourself. It will be difficult to ignore your own biases in reviewing player data, but you have to try. Confirmation bias is probably the largest hurdle here: the tendency to accept information which conforms with an existing view. If you've convinced yourself that a certain level is too difficult, you might latch on to the one player that struggled with it—even if twenty others breezed through without issue. Your best strategy here is to make sure that you're always backing up any conclusions you've made directly with the data, and that those justifications don't look ridiculous in context. Bumping your "favourite" issue to top priority while the issues encountered by dozens more players languish below isn't going to get you anywhere useful, and it certainly won't make your reports very convincing.

After you've crunched all the interview responses, gameplay recordings, and observation notes together, put a feedback list together comprising any issues or notable positive comments. The level of detail here, and the priority needed to make the cut for team discussion, will depend on the time and patience you have available. At this point, your job is done. Or at least, it's done for the next couple of days, before the iterative design cycle starts anew and you'll need to be ready for the next round of testing.

11.3 The melting pot of methods

The diversity in data collection techniques we have discussed is mirrored in the combination of those techniques. There are many different approaches to structuring a game evaluation, several of which we'll run down here for your reference.

As a reminder, no matter your approach, there will be a few steps common to every evaluation. First, you'll need to pick a basic research question or two with your team. You'll design your evaluation, perhaps following one of the structures we will now discuss. Based on the methods you'll be using, set aside the requisite amount of time, space, and any tools you'll need before reaching out to participants. You can recruit for playtests via social media, or among existing members of your game's community. If you're desperate, you *can* dip into a pool of gaming-interested acquaintances, but treat this as an absolutely final resort, and stay away from anyone with game development experience (they know too much).

After you've gotten everything ready, and with your trusty notepad in hand, you'll be ready to learn about your game. What you'll aim to learn will be dependent on that all-important research question, supported by the test structure that best suits your needs.

First-time user experience (FTUE) evaluation. Just as it says on the tin, an FTUE test aims to figure out if the initial experience you've crafted for players is effective. In this context, "effective" means that players will learn how to play, work through the first challenges they're given, and gain the motivation to keep playing after that. You can run an effective FTUE evaluation with a relatively small group of people; half a dozen participants from your target audience should give you a good idea of whether you're on the right track.

Typical methods used in an FTUE test are observation and interviews, which can be complemented by think-aloud and questionnaires. It is especially important that you recruit participants who haven't seen the game before, or you'd be forsaking the FTU part and just conducting an E test, which isn't nearly as flashy. You should also try and keep gameplay short; depending on how lengthy your game's opening moments are, "short" might mean anywhere from 15 minutes to an hour. If you have no explicit intro material, or that material is very short, just let players play for a time on the shorter end of that scale. If your explicit intro material is longer than an hour, you'll probably want to seriously reconsider your design, but go ahead and test as much of it as you can (being sure to watch out for player boredom).

If your FTUE session is on the longer side, you might want to consider stopping midway for a skill-check interview asking players to explain what they've learned about the game so far. After gameplay, interview players on their experience. Ask the basic trio of interview questions as a starting point (like/dislike/change). To validate player learning, you can ask participants to quickly explain what they had to do in the game and why. Any spots of confusion or omission should be noted as concepts that could be better communicated by the game. If this isn't your first run of FTUE tests, focus on any features that have been added or changed—and don't double-dip for participants from previous rounds.

As we learned in Chapter 3, the first few minutes (or hours) of a game are instrumental in getting players to enjoy their time with your game. Figuring out whether those opening few minutes are successful is critical, and one of the reasons to shoot for having a vertical slice of your early experience as soon as possible. Once you have this in hand, an FTUE evaluation should be the next thing on your roadmap.

Usability evaluation. As far as test structures go, this is the most straightforward. The goal of a usability test is to evaluate the functional efficacy of your interaction design. More simply, it's to find issues with the practical experience of playing your game. Do players have trouble understanding what to do? Are the controls awkward to use? Is your feedback sufficiently clear? A usability test is less about figuring out whether people enjoy your game, and more about whether they can play it without having problems.

Like an FTUE evaluation, the most common methods employed in a usability test are observation, think-aloud, and interviews. An additional similarity is that usability evaluations can be very effective even when only a handful of participants are available. The target of usability evaluation comes down to interaction, and so the things you'll be most commonly focused on will include the subjects of Chapters 4 and 5, feedback and control design.

The enjoyment-oriented counterpart of a usability evaluation is a user experience (UX) evaluation, and you can structure such a test quite similarly. You'll be asking different questions, focused on things like engagement rather than various iterations of *"Did you feel like you could do X effectively?"* And in case you're wondering, yes, you can evaluate a bit of both in the same test. If you're an indie with a budget, asking questions about both usability and UX in a single playtest is probably a good idea, since practically speaking you likely won't have the funds or the connections to funnel through a dozen players a week all throughout development. Keep in mind, though, that the more subjective nature of UX-oriented questions might mean you'll need more participants to find a clear answer to certain questions, as we discussed earlier.

Rapid iterative testing and evaluation (RITE). The *testing and evaluation* bit may be a little redundant, but switching out "evaluation" for "analysis" would have left us with RITA, which sounds too much like the name of a maniacal AI here to usurp humanity. RITE is a testing structure which embraces iteration to the extreme, with the goal of continuous design improvement. Designers are involved in the testing process, with each iteration lasting only a couple of days. At the start of a cycle, areas of interest related to recent changes are highlighted. A playtest is conducted with a few players over the course of a day or so, and feedback is discussed with the design team to make small changes. After changes are made, the cycle starts again.

Methodologically speaking, RITE playtests are basically usability tests, just on an accelerated timescale. Only a few participants are recruited for practical reasons, and practically speaking, you might be recycling players between different cycles. This isn't *always* a bad thing—bringing someone back after changes have been made to see if there's a subjective improvement is valuable. Just be sure to also bring in fresh eyes, or else risk putting out a game that's perfect for long-time playtesters Rick and Diane, but hated by everyone else.

While it's great during periods where rapid change is possible, RITE isn't right at every point in development. If you're in a long series of sprints focused on polish, RITE probably won't be very helpful, nor will it do you any favours when you're in the middle of cobbling together your first vertical slice. But for something like early gameplay balancing, RITE can be the perfect way to test out your changes as soon as they're ready.

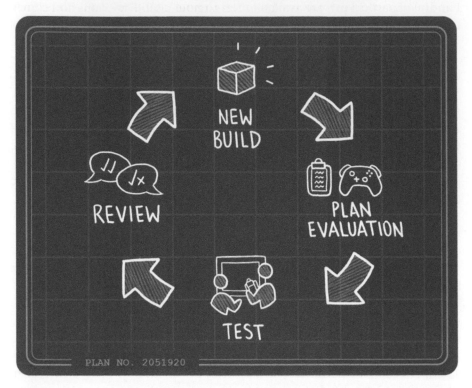

Figure 11.3 Iterative testing, and the last circle diagram in this book. We promise.

A/B testing. In an A/B test, you need to have multiple alternatives of something between which you're trying to establish preference: a control scheme, a HUD, a different player companion, et cetera. Should you have more than two variants of said thing, you can feel free to use the term A/B/C test or similar, but beware that professional researchers will make fun of you for it. You can think of this sort of test like sitting in a room while a psychiatrist shows you two inkblots. Except this time, you're the psychiatrist. And instead of saying "The one on the left is my parents fighting," your participants will say something like "Using the gamepad felt really awkward."

The methods used in an A/B test typically resemble a usability test broken into chunks for different conditions. Let's say you have two different control schemes proposed for gamepad, and you want to select one as the default to ship with the game. Each participant will play the game twice, once with your "A" controls, and once with your "B" controls. Each time they play, you'll ask them briefly about their experience with the controls, and at the very end of the session, you'll ask them to compare. Based on how participants react to each of the control schemes alone, and in comparing the two, you'll assess which one is more effective.

There's a couple of important things to note here. First, you *can* test with two separate groups of people, one for the "A" option and one for the "B."[4] However, especially for a subtle difference, you will probably generally want to opt for a larger group of players to experience both. The more critical point to make is that you need to account for so-called *ordering effects*: the order in which participants play each condition might affect their experience! After having played once, players will know more about the game, and so might have an easier time with the second condition than they otherwise would. They might also be fatigued later on in the test, or growing bored. To stop this from having an effect on the results of the evaluation, you should counterbalance the order that people will play each of your conditions. Half of your participants should play with A first, while the other half play with B first—this will help eliminate any effects of learning and fatigue from fuzzing your results.[5]

Concept testing. If you've been thumbing through the first few test designs bemoaning your lack of a working prototype, then this is the solution for you. Concept testing is made for the early stages of a new idea or a feature development, when you've got nothing but a few sketches, story descriptions, and some wood carving your producer made in their garage. The goal of a concept test is to validate whether potential players are interested in the idea of something: different mechanics, characters, art style candidates, and so on.

The methods employed in a concept test are typically surveys (questionnaires disseminated online to a large group of people) and focus groups. You'll embed a few items of interest in a questionnaire, or haul that wood carving into a boardroom with one-way glass and set loose a dozen members of the precious 18–34 demographic to talk about it for an hour. Depending on your definition of interesting, you might find it interesting to know that concept testing often overlaps with the soul of A/B testing. That is to say, the focus of a concept test might be to explore alternatives in something like art style or soundtrack, presenting participants with lots of options to gauge overall interest in each.

Expert evaluation. Playtesting is the most effective way to figure out if your game actually works, but it's also expensive, time-consuming, and not infallible. Expert evaluation certainly isn't infallible either, but it can be

---

[4] Academically, this approach would be called a *between-subjects* evaluation, as opposed to a *within-subjects* one.

[5] Should you have more than two conditions, look up a Latin Square generator. You'll thank us later. Probably.

a quick way to find opportunities for improvement, and it can also prove to be relatively cheap—particularly if you've got the right sort of expert on your team. An expert evaluation will involve some of those expert methods we discussed earlier, like heuristic evaluation or cognitive walkthroughs. An example case where expert evaluation would be especially useful might be before scheduling a usability test with actual players. If you can identify a few easy-fix issues from expert analysis, those issues won't crowd out subtler details that your usability test will then be able to uncover. For instance, before running a usability test targeting your UI, an expert evaluator could prepare a series of cognitive walkthroughs comprising UI-centric tasks like reorganizing the player's inventory or navigating the options menu.

Long-term and large-scale approaches. Should you want to evaluate your game in the longer term, you might consider something like a *diary study*, where participants walk away with a copy of your game, play it for hours on their own time, write down their experiences with the game (like in a diary) and ideally report back for interviews. This can be great for the course of a few days or weeks, but in the much longer term (i.e., during a closed or public beta, or after release) you'll want to turn to the likes of game analytics and surveys. If you've ever clicked past a disclaimer along the lines of "anonymous data collection for the purposes of product improvement," then you've already had experience supplying your own gameplay metrics for evaluation. Or you've been feeding training data to some sort of foreign intelligence organization.

An excellent application of long-term evaluation driven by game metrics is balancing gameplay in a multiplayer title like *Overwatch* or *League of Legends*. With every match played, you can have information on which characters are more likely to be on a winning or losing team, or which maps seem to grant certain teams or characters an advantage. You can use this information as a starting point for where balancing tweaks are warranted, or even dig into questions like whether players of a higher competitive rating have certain unexpected gameplay preferences. Pursuing this type of long-term evaluation and improvement can help a game maintain a vibrant community long after its release.

Even if executed perfectly, the evaluation approaches we've described here won't guarantee that your game is a smash hit. They won't guarantee financial success, or universal critical acclaim. Game development, like most other businesses, is too dependent on luck and a certain *je ne sais quoi* for any such guarantees to be made. However, testing can guarantee one thing which is utterly invaluable, and that is to make your game better than it otherwise would be. And with our goal as designers being to make a great experience for our players, we can't ask for a better promise.

Expert Profile: Graham McAllister—Having a clear vision

Creator of TeamSync

Game development is a field with many sides to it: design, art, programming, animation, and writing, among others. Graham McAllister has spent his time in games firmly on the science side, with the goal of understanding what makes great (or terrible) game experiences. In 2012, after almost ten years of experience as a computer science lecturer, he founded Player Research, a company offering playtesting services to the video game industry. Five years later, the company expanded with a new lab in Montréal, shortly after acquisition by industry conglomerate Keywords Studios. Graham had made a name for himself, captaining a prominent and rapidly growing user research firm. It might be a bit of a shock, then, to learn that Graham thinks user research isn't working particularly well.

When we sat down with Graham, he pointed out an embarrassing conundrum in the industry. If user research aims to find design flaws and assess the player experience before a game's release (it does), and large studios have healthy budgets for it (they do), then why do we see so many big-budget games flop with critics and audiences at release? (He offers EA's *Anthem* as the most memorable recent example.) It's not as if user research is a new field; it may not be as established as many bastions of science, but studios have been investing in playtesting and UX experts for decades now. And yet, games like *Anthem* send the clear message that something in the game development process is lacking. Looking at the state of modern user research, Graham says that "it's not the most effective way of making a game [better]."

In his time at Player Research, Graham noticed a pattern: user research often came too late in development. By the time usability and UX testing rolled around, the only feasible changes were relatively small ones, but many games suffered from much larger problems in their core design. To help studios get design feedback earlier in development, Graham started offering heuristic reviews, a method which relies on principles of design and human psychology rather than actual players as the source of input. However, even that comes too late for many studios, so Player Research added concept testing and competitor analysis services which can be done very early in the development process.

By speaking with many studios of all sizes, budgets, and experience levels, Graham soon found himself troubled by a new problem that seemingly no amount of UX research could fix. An alarming number of developers struggled to describe their creative vision. When asking big-picture questions like "What game are you making?" and "Who is it for?," he found that different team members would give wildly different answers. Often, those answers would rely on ambiguous words like "engaging," "deep," and "exciting," leading to each member of the team interpreting these terms differently. The problem however, is that each team member is often not aware that their interpretation is different from their teammates, resulting in the game being pulled in different directions. Graham says that such unstructured, messy descriptions ultimately lead to unstructured, messy products.

Without a clear creative vision, Graham says good user research is impossible. He says that too many user research discussions focus on improving testing methods, instead of looking at how the design process and user research are linked in the first place: "If you don't know what your game is about, you certainly don't know how to measure [user experience]. You don't know if you're on track." So even though user

(Continued)

327

(Continued)

research might not be working, Graham doesn't see user research itself as the problem. "The problem is with the team, in particular, how the team works together to define and then deliver their creative vision."

Being a field with so very many sides, game development is a notoriously messy process. We dream of clean, systems-oriented, user-centric design. But creating a game is more like trying to build a castle in the middle of a forest fire; it's chaotic, beautiful in its own way, and at least a little tragic. And without a clear picture of what that castle (or game) should look like, having the most talented team in the world can't save a project without clear direction. That's where his new framework, TeamSync, comes in. With TeamSync, Graham wants to "bring the science into the team," applying analytical methods from organizational psychology and user research to development teams rather than players. The objective, broadly speaking, is to ensure the whole team is aligned in the same direction, and ultimately deliver a better game.

To understand this design re-think, we should start with how Graham sees interaction design. He visualizes a game as a pyramid of sorts with user experience at the top. Interaction design is a stone in the layer just below, which Graham initially describes as synonymous with 'controls'. He notes that things like audiovisual feedback are tightly coupled to our experience of game interaction. Many of the most satisfying interactions—he mentions axe-throwing in *God of War* and web-slinging in *Spider-Man*—depend on much more than button presses to delight players.

This thinking is at the heart of Graham's philosophy, and the framework he's developing with TeamSync. He mentions that the definition of interaction design typically refers to the feedback loop between the player and the system, while TeamSync considers interaction design at the *team level*. In other words, his aim is to tackle 'team interaction design' to enable precise communication and more effective interactions within a team. In our discussion, we talked about common development problems ranging from feature creep to running out of time for all but the smallest changes suggested by user researchers. Graham's side of the discussion usually involved gesturing with a few colourful and top-secret papers from his work on TeamSync, tracing those issues back to the evident progenitor of many design evils. He eloquently pinned one setback after another on the absence of a clear creative vision, painting himself as an optometrist of sorts for the games industry. Take feature creep for example, where a game's design becomes bloated with things destined for later deletion or disappointment: "If it doesn't fit into the vision, maybe it doesn't matter [...] why are you spending time designing something that maybe isn't that important?"

When we spoke to him, Graham was still busy getting the framework together for his new venture. As for anyone looking to remodel their design process in the meantime, he advises making sure the team checks even their most basic assumptions from the outset. Above all else however, ensure everyone on the team shares a clear vision of the game. If you can do this, the team will enjoy a smoother development journey and your players will experience a better game.

Further reading

Games User Research edited by Anders Drachen, Pejman Mirza-Babaei, and Lennart E. Nacke (Oxford University Press). ISBN: 978-0198794843.

A comprehensive book on the methods and ideology of games user research, with a focus on developing a good process for commercially oriented work.

Game User Experience Evaluation edited by Regina Bernhaupt (Springer).

ISBN: 978-3319362939.

Another overview of GUR methods which is arguably more academic in nature. The last part of the book contains some domain-specific applications which are useful for specific projects, like co-located multiplayer, exercise games, and novel controller design.

Discovering Statistics using IBM SPSS by Andy Field (4th ed., Sage). ISBN: 978-9351500827.

Despite the name, you won't have to use SPSS to get a good deal out of this book. The first couple of chapters are a great rundown of basic data analysis and statistics, while the rest of the book explains more sophisticated techniques which may prove useful if you're especially interested in dealing with large-scale quantitative data (if you're a telemetry buff).

How to be a Games User Researcher by Steve Bromley. ISBN: 979-8556962040

A highly accessible book on how games development works and where research can fit in. The book also offers great tips for people interested to start a career in user research.

Exercises

Become the expert

Try your hand at an expert evaluation using a set of *heuristics*, criteria which act as rules of thumb for good game design. Look up an existing set of heuristics, such as the PLAY heuristics first presented at the CHI conference in 2004. Read through the heuristics to familiarize yourself with them.

Pick a game you haven't played before, and play it for an hour or two. Take notes as you play, paying attention to what works and what doesn't. If anything jumps out as related to one of the heuristics you've selected, make sure to take a note of that as well.

After playing, compare your notes to the set of heuristics and see if you can relate them to those heuristics. Which ones does the game violate, if any? Which does it do well? Write out a list of any issues you have identified and estimate their priority based on how often they occur and how severely they impact the player's experience.

(Continued)

329

(Continued)

Guerrilla playtesting

Recruit a (willing) friend and have them act as a playtesting participant for you. Pick an existing commercial game, and run a FTUE-type test with your friend. Take this opportunity to play around with a "proper" playtesting setup. Create a comfortable area for your friend to play, set up software to record their gameplay, take notes while they play, and have questions ready to interview them.

 Afterwards, create a list of issues and suggestions to improve the experience based on watching your friend play (remember that in reality, you will very rarely jump to absolutes based on data from one person). Discuss your findings with your friend. If you were the game's developer, what would your next steps be?

12

What Comes Next?

In the summer of 1964, millions flocked to New York City for the World's Fair, a celebration of human culture and technology. Dripping with post-war optimism, the fair showcased developments in transportation, computing, and communications. Epcot-style pavilions housed Florida flamingos, art on loan from the Vatican, and of course, "The World's Largest Cheese," courtesy of Wisconsin. Among all its exhibitions, one of many memorable moments at the fair was a demonstration staged in May by Bell Aerosystems: the *Rocket Belt Man*.

Rocket Belt Man was, as you might expect, a man with a rocket belt. The rocket belt in this case consisted of three fuel tanks and two nozzles to direct outflow downwards and away from the user. In other words, it was a jet pack. To a crowd of live onlookers, and thousands more on television, the 16-second flight was a promise of the future. Bell had worked on their prototype for military use, but the rocket belt wasn't just a military experiment. Culturally, demonstrations like this were glimpses into the chrome-plated, white-walled utopia of the coming decades, where parcels would arrive via flying car and your daily commute would involve a jetpack of your own.

It's been 60 years since the height of space age futurism, and we're still waiting on those jetpacks. Missing out on personal rocket belts is disappointing, but hardly surprising. Putting aside a near-endless list of impracticalities, jetpacks-for-all was merely one of many overly imaginative predictions that never came to be. *Back to the Future* envisioned hoverboards in the 2010s, and we ended up with hands-free electric scooters that grant their owners a classy frat boy sensibility on the way to pay six dollars for coffee.

Plenty of projections of the opposite sort also proved fruitless, as every new technology in the past 5,000 years has been shunned by naysaying contemporaries as a temporary curiosity. Electric light, radio, film, automobiles, and television were all decried as fads by frightened men in spectacles clutching their copies of Gutenberg's Bible (presumably convinced that it might

The Game Designer's Playbook. Samantha Stahlke and Pejman Mirza-Babaei, Oxford University Press.
© Samantha Stahlke and Pejman Mirza-Babaei (2022). DOI: 10.1093/oso/9780198845911.003.0012

disappear at any moment, as the printing press was surely a fad). It's strange that such fellows seemed less vocal on the subject of Pet Rocks and table-sized Jello salads filled with ham and olives, but you can hardly blame them for assuming those would stick around.

Some visions of the future were closer to what we ended up with, often coming from science fiction. "Communicators" in *Star Trek* weren't all that far from the flip phones dominating the turn of the millennium. *The Jetsons* presented a shockingly cogent interpretation of smart home technology for a cartoon, albeit boasting far more emotionally intelligent cleaning robots than the ones we have today.

In gaming, the predictions encoded by industry in their designs over the past decades have varied similarly in quality. Of the consoles that touted themselves as the new standard in hardware design, some weren't that far off the mark. Sony's original Dualshock controller in 1997 introduced the "two sticks, four buttons, and a directional pad" formula that's persisted for the last quarter of a century. Some designs that tried to leap further into the future by experimentation, like the Wii with motion controls, were wildly successful. Others turned out to be expensive mistakes, like the Virtual Boy, Nintendo's fever dream tabletop VR headset, or Sega's Activator, an erratic attempt at full-body motion control.

Assertions and hopes about the future made by players, corporations, and the media have likewise fallen evenly across the gradient between realism and ridicule. For all the fearmongering from writers that had never picked up a controller in their lives, video games never did manage to rot the brains of children or raise a generation of gun-toting gremlins hellbent on destruction. Meanwhile, market whisperers who claimed mobile games would eventually generate massive revenues turned out to be right. Those who hopped on the toys-to-life bandwagon popularized by franchises like *Skylanders* mostly accomplished little more than filling the ocean with plastic, with the possible exception of Nintendo's Amiibo, which also filled players' homes with plastic.

What we can extract from all of this is that attempting to predict the future with any degree of reliability is a useless effort. There's a reason hindsight serves as the basis for so many of our lamentations; try as we might, humans are not soothsayers, irrespective of expertise. Our collective ability to see into the future is just about as effective as a blindfolded capuchin playing darts—figure about random chance; sometimes slightly better, and sometimes slightly worse.

You're probably wondering where we're going with this discussion, which insofar has perhaps been a bit on the cynical side for a final chapter. The more optimistic note is this: for all the pitfalls in spinning a vision of the future, we try anyways, because it's fun. Everyone wants to pretend they're

Nostradamus, at least a little bit, and speculation breeds innovation. As such, this chapter will explore how technology, games, and the industry have changed in recent years, and what these changes might say about the future of game interaction.

For our purposes, we'll lean on the conservative side of things to try and facilitate a realistic examination of the design trends that exist today. Should you return to this book years from now, feel free to marvel in how our tempered wisdom has remained relevant, or laugh hysterically at our failure to even mention the rise of virtual anime esports players to the seat of international government. Hopefully a few of those darts we throw will land, and if not, hopefully they'll still provide some food for thought on how your own designs might evolve in the coming years.

Like sands through the tiny plastic hourglass that comes with *Boggle*, these are the plays of our lives.

12.1 Pocket supercomputers strapped to your face

Advances in the technology behind games help shape what we see, hear, and do while playing. Looking back on what seemed like relatively gradual shifts at the time, the past five decades have been a period of radical, accelerated change. That change brought us from arcade cabinets to consumer electronics, which became wildly more powerful and diverse as the years rolled on. As the devices that powered games evolved, so too have the ways in which we interact with them. Dials gave way to joysticks and buttons, and eventually touchscreens, gestures, and motion. Games became longer, more complex, more compelling imitations of the fantasy worlds. Equally important to all that improving technologies could give was what they could remove, erasing limitations of the past and letting our designs achieve something closer to the perfection of imagination.

Of the more recent shifts in game technology, the mobile revolution is arguably the most pervasive. Since *Angry Birds* and their ilk first slingshotted onto the scene, smartphone games have become the de facto face of the games industry, whether we like it or not.[1] Mobile games make more money than either console or PC gaming, with smartphone and tablet releases accounting for nearly half of the industry's total revenue. By the time this book hits a shelf or agonizingly bright screen near you, that figure will probably have become "just over half," if not substantially more.

From a general design standpoint, the biggest change here is obvious—extreme portability. Somewhat ironically, the emergence of accessible pocket

---

[1] We don't. Can't the Virtual Boy at least have this?

333

computers seems to have effectively killed the handheld gaming industry, suffocating once-popular devices like the Playstation Vita and Nintendo 3DS. Unless you were willing to haul a CRT on the subway, handheld consoles used to be the only option for gaming on the go. When smartphones came along, it was only a matter of time before consumers' limited money and pocket real estate would have to settle for the device that could do everything, even if it didn't feel quite as special.

Phones and tablets aren't the only surviving way to play games in a portable form factor, of course. Gaming laptops are a niche purchase for plenty of techie professionals and hobbyists that value the ability to play PC games while on the couch. And in their usual fashion, Nintendo's latest-generation device flouts the traditional set-top box design of Microsoft and Sony's offerings with the Switch, a hybrid that works as a console or handheld.

Figure 12.1 Hardware has come a long way since the days of the Commodore 64 (top left) and Nintendo Entertainment System (top right). Modern hardware demonstrates years of design experience in refining ergonomics and embracing new technology. The Xbox One controller (bottom left) is one embodiment of years of design finesse, while the Oculus Rift (bottom right) is one entry in the still-fresh frontier of virtual reality.

Credit: Image of the Commodore 64 cropped from original by Federigo Federighi (CC BY-SA 4.0). Image of NES controller by Denis Apel (CC BY-SA 3.0). Image of Xbox controller by Luzankia (CC BY-SA 4.0). Image of Oculus Rift cropped from original by Evan-Amos (public domain). All original images obtained via Wikimedia Commons.

For game interaction designers, these changes bring about some interesting challenges and opportunities in shifting away from the paradigm of playing games on biggish screens in quietish rooms. Designing for mobile means designing for a host of screens, many of which are small, and figuring out how to map a set of complicated interactions to a touchscreen without relying on dozens of infuriatingly small buttons. Peripherals for smartphone gaming haven't really taken off, outside of a very niche audience, and you probably won't ever be able to count on your player base carting around a wireless controller for *Fruit Ninja: 2035*.

Play habits are another progenitor of considerations for interaction design here. The nature of mobile communication and the development ecosystem it has created has served to mutate our relationship with technology and whittle humanity's collective attention span to a very self-absorbed toothpick. Notifications used to be utilitarian, letting us quickly scan for a missed call from family or an important work email. Once app developers realized they could hijack notifications to create a false sense of urgency, we were cursed with a constant barrage of popups baiting us into opening a social media app on some flimsy assurance that we're missing critical updates to a friend-of-a-friend's brunch diary. Games are no exception, with the likes of login bonuses and promises of limited-time exclusives cluttering up the top quarter of the screen until you're pressured into boosting someone's daily active user count.

Luckily, this doesn't mean you have to toss your daily bonus-based design effort on the trash fire of instant gratification. Varied play habits give us the chance to create experiences that veer away from tradition. Before mobile games, we were more or less locked into designing games often played for hours at a stretch. A return to the arcade-style ethos of short play sessions with high skill ceilings is a perfect fit for play on mobile devices. When thinking about how players interact with such creations, can we consider their surroundings and activity? Might we see more phenomena like *Pokémon Go*, which encourage real-world exploration (Outdoors? In the sunlight? Perish the thought!) as a core part of gameplay?

On the wilder side of things, we might speculate that the future of mobile devices will eventually lead to an established market in wearables. Should they ever be able to spread to the general public from the wrists of upper-middle class tech enthusiasts, we might see something along the lines of a second Tamagotchi craze. And as all of the devices we use veer ever-closer to a set of black rectangles differentiated only by size, perhaps we'll see a rebellion from hardware designers making some visible effort to innovate in their form factors. With a few exotic foldable screens starting to hit the enthusiast circuit already, maybe we can expect to eventually see the revival of specialized handhelds for gaming as part of a design renaissance.

Another development common to all of our devices is the widespread availability of ludicrously high-speed internet. This has allowed for the mass proliferation of online multiplayer games; while such modes were once a treat, these days it can feel like one too many shooters put all of their efforts into online play without much in the way of a single-player experience. So long as advertising is honest, this isn't such a terrible thing, creating more diversity in the type of play you can expect from titles that focus more on an individual or group experience.

For designers, this also means that we can probably expect the importance of remote player-to-player communication to keep growing. Designing systems for players to interact with one another is often equally critical as creating those for players to interact with the game itself. Text chat and emotes don't cut it anymore; things like interactive maps and sleek, context-aware ping communications are practically standard. For these types of features, the game serves only as a mediator, and your design skills must adapt to the unpredictable humans at each end of the interaction.

The age of always-on internet has brought other changes as well; always-online games, or "games as services," have practically become the default for AAA releases. Consequently, developers can more easily provide players with new content and updates, constantly responding to player needs and keeping communities thriving for longer. On the flip side, the tantalizing notion of easy patches means a temptation to release products that aren't quite ready. And to justify continued development, continued revenue may take the form of predatory microtransactions. Striking a balance between the positive and more concerning aspects of games as services, for the present moment, seems to be something developers are still trying to figure out.

As a partner to the online service model of individual games, we're also seeing a rise in early attempts at cloud gaming subscriptions. In a few words, you might think of this as "Netflix for games." In a few more, cloud gaming means using your device as nothing more than a relay station; it communicates your inputs to a server which actually runs the game, and then receives video (and sound, and sometimes a signal for controller rumble) to play back at you.

From a practical design standpoint, this presents similar challenges as the rise of mobile devices. If an experience originally designed for PC and console makes the leap to cloud gaming, it needs to adapt to a wider variety of devices and play contexts. You can recommend a traditional setup all you like, but if you really want to be inclusive to the crowd you've expanded into, things like UI scaling and visual cues to replace spatial audio feedback will be necessary considerations. Depending on how far this trend swings, we might eventually see cloud gaming become the standard. Hopefully we'll never see a dystopian hellscape where nobody actually *owns* a real computer or copies of the games they play, but it is an unfortunate possibility.

Speaking of dystopian hellscapes, we might also speculate about a future where virtual reality has supplanted real reality, à la *The Matrix* or *Ready Player One*. More realistically, we could suggest that a steadily growing library of VR titles and improving hardware will finally allow the market to reach critical mass. VR devices may one day become as commonplace as consoles are today. If this happens, we might see versions of today's wacky VR peripherals become standard: things like omnidirectional treadmills, haptic gloves, full-body trackers, and next-generation *Duck Hunt*-style gun attachments for controllers. With this future might come something more exotic, like the use of brain-computer interfaces for more streamlined output, or a long-anticipated breakthrough in true holograms breathing new life into mixed reality. Should any of this come to pass, the challenges we face will be a continuation of those we explored in Chapter 7—adapting to new control methods, working with gestural input, taking advantage of player immersion, and avoiding unpleasant side effects like VR sickness.

Supporting all of these advances are continued innovations in game and engine programming. Physically-based rendering techniques bring increased realism to how we deal with materials from metal to blood and everything in between. Raytracing simulates the behaviour of actual light as it bounces through an environment, instead of approximating it with the fakery we've come to know and love. There's still plenty of fakery at work today to let us grab a taste of raytracing on consumer hardware. But when we can push more pixels, and crank up the detail of assets created by artists, raytracing might effectively make visual realism a completely solved problem in the next couple of decades.

Figure 12.2 *Minecraft* as seen by us lowly peasants of the everyday gaming world (left) and those with raytracing-capable GPUs (right.).

Credit: *Minecraft* was developed and published by Mojang Studios.

Moving on from here, the sensory boundaries between playing a game and watching (or living) an action movie will narrow further. As we dazzle players with our visuals, our designs must grow to take advantage of their potential. In a future where players will never be able to make out another polygon or catch a pixelated shadow, things like feedback design and representing unrealistic action in a way that feels tangible will become even more important.

12.2 Buy low, sell high

As our technology has evolved, so too has the games market transformed into something barely resembling its former self. Long after the hobby of playing games broke into the mainstream, the craft of making games was still reserved for a select few in the industry. Aspiring developers lacked access to the wealth of tools on offer today, and education in programming was far from standard in elementary or secondary schools. Even if you managed to learn and create something on your own time, when it came to distribution, you were out of luck, unless you could manage to get an audience with a publisher.

All of this changed when digital distribution stumbled onto the scene with PC services including Steam and GOG.com, and their console counterparts like the Xbox Games Store. Of the major players in the PC market, Steam is the eldest, and for the time being, most widely known. From humble origins as an update service for Valve's games in 2003, Steam branched out to negotiate distribution for third parties in the coming years, eventually gaining traction with large publishers. By the onset of the next decade, Steam cemented itself as a premier digital storefront, boasting tens of millions of users.

The advent of digital distribution accelerated the process of democratizing game publishing. Indie developers no longer had to throw an executable up on their website and hope for the best. Better distribution and more widely available tools meant that anyone could develop a game, and just maybe manage to get it on a digital storefront. One of the first breakthroughs in this respect was *Braid*, often credited as the first "big" indie game of the modern era. Released in 2009, *Braid* is old, though not so old in the greater scheme of things. Alongside its name, you'll hear other indie darlings of the period, like *Limbo (2010)*, *Super Meat Boy (2010)* and *Fez (2012)*.

Since the first shots fired in the indie revolution, game distribution was quickly democratized thanks to programs like Steam Greenlight and Xbox Live Indie Games. From here, the market exploded in diversity, as small developers could hoist their creations onto commercial storefronts with

Figure 12.3 Two breakthrough video games from the first wave of indies' rise to visibility and mass market appeal: *Fez* (left) and *Limbo* (right).

Credit: *Fez* was developed by Polytron and published by Trapdoor. *Limbo* was developed and published by Playdead.

relatively little expense. As restrictions relaxed across the board, the marketplace grew more saturated. Today, we might say that anyone can fuel their passion into a game and make it available for all to see. More pragmatically, we might say that digital stores everywhere are flooded with asset flips and poorly conceived clones that slowly choke the life from more earnest efforts unlucky enough to miss out on the fickle luck of getting noticed on social media. All of this coincides with the industry's continued growth, having recently broken $100 billion annually and projected to keep expanding in the years to come.

Our question then becomes how we can possibly carve out a space for ourselves in the crowded ocean of the games industry. Fortunately, all of this growth has been supported by some changes in marketing friendly to developers of all sizes. The more traditional means of throwing large sums of money at advertising in the form of television spots, massive online campaigns, and creator sponsorships are still in full force, but they're no longer the only options available. Gaming has its own version of influencer marketing in the form of content creators like streamers and independent reviewers. Get enough social media traction to have your case heard by a popular personality, and they just might stick your game in front of an audience of millions.

There is, of course, a great deal of luck involved in the success of such efforts, though if you can juice up your design with things to make it more of a sensory treat (Chapter 4) or something naturally suited to streaming (Chapter 8), you'll have a better shot. As market saturation increases and media dissemination moves further online, these tactics will become even more important. Your skills in designing interactions that are satisfying and watchable won't just contribute to a good player experience; they'll become ever-more instrumental in getting noticed in the first place.

Along with this transformation in marketing has come once-unthinkable shifts in how and when games make their money. Releasing a game before it was finished would have once been a commercial death knell; now, early access is a way for developers to fund further development through sales (or take the money and run). Meanwhile, spending your money on a game before it's been released remains a standard practice in the form of pre-orders, the ridiculousness of which is somehow mitigated in the public eye by dangling a few cosmetic exclusives alongside calls for pre-release sales. The culture of incentivizing pre-orders, early access, and constant online marketing has created a tendency for voracious anticipation of new releases. But just as hype can turn release into a celebration (*Mass Effect 2*, *Overwatch*, *The Witcher 3*, *Half-Life: Alyx*), it can also create catastrophe around games that fail to impress at release (*Anthem*, *No Man's Sky*[2], *Fallout 76*, *Cyberpunk 2077*) or underwhelming murmurs around games that weren't quite what players expected (*Death Stranding*[3]).

With what feels like a growing number of hype trains gone wrong with every passing year, players have gained a bit of understandable skepticism around things like early access and pre-orders. It's easy for such strategies to seem like schemes focused on making money instead of games—and perhaps none has become more scrutinized than the implementation of microtransactions. First becoming commonplace in classic virtual worlds like *Habbo Hotel* (2001) and *Second Life* (2003), these small purchases took off in concert with the mobile market, as games like *Clash of Clans* (2012) adopted a "free-to-play" (F2P) model.

Many F2P games are, of course, free games in the same way that a cardboard box with wheels is a car. You can technically make your way to work in one, but if you want to have any sort of enjoyable experience, you're going to have to shell out a lot more money to have one. The F2P model quickly spread out of the mobile ecosystem with the likes of *Hearthstone* (2014), a virtual trading card game which practically forces players to shell out four times as much on cards as they'd willingly spend on a complete experience out of the box. Live-service games like *Fortnite* (2017), also adopted a microtransaction-focused F2P economy. Meanwhile, games with an upfront price have integrated microtransactions for things like cosmetics as a way to generate additional revenue. In theory, this can be an effective

---

[2] While it certainly suffered around launch, the team behind *No Man's Sky* in particular should be commended for the updates and support they have provided since, turning the game into something which is deservedly and almost universally loved.

[3] It might not be everyone's cup of tea, but this mixed reception shouldn't be taken as a negative judgement of *Death Stranding* itself; if anything, it speaks more to the problems surrounding hype in the gaming community as a whole.

way to fund continued development. In practice, though, it's often a quick slide into so-called dark design patterns: decisions that intentionally make players' experience *worse* to bait them into spending money. Fear of missing out on seasonal cosmetics tempts players to buy up randomized unlocks. Some games have the audacity to artificially limit the pace of progression while offering paid "time-savers" to speed things up, as in *Assassin's Creed: Odyssey* (2018), a game which already carries a full price tag up front.

With all of these changes, there's nothing much that we can say from a design perspective except to tread carefully. Should you have any sort of creative control over the projects you work on, bear in mind that a shift in business models doesn't necessitate a complete abandonment of ethics. If you're a burgeoning designer, remember that your priority is creating satisfying interactions, and not promising players that they'll finally have a great experience for just a few more dollars on top of what they've already spent.

On the speculation side of things, we can summarize the recent changes highlighted here in three words: expansion, saturation, and discontent. Putting these factors together, we might make comparisons to economic bubbles of the past, or more ambitiously say something about the former Soviet Union. On the latter point, we probably won't be seeing the ghost of Boris Yeltsin making any appearances at GDC. In regard to the former, though, the games market has seen some spectacular volatility in the past.

1983 marked the start of a massive industry recession that went on for 2 years, sparked by a market flooded with rivaling consoles and rushed products. Today, the industry is far more established, and product quality is incomparable to what it was 40 years ago. Nonetheless, as hype trains derail, app stores reach saturation points, and a growing number of distributors battle for exclusives, we might be on the verge of large-scale shifts. Whether this will take the form of a crash, further changes in market share, or a change in the landscape of corporate ownership remains to be seen. Some of the most substantial changes in what players actually end up with, though, have resulted not from an evolving marketplace, but from the ethos of game design itself.

12.3 Game changers

The way we think about and design games has come to reflect an expanded understanding of the role they serve in our lives. Video games started out as diversions, technical curiosities that let us experiment with play in a new way. But as technology improved and designs grew more complex, games begun to serve other purposes as well. Games started to showcase impressive digital art and music, often alongside stories that were far too deep to be called diversions anymore. A new question arose: were video games a form of art in themselves?

Answering this question without diving into pedantry is relatively straightforward. If art is an expression of human creativity meant to be appreciated by its audience, then of course video games are art. Whether based on their beauty, intellectual curiosity, or ability to evoke emotion, video games meet this definition.

And yet, the classification of games as an art form was the subject of a rather contentious debate, the echoes of which are still bandying about today. By the early 2010s, fears that video games were some sort of propaganda designed to turn us all into violent criminals had grown passé. Around this time, the art debate popped into the public eye, as if all that negative energy about games eventually had to be redirected. Some of these debates were marked with an unsettling sort of elitism, as if games were too popular, too commonly accessible and accepted by the middle class to possibly be considered on the pedestal of the arts. Others were focused on frustratingly myopic semantics, insisting that some technicality or another in the encyclopedia definitions of "art" and "play" could make the two mutually exclusive.

Most of the anti-art argumentation, though, came back to some embodiment of the idea that games aren't a form of art because their primary purpose is to provide entertainment as a product. One could hold up several examples here of games that aren't really intended to be artistic; ignoring the technical skill on display from artists and animators, is *Call of Duty* artistic? Is *Fortnite* artistic? Following this logic, any art form which has been sufficiently commercialized should be disqualified. But in the absence of a pitchfork-bearing mob decrying the classification of films as art on the basis of *Sharknado*'s existence, perhaps we can accept that games are no less a form of art than anything else in our hyper-commodified present day.

Coinciding with the death throes of this debate and the uptick in indie releases is a growing library of games that could be described as more traditionally artistic. *Cuphead*, for example, features painstakingly hand-drawn animation and live-recorded original jazz music, paying homage to cartoons of the early twentieth century. *Gris* explores a story about grieving a loved one, set against massive beautifully illustrated backdrops reflecting its narrative themes. *This War of Mine* tells an unstructured story about the horrors of war from the perspective of ordinary civilians. And some games, like *The Witness* with its layered puzzles and crumbling statues showing different poses from different perspectives, encode abstract messages about the nature of games and play.

Games like this usually still strive to be fun and engaging—certainly the examples above do—but what makes them remarkable is less the core of their interaction, and more so what surrounds and motivates that interaction. As the art of game development matures, one way to push the medium forward is to embrace this focus, paying even more attention to the factors enveloping the act of play. In other words, as a designer, you might come to focus less on the functionality of "doing" and "communicating" in game interaction. Instead, think about how players perceive and think about a game's world, and what emotional response or artistic appreciation you hope to derive. In the coming years, innovation in game design will be, in part, a question of artistry.

Of course, this isn't to say that games have reached the apex of mechanical design. Promising opportunities can be found in pushing the limits of those more functional aspects of game interaction. One way this is already being explored is in games that experiment with real-world impossibilities that play with the laws of physics. *Portal* is a notable early example, centred around the mechanic of placing portals: effectively, wormholes that allow for instant transportation between two places.

Since *Portal*, we've seen *Antichamber* and *Manifold Garden*, two games that play with the idea of non-Euclidean geometry to create environments for players that have impossible connections and infinite spatial loops. More recently, *Superliminal* built its puzzles around forced perspective, where players can move objects around and change their physical size based on their apparent size on-screen. Messing around with physics isn't just interesting, it can grab players' attention: a large part of the appeal of aforementioned indie phenomenon *Braid* was its core mechanic, which allowed players to reverse the flow of time.

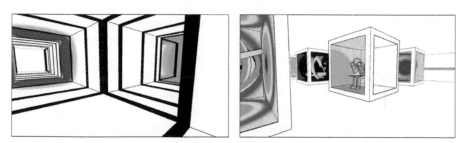

Figure 12.4 *Antichamber* uses a mimic of non-Euclidean geometry to create spaces that connect in impossible ways and change when viewed from different perspectives or in different conditions.

Credit: *Antichamber* was developed and published by Demruth.

On top of broadening our understanding of artistic potential and mechanical possibility, time has also revealed the ability of games to contribute to society in different ways. Games can be used for education, training, therapy, and exercise. This revelation in the diversity of purposes that games can serve has been complemented by a welcome change in who's playing games, or at least a change in our awareness of the people who play games. The cultural ideal of gaming was once maddeningly confined to the image of a tech enthusiast, locked in a basement away from any shred of daylight, surrounded by bags of cheese puffs in the immaculate blue glow of a screen. Today, we understand that this exclusionary view is inaccurate (and a bit harmful), as the real faces of gaming are far more diverse. Children, seniors, students, professionals, and caretakers—from all walks and at all stages of life, people enjoy playing games. The needs of different individuals will be reflected in their preferences, but the act of gaming itself is far from exclusive.

Certain types of games can cater to the needs and better the lives of individuals from different groups. The edutainment craze of the 90s has resurfaced in the form of mobile games targeting school-aged children, like *Khan Academy Kids* and *Prodigy Math Game*. Meanwhile, games promoting at-home exercise, like *Wii Fit* and *Wii Sports*, are designed with accessibility for gamers with less experience (like many older adults and seniors) in mind. As demographics continue to shift in the coming years, designers may have interesting questions to address. Will the idea of most children as "novices" become outdated as technical literacy becomes an increasing part of childhood at home and in school? How will the entertainment and technology needs of those who grew up playing games in the eighties and nineties change, if at all, as they become seniors in another few decades?

Related to the idea of games as tools for education or staying active is the notion that they can promote positive social change. While games, or perhaps more accurately "playful applications," developed solely to this end do exist, they are often birthed from academia and deployed in specific contexts. We probably can't drop any names here that readers would be sure to recognize, though you will find some literature related to such projects in the reading recommendations following this chapter.

More widely known are commercial titles which explore important subjects, aiming to promote awareness or often a deeper understanding and empathy in players. Mental illness has been seriously explored in titles like *Celeste* and *Hellblade: Senua's Sacrifice*. *Hellblade* is particularly notable for its development team's efforts to produce a grounded portrayal of the protagonist's psychosis by connecting with academics, non-profit organizations, and individuals with mental illnesses. In a similar fashion to user-centred design approaches, such tactics can help games that deal with serious issues to ensure that their messages are more informed, effective, and emotionally powerful.

In addition to challenging our conception of important issues, games can also challenge our definition of the word "game" itself. We're no longer at the point where new genres are being invented from the ground up every couple of years, but we still routinely see the emergence of new paradigms that reimagine some aspect of game interaction.

Improved technology that let us tell audiovisual stories more easily saw the rise of visual novels and "walking simulators," where gameplay might be pared down to basic navigation and dialogue in favour of focusing on character and world development. A strange hybridization of point-and-click adventure mysteries with true crime-esque drama brought us games like *Her Story*. In these interactive explorations of story fragments, your ultimate goal is not to eventually catch some big bad or embark on a thrilling chase, but to unravel a series of events that's already played out for your own understanding.

For any designer, especially one new to the industry, the wealth of games brought by the last few decades can seem overwhelming. Suffocated by market saturation, it might feel like most things have already been done at this point. Survival sandbox games march one after another trying to fill the shoes of *Minecraft*. Expectations have been subverted in every genre, to the point where subversion *is* the expectation. An FPS where you don't shoot anyone (*Portal*), an RPG where you don't kill anyone (*Undertale*), a grand adventure squashed into 60 seconds (*Minit*).

And yet, for every "what if" that games have already answered, games can still surprise us. Plenty of unanswered questions remain for us to explore. Failing that, there's no law that says a game needs to tread totally unexplored ground to surprise and delight its players. Not every game needs to incorporate some physical impossibility or genre-twisting innovation to be seen as good design, leave its mark on the art of games, or most importantly, give players a good experience. In the end, the recent explosion of diversity in design is less overwhelming and more a reminder of the freedom we have to create something, no matter how strange or specific, that brings players joy.

12.3.1 ... So what comes next?

Throughout this book, we've looked at many different aspects of game interaction. Our basic interaction model comprises five steps: game-to-player communication, player decision, player-to-game communication, action, and result. Information about the result of each action feeds into the information players can use to make their next decision, creating a cycle. Moving forward, we might think about how each of these stages could be affected by the changes we see in technology, industry, and game design.

The boundaries across which games communicate with us are shrinking; feedback can be far more realistic, and up close, than it once could. Experiencing a game through a head-mounted display and headset feels distinctly more personal than doing so via distant television screen and speakers. Likewise, the physical and psychological gaps we need to cross in communicating with games are narrowing. Instead of mapping actions through hardware intermediaries like joysticks, the mapping of action to action via gestural controls is becoming more widespread. Taken to the technological extreme, we might see proof-of-concept in the next few decades for rich brain-computer interaction (BCI) in games. As of this writing, at least one major commercial effort[4] exists in researching scalable BCI production, alongside many academic endeavours aimed at medical interventions. Whether this work will eventually save lives, or let us finally play games undetected during performance reviews at work, remains to be seen.

Having covered communication, we only have control over two of the remaining parts of the interaction process. Outside of the power of suggestion, we can't directly meddle with player decision-making, at least, not without some MK-Ultra tech to complement our BCI chips, should they ever get here. This leaves us with action and result, the stages most relevant to changes in game design itself. As game design diversifies into new subgenres, intentions of purpose, and target demographics, the possibility space of the actions and consequences we design for will continue to grow. This isn't to say that individual games will grow more complicated by necessity, but rather that we will see more nuance distinguishing between similar types of action in different contexts. For instance, we can already see far more diversity in the feel of gunplay between shooters today as opposed to their arcade counterparts of old. We can expect this type of diversity to persist and grow across all types of game interaction.

With some basic understanding of how game interaction might change in the coming years, let's take a moment to envision how this might manifest in the games we create and play.

In Chapter 3, we talked about the challenge of captivating players early on and keeping them invested for hundreds of hours of play. As the market grows more saturated, players become wise to our tricks, and the age of social media threatens to shrink attention spans, how will we adapt? Some games may further erase the traditional tutorial, throwing players into the fire as quickly as possible to get them engaged in the action. Some games might try to go in the opposite direction, creating a series of hand-holds with well-timed rushes of dopamine to emulate the onboarding experience of many mobile titles. And to achieve longevity, we may see more games embracing an early access model whereby they can grow a community and keep players

---

[4] Should you be reading this before society collapses into a lawless wasteland and you still have internet access, that effort is Neuralink, and it's championed by exactly who you think it would be.

interested by offering a steady stream of updates as development continues after initial release.

What we see, hear, and otherwise sense in games may also change radically in the coming years. In Chapter 4, we discussed game feedback, focusing primarily on audiovisual communication. As technology improves, we may see more communication in the form of haptics. Particularly for VR interactions, "high definition" haptics could be valuable to let us mimic things like the weight, shape, and texture of virtual objects with a little sensory trickery. Maybe one day there will be appeals made to our other senses as well; personally, we're still holding on hope for that resurgence of Smell-O-Vision, probably courtesy of Nintendo.

On the other side of interaction, the way we control games will also continue to evolve. Motion controls ten years ago were fun, but often felt gimmicky. Modern incarnations have become more sophisticated, while preserving that spark of naturalistic novelty they've always had. With better sensors and image processing, we'll probably see much finer gestural controls become established in the next couple of decades, particularly for VR. Or at least, we can hope so, lest the idea of practicing virtual sorcery through the intricate pantomime of martial arts remain nothing more than a dream.

One of the things that all of this communication lets us accomplish is to tell stories to our players. Technical limitations once hampered how rich and complex these stories could be, assuming we still wanted room for graphics and mechanics. For a while at least, many game narratives could be boiled down to three words without losing out on anything really integral to the plot: "save the princess," "kill that guy," "make number bigger." There's nothing inherently wrong with this, and certainly even many games today are worthwhile experiences without much in the way of story holding them together. But since we now have the room and resources to weave more subtle narrative threads, game writing is starting to catch up. And with a market established for games that tell stories with real emotional impact, we can expect to see more diverse voices and more serious topics represented moving forward. If you've been waiting on wanting to be heard, you're in the perfect era to work your own personal story into the games you create.

The technological developments we explored in the latter half of this volume, relating to virtual reality, streaming, and artificial intelligence, might also give us some clues about the future. Any attempts to characterize these trends as fads might prove just as humorous as the critics of automobiles and televisions a century ago. Maybe one day we'll see true plug-yourself-in VR, and if we're lucky, maybe it won't precipitate the total collapse of society. If streaming continues its rise as a new normal of media distribution, content creation might become a far more mainstream hobby, leading to a democratization of entertainment unlike any we've seen before. And as

AI develops increasingly realistic behaviours to complement our increasingly realistic graphics alongside everything else, we'll come even closer to that tantalizing promise of one day making games indistinguishable from reality. Or, maybe these trends will simply stabilize or sputter out, remaining as fond memories of our current cultural landscape and nothing more.

That's the tricky thing about predicting the future—it's always so much easier after you're already there. But, on our journey to explore the nature of play and our relationship with games, hopefully you'll take away some knowledge that will help make that future just a little bit more enjoyable. We might not be able to say for sure where we're going. But no matter where we end up, it's going to be somewhere fun.

Expert Profile: Jason Della Rocca—Optimizing for success

Industry consultant and co-founder of Execution Labs

In the 1990s, a young Jason Della Rocca walked into an accounting firm for the first day of his university internship. Later that day, he quit, walked out, and swore off accounting forever.

The decisions we make can change the course of a day, or the course of our entire lives. In Jason's case, his decision led to switching majors from accounting to business computing. Once graduated, he worked in the emerging space of 3D graphics hardware. On his first day at Silicon Graphics, a colleague brought in a pre-release version of the Nintendo 64, and Jason knew he was on the right track.

After some time working in hardware, and briefly in networking middleware, Jason became an executive of the International Game Developers Association (IGDA), eventually taking the top seat. During his tenure, he worked on building bridges between the industry and academia for research and talent recruitment, simultaneously serving on several committees related to games research. In 2009, Jason stepped down from his directorship at the IGDA. A few years later, he worked with co-founder Keith Katz to start Execution Labs, an early-stage investor and accelerator for independent game developers.

These days, Jason still works closely with indies, as an industry consultant helping developers to improve their business mettle and connect with publishers and investors. On top of that, he's become an ambassador of sorts for the games industry itself, working with governments around the world to make recommendations on economic policy and ecosystem development. Jason says his work in this respect is greatly influenced by his hands-on time with studios, advocating for the support of incubators, seed funds, and mentorship opportunities.

Perhaps the best way to describe Jason's role in the industry is as a champion of success, both at the small scale of independent studios and in the much larger world of government policy. Fittingly, much of our discussion with Jason centred around the concept of success. But Jason recognizes that concept as inherently and frustratingly elusive: "The question of success cannot really be answered, because success is very subjective, or very contextual."

He goes on to explain that the metrics for success can be strikingly different between investors and development teams. In his time at Execution Labs, Jason watched (and

(Continued)

helped) several indie studios reach varying levels of commercial success. He mentions Montréal developer Kitfox Studios as an example of an "unbelievable success" emerging from the group, having become a self-sustaining studio with a creative portfolio of games and supportive company culture. But Jason notes that the success of studios like Kitfox usually isn't enough to keep an investment firm going. Investment is a numbers game, and a risky one at that, dependent on finding the occasional runaway smash-hit. Luckily, it seems that Jason's role hasn't made him cynical in this regard, valuing the kind of modest, sustainable success that can keep small development teams going.

Irrespective of how you define success, Jason says that studios can, often unwittingly, stack the odds before development even starts. At the idea stage, just a bit of competitive analysis can indicate whether something will be commercially viable. Jason mentions a studio he interacted with set on developing a couch co-op party game, noting that a five-minute search on SteamSpy[5] would show almost no player interest in the category. He says that getting developers to do this pre-emptive research, and accept its results, is challenging: "It's hard to stop a developer and say, when you've got a great idea, stop. Go on Steam, go on SteamSpy, do a bit of homework, look up the numbers. Because you're taking a bit of the soul, or the passion, away from it."

Another point of failure Jason has observed in his work with indies is an aversion to what he calls "optimizing for success." He notes that smaller studios often try, sensibly, to align their production with what they can reasonably finish on a small budget and tight timeline. But sometimes, this mentality leads developers away from pursuing ideas that could boost their game's commercial viability. He's witnessed this firsthand, watching studios struggle to scale up even with investor backing, crumbling under the pressure of increased scope or a shifting design plan. Jason suggests that, almost counterintuitively, it is better to spend more time researching and imagining what could succeed early in the development process, and work backwards from there.

At least to a degree, avoiding catastrophe is a matter of creativity just as much as business acumen. Jason emphasizes that early development choices are pivotal, perhaps in the same sense as quitting an internship or pushing past coworkers to glimpse a Nintendo 64: "The most important marketing decision you will ever make is your game design."

While Jason points out that he's not a game designer, he notes that part of his role as a mentor relies on "investigating games" and helping developers to get their products into shape before approaching potential partners, like publishers, investors, or platforms. His view of game design, particularly interaction design, is a holistic one: "You're thinking about the interface between the game and the player. And you are being very deliberate and thoughtful [about] what that is, how it works, what it looks like." He sees game interaction as "more than just pushing buttons," noting that much broader concepts like social and cultural factors shape the way we play.

Jason also remarks on how much the field of game design has changed over the last two decades. "In the early days, there was very little language of design," he says, jokingly referring to the game designers of yore as "Cavemen and women just sort of banging sticks and trying to discover fire." With the formalization of design—he gives the MDA (mechanics, dynamics, aesthetics) framework as an early example—came

---

[5] SteamSpy (https://steamspy.com) hosts analytics, such as player counts, for the Steam distribution platform.

(Continued)

(Continued)

an improved ability to critique game experiences and create new ones. Alongside a more organized understanding of design, Jason says the introduction of HCI tactics like user research, and the advent of analytics to help developers understand player behaviour, have helped the field to mature. He recalls an issue of Wired from 2007 describing the "Science of Play" at Microsoft atop a bespoke Master Chief on the cover as one of many moments that helped shift the field away from purely gut-driven design.

One of the most substantial changes Jason sees in game design is a shift towards thinking about our players more than ourselves when creating games. He says that the most important quality in a designer is empathy, noting that too many developers still "create from within" exclusively thinking of their own wants, and need to "realize it's not about them." A successful designer, Jason says, needs to ask questions like "What do [I] want the player to feel? What kind of experience do [I] want them to have? What game [...] do I need to build to elicit that response?"

Deep introspection aside, for anyone who's looking to make the killer marketing decision that is their game's design, Jason says that one of the best things you can do is to step away from the screen once in a while. "Experience life. Consume other media and content and works of art, and be inspired by other things." He notes that legendary game designers like Will Wright and Shigeru Miyamoto often cite sources like gardening for their best ideas, and says with a chuckle that developers should "put down the controller and read a book" to find inspiration outside games.

When the time comes to follow through on that inspiration, Jason says you should ask one question above all else: "What do we need to do to have a game that succeeds?" Think of your players, think of the experience you want for them, and work to achieve success—whatever that means to you.

Further reading

What's Next in Game Design? Keynote delivered by Will Wright (GDC, 2006).

Now over a decade old, the speculation of legendary simulation game design pioneer Will Wright still holds up, and is perhaps more interesting with the power of hindsight.

Future Gaming: Creative Interventions in Video Game Culture by Paolo Ruffino (Goldsmiths Press). ISBN: 978-1906897550.

A critical look at the study of games in general and the representation of games in popular culture. A sort of counterweight to unbridled optimism and the games media.

Improving literacy in rural India: Cellphone games in an after-school program, conference paper by Matthew Kam et al. (ICTD, 2009, IEEE). DOI: 10.1109/ICTD.2009.5426712.

An interesting instance of a game for social development, and one of those academic development examples promised earlier in the chapter.

Exercises

Think the change you want to see in the world

Pick a social issue that you care about. Brainstorm different ideas for games that would spread awareness, educate players, or motivate them to donate their time or resources to a cause. Try to think about how you could communicate your message in a meaningful way through interaction, instead of just hitting players over the head with text or voiceover calling them to action.

Look for any other games related to the issue you chose. Are any of them similar to your ideas? Do any of them surprise you? Try playing one. Do you think it's effective in getting its message across? How would you improve on it?

Possible impossible

Using the engine of your choice, prototype an "impossible" mechanic which plays with the rules of physics, time, causality, or nature in the real world—think portals, going back in time, and so on. Your prototype doesn't have to look nice or even work that well; just get something together that gets your idea across. How could you create puzzles using this mechanic? How do you think you'd develop this mechanic over the course of an entire game to give players an interesting and distinct experience?

No infringement intended

One of the best ways to learn game development, and come up with new ideas— at least in our humble opinion—is the creation of mods. Many games support mods officially; for instance, on Steam, games with Workshop content will often have a suite of tools to help you get started in creating your own custom content. Naturally, many games which *do not* officially support modification in any way still have active modding communities. While we cannot really endorse some of the things that go on to make mod development possible in these cases, at least one of the authors will confess to having employed such tactics for personal learning purposes.

Regardless of how you go about creating a mod, though, this really is one of the best things you can do to sharpen your design and development skills. Working within the universe of an existing game provides just enough constraints to keep your creativity on track, while the undoubted hiccups you'll face along the way in technical feasibility provide surprising design challenges.

Glossary

Action genre. A genre of games distinguished by its focus on physical challenges, such as the timing of precise inputs. Examples of sub-genres include shooters, platformers, fighting games, and racing games.

Affordance. The implication of function through design. For example, a protruding handle on a door suggests that it can be opened by pulling on the handle. One of Norman's six design principles.

Agile development. A software development ideology that prioritizes flexibility. Characteristics of agile development include frequent communication and working to accomplish relatively small milestones in quick succession, contributing to a larger whole. Contrast with *waterfall development.*

Artificial intelligence. A broad category of algorithms that allow computers to function autonomously in completing certain tasks. One general definition is the ability of computer systems to acquire and apply knowledge to solve problems.

Consistency. The adherence to conventions established within a design (internal consistency) or by other designs or the real world (external consistency). For example, using a red heart to symbolize health in a game is externally consistent with many other games. One of Norman's six design principles.

Constraints. Restrictions imposed on the actions of a user (player) with the intention of preventing error or enhancing user experience. For instance, a game may restrict players from damaging their teammates to avoid accidental friendly fire (whether this is a good decision depends on the specific experience). One of Norman's six design principles.

Continuous communication. Giving information to the player about the game state on an ongoing basis. Relevant information might include things like health, ammunition, time of day, and so on. A common example is a heads-up display. Contrast with *responsive communication.*

Core mechanic. The main interaction around which a game's design is built. For instance, the core mechanic of *Super Mario Bros.* is platforming. The core mechanic in *Call of Duty* is gunplay (shooting).

Direct input. The immediate translation of real-world physical action into in-game action. For example, pushing forward on an analog stick to move one's character forward in a game's world. Contrast with *virtual input.*

Feedback. Information given by a system in response to user action, with the intent of communicating a change in the state of the system or the consequences of that action. For instance, hearing a sound to indicate that your character has fired their gun. One of Norman's six design principles. Also see *responsive communication.*

First-person. A category of games characterized by the player viewpoint matching their character's viewpoint; players see "through their character's eyes."

First-person shooter. A shooter game (i.e., generally focused on gunplay and combat) with a first-person perspective.

First-time user experience. A term used to describe a user's initial experience and perceptions of a piece of software, such as a game. Includes things like learning how a game works, and a player's decision as to whether they would like to continue playing. Also see *onboarding*.

Flow. A state of total psychological absorption in the task at hand, characterized by a trance-like state. Caused by a balance in the challenge offered by a task and the skill of the individual performing it. Often associated with peak performance in playing a game.

Free-to-play. A monetization model where a game is free to initially download or play, but encourages the user to make purchases that "enhance" their experience. Many F2P games incentivize repeated purchases, rather than one-time unlocks (e.g., premium currency that can be used to buy expendable items).

Games user research. A field concerned with the evaluation of games, aimed at understanding the reasons for player behaviour and how players react to the games they interact with.

Heads-up display. An overlay present on a player's view of a game. A HUD might include things like a health bar, ammo counter, and minimap of the surrounding area. The function of a HUD is to convey information that players will find useful (see *continuous communication*).

Human-computer interaction. A field concerned with understanding the relationship between humans and computer technology. HCI is an all-encompassing domain comprising the evaluation of existing technology, the development of new experimental technologies, understanding how computers can improve our lives, and so on.

Interaction. Two-way communication between two entities. For instance, two people can interact by talking to one another. A person can interact with a computer (or game) by performing an action and receiving feedback on the results of that action. For instance, pressing a button on a controller and seeing your character cast a spell is an example of a game interaction.

Interface. A boundary across which two entities can interact, or more simply, something that facilitates interaction. For example, a menu with clickable buttons is an interface.

Iterative design (or testing). A development methodology characterized by cycles of ideation, prototyping (or testing), and review. No matter whether applied to design, testing, or some other aspect of the development process, the focus is on continual improvement. Iterative approaches typically seek to frequently validate new changes, and improve on previous work.

Machine learning. The ability of a computer to learn to perform a task without being explicitly programmed to do so. An example is a neural network that learns to classify previously unseen images based on training with examples labelled by a human.

Magic circle. A theoretical concept describing the "space" of a game outside of reality. This space may be more or less detached from reality based on the rules of the game. Boundaries delineating the magic circle from reality may be physical (e.g., the borders of a basketball court) or intangible (e.g., the understanding that only voluntary participants are included in a game of tag).

Mapping. The relationship between controls and their function. This is most often expressed in terms of spatial relationship (e.g., similar functions should be grouped together in space). It can also be expressed in terms of form (e.g., if an analog stick is available, it is better suited to multidirectional movement than a ring of buttons). One of Norman's six design principles.

Mechanic. An action that players can take in a game, or a word used to describe a set of related actions. For instance, the gunplay in a shooter could be described as "shooting mechanics."

Massively multiplayer online game. Any game that relies on a large online playerbase to facilitate multiplayer interaction. The delineation between an MMO and an "online multiplayer game" can be muddy, especially today. Colloquially, the very large number of players and tendency to play with strangers is what distinguishes an MMO (e.g., *Super Smash Bros.* is not commonly referred to as an MMO, but *League of Legends* is). Sometimes used as shorthand for MMORPG (massively multiplayer online role-playing game).

Onboarding. The process of getting players "on board" to play a game, usually in reference to teaching players about mechanics and showing players what a game has to offer to encourage continued play. Also see *first-time user experience.*

Platformer. A subgenre of action games distinguished by a focus on platforming (e.g., navigation challenges involving jumping between ledges and "platforms"). Examples include the *Super Mario* series, *Banjo-Kazooie,* and *Hollow Knight.*

Port. A version of a game developed for a platform other than its original release platform(s). Often, development work is done by a studio not involved with the original game. Colloquially, the words "port" and "version" are sometimes used interchangeably.

Procedural generation. The use of algorithms to generate game content, such as levels, items, or even assets. An example is the world map in *Minecraft.*

Responsive communication. Giving information to the player in response to their action, typically immediately. Relevant information might include the success or failure and consequences of their action. A common example is sound effects and animation after striking an enemy. Contrast with *continuous communication.*

Role-playing game. A genre of games distinguished by a focus on immersing oneself in the role of one's character. Often characterized by complex systems of character skills allowing for a wide array of specializations, allowing players to build a character (and narrative) specific to them. A classic example is *Dungeons and Dragons.*

Sandbox game. A genre of games distinguished by the freedom of the player to experiment within a set of systems, often with very loosely defined rules and optional or no-win conditions. Examples include games like *The Sims* and *Tycoon* series, *Minecraft,* and *Garry's Mod.*

Simulation game. A genre of games distinguished by imitation of activities from the real world (though fantasy settings can also be used). Colloquially, a defining factor is often a focus on activities that might otherwise be thought of as mundane. For instance, a shooter simulates gun combat, but most shooters are not classified as simulation games. A management game that simulates organizing finances and producing goods for a business is classified as a simulation game, however.

Third-person. A category of games characterized by a player viewpoint that allows the player to see their character. Often in 3D games, the game's camera (player view) is positioned just behind their character, though top-down and side-scrolling views are common.

Tutorial. Part of a game meant to teach the player about the rules or mechanics. Tutorials may be very explicit (e.g., requiring the player to read instructions) or implicit (e.g., setting up a scenario which hints at a solution that also serves as a learning experience).

Usability. A term used to describe how well a piece of software, such as a game, facilitates effective user interaction. More specifically, *usability* often covers these goals: effective to use, efficient to use, safe to use, having good utility, easy to learn, and easy to remember how to use. Generally speaking, good usability means that players will understand what they need to do, and be able to perform the actions necessary to accomplish their goals. Bad usability means that players may have difficulty understanding what is being asked of them, or have undue troubles executing the needed actions. Balancing usability in games can be especially challenging, since difficulty in execution is often intended (e.g., a boss fight). Can be loosely thought of as the objective counterpart to *user experience*.

User experience. An all-encompassing term describing the quality of a user's interactions with something (e.g., a player's interactions with a game). User experience includes desirable aspects like enjoyable, satisfying, motivating, exciting, engaging, rewarding, and the ability to express oneself. In game design, a good user experience is paramount in whether a game can be said to be "good." However, it can be difficult to measure and validate, due to things like variation between individual players and the specific intent of designers. Can be loosely thought of as the subjective counterpart to *usability*.

User interface. Broadly speaking, any interface (including a physical device like a keyboard) between humans and computers is a user interface. Colloquially in games, the term UI usually refers to virtual interfaces that allow players to communicate with a game (or vice versa). For example, parts of a game's UI include its HUD and menus.

Virtual input. The translation of interaction with virtual elements (e.g., on-screen buttons) into in-game action. Use of a physical device (e.g., mouse, controller) serves to facilitate interaction with virtual elements, which act as an intermediary between physical action and in-game action. For instance, manipulating icons with a mouse to rearrange a character's inventory. Contrast with *direct input*.

Virtual reality. A platform for experiencing games characterized by sensory immersion, most commonly facilitated through a head-mounted display (headset) which places screens directly in front of the user's eyes.

Visibility.   The perceptual obviousness of an element. Good visibility is key to ensuring that information can be quickly and easily understood. For instance, white text on a black background has good visibility, while dark grey text on a black background has poor visibility. One of Norman's six design principles.

Waterfall development.   A software development ideology characterized by linear progression through a series of stages from conceptualization to final release. Strict waterfall approaches are very rigid, and can have difficulty embracing iterative approaches. Contrast with *agile development.*

List of Acronyms

AI	Artificial intelligence
API	Application-programmer interface
AR	Augmented reality
ARPG	Action role-playing game
BCI	Brain-computer interaction
CHI	Conference for Human-Computer Interaction
DDA	Dynamic difficulty adjustment
FOV	Field-of-view
F2P	Free-to-play
FPS	Frames per second
FPS	First-person shooter
FTUE	First-time user experience
GDC	Game Developers Conference
GOAP	Goal-oriented action planning
GUI	Graphical user interface
GUR	Games user research
HCI	Human-computer interaction
HUD	Heads-up display
IGDA	International Game Developers Association
JRPG	Japanese role-playing game
ML	Machine learning
MMO	Massively multiplayer online (game)
MOBA	Multiplayer online battle arena
MR	Mixed reality
NPC(s)	Non-player character(s)
PCG	Procedural content generation
PvE	Player versus environment
QA	Quality assurance
RITE	Rapid iterative testing and evaluation

List of Acronyms

RPG	Role-playing game
UCD	User-centred design
UI	User interface
UX	User experience
VR	Virtual reality

Ludography

1-2 Switch. (2017) Nintendo. Switch.

Agar.io. (2015) Matheus Valadares (pub. Miniclip). Browser.

Alien: Isolation. (2019, Switch ver.) Creative Assembly (orig.), Feral Interactive (port) (pub. Sega). Switch.

Among Us. (2018) InnerSloth. PC/Mobile.

Angry Birds. (series, first game 2009). Rovio Entertainment. Mobile.

Animal Crossing. (series, first game 2001). Nintendo. Console.

Anthem. (2019) BioWare (pub. Electronic Arts). PC/console.

Antichamber. (2013) Demruth. PC.

Assassin's Creed. (2008) Ubisoft Montréal (pub. Ubisoft). PC/console.

Assassin's Creed II. (2009) Ubisoft Montréal (pub. Ubisoft). PC/console.

Assassin's Creed: Odyssey. (2018) Ubisoft Quebec (pub. Ubisoft). PC/console.

Astroneer. (2019) System Era Softworks. PC/console.

Batman: Arkham Knight (PC). (2015, PC ver.) Rocksteady Studios (pub. Warner Bros.). PC.

Battlefield V. (2018) EA DICE (pub. Electronic Arts). PC/console.

Bayonetta. (2009) PlatinumGames (pub. Sega). Console.

Beat Saber. (2019) Beat Games. PC/console (VR).

Bejeweled. (2001) PopCap Games. Browser.

BioShock. (2007) 2K Boston, 2K Australia (pub. 2K Games). PC/console.

Bioshock Infinite. (2013) Irrational Games (pub. 2K Games). PC/console.

Blade + Sorcery. (2018) WarpFrog. PC (VR).

Boggle. (board game, 1972) Parker Brothers.

Boneworks. (2019) Stress Level Zero. PC (VR).

Boom Beach. (2014) Supercell. Mobile.

Borderlands. (2009) Gearbox Software (pub. 2K Games). PC/console.

Braid. (2008) Number None. PC/console.

Bravely Default. (2012) Silicon Studio (pub. Square Enix, Nintendo). Handheld.

Brawl Stars. (2017) Supercell. Mobile.

Brütal Legend. (2010) Double Fine Productions (pub. Electronic Arts). PC/console.

Call of Duty. (series, first game 2003) Infinity Ward et al. (pub. Activision). PC.

Call of Duty: Warzone. (2020) Infinity Ward, Raven Software (pub. Activision). PC.

Candy Crush. (2012) King. Mobile.

Carcassonne. (board game, 2000) Hans im Glück.

Carrion. (2020) Phobia Game Studio (pub. Devolver Digital). PC.

Celeste. (2018) Matt Makes Games. PC/console.

ChefSquad. (2021) Vertigo Gaming. PC.

Choice Chamber. (2015) Studio Bean. PC.

Cities: Skylines. (2015) Colossal Order (pub. Paradox Interactive). PC.

Civilization. (series, first game 1991) Sid Meier et al. (pub. MicroProse et al.). PC.

Civilization V. (2010) Firaxis Games (pub. 2K Games). PC.

Clash of Clans. (2012) Supercell. Mobile.

Clash Royale. (2016) Supercell. Mobile.

Clone Drone in the Danger Zone. (2017) Doborog Games. PC.

Clustertruck. (2016) Landfall Games (pub. tinyBuild). PC.

Commandos: Behind Enemy Lines. (1998) Pyro Studios (pub. Eidos Interactive). PC.

Cook, Serve, Delicious!. (2012) Vertigo Gaming. PC/mobile.

Cook, Serve, Delicious! 2!!. (2017) Vertigo Gaming. PC/console.

Cook, Serve, Delicious! 3?!. (2020) Vertigo Gaming. PC/console.

Cookie Clicker. (2013) Orteil. Browser.

Cooking Mama. (series, first game 2006) Cooking Mama Ltd. (pub. Taito et al.). Handheld/console.

Cooking Simulator. (2019) Big Cheese Studio (pub. PlayWay S.A.). PC.

Counter-Strike. (2000) Valve. PC/console.

Counter-Strike: Global Offensive. (2012) Valve, Hidden Path Entertainment (pub. Valve). PC/console.

Crash Bandicoot 2. (1997) Naughty Dog (pub. Sony). Console.

CSR Racing. (2012) Boss Alien (pub. NaturalMotion). Mobile.

Cuphead. (2017) Studio MDHR. PC/console.

Cyberpunk 2077. (2020) CD Projekt Red. PC/console.

Dark Souls 3. (2016) FromSoftware (pub. Bandai Namco Entertainment). PC/console.

Dead Cells. (2018) Motion Twin. PC/console.

Dead Space. (2008) EA Redwood Shores (pub. Electronic Arts). PC/console.

Death Stranding. (2019) Kojima Productions (Sony). Console.

Deep Rock Galactic. (2020) Ghost Ship Games (pub. Coffee Stain Publishing). PC/console.

Destiny. (2014) Bungie (pub. Activision). Console.

Dig Dug. (1982) Namco. Arcade.

Dishonored. (2012) Arkane Studios (pub. Bethesda Softworks). PC/console.

Divinity: Original Sin. (2014) Larian Studios. PC.

Don't Starve. (2012) Klei Entertainment. PC/console/Mobile.

Donkey Kong. (1981) Nintendo. Arcade.

Doom. (series, first game 1993) id Software et al. (pub. id Software et al.). PC/console.

Doom. (2016) id Software (pub. Bethesda Softworks). PC/console.

Doom Eternal. (2020) id Software (pub. Bethesda Softworks). PC/console.

DotA 2. (2013) Valve. PC.

Drawful. (2014) Jackbox. PC.

Dreadhalls. (2017) White Door Games. PC.

Dreams. (2020) Media Molecule (pub. Sony). Console.

Duck Hunt. (1984) Nintendo. Console.

Dungeons and Dragons. (tabletop game, 1974) Tactical Studies Rules, Inc.

Dwarf Fortress. (2006) Bay 12 Games. PC.

The Elder Scrolls. (series, first game 1994). Bethesda Softworks et al. PC/console.

The Elder Scrolls III: Morrowind. (2002) Bethesda Game Studios (pub. Bethesda Softworks). PC/console.

The Elder Scrolls IV: Oblivion. (2006) Bethesda Game Studios (pub. Bethesda Softworks, 2K Games). PC/console.

The Elder Scrolls V: Skyrim. (2011) Bethesda Game Studios (pub. Bethesda Softworks). PC/console.

The Elder Scrolls V: Skyrim VR. (2017) Bethesda Game Studios (pub. Bethesda Softworks). PC/console (VR).

Elite Dangerous. (2014) Frontier Developments. PC/console.

E.T. the Extra-Terrestrial. (1982) Atari. Console.

Fall Guys: Ultimate Knockout. (2020) Mediatonic (pub. Devolver Digital). PC/console.

Fallout. (series, first game 1997) Interplay Entertainment et al. PC/console.

Fallout 3. (2008) Bethesda Game Studios (pub. Bethesda Softworks). PC/console.

Fallout 4. (2015) Bethesda Game Studios (pub. Bethesda Softworks). PC/console.

Fallout 4 VR. (2017) Bethesda Game Studios (pub. Bethesda Softworks). PC (VR).

Fallout 76. (2018) Bethesda Game Studios (pub. Bethesda Softworks). PC/console.

Far Cry. (series, first game 2004) Crytek et al. (pub. Ubisoft). PC/console.

Far Cry 4. (2014) Ubisoft Montréal (pub. Ubisoft). PC/console.

Far Cry 5. (2018) Ubisoft Montréal, Ubisoft Toronto (pub. Ubisoft). PC/console.

Farmville. (2009) Zynga. Web.

F.E.A.R. (2005) Monolith Productions et al. (pub. Vivendi Games). PC/console.

Fez. (2012) Polytron Corporation (pub. Trapdoor). PC/console.

Final Fantasy. (series, first game 1987) Square Enix (formerly Square). Console/handheld.

Firewatch. (2016) Campo Santo (pub. Panic). PC/console.

For Honor. (2017) Ubisoft Montréal (pub. Ubisoft). PC/console.

Forager. (2019) Hopfrog (pub. Humble Games). PC/console.

Fortnite. (2017) Epic Games (pub. Epic Games, Warner Bros.). PC/console/mobile.

Frogger. (1981) Konami, Sega. Arcade.

Fruit Ninja. (2010) Halfbrick. Mobile.

FTL: Faster Than Light. (2012) Subset Games. PC.

Galaga. (1981) Namco. Arcade.

Galaxy on Fire. (series, first game 2009) Deep Silver Fishlabs. Mobile/PC.

Galaxy on Fire 2. (2010) Deep Silver Fishlabs. Mobile/PC.

Garry's Mod. (2006) Facepunch Studios (pub. Valve). PC.

Getting Over It With Bennett Foddy. (2017) Bennett Foddy. PC/mobile.

God of War. (series, first game 2005) Santa Monica Studio et al. (pub. Sony et al.). Console.

God of War. (2018) Santa Monica Studio (pub. Sony). Console.

Grand Theft Auto. (series, first game 1997) Rockstar North et al. (pub. Rockstar Games). PC/console.

Grand Theft Auto V. (2013) Rockstar North (pub. Rockstar Games). PC/console.

Gris. (2019) Nomada Studio (pub. Devolver Digital). PC/console.

Habbo Hotel. (2000) Sulake Corporation. Browser.

Hades. (2020) Supergiant Games. PC.

Half-Life. (series, first game 1998) Valve. PC/console.

Half-Life. (1998) Valve. PC/console.

Half-Life 2: Episode Two. (2007) Valve. PC/console.

Half-Life: Alyx. (2020) Valve. PC (VR).

Halo. (series, first game 2001) Bungie et al. (pub. Xbox Game Studios). Console.

Hatoful Boyfriend. (2014) Mediatonic (pub. Devolver Digital). PC.

Hay Day. (2012) Supercell. Mobile.

Hearthstone. (2014) Blizzard Entertainment. PC/mobile.

Hellblade: Senua's Sacrifice. (2017) Ninja Theory. PC/console.

Hollow Knight. (2017) Team Cherry. PC/console.

Horizon Zero Dawn. (2017) Guerilla Games (pub. Sony). Console.

Hotline Miami. (2012) Dennaton games (pub. Devolver Digital). PC.

HQ Trivia. (2017) Intermedia Labs. Mobile.

Human: Fall Flat. (2016) No Brakes Games (pub. Curve Digital). PC/console.

I Am Bread. (2015) Bossa Studios. PC/console.

I Expect You to Die. (2016) Schell Games. PC/console (VR).

InFamous. (series, first game 2009) Sucker Punch Productions (pub. Sony). Console.

Inside. (2016) Playdead. PC.

The Jackbox Party Pack. (series, first game 2014) Jackbox Games. PC.

Jet Island. (2018) Master Indie. PC (VR).

Just Cause. (2006) Avalanche Studios (pub. Eidos Interactive). PC/console.

Katamari Damacy. (2004) Namco. Console.

Keep Talking and Nobody Explodes. (2015) Steel Crate Games. PC/console.

Khan Academy Kids. (2018) Khan Academy. Mobile.

King's Quest V. (1990) Sierra Entertainment. PC.

Kingdom Hearts II. (2005) Square Enix. Console.

LA Noire. (2011) Team Bondi (pub. Rockstar Games). Console/PC.

League of Legends. (2009) Riot Games. PC.

Left 4 Dead. (2008) Valve South (formerly Turtle Rock Studios) (pub. Valve). PC.

Left 4 Dead 2. (2009) Valve. PC.

LEGO Star Wars Battles. (2020) Playdemic (pub. TT Games). Mobile.

Life Is Strange. (2015) Dontnod Entertainment (Square Enix). PC.

Lightseekers. (2019) PlayFusion. PC/Mobile.

Limbo. (2010) Playdead. PC/console.

Manifold Garden. (2019) William Chyr Studio. PC/mobile.

Marbles on Stream. (2018) Pixel by Pixel Studios. PC.

Mario Kart. (series, first game 1992) Nintendo. Console.

Mario Kart: Double Dash. (2003) Nintendo. Console.

Mario Kart 8. (2014) Nintendo. Console.

Marvel vs. Capcom. (series, first game 1996) Capcom et al. Console/PC.

Mass Effect 2. (2010) BioWare (pub. Electronic Arts). PC/console.

Mass Effect 3. (2012) BioWare (pub. Electronic Arts). PC/console.

Metal Gear. (series, first game 1987) Bluepoint Games et al. (pub. Konami). Console/PC.

Metal Gear Solid V: The Phantom Pain. (2015) Kojima Productions (pub. Konami). Console/PC.

Microsoft Flight Simulator. (2020) Asobo Studio (pub. Xbox Game Studios). PC/console.

Minecraft. (2011) Mojang (pub. Mojang, Microsoft, Sony). PC/console/mobile.

Minit. (2018) Jan Willem Nijman et al. (pub. Devolver Digital). PC/console.

Mirror's Edge. (2008) DICE (pub. Electronic Arts). PC/console.

Mirror's Edge: Catalyst. (2016) EA DICE (pub. Electronic Arts). PC/console.

Monopoly. (board game, 1935) Parker Brothers.

Mortal Kombat X. (2015, PC ver.) NetherRealm Studios (orig.), High Voltage Software (port) (pub. Warner Bros.). PC.

Moss. (2018) Polyarc. PC/console (VR).

Mugen. (1999) Elecbyte. PC.

Nier: Automata. (2017) PlatinumGames (pub. Square Enix). Console/PC.

Night in the Woods. (2017) Infinite Fall (pub. Finji). PC/console.

No Man's Sky. (2016) Hello Games. PC/console.

No More Heroes. (2007) Grasshopper Manufacture (pub. Ubisoft et al.). Console.

Noita. (2020) Nolla Games. PC.

Noughts and Crosses (OXO). (1952) A.S. Douglas. EDSAC.

Observation. (2019) No Code (pub. Devolver Digital). PC.

Octodad: Dadliest Catch. (2014) Young Horses. PC/console.

Okami. (2006) Clover Studio (pub. Capcom). Console.

Okami HD. (2017, PC port) Capcom and HexaDrive (pub. Capcom). PC.

Old School Runescape. (2013) Jagex. PC.

Onward. (2016) Downpour Interactive (pub. Coatsink). PC (VR).

Opus Magnum. (2017) Zachtronics. PC.

Ori and the Blind Forest. (2015) Moon Studios (pub. Microsoft Studios). PC/console.

Osu! (2007) Dean "Peppy" Herbert. PC.

Overwatch. (2016) Blizzard Entertainment. PC/console.

Pac-Man. (1980) Namco. Arcade.

Papers, Please. (2013) Lucas Pope (pub. 3909). PC.

Parcheesi. (board game, 1874) Selchow & Righter.

Party Hard. (2015) Pinokl Games (pub. tinyBuild). PC/console.

Pavlov VR. (2017) Vankrupt Games. PC (VR).

Pentalath. (board game, 2007) Cyberite Ltd.

Persona 5. (2016) P-Studio (pub. Atlus et al.). Console.

Phasmophobia. (2020) Kinetic Games. PC.

Pistol Whip. (2019) Cloudhead Games. PC (VR).

A Plague Tale: Innocence. (2019) Asobo Studio (pub. Focus Home Interactive). PC/console.

Planet Coaster. (2016) Frontier Developments. PC.

Planet Zoo. (2019) Frontier Developments. PC.

Plants vs. Zombies 2. (2013) PopCap Games (pub. Electronic Arts). Mobile.

Pokémon. (series, first game 1996) Game Freak (pub. Nintendo and The Pokémon Company). Handheld/console.

Pokémon Go. (2017) Niantic et al. Mobile.

Pokémon Red. (1998) Game Freak (pub. Nintendo). Handheld.

Pokémon Sword and Shield. (2019) Game Freak (pub. Nintendo and The Pokémon Company). Console.

Pong. (1972) Atari. Arcade.

Portal. (2007) Valve. PC/console.

Portal 2. (2011) Valve. PC/console.

Prodigy Math Game. (2020) SMARTeacher Inc. Mobile.

Psychonauts. (2005) Double Fine Productions (pub. Majesco Entertainment). PC/console.

Quake. (1996) id Software (pub. GT Interactive). PC.

Quiplash. (2015) Jackbox Games. PC/console/browser.

QWOP. (2008) Bennett Foddy. Browser.

Rainbow Six Siege. (2015) Ubisoft Montréal (pub. Ubisoft). PC/console.

Resident Evil. (series, first game 1996) Capcom. Console.

Resident Evil 4. (2005) Capcom. Console.

Resident Evil 4. (PC ver., 2007) Sourcenext (pub. Ubisoft). PC.

Resident Evil 4: Wii Edition. (Wii ver., 2007) Capcom. Console.

Red Dead Redemption 2. (2018) Rockstar Games. PC/console.

Robo Recall. (2017) Epic Games. PC (VR).

RollerCoaster Tycoon. (series, first game 1999) Chris Sawyer Productions et al. (pub. Hasbro et al.) PC/console.

Second Life. (2003) Linden Lab. PC.

Sekiro: Shadows Die Twice. (2019) FromSoftware (pub. Activision). Console/PC.

Shariki. (1994) Augene Alemzhin. PC.

Simon. (board game, 1978) Ralph H. Baer and Howard J. Morrison.

Skribbl.io. (2017) Ticedev. Browser.

Snake Pass. (2017) Sumo Digital. PC/console.

Sonic. (series, first game 1991) Sega. Console.

Sonic the Hedgehog ("Sonic '06"). (2006) Sonic Team (pub. Sega). Console.

Sonic the Hedgehog. (2013 remaster) Christian Whitehead, Headcannon (pub. Sega). Mobile.

Sorry! (board game, 1929) W.H. Storey & Co.

Souls. (series, first game 2009) FromSoftware (pub. Bandai Namco). Console/PC.

Space Invaders. (1978) Taito. Arcade.

SpaceChem. (2011) Zachtronics Industries. PC/mobile.

Spacewar! (1962) Steve Russell et al. PDP-1.

Spelunky. (2008) Mossmouth. PC/console.

Spider-Man. (2018) Insomniac Games (pub. Sony). Console.

Spore. (2008) Maxis (pub. Electronic Arts). PC.

Starbound. (2016) Chucklefish. PC/console.

Starcraft. (series, first game 1998) Blizzard Entertainment. PC.

Stardew Valley. (2016) ConcernedApe. PC/console.

Stream Animals. (2020) Smash Bolt Games. PC.

Street Fighter. (series, first game 1987) Capcom et al. Arcade/PC/console.

Street Fighter III: Third Strike Online Edition. (2011) Capcom. Console.

Subnautica. (2018) Unknown Worlds Entertainment. PC.

Super Mario. (series, first game 1985) Nintendo. Arcade/console.

Super Mario 64. (1996) Nintendo. Console.

Super Mario Bros. (1985) Nintendo. Arcade.

Super Mario Galaxy. (2007) Nintendo. Console.

Super Mario Maker. (2015) Nintendo. Console.

Super Meat Boy. (2010) Team Meat. PC/console.

Super Motherload. (2013) XGen Studios. PC/console.

Super Smash Bros. (series, first game 1999) HAL Laboratory et al. (pub. Nintendo). Console.

Super Smash Bros. Ultimate. (2018) Bandai Namco and Sora Ltd. (pub. Nintendo). Console.

Superliminal. (2019) Pillow Castle. PC.

Superman: The New Superman Adventures ("Superman 64"). (1999) Titus Interactive. Console.

Tabletop Simulator. (2015) Berserk Games. PC.

Team Fortress 2. (2007) Valve. PC/console.

Tennis for Two. (1958) William Higinbotham. Analog computer.

Terraforming Mars. (board game, 2016) FryxGames.

Terraria. (2011) Re-Logic. PC/console/mobile.

The Binding of Isaac: Rebirth. (2014) Nicalis and Edmund McMillen (pub. Nicalis). PC.

The Lab. (2016) Valve. PC (VR).

The Last of Us. (2013) Naughty Dog (pub. Sony). Console.

The Last of Us 2. (2020) Naughty Dog (pub. Sony). Console.

The Legend of Zelda. (series, first game 1986) Nintendo et al. Console/handheld.

The Legend of Zelda: Breath of the Wild. (2017) Nintendo. Console.

The Legend of Zelda: Skyward Sword. (2011) Nintendo. Console.

The Long Dark. (2017) Hinterland Studio. PC/console.

The Sims. (series, first game 2000) Maxis et al. (pub. Electronic Arts). PC/console.

The Sims. (2000) Maxis (pub. Electronic Arts). PC.

The Sims 3. (2009) Maxis et al. (pub. Electronic Arts). PC/console.

The Stanley Parable. (2011) Galactic Cafe. PC.

The Witcher. (series, first game 2007) CD Projekt Red. PC.

The Witcher 3. (2015) CD Projekt Red. PC/console.

The Witness. (2016) Thekla Inc. PC.

This War of Mine. (2014) 11 Bit Studios. PC/console.

The Legend of Zelda: Ocarina of Time. (1998) Nintendo. Console.

The Legend of Zelda: Twilight Princess. (2006) Nintendo. Console.

Tomb Raider. (series, first game 1996) Core Design et al. (pub. Eidos Interactive and Square Enix). Console/PC.

Ultimate Chicken Horse. (2016) Clever Endeavour Games. PC/console.

Uncharted. (series, first game 2007) Naughty Dog (pub. Sony). Console.

Uncharted 2: Among Thieves. (2009) Naughty Dog (pub. Sony). Console.

Uncharted 3: Drake's Deception. (2011) Naughty Dog (pub. Sony). Console.

Undertale. (2015) Toby Fox. PC/console.

Valorant. (2020) Riot Games. PC.

Watch Dogs: Legion. (2020) Ubisoft Toronto (pub. Ubisoft). PC/console.

What Remains of Edith Finch. (2017) Giant Sparrow (pub. Annapurna Interactive). PC/console.

Wii Fit. (2007) Nintendo. Console.

Wii Sports. (2006) Nintendo. Console.

World of Warcraft. (2004) Blizzard Entertainment. PC.

XCOM: Terror from the Deep. (1995) MicroProse. PC/Console.

Xenoblade Chronicles. (series, first game 2010) Monolith Soft (pub. Nintendo). Console.

Yavalath. (board game, 2007) Cyberite Ltd.

Zoo Tycoon. (series, first game 2001) Blue Fang Games et al. (pub. Microsoft Studios). PC/console.

Zoo Tycoon 2. (2004) Blue Fang Games et al. (pub. Microsoft Studios). PC.

Subject Index

Game Index

Because you've made it to the very, very end of this book, here's a coloring page for you. Feel free to tear it out and stick it on your fridge, whiteboard, face or any other surface you like. And send us a picture (you can find us at gamedesignplaybook.com) if you get a chance, we're lonely.